O9-BUD-889

AMERICAN
QUEEN

# AMERICAN QUEEN

*The Rise and Fall of Kate Chase Sprague, Civil War "Belle of the North" and Gilded Age Woman of Scandal*

John Oller

**DA CAPO PRESS**

A Member of the Perseus Books Group

*A Note on the Text*

Nineteenth-century letters and diaries can pose a challenge to twenty-first-century readers, and for that reason I have made certain changes to the original text for convenience and clarity—modernizing spellings (e.g., changing "can not" to "cannot," or "to-night" to "tonight"), substituting "and" for "&," supplying missing question marks where they were clearly implied in the original, and making other miscellaneous punctuation changes. In no case was a text changed where I thought it might alter the author's original meaning. Original capitalizations were generally left intact, even for words that ordinarily would be lower-cased today, on the theory that they reflected an intended emphasis by the writer. Underlinings in the original appear as italics here. All emphases in quotations are from the original.

Frontispiece: Kate Chase, photographed by Matthew Brady in 1860 (Courtesy of Library of Congress)


Printed in the United States of America. For information, address Da Capo Press, 44 Farnsworth Street, Third Floor, Boston, MA 02210.
*Book design by Cynthia Young*

Library of Congress Cataloging-in-Publication Data
Oller, John.
American queen : the rise and fall of Kate Chase Sprague, Civil War "Belle of the North" and gilded age woman of scandal / John Oller.
pages cm
Includes bibliographical references and index.
ISBN 978-0-306-82280-3 (hardcover) — ISBN 978-0-306-82281-0 (e-book)
1. Sprague, Kate Chase, 1840-1899. 2. Chase, Salmon P. (Salmon Portland), 1808–1873. 3. Sprague, William, 1830-1915. 4. Socialites–United States–Biography. 5. United States–Politics and government–19th century. I. Title.
E415.9.S76O55 2014
973.5092–dc23
[B]
2014012054

Published by Da Capo Press
A Member of the Perseus Books Group
www.dacapopress.com

Da Capo Press books are available at special discounts for bulk purchases in the U.S. by corporations, institutions, and other organizations. For more information, please contact the Special Markets Department at the Perseus Books Group, 2300 Chestnut Street, Suite 200, Philadelphia, PA 19103, or call (800) 810-4145, ext. 5000, or e-mail special.markets@perseusbooks.com.

10 9 8 7 6 5 4 3 2 1

*To my mother*
*and in memory of my father*

## CONTENTS

PROLOGUE

# A Woman in the Arena

The old woman held the reins of the rickety, one-horse carriage with her soiled, white kid gloves as she wound her way down the hill in the direction of the nation's capital. She wore a purple plumed hat over her blonde wig, her face heavily painted with rouge, her dress badly out of fashion. As the buggy rolled along the driveway, overgrown with weeds and bordered by a broken-down fence, the aging mare trudged past chickens running freely about the property. Atop the hill stood a decaying brick country home, its outline obscured by the thicket of scrub and fallen tree branches.

In the distance the woman could see the glistening white dome of the Capitol, where she had spent so many hours listening to Senate speeches, watching impeachment proceedings, witnessing presidents being sworn in, and gazing upon those who had lain in state. She had known so many of them: every president from Lincoln to Grover Cleveland and countless other eminent nineteenth-century men: the great abolitionist senator Charles Sumner, the war generals Grant and Sherman, cabinet members Seward and Stanton, and powerful journalists such as Horace Greeley, literary giants such as Longfellow and Twain, and assorted statesmen, diplomats, and financiers. She had entertained men such as these at her famous Washington salons, where she held court as a political hostess and established her reputation as the most brilliant woman of her day. The daughter of Lincoln's treasury secretary, the Belle of the North during the Civil War, she became America's version of the salonnières—the madames and duchesses who flourished in Europe as arbiters of high social discourse. Among contemporaries, she was compared to the celebrated French Empress Eugénie, wife of Napoleon III and influencer of foreign affairs. "No Queen has ever reigned under the Stars and Stripes," one newspaper eulogized after her death, "but this remarkable woman came closer to being a Queen than any American woman has."

Much of it had to do with her appearance: tall, slender, a long, swanlike neck and fetching, hazel eyes hidden beneath thick, drooping lashes. Men thought her beautiful, but it was not so much that she was a classic beauty—her nose, for one, was "slightly inclined to pug," as James Garfield once commented, a feature others thought added a touch of piquancy to her face. Like the *Mona Lisa*, to whom she was also compared, she appeared fascinating and irresistible, with "something of the strangeness which has been said to belong invariably to beauty of the highest order."

There was also a hint of condescension in her manner—in the pose of a head that, with its proud tilt, seemed slightly imperious, and in the aloof, half smile she habitually wore. Her voice was mellow and musical; she enunciated beautifully, spoke faultless French, and was fluent in German. An acknowledged queen of fashion, she adorned herself in the most superb gowns, imported by the dozens from Parisian couturiers, always matching the color of her millinery and jewelry. Yet even simply dressed, she was the envy of other women, as when she upstaged her rival, Mary Todd Lincoln, by appearing at a White House reception in a modest costume, with hardly more than a flower in her hair, yet remaining the center of attention. "Poor, weak Mrs. Lincoln was simply swept into the corner when this imperious young beauty appeared, leaning upon the arm of the great secretary," it would be written later.

Her looks and adornments created a total package that was greater than the sum of its parts. Enhancing all of it was a magnetic personality that drew people to her. Admirers commented on her keen intellect, the breadth of her sparkling conversation, and her diplomatic skills. When she entered the room a hush would fall over the crowd, but, like a monarch in a receiving line, any trace of haughtiness dissolved into grace and charm once she met a person one-on-one. As a male political friend marveled, "when she is talking to you, you feel that you are the very person she wanted to meet. That she has forgotten your existence the next moment is an afterthought."

Beneath the charming exterior, though, was a calculating politician. As was once said of her, "She could talk about anything at all and make it seem sweet music—yet she could scheme like a cigar-chewing convention rigger." Of course, no nineteenth-century American woman could ever hope to possess the power of a true monarch—a Queen Victoria or, from earlier history, an Elizabeth I or a Catherine the Great. And before the twentieth century, American women could not even vote, much less hold political office. Yet at the dawn of that new century, due to her scientific knowledge of the subject, she enjoyed a political power that no American woman to that time had ever possessed. It grew out of her upbringing and training: as a young girl and daughter of a politician, she had met the most famous men of her time—Henry Clay, John C. Calhoun, and Daniel Webster, the noted orator, who sent her his speeches to read when she was attending an exclusive boarding school in New York. At age fifteen, when her widowed father was elected governor of Ohio, she became the mistress of his household and his official hostess, a position she continued to hold in Washington during the war. Having "mastered the art of seducing men's minds," she used her personal allure to advance her father's political ambitions, hoping one day to make him president of the United States. Certainly she thought, as did he, that he would make a better president than Lincoln and that she was a more suitable First Lady than the dowdy Mrs. Lincoln.

Beauty, charisma, power—all these she possessed. But to truly emulate a queen one needs, above all else, wealth. This she had lacked until she married, at age twenty-three, one of the richest men in the country in the social event of the Civil War. Many would claim she married only for money, which she needed to fuel her father's presidential aspirations. But her diary, undiscovered for nearly a century, would tell a different story: she had been genuinely in love at the time of her wedding. The money did not hurt, of course, and with her husband's fortune she would live a life of virtual royalty for more than a decade. Alas, he would not prove to be a king; the marriage would crumble, the money would disappear. After a sex scandal with another powerful figure, she became a social outcast, and her political influence waned. Finally the beauty faded as well. And so she found herself on this day in 1897, old beyond her years at fifty-seven, alone, obscure, and living in poverty—driving her shabby carriage not to the Capitol that was once her haunting grounds but to the outskirts of Washington to peddle milk and eggs. With these and the vegetables she grew at home, she was trying her best to eke out a living.

Yet if she was bitter, she showed no signs of it. In her diary many years earlier she acknowledged a need to "force back the old bitterness of spirit" she had not yet succeeded in conquering. As she admitted, "proud, passionate, intolerant, I had never learned to submit." In later years, as her need for public recognition subsided, her spirit softened. In her solitude and altered circumstances she found an inner peace that had eluded her most of her turbulent life. But nothing could ever change her proud bearing nor could the whirligig of time rob her of the memories of when she was at the center of the political arena, busy working her enchanting magic.

* * *

**NEW YORK, JULY 5, 1868**—The room was insufferably hot when Kate Chase sat down to write a letter to her father from her guest lodgings near Union Square in New York City. The mercury had reached ninety-nine degrees that Sunday afternoon, and, as she told him, "Day before yesterday, yesterday and today have been as hot as weather can well be, too hot by far, for the warm work on hand here." Despite her discomfort, "work" was more than enough to keep her going. The Democratic National Convention had opened the day before to choose a candidate for president, and Kate Chase was there to make sure that candidate would be her father, then chief justice of the Supreme Court, Salmon P. Chase. She was twenty-seven years old.

"There is a noble work being done here by your friends," she continued, "and whether success or failure crowns their efforts, they will be always proud to have had a hand in it." She would not enter into details, she said, but reassured her father that "everything, as far as developed looks well—only New York—friends inside that close corporation say their action is cautious, those outside call it *timid.*" In the political-speak that was her wont, she was referring to the New York delegation, which held the key to the nomination. Upon her arrival in the city a few days before, as one newspaper reported, she had "immediately sent for" the delegation's shrewd head, Samuel J. Tilden, as well as Wall Street banker and

Democratic Party National Chair August Belmont, and in long interviews she sought to enlist their support for her father's cause.

The newspaper writer's choice of words, "sent for," was intentional, for powerful men came to see Kate Chase, not the other way around. Belmont seemed on board for Chase, but Tilden, whom the *New-York Tribune* called "the airiest, coolest, wiliest-looking delegate in the Convention," was noncommittal. Kate would need to work on him.

If anyone could corral the necessary support, it was Kate Chase. She had gone to New York, as her father's unofficial campaign manager, to achieve a goal that had eluded him in his three previous presidential bids—all as a Republican. Those rudderless attempts lacked someone who could crack the whip when needed. Kate saw that as her task this time. As she later recalled of that 1868 convention, "I knew that the men who were managing my father's interests were not so well organized as they should be, and I wanted to be present to prevent any trouble and take advantage of any situation that might come up."

To be close to the action, she was staying at a relative's townhouse on lower Fifth Avenue, just a few blocks west of the convention site at the brand-new Tammany Hall on Fourteenth Street. Kate also took out a suite of rooms a little farther uptown at the Fifth Avenue Hotel, the most modern and luxurious hotel in the city. It featured private bathrooms in every bedroom and a "vertical steam engine," as the passenger elevator was called, connecting its six stories. The hotel served as headquarters for her father's backers while they courted convention delegates who came from across the country to choose a man to go up against the Republican nominee, General Ulysses S. Grant.

Kate was visibly in charge of the Chase-for-President operations, using all her unrivaled powers to secure her father's nomination. Her Fifth Avenue Hotel suite was crowded day and night with campaign workers and convention delegates. "Some delegates were coaxed, to others promises were given, and upon all were brought to bear the power of her conversation and the charm of her irresistible beauty," one memoirist recounted. "What a Magnificent woman Kate has become," one of Chase's friends wrote to him, insisting that "with her shrewdness and force, and with ninety days' time, I could have you nominated by acclamation and elected by an overwhelming majority." Billy Hudson, then a cub reporter for the *Brooklyn Eagle* covering his first convention, recalled years later being mesmerized by the sight of Kate in action. "There, in supreme control, was Chase's daughter, in the flush of beautiful womanhood, tall and elegant, with exquisite tact, with brains of almost masculine fiber, trained in the political arts by her father, who had long been a national figure."

Like many, Hudson had difficulty reconciling the career of Salmon Chase—antislavery champion, a leading founder of the Republican Party, and Lincoln's treasury secretary—with the fact that he was before the Democratic convention, "cap in hand, deferentially supplicating a nomination." The Democrats at that time were largely opposed to equal rights for black Americans. Many of those attending the convention—like former Confederate general Nathan Bedford Forrest, founder of the Ku Klux Klan—stood for everything Chase had fought against his entire life. In the opening keynote address Belmont gave a rabble-rousing speech in which he called African Americans "a debased and ignorant race, just emerged from servitude." So *this* was the party, *these* were the people, Billy Hudson mused, that Salmon Chase now sought to represent? But all these perplexities disappeared for the young reporter the moment Kate entered the Chase headquarters. Hudson would later recall that he "fell under her sway, a willing captive." If she wanted her father to have the nomination, that was good enough for him.

To a more established society journalist Kate seemed, on the surface, "the most graceful, distinguished, and queenly woman" she had ever seen. And yet Kate was a woman in anguish over her private life. In her diary a few weeks before, she had despaired of "the absence from my life of a pervading, tender, devoted love." She had suffered outrages and insults from her habitually drunken, womanizing husband and vowed that "if I cannot be a respected and honored wife and treated as such I will not be this man's mistress."

"This man" was William Sprague, the former governor of Rhode Island, now a Republican US senator from the same state. One of the wealthiest men in America, he was heir to a multimillion-dollar textile manufacturing empire in New England. Their wedding in the nation's capital in November 1863—attended by President Lincoln a week before his Gettysburg address—was a union between the undisputed Belle of Washington and the dashing "boy governor" who had distinguished himself at the Battle of First Bull Run. Now, less than five years later, the marriage was in tatters. But Kate could not think about any of that now—there was too much important work to do in New York.

While Kate toiled in the heat of New York that Fourth of July week, her husband, conspicuous by his absence, was at their oceanside estate in Narragansett, tending to business and staying with their three-year-old son, Willie. Sprague's brother Amasa was at the convention, though, and was working night and day on Chase's behalf. "The young men are the life of this movement," Kate wrote her father on her arrival in New York. "Things look a good deal clearer, and Amasa insists that *he* 'will know tonight which way the cat will jump'—The point now is to select *the* man to be spokesman in the convention." From memory she rattled off the names of various southern politicians she thought would be useful: "Mr. Hunter, Col. Cabell, Bradley Johnson, and Gilmer," although Edgerton, a former midwestern congressman, was "bitter as gall, and swears he would not vote for you under any circumstances." Such unalloyed opponents were rare, she assured her father. "The popular voice here is all one way, most singularly enthusiastic," she wrote. But the Chase backers needed to control their enthusiasm, she cautioned. Her game plan was to hold Chase's name back from the convention at first and await a deadlock, as she was afraid her father's more passionate followers would stage a premature floor demonstration and offend the supporters of Ohio's George Pendleton, the frontrunner. "The Pendleton men," she had ascertained, were "very fractious."

With all this heady business at hand, Kate did not have time for the diversions of entertainment or escapes from the stifling heat sought by the many delegates and tourists who had flooded New York that weekend. For fifteen cents a ticket, families could catch a special holiday minstrel show of "patriotic negro eccentricities" at Tony Pastor's Opera House in the Bowery, whose proprietor boasted fans and ice water in abundance. The nearby New Stadt Theatre was reenacting the Battle of Bunker Hill with a mechanical diorama and genuine muskets and powder, while the Olympic Theatre on lower Broadway featured clown comedian George L. Fox pantomiming Humpty Dumpty on stage with a roller-skating ballet and live pigs. Others seeking to cool off might catch a steamboat excursion to West Point, while strollers through Central Park could pursue temporary relief in ice cream saloons or beer gardens.

Instead, Kate was sweating things out inside Tammany Hall, known as the "Wigwam." Filled to capacity, its oven-like atmosphere was made worse by the heavy bunting covering the window openings that trapped the stale air inside. Yet many on the outside were clamoring to get in. The most eager were the small-town newspapermen from all corners of the country who had to be held back by the cordons of police who had never heard of their publications. Meanwhile, on nearly every street corner, maimed Union veterans played hand organs, seeking charity from followers of the party of rebellion.

As anticipation mounted for the goings-on inside the convention hall, so did Kate's hopes for her father's nomination. The *New York Times* reported that delegates were discussing Chase's name favorably in hotel hallways, and one of Chase's operatives wrote him to say, "My parlors are thronged all the time." As the convention got under way, the *New-York Tribune* reported that "All the Southern men who arrive here speak of [Chase] as the only man they will support, and gentlemen from that section are tonight freely laying wagers on his nomination."

These were the hopeful thoughts that sustained Kate as she finished off her letter to her father on the sweltering fifth of July. Her final consideration that evening was for him, waiting back in Washington. "I am so glad that it does not fall to you to bear the burden and heat, and I love to think of you quietly at home, perhaps enjoying a game of Croquet or ten-pins. Lovingly your child Katie."

On the morning of the day Kate penned her letter, Salmon Chase would have gone to church after reading morning prayers to every member of his house, down to the humblest servant. As he sat in his townhouse in Washington, Chase's thoughts also ran to his beloved daughter. Kate Chase was the love of her father's life, the pride of his heart. Much of his worship of her stemmed from having lost three wives to early deaths as well as four of his six children by the time he was forty-four. But it went beyond that. Kate, the older of his two surviving daughters, was the child made in his own image, the one with the greatest chance to embody his ideal of an accomplished, Christian woman. By 1868 the "accomplished" part was well taken care of; it was the "Christian" part he was worried about. She attended too many wretched late-night parties, he thought, and did not spend enough time tending to duties on her homefront. And here she was at the convention, "acting too much the politician," he told her. How he wished she were with him in Washington or in Rhode Island seeking out the cool ocean breezes with her husband and son. She had intended to go there to see the boy, but, as she explained to her father, "I really could not make up my mind to leave just now." No, she knew, she did not belong in Narragansett or Washington at this hour; she was right where her father needed her most. She hoped the country would have "the *Courage* to do right" and signed off on her letter to him: "Affectionately and ambitiously for Country—the Democracy, and its Noblest Patriot and Statesman."

The rest of the country did not necessarily see it her way. At six feet two, Salmon Portland Chase was a presidential aspirant out of central casting, with the look of a Roman statesman and a dignified manner to match. But, unlike Abraham Lincoln, he was humorless and lacked the common touch. He had a sanctimonious streak that even admirers found off-putting. Known for frequently switching parties over the past three decades, he was viewed by many as an opportunist. This perennial candidate was, thought Lincoln, "a little insane" when it came to the presidency. Now Salmon Chase's gnawing lust for that office was tempting him to compromise his principles and seek the nomination of a party heavily populated with racists and traitors.

There were those who thought it was Kate who was the driving force behind her father's ambition. Because Chase was a widower, Kate would, if he entered the White House, become his official hostess and the nation's First Lady. One woman journalist wrote that her desire for that position amounted "almost to a mania." Kate recognized that, with her father's path to the Republican nomination blocked by the war hero Grant, he needed to switch parties to have a shot at the prize. To Kate, politics was less about ideology than electing the right person, which she believed her father to be.

Chase wrote Kate during the 1868 convention to say he would be happy to stay on the Supreme Court. "You know how little I have desired a nomination and how averse I have been to making any efforts to secure it," he wrote. But he was protesting too much. A few months before the convention one of Chase's Ohio friends advised the chief justice to stay on the bench because his chances of being nominated for president were slim. But Chase spent an hour trying to convince his visitor he was wrong and that he could and would receive the nomination. Another close friend who spoke to him in May 1868 found him "entranced by White House dreams."

Kate pretended to go along with her father's professed lack of interest in higher office. "I am glad you are not going to be greatly disappointed if the nomination is not for you," she wrote him on the eve of the convention. But she had heard too many similar disclaimers from her father, for too many years, to place any reliance on them. She concluded her letter, "I should like to see this bright jewel added to your crown of earthly distinction, and *I believe it will* be. But we can love and be very happy and just as proud of you without it. Will the *Country* do as well?"

**MONDAY, JULY 6**—The day was devoted to preliminaries: selection of the presiding chair (ex-New York governor Horatio Seymour), setting of procedural ground rules, and the reading of resolutions decrying the Republicans' Reconstruction policy of granting power to "ignorant negroes" in the South. Kate must have cringed at such expressions, so at odds with her father's views of a lifetime. One might ask why she did not leave the convention, pack up her bags, and telegraph her father to say he should want no part of any party such as this. But it was too late for any such second thoughts.

It would be more interesting to know Kate's reaction to another resolution presented that day by the Women's Suffrage Association. Seymour, the chair, announced he had a letter from that organization, signed by Susan B. Anthony, at which point some delegates laughingly called out, "Read it! Read it!" The convention secretary read the letter, which demanded the enfranchisement of the women of America, "the only class (not guilty of crime) taxed without representation, tried without a jury of their peers, governed without their consent." One delegate recalled that at the time it was regarded as a joke and was ignored.

Unlike the all-male delegates, Kate probably did not laugh at these ladies, but neither did she embrace them. In all her years Kate never spoke out in favor of women's suffrage, and was at best a bystander in the movement. Three years after the convention she would decline to add her name to a Senate petition, signed by over a thousand women, in support of giving women the vote. It was not that she opposed the suffragists' goals, but she preferred different means. She thought women could be more effective behind the scenes, in salon parlors and back rooms, using informal suasion rather than demonstrative protest. Her role at the convention was a case in point: as a woman, she was not allowed on the convention floor, although she could watch from the gallery, and when back at her hotel she was in hourly communication with Tammany Hall by messenger.

One reason for her growing optimism was the weak competition her father faced. Ohio's Pendleton was a prominent "Copperhead" who had opposed the war, served as General George McClellan's vice presidential running mate against Lincoln in 1864, and led opposition to the passage of the Thirteenth Amendment abolishing slavery. His record endeared him to hard-core Democrats but made him a weak candidate to do battle against the war hero Grant in the general election. And although Pendleton enjoyed strong support from western delegates, his advocacy of repayment of Civil War bondholders in paper "greenbacks" rather than gold made him anathema to eastern money men such as Tilden and Belmont. Another western man, Indiana senator Thomas Hendricks, was a popular mainstream Democrat, but he faced strong hostility from the Pendleton forces. The main argument in favor of Pennsylvania's General Winfield Scott Hancock, one of the North's heroes of Gettysburg, was that he was electable, but the *New York Herald* thought choosing him as the challenger to Grant would be like "taking the lieutenant to run against the captain."

The man Kate had to worry about most was, ironically, someone who was not even running and who, shortly before the convention, announced his support for Chase. Former New York governor Horatio Seymour was the most popular national Democrat in the country, someone who could have the nomination with the merest indication he would accept it. But he said repeatedly he would not. The fifty-eight-year-old Seymour, from Utica, New York, was an elegant and courtly gentleman, always flawlessly dressed. His grandfatherly exterior, however, concealed a steely Copperhead who had fought Lincoln at every turn and infamously addressed the New York draft rioters of July 1863 as "my friends." The pro-Chase *Herald* also thought Seymour "as dry as the dead leaves of autumn," a "fossil politician of a bygone age" who would inspire no enthusiasm among the people.

Although leading Democrats continued to pepper Tilden with letters advocating Seymour's nomination, Kate seemed satisfied with Seymour's demurrals. Seymour was staying at the Greenwich Village home of John

Van Buren, Chase's floor manager at the convention, and, as Kate wrote her father, Van Buren insisted that Seymour was sincere in his intention not to be a candidate under any circumstances.

On Monday afternoon the convention adjourned until Tuesday morning, whereupon the delegates repaired to the hotel barrooms and balconies to discuss the various candidates' prospects. A reporter asked Kate about her father's chances of success. "It is all a question," she said, "whether the Democratic party has the sense to seize its opportunities. I fear that when the South seceded the brains of the party went with it. Since then it has rarely missed an opportunity to blunder."

* * *

One person who would not have minded the Democrats blundering was New York senator Roscoe Conkling. A rising star in the Republican Party, he had more than a passing interest in the Democratic convention, as Horatio Seymour happened to be his brother-in-law. Their opposing political allegiances might have made for awkward conversation at family get-togethers, except that Conkling was living apart from his estranged wife, Julia, Seymour's sister, who preferred to stay in Utica while Conkling was in Washington.

As Conkling sat at his Senate desk that first week of July, he would watch and await the outcome of the Democratic gathering. A notorious ladies' man, whose handsome looks, impressive physique, and powerful oratory would earn him the title "Adonis of the Senate," he undoubtedly had his eye on Kate Chase Sprague. It could not have escaped his notice when it was reported in the press, two years earlier, that Mr. and Mrs. Sprague were about to divorce. The couple seemed like such an obvious mismatch that there had to be something to the rumors. Kate Chase was a woman Roscoe Conkling would have to get to know better.

**TUESDAY, JULY 7**—As the balloting for president got under way that morning, Kate sent her father an upbeat letter. "The excitement here is intense—The outside pressure is very great," she wrote, "and 'Chase' is the pass word in the throng gathered about Tammany Hall." There were "snares and pitfalls everywhere," she cautioned, but "the feeling improves every hour and there is a growing confidence everywhere that you will Ultimately be the choice."

The pitfalls related to both people and platform. Kate was frustrated with her inability to locate Van Buren, who was not around the convention much, and she had the same problem with Frederick Aiken, a lawyer and newspaper editor who served as a sort of master of ceremonies who introduced Kate to out-of-town delegates at her Fifth Avenue Hotel parlor. He also was secretary of the Chase "committee of one hundred," headquartered at the Chanler House, another base of operations set up on Fourteenth Street across from Tammany Hall. But Kate wrote her father on Tuesday, July 7, to say that Aiken was "too indiscreet to be trusted by you in any way." He would disappear for long stretches, she explained, then resurface, still hungover from drinking, to ask for reimbursement of headquarters expenses.*

As for the platform, adopted by the convention Tuesday morning, it was not a Chase-friendly document. It declined to endorse the chief justice's cherished principle in favor of voting rights for black Americans. It also contained inflammatory language denouncing "negro supremacy" and attacking the Reconstruction Acts as "unconstitutional, revolutionary, and void." But Kate was trying to convince her father not to be too fastidious over the wording. Her goal was getting him nominated, not standing on ceremony. She had excerpts of the platform telegraphed to him on Tuesday morning so he might have time to become comfortable with it. In a "P.S." she suggested that as soon as he saw the platform in the press that night, he send "such a telegram as may be advisable and *necessary* to be read in *open Convention*." Kate considered the time for vacillation to be over; her father needed to inform the delegates, as clearly as possible, that he was prepared to carry the Democratic banner into the fall election.

Chase did not respond as she might have hoped. He wrote Van Buren to say that, based on what he had seen, the platform was "in the main, very good," but he was not prepared to sign off on it until he had seen the entire document. To Kate he expressed even less enthusiasm. "I can accept well enough the platform," he wrote, "but I can't say that I like it." He was willing to have his name put forward if he was assured of being nominated but was worried at the prospect of endorsing a discreditable

---

*A former Union army officer with a checkered past, Aiken had gained fame defending Mary Surratt, the Washington, DC, boardinghouse owner who was tried and hung as a conspirator in the assassination of Lincoln.

platform, compromising his honor, and still losing. As a result, he placed his supporters on a tight leash, cautioning Kate not to "do or say anything which may not be proclaimed on the housetops." He was not making her job any easier.

In the meantime balloting for the nomination had begun. Six inconclusive tallies were recorded that Tuesday, producing no major surprises. Each followed the same pattern: a clear lead for Pendleton, but less than a majority and far short of the two-thirds needed to nominate. In second place was Hancock, followed by Sanford Church (New York's favorite-son candidate), then Hendricks. Around midafternoon the convention adjourned to Wednesday at 10 a.m. Aiken telegrammed Chase to let him know his name had "not yet [been] presented—all going well . . . carried our point in gaining time." Full of optimism, the Chase forces would be back at it again the following day.

* * *

Far away in Minnesota, Kate's half-sister, twenty-year-old Janet Ralston Chase, known to the family as "Nettie," was blissfully uninvolved with the hubbub of the Democratic convention. She was visiting relatives, hiking and exploring Indian country, and exhibiting her budding artistic talent with sketches of waterfalls and real wigwams, not those of the Tammany Hall variety. The breeziness of her letters back home reflected her carefree personality, so different from her father's or Kate's. "Do you know I think I have inherited a soupçon of the old pioneer spirit," she wrote her father, "for when I feel myself beyond civilization, a kind of wild delight comes over me, my Indian wakes and gives a warhoop." She told of stopping at an inn at midnight under the aurora borealis and having a hot supper made for her group by a farmer's wife who "told us she had a Sister living in the *West*. I suppose she considers Minnesota as the East." She had received a letter from her father the prior night that presumably included a discussion of politics, and, without commenting on its contents, she said she "liked the envelope best of all." That was typical Nettie. She was happy enough in Minnesota, making her outdoor sketches "on the back of a note book with the end of a burnt match." And glad not to have to worry about delegations, platforms, and candidates in the Wigwam on Fourteenth Street.

**WEDNESDAY, JULY 8**—As the week progressed, the weather began to cool off outside Tammany Hall, but inside the convention things were heating up. On the seventh ballot, taken Wednesday morning, Pendleton increased his lead, which worried the New Yorkers. On the next ballot New York switched its support from its favorite son, Church, to Indiana's Hendricks, who vaulted into second place and headed off any rush to Pendleton.

The ninth through eleventh ballots showed little change. It was now midafternoon, and Kate was waiting for a letter from her father expressing support for the platform. But before anything came the secretary began to call the roll for the twelfth ballot: "Alabama: Eight for Pendleton. Arkansas: Five for Hendricks." Then the leader of the California delegation stepped forward. Of the five votes the state had to cast, three went to Pendleton, one and a half to Hendricks, and, in a surprise announcement, one-half vote would go to . . . Salmon P. Chase.

Prolonged cheering rose from the galleries and hall. As it began to subside, a few scattered hisses were heard, prompting a renewal of applause. A Chase man recalled it as "a scene of delirious excitement, which lasted unremittingly for ten minutes" and brought the proceedings to a halt. "It was a strange and extraordinary occurrence; and thoroughly bewildering to most of the members of the convention."

As she joined in the applause that afternoon, Kate was not bewildered at all; she was exhilarated and maybe a bit misty-eyed. For, despite her reputation as a cold, Machiavellian schemer, she had a sensitive inner emotional core and cried easily at the theater. This was a moment to shed tears of joy. For now, surely, the convention would jump on the Chase bandwagon and nominate her adored father. He would, indeed, defeat General Grant, and Kate would, at last, become the First Lady of the land.

It was a position for which her whole life to that point had prepared her. In fact, her training had begun nearly two decades earlier, not more than a ten-minute walk from the convention hall where she now stood, cheering her father's name.

# PART 1

# MISS CHASE

CHAPTER 1

# "Qualified to Ornament Any Society"

Mademoiselle Henriette Desportes (or Deluzy, her alias in Paris), stepped off the steamer *Zurich* in New York harbor in mid-September 1849, carrying a Manhattan address with her: 10 Gramercy Park. Her new life in America could only be better than the one she left behind in France, where she was a suspected accomplice in that country's notorious murder of the century.*

To gain work in America, Henriette needed to find an employer who would judge her not on her past but on her merits: as a teacher of art and French and as a woman of ready wit and intellect. She had found the right place—10 Gramercy Park was the home of Miss Haines's School for Girls as well as its headmistress, Henrietta B. Haines. One of the most exclusive and fashionable girls' private boarding schools in the country, it was, importantly, a meritocracy.

At the same time thirty-six-year-old Henriette Desportes set sail for New York, nine-year-old Kate Chase was preparing to head to the same

---

*She had been the governess of the children of a French duchess who was found bludgeoned to death in her Paris mansion just weeks after Henriette left her household because of suspicions of an affair with the duchess's husband, the Duc Theobald de Praslin. The Duc, clearly guilty of the crime, committed suicide by swallowing poison before he could be brought to trial. Henriette was jailed, repeatedly interrogated, and finally let go for lack of evidence.

place. Unlike Henriette, young Kate was going there not to rebuild a life but to start one. Nevertheless, the concept was the same. Most of her classmates were day pupils from the wealthiest, old-line New York families, with Dutch settler names like Van Horn, Schuyler, and De Peyster, the English DeLancey and Jay, and the French Lorillard. Kate would be a minority—a hick from the West, as Ohio was considered in those days. The New York girls would return home at night to their families, whereas Kate would be on her own, one of only a handful of actual boarders. She was also younger than most of the other students. She would need to prove herself, but if she had what it took, she could become the equal of any girl there.

Beginning with the January term in 1850, Kate's and Henriette Desportes's tenures at Miss Haines's School overlapped for about a year and a half, during which the former governess taught the girls French and supervised their daily walks, two abreast, around Gramercy Park. Those walks, along with the classroom scenes inside Miss Haines's School, would be immortalized nearly a century later in Rachel Field's novel, *All This, And Heaven Too*, and in the 1940 Bette Davis film of the same name. Although Field, Henriette Desportes's great-niece, based her book on fact, the movie would mistakenly portray Haines as an elderly spinster. Single she was—divorced after a brief marriage to a Christian missionary in her early twenties. But Henrietta Haines in 1849 was only thirty-three, younger than Mademoiselle Desportes. Yet already by 1849 her boarding school had acquired a reputation for excellence. She also boasted of its new setting in a handsome, five-story brownstone overlooking Gramercy Park, then as now a serene oasis in a bustling metropolis.

The surroundings may have been pleasant, but the Spartan school regimen was anything but. Up at 5:30 a.m., the girls studied until seven, followed by prayers and a continental breakfast of buttered bread, honey, and café au lait. They took the first of their two daily walks at eight in the morning, promenading six times around the park, then several blocks north up Lexington Avenue and back for the beginning of school. In class until about 2 p.m., they took their second walk of the day, returning by three for some free time, followed by a study hour that, as one girl recalled, was "pretty severe for we could hardly breathe" without the teacher's permission. After dinner they had an hour of French conversation, more study or listening to Miss Haines read aloud, then tea and prayers until bedtime at 8 p.m. On Tuesday "parlor nights" the girls could stay up an extra hour to sew, knit, or sketch. Some evenings they would perform little scenes or "tableaux." Weekends involved much church going and singing. It was an exacting program, but the students kept coming back, year after year. An instructor recalled that the girls enjoyed well-cooked, generous meals and were "*taught table manners!*" The school was often called "the Manners School."

Miss Haines displayed a violent temper at times. But Julia Newberry, a student who feared the tall, blackly clad headmistress at first, found her "*supremely* gracious." As the young girl recalled, Miss Haines "called me 'my dear' all the time. She sat on the sofa and her eyes twinkled."

The school's educational curriculum combined hard learning with more artful instruction designed to prepare the girls for society. In addition to French, Kate studied Latin, geography, history, math, English grammar, spelling, penmanship, and composition. She read Oliver Goldsmith's "Deserted Village" as well as Longfellow, Dickens, and Emerson. She received religious instruction and heard visiting lectures on theology, glaciers, and geology. Piano and dancing—cotillions and waltzes—were also on the agenda. Particularly relevant to her later skills as a hostess, she was taught elocution—the art of speaking and pronunciation.

Kate's father sent her there not just to get her out of his hair but also as part of his grand plan for her. Although conservative in style and tone, Henrietta Haines's school was part of mainstream progressive thought in women's education, following the lead of such proponents as Cincinnati's Catharine Beecher, the sister of Harriet Beecher Stowe and famed clergyman Henry Ward Beecher, all acquaintances of Chase. In a book published the year after Kate's birth, Catharine Beecher advocated sending girls to boarding schools not only to learn home economics but also to receive instruction in the natural sciences and language arts so they might "develop a parlor-based culture that would spread their influence over the entire nation." It was as if she were writing prophetically about young Kate Chase.

From her time in New York, Kate also took away a taste for culture, sophistication, and the finer things in life. A small-town girl in the big city for the first time, she gained exposure to theater, opera, and other entertainments. She and her schoolmates had front-row seats to hear Jenny Lind, the celebrated Swedish soprano, make her American debut at the

Castle Garden in Battery Park. It was in New York too that Kate developed her interest in expensive clothes and fashion. In 1854 Catharine Beekman, a year younger than Kate, recalled in a letter to her mother how, for one of their tableaux, some of the girls had sent to Boston for dresses and spent "at least a month getting them up." Kate was probably one of those doing the getting up. A year later her father asked her to validate a more than $300 bill she had run up for clothing (equivalent to $8,000 in 2014 dollars), including "24 yds of cross-barred muslin [fabric], 18 yds of linen, silk dress, Miss Wharton's bill for making dresses . . . 4 pairs of boots and shoes . . . 2 bonnets," plus incidentals such as combs, bows, and a parasol. The teenaged Kate responded peremptorily, "I have examined this bill and find everything correct. C.J. Chase." It was the first of many times her extravagance would be called into question.

The four and a half years Kate spent at Miss Haines's School had an incalculable impact on her. It was here that she acquired the deportment and conversational skills she would use to her advantage the rest of her life. She shared the stage with other young, intelligent girls, most of whom were well ahead of her in worldliness and sophistication when she first arrived. And she proved she could be one of them.

Although Kate would later express pride at having attended this celebrated school, her memories of her time there were not all fond ones. Described as "a little devil," she found the atmosphere stifling. Miss Haines, to whom the girls had to curtsy, emphasized "three deadly sins": crossing the legs, lifting the hands from the lap, and running instead of walking gracefully. "What little prigs we were!" recalled one girl. Kate may not have liked her classmates much, for she roomed most of her time not with other girls but with her French teacher, Camille de Janon, who took over in 1851 when Henriette Desportes married a minister and became a highly regarded salon hostess herself. Although Kate made a couple of girlfriends, she formed no lasting relationships from her years at the Haines School. In fact, for most of her life she had very few close female friends. "She would frankly tell me," her youngest daughter later recalled, "that she always detested women, however much she might like men."

Kate's relationship with Miss Haines also was problematic. Kate was lonely in New York, but in December 1852 the headmistress denied Kate's request to go home for Christmas, saying she did not think Kate deserved that pleasure at that time. Chase told his daughter he was sure she must have done something wrong or neglected some duty. He wrote her to say he would acquiesce in Miss Haines's views and that she should as well. It is unlikely that Kate, homesick in New York while her classmates returned to their families for Christmas, took kindly to this advice.

Kate's memories of the Haines School also were tarnished by the steady stream of letters—critical, reproachful, and sometimes downright cruel—that she received from her father during her years there. His letters would always be leavened with words of love and encouragement and relieved by occasional praise, but they were not the sort of letters a lonely young girl would wish to receive from an absent father she adored.

During her first year of school in New York, in 1850, Kate's father cautioned her not to be selfish, scolded her for not writing more frequently, judged her letters as poor, and admonished her for being untruthful. On her tenth birthday, writing from his Senate chamber in Washington, her father had this to say to her: "You have said a good deal in your letters in excuse of your delays and bad writing. I do not like excuses. They are not often strictly true, and they are almost invariably in bad taste." He told her she had not yet "cultivated those habits of self denial" necessary to keeping up a daily journal, as he always did. "There is another thing which I want to speak to you about," he continued. "You do not always speak the exact truth. This is a *very-very* bad *habit.* If you do not overcome it, it will grow upon you and will ruin you forever." He did manage to notice some improvement in her handwriting from her last letter and, having otherwise faulted her letter, was glad to conclude it with a compliment. He forgot to wish her a happy birthday, however—not the last time that would happen.

Three weeks later he was back at her. "You have not in any letter, taken any notice of what I wrote some weeks since on the subject of your negligence in not writing punctually and some other matters. What is the meaning of this? The least it *can* mean is that you are very thoughtless." He closed by saying that when she wrote him better letters he would try to improve the quality of his.

Kate was not the only family member who came in for such treatment. Around the same time, for example, in a letter to his twenty-nine-year-old wife, Kate's stepmother, Chase pointed out that she had spelled "Tuesday" as "tewsday." A few years later he would tell nine-year-old Nettie, Kate's sister, that her last letter was "not nearly as good as some little girls write who are no older than you are." He would later disparage one of Nettie's letters as careless and ragged looking and, on another occasion, would accuse her of "heedlessness." But his most severe and consistent criticism was reserved for Kate, if only because he expected so much more from her.

He gave Kate credit on those infrequent occasions when he thought it due, telling her in early 1851 that her last two letters were among her best. But the praise never lasted long and invariably was overridden by criticism in ensuing exchanges. Sometimes he faulted her handwriting, as when he wrote in March 1851 to say that her letters were too small and pinched looking. Another time he told her she needed to take more care in joining all the letters of each word, for in her last letter she had written "pleasure" as "pleas ure." These were hypocritical comments, coming from someone whose own handwriting was notoriously illegible. Anticipating this very argument from Kate, he instructed her to "follow my precept rather than my practice."

But his most stinging criticisms were not of Kate's handwriting but of her style. He repeatedly lamented the dullness of her prose and prodded her to enliven her letters with greater detail about everyday life. "You set down only naked facts without any embellishment whatever," he wrote. Like the diners who complained about the restaurant where the food was no good and of such small portions, he said her letters were both poorly written and too infrequent. "I hope the other little girls, under Miss Haines's care, are more punctual and better correspondents than you are," he wrote her in September 1851, adding, "If not[,] their parents will not be very well satisfied with them." But when the letters came he wasn't satisfied. They were too wooden, he said; she needed to "write exactly as you would talk, and tell me, just as you would in conversation, of all I wish to know." In a particularly scathing post he called her letters "mere dry bones" and reflective of "habitual disregard of your father's wishes." He added that in his view she was certainly old enough (at age twelve) to realize the pain she caused him.

None of Kate's letters from this period have survived, so her side of the story is untold. But at least one of her excuses may be inferred from one of her father's letters. She defended the lack of spontaneity in her writing on the grounds that Miss Haines read all of her students' outgoing correspondence before it was sent. Kate also knew that her serious-minded father would have no interest in hearing about the sorts of things that engaged a young girl—dresses, fabrics, and dances—subjects the other girls could write about to their mothers. Although he would come to admire her intellect, Kate's father did not encourage his daughter to think creatively, outside the box of religious dedication and worldly striving that he constructed for her.

As Kate grew older, Chase adopted an even more biting tone with her. In September 1853, the start of what would prove to be her final year at the Haines School, he called her last letter, written on her birthday, "rather a poor beginning for your new year. . . . I don't wonder you were 'ashamed to send this miserable scrawl' especially as the first letter of a young lady of thirteen." Three months later he said that, based on a specimen of her French translations, "I am afraid you do not think enough." He commanded that "what you do at all, do well."

Her father's constant remonstrations, over a period from 1850 to 1854, had to wear on Kate. Her years at the Haines School may have been useful, but they were often painful—good for grooming but not emotionally satisfying.

It also did not help that her father compared Kate's more complicated personality with the sweet, good-humored nature of her younger half-sister. After receiving a letter in October 1853 that Kate thought she had infused with levity, he told her he found it "short and not *very* funny." But Nettie was "the most winsome little creature" one could imagine, he wrote Kate a couple of weeks later. The following year, shortly after Kate left the Haines School, he again praised Nettie while taking a direct swipe at Kate. "Artless, guileless, truthful, affectionate, and winning[,] she [Nettie] gains all hearts. It is by loving others that she makes others love her. There is a lesson in this, dear Katie. Can't you tell what it is?"

Kate's last month at the Haines School came in June 1854. In early July Chase received her report card, which he disparaged as unacceptable even though she ranked eighth in her class. As a young man, Chase had said that he wanted to be "first wherever I may be," and now he wanted no less from Kate. "The time has come," he told her that July, "when you must put on your thinking cap and use your brains, and qualify yourself for a part in society." He wanted her to lead a useful and refined life. "I desire that you may be qualified to ornament any society in our own country or elsewhere," he told her. As usual, in the same letter in which he bemoaned her grades, he tempered his lament with a bit of praise, saying he was pleased with a composition of hers, entitled "The Hand." Then he took most of it back, expressing doubt that she could have written it herself. "Were you not helped in it?" he asked. "If not absolutely your own, how much was?"

Yet all the questioning and reproach Kate received from her father did nothing to diminish her love for him. As far as she was concerned he was immune from censure. She may have been reluctant to counter him for fear he would transfer all his attention and devotion to Nettie. But it went beyond any sibling rivalry. As much as Kate may have recoiled from her father's criticism, she proceeded to internalize it, for fundamentally she accepted his notions of perfectionism. She was too much like him to do otherwise. Kate too was ambitious, sought perfection, and, though clever in speech, had little sense of humor, at least when it came to herself. She would strive for perfect salons, perfect clothes, a perfect marriage. And so, without a trace of irony, she could write her younger sister Nettie, as she did a few years later, to say "Your last letter was a great improvement upon the others, still the spelling is not perfect." She would one day compliment her own son on the neatness and care of his latest letter while criticizing its style. "Grandpapa would complain of my schoolgirl efforts and say, 'don't let your letters be all *dry bones* my daughter, put *some meat* on *them*,'" she wrote Willie when he was approaching twelve. "I repeat his advice to you my dearest Willie," she continued. "Write as you would talk. Tell what interests you and be sure it will interest your parents who follow your every little act."

"You, I think, are like me," Chase told Kate, when she was but ten, beginning her second year of school with Miss Haines. He saw her even then as mirroring himself, including his flaws. "I wish you could put a little more life into your letters," he wrote her, "but I cannot blame you much seeing there is so little life in mine."

That there was little life in Salmon Chase's letters was true, but it was easy enough to understand. As he wrote his friend Charles Sumner, the great abolitionist senator, in 1850, death had been pursuing him incessantly his entire life. And given that ever-present shadow, one needed to do as much as possible in the little time one had. "I wish to see you as accomplished as a lady whom I saw in Philadelphia—a Miss Furness who understands French, Italian and German, converses in all three languages, writes beautifully and talks as well as she writes," he wrote Kate in her final year at the Haines School. "I hope you will not merely equal but excel her before you are twenty," he wrote. "But don't think because twenty to you is seven years off you have plenty of time to spare. No, indeed. Every minute is precious. You must not lose any of them." Ever since his childhood in New Hampshire, Salmon Chase had striven to achieve for himself what he now sought for Kate and what Rachel Field believed her Great-Aunt Henriette Desportes finally achieved in America as well: both earthly accomplishment and eternal grace—all of this, and heaven too.

CHAPTER 2

# "I Shall Strive to Be First Wherever I May Be"

So close was the bond between them, so indelibly linked are they in history, that to understand Kate one must come to know her famous father, Salmon Portland Chase.

He was born in Cornish, New Hampshire, on January 13, 1808, a year before Abraham Lincoln, and had several things in common with his future rival. Both were sons of farmers and disliked farm work. Chase lost his father at age nine, the same age at which Lincoln's mother died. Both youths grew up tall, sought to escape their rustic backgrounds, and gravitated to the law. Neither had an impressive speaking voice: Lincoln's was a high-pitched, midwestern twang, whereas the deep-voiced Chase struggled to overcome an "almost childlike little lisp." But there the similarities mostly ended.

The third youngest of ten children, Salmon obtained a solid formal education, something Lincoln never had. Although his father had only a country boy's schooling, most of Salmon's uncles attended Dartmouth College. One of them, Salmon, was a prominent lawyer in Maine and the source of the name Chase always disliked because it sounded "fishy." Another was a US senator from Vermont, and others were learned professionals—doctors and clergymen.

Chase's father, Ithamar, was a successful farmer, church warden, and local office holder. Esteemed by his Cornish neighbors, he represented them for a number of years in the New Hampshire legislature. But he left it all behind in late 1815, when he moved his family to Keene, some thirty miles away, to invest in a glass factory and run the hotel-tavern his wife had inherited. The glass factory soon failed, and Ithamar descended toward bankruptcy. In 1817 Ithamar died following a massive stroke at age fifty-four, leaving his widow and children impoverished and threatening Salmon's educational progress. But one of his uncles, Episcopalian Bishop Philander Chase (a bizarre name for a preacher) agreed to bring the fatherless twelve-year-old Salmon to Worthington, Ohio, near Columbus, where the bishop headed a boys' school and kept a farm in addition to ministering to his small flock. At Worthington and, later, at Cincinnati College, where Bishop Chase assumed the presidency in 1822, young Chase continued a classical education that, in New Hampshire, had already included Latin, Greek, and Euclidean geometry.

Unlike Lincoln, who had no religious inclinations to speak of, Salmon Chase embraced the Christian faith. His mother, Janet Ralston Chase, was a pious and cultured woman who had him baptized into the Episcopal Church, and Uncle Philander imbued him with strong spiritual impulses. Whereas Lincoln's stepmother was a kind and loving woman, helping foster young Abe's famous amiability, Bishop Philander was, as Chase would later recall, a "tyrannical" figure. Physically imposing at over six feet tall, the bishop secured Chase's obedience but not his affection. He was a strict taskmaster who kept young Salmon busy with rigorous study and monotonous farm chores. When his nephew was disobedient or indolent, Bishop Chase beat the boy or locked him up, justifying such punishment by quoting the Bible. Still, Salmon considered his uncle to be a good man and was heavily influenced by him. Philander Chase's tendency to view the world in black and white ethical terms would find expression in Salmon Chase's own off-putting moral certitude. And his uncle's demand for perfection would show up in Chase's letters to his daughters. When Chase admonished Kate and Nettie to do better, he was hearing echoes of Philander Chase in his ear.

Chase hated his time in Ohio. He counted the days until he could return to New Hampshire or find work elsewhere. He got his wish in 1823, when Philander Chase resigned the presidency of Cincinnati College and headed to England to raise funds for an Episcopal seminary he planned to start in Ohio, which became Kenyon College. Salmon went home to

Keene, where he taught school for a while, despite being only fifteen. But he was fired after parents complained that he was administering excessive corporal punishment. As Chase remembered it, one of the older students was acting up, so he cracked him on the head with the end of a cane. Salmon had more than a little of his Uncle Philander in him.

At age sixteen Chase entered Dartmouth College as a junior. It was a liberating experience, and the two years he spent at Dartmouth were among the few times in his life Chase let loose, if only a little. He partook liberally in gossip, assigned his classmates clever nicknames, and made several lifelong friends. But despite graduating Phi Beta Kappa and eighth in his class of thirty-six, he expressed regret at wasting so much time there. To his former classmate, Tom Sparhawk, he confessed to reading too many novels and light works and told him that, considering "the shortness of time and magnitude of the work which each of us must perform," he was ashamed of his own listlessness. Even at a young age Chase had adopted the notion that life on earth was fleeting.

Salmon Chase was a determined and opinionated young man. In his first year at Dartmouth he staged a successful one-man protest to reinstate an innocent classmate who had been suspended from school. While attending college he also taught school, loathing every minute of it. He considered his students insolent and said he "would sooner undertake to teach the wild Indians, than again attempt to instruct *savages* of our enlightened land."

Chase's letters during and shortly after his years at Dartmouth reflect a chattiness and irreverence lacking in his later correspondence. He dotted them with witticisms and French phrases, talked of "old Bison's falling in love for the 99th time," and told his friend Sparhawk, after learning that one of their female acquaintances was engaged to a physician, that he would "give the end of my little fingernail to know a thing or two in relation to this match." But the serious young man always returned to the themes of duty and moral striving. Two years after graduation he summed up his philosophy in a letter to Sparhawk: "I regard this world not as a place of leisure—not as a place of selfish exertion, but as a vast theatre upon which each man has a part allotted to him to perform and duties to discharge which connect him closely with his fellowman." A year later he wrote again to say that "I am not sorry that I have been a pedagogue. It is good to have borne the yoke in one's youth." He was the ripe old age of twenty-one.

By this time Chase was living in Washington, DC, hoping to pursue a legal career. His older brother Alexander predicted he would be "a shining ornament to the profession." But Salmon needed money to support his legal studies and ended up teaching school again. He asked his Uncle Dudley, the US senator, to help him get a government clerkship, but he was turned down on the grounds that he was better off fending for himself. "I once obtained an office for a nephew of mine and he was ruined by it," Uncle Dudley told him. "I will give you fifty cents with which to buy a spade; but I will not help to put you in a clerkship." And so, despite his misgivings about teaching, he took over a class of a dozen or so boys and taught classics to them for more than two years. Among his students were the sons of Senator Henry Clay and several of President John Quincy Adams's cabinet members. He found this group more obedient than the "brats" he had taught in New England and liked the school "as well as I ever shall like any school." That was not saying much. He still detested the drudgery and thanklessness of school teaching and continued to draw complaints from parents for doling out whippings to miscreant students. He later confessed to Kate, in trying to convince her to sympathize with her boarding school faculty, that during his teaching years he went to school each morning resolved to control his temper but too often "the petty vexations and cares of the schoolroom swept away the defenses of good resolutions."

The disgruntled young instructor also had little use for almost every other Washington inhabitant and institution. His fellow teachers were a "miserable set"; Congress was full of lazy, stupid men; and the city's class structure was akin to the Hindu caste system. He met President John Quincy Adams at a White House soirée and found him "stiff as a crowbar," like an "Automaton chess-Player." The president's successor, Andrew Jackson, was an "ignoramus," a "rash, violent military chief" whose followers were a vulgar mob and whose then secretary of state, Martin Van Buren, was a "contemptible intriguer."

Though not yet politically involved, Chase was beginning to show a spectator's interest in presidential politics. His views on slavery were still unformed; although slaves were constantly on display in Washington, Chase had yet to develop the messianic hatred of the institution that preoccupied him in later years. Rather than supporting abolition, he thought it made sense to colonize African Americans on the Pacific Coast or send them back to Africa. But even three decades before the Civil War he sensed that one day the issue would split the country. He told Sparhawk he expected to "see this Union dissolved and I do not know that New England has much reason to deprecate such an event."

The bright spot in the three years he spent in Washington was his friendship with the family of William Wirt, the attorney general in the Adams administration, whose sons were among Chase's pupils. Chase in turn became a law student of Wirt's. Although the busy attorney generally spent little time supervising the young man's superficial study, Chase saw more of him at Wirt's home, where the multitalented lawyer, biographer, and man of letters became a role model for Chase in a way his uncle the bishop had never been. Wirt reminded Chase more of his late father, Ithamar, who had "ruled by kind words and kind looks" and kept Salmon "pretty straight by the mildest means." Wirt was antislavery and supported rights for Native Americans. Generous and gentlemanly, he invited the lonely Chase into his large household, where the young man recalled spending many happy hours in song around the piano, listening to poetry, and engaging in conversation.

The Wirt home was a gathering place for Washington's social elite, but of greater interest to Chase were two of Wirt's unmarried daughters, Elizabeth and Catharine. He accompanied the pair to galleries, receptions, and concerts—the first time in his life he socialized with members of the opposite sex. He wrote a college friend to say that both of them possessed highly cultivated minds, good taste, and elegant manners. Elizabeth, the older, may have been the inspiration for the diary he started on New Year's Day in 1829 (one he would maintain for the rest of his life), for in the second entry, on January 10, he wrote that she had "bright raven locks and a fine frank open brunette countenance. She moves like a wind-borne thing over the earth." Chase thought of trying to win her affection, but being unsure of his future, he felt it would be unfair to her. She also might not have appreciated the well-meaning but inept description of her that he recorded in his diary and later expanded into a poem, entitled "The Sisters," that he inscribed privately to her and Catharine. "She was not very beautiful," he wrote of Elizabeth, "and yet . . . " The poem went on to extol her other fine qualities of intellect and loveliness, but if Elizabeth saw what Chase had written about her, she could hardly have been blamed if she lost interest in him after the words "not very beautiful." A year later he was close to falling in love with another girl he found "slight and frail but exquisitely molded" and would have done so had they in one critical respect not been so dissimilar. "She is fond of the gay world," he lamented, whereas he had "no desire to partake in its vanities. She is disinclined to religion and its duties; I value them more than any earthly possession."

He tended to idealize women. As he wrote to his Dartmouth friend Hamilton Smith, man was "always the seducer, woman the seduced," and "any inference which would affect injuriously the character of the female sex would fall still more heavily upon our own." If patronizing, his attitude was more progressive than most. Whatever negative traits females possessed as a gender, he insisted, were instilled, not inborn. "Are they deceitful and dang[erous]; are their affections light, fickle or evanescent?" he asked Smith. Answering his own question, he wrote, "They often are; but why? Because man has taught them so to be. But naturally it is not so." He saw that women could be just as logical and intellectual as men; on a ride to the country shortly before his twenty-second birthday the young Chase met "two agreeable, intelligent girls who had read much, thought much and (perhaps) talked more. They made subtle distinctions with a skill worthy of old Aristotle, and syllogized as if they [had] been educated in the school of . . . Thomas Aquinas." He found this particular pair too pushy for his tastes, though, for he immediately added in his diary that he did not like "argumentative ladies." Nonetheless, in the same entry he mocked the claim that men were "entitled to an exclusive monopoly of all the wit, sense and learning in the world." And although he never encouraged his own daughters to go to college or pursue their own professional careers, this was not because he viewed them as inferior beings due to their gender; it was not the norm then for women, even from socially advanced families of means, to attend college, and Chase was far from a wealthy man himself. The widower Chase was also more than happy to have Kate and, later, Nettie serve as his domestic hostesses.

When it came to male and female relationships, Chase and Kate were mirror images of each other: he formed closer attachments with women than with men, and she too got along better with members of the opposite sex. Like most successful public men, Chase was able, as he became older, to attract a following from younger male protégés. But, with few exceptions, he never developed intimate friendships with men of his own generation and social standing. He was not one to hang out with the boys at the bar, smoke cigars, or play poker on Saturday nights. (He neither drank nor used tobacco, and he avoided—in fact, in his own home disallowed—card playing and games of chance.) Things were different with women. Without self-consciousness he could share with them his interests in softer disciplines: literature, French, poetry, religion. By his midtwenties his awkwardness around women was largely behind him, and he became attractive to the opposite sex.

There was one other girl from his youth who was the one who got away. Elizabeth Hannah Cabell, the niece of William Wirt, was the daughter of a former Virginia governor. Chase described her in his diary in 1829 as "a pretty young lady of eighteen" who was "singularly sensible and intelligent; but timid as a fawn." Eugene Didier, his private secretary many years later, wrote that she allowed him to escort her to social events and found him clever and intelligent but would not consider marrying a poor young schoolteacher with no apparent prospects. Yet for Chase, according to his secretary, "the aroma of that early love still lingered many years afterward." When, as chief justice, he was visiting Richmond with Nettie, they were paid a visit by Elizabeth Cabell's niece. Chase "recalled with tender feeling the circumstance of his youthful love and its result. When he spoke of his first sweetheart there was a pathos in the voice of the calm and dignified Chief Justice, which was as rare as it was interesting."

Though admitted to the Washington, DC, bar, Chase left the capital in 1830 and returned to Cincinnati. The main reason for his move was the departure of the Wirt family to Baltimore in April 1829, following the change in administrations, from Adams to Jackson, that ended William Wirt's tenure as attorney general. Wirt's daughters Elizabeth and Catharine relocated to Virginia, and Chase's entire social life left with them. Dazed, he attended a public auction of the furniture Wirt left behind, not to buy anything but "to pass once more through the house." He wandered into the deserted rooms where Elizabeth had dressed while he waited for her downstairs and where Wirt had maintained his study, and then he entered the garden that had been Mrs. Wirt's favorite spot. "But her step was no more among them. She was far away. . . . I went home."

Chase thought for a time of following Wirt to Baltimore and becoming a lawyer there, but he longed to be a bigger fish in a smaller pond. "I would rather be *first* in Cincinnati than first in Baltimore, twenty years hence," he wrote to Charles Cleveland, a former Dartmouth classmate, soon after turning twenty-two. "And as I have ever been first at school and college (except at Dartmouth where I was an idle goose) I shall strive to be first wherever I may be." He asked his friend not to laugh at his idea of changing his name to "Spencer De Cheyce or Spencer Payne Cheyce." That thought went nowhere, but the pompous impulse behind it would remain. So would the ambition. As he wrote his friend Smith shortly before the Wirts left Washington, "I have always thought that Providence intended me as the instrument of effecting something more than falls to the lot of all men to achieve."

And so in early 1830, after three years in the nation's capital, he found himself back in Ohio, a lawyer in search of a practice, a bachelor in search of a wife, and a man in search of greatness. All three would come to him, and in that order. But so would repeated family tragedy, for which he would seek compensation in the birth and life of a beloved daughter.

CHAPTER 3

# "How Short Then Is This Life!"

The ten years between Salmon Chase's return to Cincinnati and the birth of Kate, in 1840, were marked by impressive public accomplishment and untold private grief.

During the 1830s Chase became a moderately prosperous banking lawyer, but his interests ranged far beyond his legal practice. He founded a lyceum for popular lectures; joined the "Semi-Colon" literary society; became a Sunday school superintendent; was active in the local temperance movement; read prodigiously of history, philosophy, and theology; and, in a gargantuan task, compiled a comprehensive annotated edition of the statutes of Ohio. His schedule was so busy that for a time he planned each day's activities in writing, down to the half hour, then recorded how closely he had adhered to the program. His plan for June 26, 1840, for example, had him rising at 4:30 a.m. and bathing and dressing by 5:30. He rose a little late, so he skipped the bath to stay on schedule. The next day he was more diligent: "½ past 4 to ½ past 5—Shower bath—repetition of Psalm—dress—15 minutes past 4 to ¼ past 5—accomplished all." He ended his eighteen-hour day just before ten o'clock, when he retired to bed after recording the next day's plan.

Chase's greatest passion, however, was reserved for the growing antislavery cause. His feelings were galvanized in 1836, when angry mobs of white Cincinnati race rioters attacked James Birney, a former slaveholder turned abolitionist newspaper publisher, twice destroying his printing press. Among the disgusted observers were Chase and his fellow Semi-Colon Club member Harriet Beecher Stowe. The incident had a profound influence on both of them: she would go on to write *Uncle Tom's Cabin*, a book that made Chase cry, and he would become a national leader of the antislavery movement.

When the anti-Birney mob reached the steps of the Franklin House, where the publisher lived but was absent that night, they found the doorway blocked by the six-foot-two, twenty-eight-year-old Chase. One of the ringleaders asked for his name, and when he told them, he was warned that he would pay for his actions. "I told him that I could be found at any time," Chase recalled. When the crowd learned that Birney was not home, it calmed down and dispersed. It was an act of courage on Chase's part, for although Ohio was a free state, abolitionism was unpopular in Cincinnati, a border town heavily dependent on the slave trade with states south of the Ohio River, especially neighboring Kentucky. As a key stopping point on the Underground Railroad that transported runaway slaves from captivity to freedom, Cincinnati was plagued by constant racial tensions and periodic rioting.

Chase believed the city authorities had acted shamefully for having failed to condemn the rioters, and forever after he would hold a strong antipathy toward mob justice. He was not technically an abolitionist, he insisted, taking pains to explain in a letter to the editor that he acted to protect Birney principally out of his belief in freedom of the press. To be called an abolitionist in Cincinnati at the time, recalled the well-known Ohio journalist Donn Piatt, was tantamount to being "denounced as a thief or a burglar." In fact, although most schoolbook histories identify him with the abolitionists, Chase was never one of them, strictly speaking. Chase believed, as did Lincoln, that although the federal government should do everything it could to contain the spread of slavery and do nothing affirmatively to protect the peculiar institution, it was powerless under the Constitution to interfere with slavery in the states where it existed.

But if cautious about adopting the abolitionist label, Chase was fearless when it came to advancing the antislavery cause. "He was to speak, one night, at a little school-house some four miles from Cincinnati," Piatt recounted in his memoirs, "and notice had been served on him that if he did he would be mobbed. This had no effect on Chase. He was a brave man, and a threat of violence only made him the more determined to fill his appointment." A group of ruffians threw eggs at him through the window, and though they hit their mark, Chase wiped them from his chest with a handkerchief and went on with his speech.

"Chase was no recluse, no book-worm, no merely philosophic, speculative Abolitionist," said his Cincinnati law partner (and one-time Ohio governor) George Hoadly. "He believed in work and in methods; believed in parties, committees, machinery, organization, in newspapers, speeches, letters, persuasion; in short, in every species of agitation. He was no apostle of non-resistance or submission, but a propagandist of political war." His most visible efforts as a Cincinnati lawyer were on behalf of runaway slaves. Chase gained national recognition for his argument that the fugitive slave law, which required the return of escaped slaves to their masters, was unconstitutional as "contrary to natural right." Chase rarely turned down an opportunity to represent a runaway slave, even though such cases earned him no money and he lost—and expected to lose—almost all of them, including the famous *Van Zandt* case that went to the US Supreme Court. So habitual was Chase's handling of this class of cases that he became known as the "Attorney General for Runaway Negroes." Among his most treasured possessions was a silver pitcher given to him by the black citizens of Cincinnati, honoring his "zealous and disinterested advocacy of the rights and privileges of all classes of your fellow citizens, irrespective of clime, color or condition." In thanking the donors, Chase stated his position—radical even for antislavery advocates at the time—that black men should be entitled to vote.

The gusto with which Chase threw himself into the antislavery cause is largely attributable to his strong moral and religious impulses. He also had a burning desire to achieve something great beyond himself, and although his advocacy of equal rights for African Americans did not endear him to many voters, it allowed him to carve out a niche on the national stage. And he knew that if he remained constant to the cause, his time would come. "The movement, no doubt, must be in the beginning unpopular," he wrote his friend Charles Cleveland in 1841. "But it will go on and gain friends constantly. In a little while multitudes will come out of their hiding place and join the advancing host of Liberty."

But there was an additional factor that made him pursue his life's work with such fervor. It allowed him to lose himself in great public endeavors and submerge the terrible personal tragedies he had suffered in his private life. Indeed, Chase was dogged by the relentless way in which death constantly pursued him.

The first blow was the worst one. In 1834 Chase married Catharine Jane "Kitty" Garniss, the only child of a well-to-do businessman who lived with his wife and daughter in the same lodging house as Chase. Chase, who considered the Garniss family nouveau riche "pretenders to style," initially regarded Catharine as "an affected and shallow girl" whose large features and plain face did not please him. Another man, however, remembered her as a brilliant woman whose regal carriage contrasted with the awkward and ungainly Chase. Kitty Garniss shared that opinion of Chase, considering him uncouth and in need of some polishing up.

Much as he derided the Garnisses as social climbers, Chase secretly longed to be part of their society. His interest in Kitty Garniss grew slowly but inexorably. After she went away for a season to New Orleans, where she reigned as a belle, and he survived a near-deadly bout with rheumatic fever, promising to "live a more godly life" if he recovered, they began seeing each other more in Cincinnati at parties and friends' weddings and on rides in the country. His opinion of her changed. "How mistaken was I in this estimate!" he said of his original assessment. "How vastly did I underrate her!" The tipping point came in February 1834, when she confided that she dreamed the night before that he had wiped a drop of water from her cheek and chided her when he realized she was wearing makeup. Within a month they were married by the Reverend Lyman Beecher, father of Harriet and Catharine and their famous preacher brother, Henry Ward Beecher. In mid-November 1835 the couple had their first child, a daughter they named Catharine Jane, for her mother. The little girl would go by Kate.

Two weeks later the baby's mother was dead. Chase was not at his wife's bedside in her final moments, having been away on business in Philadelphia. Kitty was deliriously ill and incoherent after giving birth, but after a week she recovered sufficiently to urge him to go ahead with his trip. The reports he received while traveling were encouraging, but on his way back, in Wheeling, he was handed another note informing him of her death. Hurrying home, hoping against hope it was all a mistake, the stunned and guilt-ridden husband found his wife lying upstairs, lifeless. He knelt before her and "implored God to return her to me," then kissed her cold lips and forehead. But his prayer went unanswered. "Nothing was left but clay." His grief was compounded when he concluded that her death had been unnecessary, the result of what he considered virtually criminal medical malpractice. After diagnosing her with peritonitis and in an effort to reduce her fever, the doctors continued to bleed her—draining fifty ounces in all—until she passed away without a struggle or even a sigh.

For weeks afterward Chase was inconsolable, visiting her grave nearly every day. He berated himself for not being at her deathbed and blamed the doctors (and his in-laws) for her demise, characteristically based on his reading of several medical texts on childbirth. From then on he developed a habit of second-guessing others' actions and competence.

Chase was particularly haunted by the lack of assurance that Kitty died having accepted her Lord and Savior. With his social butterfly of a wife he had foolishly contented himself with a few conversations on the subject of religion and a few recommendations of religious books. If only, he wrote in his diary, he had persistently lectured her, he might have turned her into a true Christian. "But I procrastinated," he lamented, "and now she is gone." Never again would any of the women in his life—wives or daughters—be left to their own devices on the subject of eternal grace.

In September 1839 Chase, now thirty-one, married for a second time. His new bride, seventeen-year-old Eliza Ann Smith, was very different from his first wife. "Lizzie," as she was known, was an avowedly Christian woman from a middle-class family and lacked Kitty Garniss's social standing and stately bearing. But she was apparently more pleasing to the eye. Although no images of Lizzie have survived, she was described as "very lovely, of a slight figure and exquisite complexion, with fine light brown hair and marvelously bright eyes." She was affectionate and frolicsome and enjoyed playing jokes on her much older, dignified husband in an effort to lighten him up.

Lizzie took over care of Chase's four-year-old daughter, Kate. But less than five months later, in February 1840, the child came down with scarlet fever, apparently contracted from her grandfather, and died within days. A grief-stricken Chase sought sympathy from his Dartmouth classmate Charles Cleveland over his sudden loss. "Her animated playfulness—her childish talk—her winning endearments—have lent wings to many delightful moments," he wrote. Even more, Chase had looked forward to when his daughter might superintend his household and serve as his counselor and friend. "Many were the little plans I had formed with reference to her," he lamented to Cleveland. Those plans would be transferred to his second-born Kate, whose entry into the world six months later helped take Chase's mind off the loss of the first.

When Chase arrived at his home in downtown Cincinnati on the evening of August 12, 1840, following a day at his law office, he found his wife, Lizzie, "suffering a good deal of pain." She was about to go into labor for the birth of her first child. After the doctor and nurse arrived, Chase went into a separate room "and kneeling down prayed God to support and comfort my dear wife, to preserve the life of the child and save both from sin." A few hours later, around 2 a.m. on August 13, the wife of his law partner emerged from the birthing room to announce the arrival of a little daughter. "The babe is pronounced pretty. I think it quite otherwise," the new father wrote in his diary. "It is however well formed and I am thankful. May God give the child a good understanding that she may keep his commandments." He then went back to memorizing the 119th Psalm, the longest in the Bible, rebuking himself for having to frequently refer to the book.

Catharine Jane Chase, as she was christened, was the third female in Chase's life to bear that name. She was named not for her living mother, Lizzie, but for Chase's late first wife and daughter. She would always go by Kate (or "Katie" to her immediate family). And to distinguish herself from the two prior Catharine Janes, when writing out her full first name she spelled it with a "K"—either "Katharine" or "Katherine."

Two weeks after Kate's birth Chase wrote Cleveland to mention "a certain interesting little stranger who has lately made her first appearance on this stage." The arrival of little Kate renewed Chase's spirits. She grew healthily and became a delight to him and his young wife. Chase was especially gratified to find that Lizzie adhered to his religious views and was "indeed a renewed child of God." He looked forward to a friendship with her that would never end and imagined the two of them together in eternity, "looking back on the present scenes of our pilgrimage and reviewing together the scenes of our earthly existence!" But the happy scenes did not last long.

In 1842 Lizzie gave birth to another daughter and namesake, Lizzie, who died within three months. A third daughter—another Lizzie—was born in 1843 but lived just over a year. Chase barely mentioned the passing of these two short-lived sisters of Kate. Then death intruded again the following year, in September 1845, when twenty-three-year-old Lizzie succumbed to tuberculosis after a lengthy illness. Lizzie had never been healthy since catching cold around Christmas of 1840, and unlike with his first wife, Chase saw Lizzie's death coming. But that did little to lessen his grief. If his mourning was not equal in intensity to that over the death of his first wife, the sorrow was still genuine. "The Lord hath dealt very bitterly with me," Chase wrote his friend Charles Cleveland. "I write weeping. I cannot restrain my tears. . . . I have no wife, my little Kate has no mother, and we are desolate." His only solace was the confidence, which he so lacked regarding Kitty Garniss, that his second wife had died in the faith. He confirmed that trust in several conversations with her before her passing, when they had spoken of her probable departure, and in her final moments, as she struggled for a final utterance. Her last word was in answer to his question, "Is Christ precious to you now dear Lizzie? and she faintly answered 'yes.'"

Shortly after Lizzie's death Chase read the Bible to five-year-old Kate, choosing, naturally enough, the story of the long-suffering Job. She "listened and seemed to be pleased, probably with the solemn rhythms, for she certainly can understand very little," he recorded in his diary. But a few short years later he would make sure she understood the caprice of earthly existence. "Remember," he wrote her in 1851, when she was away at the Haines School in New York, "that you may die soon, and cannot, in any event, live very many years." It bordered on the macabre, but having seen nearly everyone close to him die prematurely, Chase could be forgiven for thinking that things would be no different with Kate. She therefore needed to make her peace with God, he told her, for "already eleven years of your life are passed. You may not live another eleven years; perhaps only a very small part of that time; certainly or almost certainly not many times eleven years. How short then is this life! And how earnest ought to be our preparation for another!"

Kate would never become as obsessed as her father with the notion of eternal salvation, but she would share his drive for worldly accomplishment. By the time she finished school, her father had, on the strength of his antislavery credentials, made it to the governor's mansion in Ohio. He was also on his way, he hoped, to the presidency of the United States. And throughout his quest his daughter Kate would be right there with him. She did want that "bright jewel" added to his "earthly crown," but she also wanted so much more. She would be driven in multiple directions, seeking perfection, the best, in everything. The question remained: driven to what end? What did her own earthly jewel look like?

CHAPTER 4

# The Belle of Columbus

When Salmon Chase wrote his friend Charles Sumner in early 1850 to say that death had been pursuing him relentlessly for years, he had not yet seen the last of it. In 1852, while Kate was away at school in New York, Chase's third wife, Sarah Bella "Belle" Ludlow Chase, passed away. He would never remarry.

Chase had married Belle Ludlow, a member of one of Cincinnati's prosperous founding families, in November 1846. With the exception of one incident, when Chase accused seven-year-old Kate of disobeying and making an "untrue representation" to Belle, Kate's relationship with her stepmother was a loving one. Belle did her best to treat Kate like her own child, signing her letters as "your affectionate mother" and addressing her as "my darling little daughter." In September 1847 Belle also brought Kate a baby sister, Janet Ralston Chase, who would always be known to the family as "Nettie."

Belle also got the family out of downtown Cincinnati, with its stifling summer heat, and up to Clifton, a hilly residential area of about four hundred people a few miles north of the city. The wooded, leafy Clifton area was more beneficial to the tubercular condition Belle developed in 1849, and by 1852 she was spending most of her time there with Kate and Nettie. "I wish sometimes that I were out of public life altogether, and living quietly at Clifton with you and darling little Nettie," Chase wrote Kate from his Senate office in Washington. But although he might have missed his family, Chase had no intention of exiting public life. He had followed a determined path to the Senate. After losing reelection to the Cincinnati City Council in 1840 due to his support for temperance, he left the Whig Party to help build the antislavery Liberty Party, which morphed into the Free Soil Party in 1848. (It was Chase who coined the party's slogan, "Free Soil, Free Labor, Free Men.")

Though an awkward public speaker, Chase excelled at presenting both his oral and written arguments in a logical, persuasive manner, and he had a knack for drafting effective party platforms and coining pithy political slogans. Those skills, combined with his energy and ambition, led to his election to the US Senate in 1849. The Ohio legislature, which elected US senators at that time, was closely divided between Whigs and Democrats, with Chase's Free Soilers holding the balance of power. Chase and his friends agreed to provide the Democrats with a legislative majority in exchange for the Democrats joining forces with the Free Soilers to elect Chase senator. The Whigs were furious, and their lingering resentment would bedevil Chase for years. Chase defended his conduct, explaining that he had betrayed none of his principles. In fact, he threw his support to the Democrats not only to get himself elected but also, just as importantly, because the Democrats promised to repeal Ohio's infamous "black laws," which prevented African Americans from voting, holding office, or testifying against whites in court. Chase reasoned that the cause was more important than the party or the man. It just so happened that in this case, Chase concluded, as he (and Kate) so often would throughout his political career, that the cause was best served by electing Salmon P. Chase.

Viewed as an opportunist by his new Senate colleagues, Chase became a sort of man without a party in Washington and exerted little influence there in his single six-year term. He made a futile opposition to Henry Clay's Compromise of 1850, which sought to avert civil war by, among other things, strengthening the fugitive slave laws Chase found so abhorrent. He spent much of his first couple of years searching for a cure for Belle's tuberculosis, taking her to Texas, Philadelphia, and New Jersey for various treatments. It was all in vain. In January 1852 Belle succumbed to the disease—the same one that had claimed his second wife, Kate's mother, Lizzie.

In the Senate Chase also unsuccessfully opposed Stephen Douglas's controversial Kansas-Nebraska Act of 1854, which opened up those two new territories to settlers who could choose whether to allow slavery within each territory. But he gained national recognition by attacking Douglas's bill in a widely published pamphlet that served as a template for the new Republican Party. Chase's politics were also starting to rub off on his teenage daughter Kate. After Charles Sumner was nearly caned to death in the Senate chamber following his vitriolic speech denouncing Kansas pro-slavery rioters, Kate hung a picture of him on her wall, next to a framed copy of the antislavery Kansas newspaper the rioters had shut down.

After tiring of Miss Haines's school, which she left in June 1854, Kate transferred in September to another girls' boarding school in Aston Ridge, Pennsylvania, outside Philadelphia. But she did not like it or the headmistress, Maria Eastman, any better. "You complain of Miss Eastman," Chase noted in a letter to fourteen-year-old Kate. She had drawn her teacher's disapproval for some misdeed, prompting Chase to remind her that "sometimes, you may deserve it." Chase questioned Miss Eastman's judgment in allowing card playing in her home, but he recognized that her comparative leniency—unlike Henrietta Haines, she did not read her students' correspondence—had produced a "freer and more affectionate spirit" in Kate's letters. Kate's free spirit also attracted young male admirers, one of whom sent her a note asking whether she would do him the favor of sitting next to him the following Sunday evening. Another boy wrote a poem comparing her to Venus and asking, "Whose face or form is there can rival thine?" An assistant to Mrs. Eastman remembered Kate as "so queenly, so beautiful." Ida Saxton, who grew up to marry William McKinley, the twenty-fifth president, was also a student at Aston Ridge, but as Eastman's assistant looked back on it years later, she said that if she were to have chosen one girl who might someday become First Lady, she "would certainly have named Kate Chase."

Kate's father also noticed she was improving in intelligence, manners, and physical development, and he was full of advice on how his blossoming daughter should conduct herself. "Take care of your health," he wrote her. "Be as much in the air as possible. Avoid stooping. Take such exercise as will expand the chest and give freest Motion to the lungs. Avoid tight dresses." He was no less concerned with her spiritual well-being.

"Do you feel inclined to say something bitter or unkind of someone or to someone?" he asked. "Suppress it then at once." If she felt some desire for revenge, she should suppress it too. Kate came to recognize those impulses within her and struggled for much of her life to control them.

Kate spent only one academic year at Eastman's Aston Ridge school, leaving there in June 1855. She returned to Ohio, where Chase was now campaigning for governor under the banner of the new Republican Party. In what would become a common refrain for Chase, he professed indifference to receiving the nomination but said he would accept it if the people wanted him. Chase wrote Kate a long letter in September 1855 detailing his campaign movements throughout Ohio and expressing optimism about the outcome. He was elected by a slim margin even though, ironically, he had said a few months earlier that the Republican Party was unlikely to last and that its name was poorly chosen. (He preferred the label "Independent Democrat.")

After her father assumed the governorship in 1856, Kate returned to Ohio to attend Lewis Heyl's Esther Institute in Columbus, a finishing school where she studied music, painting, and language. Her schooling was soon supplemented by private French lessons at home, almost every other evening, for several months. Living under the same roof as her father for the first time since she was nine, she became his official hostess, interior decorator, and confidential secretary. She played chess and backgammon with him at night and sat at his table, confidently entering the conversation (sometimes in French) while he talked politics with his important visitors. She played the piano and led the dinner guests in rounds of charades. One of them was William Dean Howells, a young statehouse reporter who would later become a famous realist novelist and America's leading literary critic. Howells and several other press correspondents were invited to the Chase home one Thanksgiving—Howells's first dinner in society, he later recalled—after which the assembled group, excluding only Chase, took part in the parlor game favorite. "My fear and pride were put to a crucial test in the first dissyllable, which the girlish hostess assigned me," he wrote, referring to Kate, "and nothing but the raillery glancing through the deep lashes of her brown eyes which were very beautiful could have brought me to the self-sacrifice involved." He attended Kate's next reception, "where again she laughed at my supposed dignity in refusing to dance; she would not suppose my inability."

At sixteen, Kate already was beginning to turn heads. Charles Sumner, a forty-five-year-old bachelor, had a slight crush on her, always reminding his fellow antislavery crusader Chase not to forget to tell his intelligent daughter how cordially he remembered her. Elizabeth Trotter, a woman from England who, with her father, was visiting America for the first time, spent some time with the Chases in Columbus and almost forgave her English father for immediately falling for Kate.

With nonadmirers, though, Kate could be a combative spitfire. She had little difficulty dealing with the immature high school boys who teased her for her haughty demeanor; she was ready with sticks and stones—"missiles," one of her antagonists recalled—"and words ready for use—the words were most deadly." She had more trouble with her female peers, who envied her beauty and talent and spread malicious gossip about her. Appointed by her father as recording secretary of a women's benevolent society, she proceeded to offend the women members by vigorously defending a doctor they had excoriated. Indeed, she came to hate her female persecutors. A sympathetic friend from the time remembered her as "a magnificent girl, a little too independent to care what the world said about her to make her cautious." She was not as diplomatic in her youth as she later became, this friend recalled, "but was outspoken, and almost defiant, if anyone attempted to turn her from a cherished purpose." Another Columbus woman spoke of Kate's reckless disregard of public opinion. It was an attitude that did not always place her in good stead. Kate herself would confess later in life that she had never cared for the "opinion or goodwill" of others. "I ran my head against a stone wall," she said. "It did not hurt the wall but it has hurt the head."

She also ran into trouble in Columbus when, at age sixteen, she openly consorted with an older married man, Richard Nevins. Dick Nevins was a handsome, dashing, twenty-eight-year-old local printer with a wife and young baby. He took Kate carriage riding and visited her at the Chase home when her father was away. It was said that after Chase banished Nevins from his household, Kate and her suitor arranged to meet at the house of one of her friends, where Nevins would drive past in his buggy awaiting Kate's signal by handkerchief.

Kate was both a source of pride and an occasional headache for her father at this time. He instructed her to go nowhere and do nothing that would attract adverse attention, for she was at a time in her life when all her acts would be closely observed. But she often ignored the advice. He caught her waltzing too closely at an evening social with one of her partners and forbade it. "Trouble at dinner," he noted in his diary one night in early 1857, over "Nevins walking with Kate." A few days later at breakfast she asked how she had offended, and he told her by "false conduct" but did not have time then to explain. That evening, after her usual French lesson with Professor Mot, Chase had a long talk with her, and she seemed genuinely sorry and repentant. She might not have cared much for the opinion of others, but it mattered greatly to her what her beloved father thought.

He thought highly of her, even if he had a hard time showing it. A few months later, following his reelection as governor, Chase delegated to Kate the task of furnishing their new home, an impressive Gothic revival mansion at Sixth and State Streets in downtown Columbus that he had purchased to replace their rented quarters. (Ohio had no official governor's residence at the time.) "I fear that I am trusting a good deal to the judgment of a girl of 17," he wrote her in December 1857, "but I am confident I may safely trust yours." He gave Kate various lists and memoranda with detailed instructions on what furniture, carpeting, and draperies to buy and how much to spend, telling her to keep his lists so he could see how well she had managed to carry out his instructions. He wanted her to learn, but he could not resist trying to micromanage the process himself. "Have I mentioned that the Stair case has 22 steps and of course needs 22 rods instead of 20?" he wrote her. "Let me again remind you *not* to buy anything in Cincinnati which you can as well buy in Columbus," he added. Another letter instructed her to "Remember this: The carpet for the parlor is to be cut but not sewed. Notice this and have it done."

With the death in February 1859 of Chase's unmarried sister Alice, who occasionally lived with him to help raise his girls, Kate was now sole mistress of his household. She was also serving as a surrogate mother to Nettie, who was being schooled in Columbus at the Esther Institute, the same one Kate had attended. Kate went off to school in New York when Nettie was only two years old, and while Kate was at school in Pennsylvania, Nettie was living with relatives in Ohio, so the two half-sisters were almost strangers when they came to live together in Columbus during Chase's governorship.

Chase now was not only relying on Kate for domestic help but also using her as a sounding board for his own political thinking. Her growing influence with him was evidenced by her successful intervention, sometime in his second term, on behalf of a man she thought had been unjustly imprisoned for murder. Chase initially refused to interfere, but Kate prevailed upon him to reconsider, and he granted a pardon.

By this time too Chase was looking forward to the 1860 presidential election. In 1856, as the leading western antislavery man, he had felt entitled to be named the first-ever presidential candidate of the Republican Party and was convinced his prospects were good. But he was crestfallen when the nomination went to the famous explorer and political novice John C. Frémont. It could not have escaped Chase's notice that Frémont's candidacy was aided by an independent, politically savvy woman, his wife, Jessie, who served on a committee to monitor her husband's speeches and prevent his expected gaffes. Jessie Frémont was, if not a conscious role model for Kate, at least a forerunner.

Chase's failure to gain the 1856 nomination had been due to several factors: the perception that he was too much of an antislavery radical to win a national election; his lack of personal popularity and warmth; an absence of organization among his supporters, owing to Chase's overconfidence; and divided support from within his own Ohio delegation, heavily made up of ex-Whigs. All of these same problems would continue to plague him in future presidential runs, but for the time being Chase had high hopes for 1860. Although the Ohio governor had little actual power in those years, Chase used his office as a platform to push a progressive Republican agenda—education and prison reform, the rights of women and the mentally disabled, and, of course, opposition to slavery—that solidified his national standing. His stature grew when he became the first Ohio governor to have his office in the newly dedicated Ohio Statehouse, a magnificent Greek revival marble structure nearing completion after almost twenty years of construction. Chase made a triumphant appearance at the new capitol for the dedication ceremonies in January 1857, arriving with Kate and Nettie in a sleigh that brought them through the snow-covered streets of Columbus, under military escort, to the gloriously illuminated building and four thousand onlookers who braved the weather for the festive occasion.

Chase lost no time planning his 1860 run. In typical Chase style he wrote his Dartmouth friend Charles Cleveland in November 1857, barely two weeks after his reelection as governor by a slim margin, to say that although he did not wish to pursue the presidency if it would prejudice the cause, people were already urging his nomination. He asked Cleveland to conduct some confidential intelligence to ascertain the exact state of opinion as to his candidacy. "Of course I do not wish to be named as seeking this information," Chase cautioned his friend.

Chase was easily flattered by anyone who told him he could, would, or should be elected president, and although he could permit himself to denigrate his own chances, he became annoyed when friends or supporters did so. After a breakfast at Chase's Columbus home Carl Schurz, the renowned German revolutionary and American statesman, told Chase that if the Republican convention in Chicago wanted an antislavery man, they would nominate New York senator William Seward, and if not, they would not nominate Chase. Chase was taken aback, but he continued to write letters to friends urging them to lobby Schurz to support his candidacy.

Schurz vividly recalled meeting Kate for the first time that day in Columbus. Chase took him into the breakfast area and told him his daughter would be down momentarily. As Schurz recalled in his memoirs,

> Soon she came, saluted me very kindly, and then let herself down upon her chair with the graceful lightness of a bird that, folding its wings, perches upon the branch of a tree. She was then about eighteen years old, tall and slender, and exceedingly well formed. Her features were not at all regularly beautiful according to the classic rule. Her little nose, somewhat audaciously tipped up, would perhaps not have passed muster with a severe critic, but it fitted pleasingly into her face with its large, languid but at the same time vivacious hazel eyes, shaded by long dark lashes, and arched over by proud eyebrows. . . . She had something imperial in the pose of the head, and all her movements possessed an exquisite natural charm. . . . After the usual polite commonplaces, the conversation at the breakfast table, in which Miss Kate took a lively and remarkably intelligent part, soon turned upon politics, and that conversation was continued during a large part of the forenoon in the Governor's library.

Schurz was an admirer of Salmon Chase but became a lifelong platonic worshipper of Kate, who came to count the rapid-talking, easily excitable, fellow piano player among her closest male friends.

Kate recognized, in a way her father did not, the overriding importance of interpersonal relationships in politics. She convinced him to visit Washington in the spring of 1860 to press the flesh and promote his candidacy directly with congressional supporters. Accompanying him to a dinner party hosted by the affable William Seward, Chase's chief rival for the nomination, Kate impressed the New Yorker with her cultivated manner. If only Chase could have borrowed some of Kate's sociability for himself, he might have enjoyed greater political support. But he could never shed the stiff, pompous manner that made him unattractive to the voting masses. Just as one Ohio Republican said in 1856 that Jessie Frémont would have made a better candidate than her husband, John, people who met them both undoubtedly thought Kate would have been a more popular vote getter than her father.

Although Seward remained the favorite heading into the convention, Chase had as much to fear from the candidacy of Missouri's Edward Bates, an ex-Whig whose moderate positions made him a potential compromise choice. Bates also had the support of Horace Greeley, the powerful editor of the liberal and antislavery *New-York Tribune*. In later years Greeley would become one of Chase's most loyal supporters and a warm personal friend of Chase and Kate, but in 1860 he wanted the Republicans to win and was concerned that Chase's reputation as an abolitionist made him seem too extreme to the general electorate. Chase came close to exacerbating that reputation when the press discovered he had donated money to John Brown, who led a disastrous raid on Harper's Ferry in 1859. To show her own support, Nettie, with Kate's help, constructed a little fort in the conservatory of their Columbus home and raised a flag on the citadel on which the defiant phrase was painted, "Freedom forever; slavery never." After a friendly visitor raised his eyebrows at the little declaration of war, Chase called his children to him that evening and explained "how impossible it was to right a great wrong the way poor old John Brown had attempted to do." Chase managed to disassociate himself from Brown by publicly condemning his Harper's Ferry expedition.

In early 1860 Chase was not too worried about another contender, a former one-term congressman and backwoodsman from Illinois named

Abraham Lincoln. Chase had campaigned for Lincoln in his Illinois Senate race in 1858 against Stephen Douglas, earning the gratitude of his fellow Republican, but he wrongly predicted to Kate that Douglas would be defeated. Lincoln's national ambitions appeared stalled, but he quietly began building an effective political organization of the type Chase would never enjoy. The awkward-looking prairie politician also wisely accepted an invitation to speak in February 1860 at New York's Cooper Union, where he stirred the packed hall with a rousing address and gained credibility among eastern Republicans. Chase turned down a similar invitation to speak in New York City prior to Lincoln, missing a valuable opportunity. But he strengthened his chances by winning back the US Senate seat in Ohio held by Democrat George Pugh, one of his former law students.

In the end Chase did not come close to winning the nomination. After the first ballot in Chicago that May, he was in fourth place, far behind the leader Seward and second-place Lincoln. On the second and third ballots Chase's support declined while Lincoln steadily vaulted into first, ahead of Seward and only a couple of votes short of victory. In a final indignity to Chase, four Ohio delegates switched their votes to Lincoln, putting him over the top. In congratulating Lincoln afterward, Chase could not resist slipping in a self-pitying reference to the fact that the Ohio delegation, unlike Lincoln's Illinois contingent, had failed to support their favorite-son candidate. Chase retained a lingering bitterness over his belief that he would have won the nomination but for what he considered the treachery of the Ohio delegates, particularly Senator Ben Wade, a former Whig, who drew off some of Ohio's support for himself. Once again, Chase felt he had been denied a prize owed to him that in his mind should have been awarded him without him having to put up much of a fight.

Kate saw lessons in the 1860 defeat she would draw upon when it became her turn, eight years later, to directly manage another of her father's bids for the presidency. She appreciated the problems created, as in 1856, by her father's overconfidence and his backers' lack of organization. She learned that if he wanted a nomination, he would have to go after it rather than waiting for it to come to him. She also appreciated the dangers of appearing to be too radical, too unyielding on principle, and henceforth she would concentrate more on political strategy and tactics and less on ideological purity. But she could not do much about her father's lack of warm personal appeal; dignified, statesmanlike competence would have to remain his calling card. And she would share his tendency to attribute his failures to the perfidy, real or imagined, of others.

Despite his defeat, Chase campaigned enthusiastically for Lincoln in the November general election. As Lincoln began to put a cabinet together, radical Republicans such as Charles Sumner and Horace Greeley demanded that Chase be given a top post. The most prestigious cabinet position, secretary of state, went to Seward, but Chase ended up with the second-highest honor, that of treasury secretary. Chase was miffed when Lincoln originally asked him whether he would accept the position even though Lincoln, still constructing his cabinet, was not yet prepared to offer it. Chase made noises to friends to the effect that he didn't want the treasury job and preferred to remain in the Senate. But privately he concluded he would have greater influence and prominence within the cabinet than outside it; indeed, Chase lobbied for the position, and Lincoln nominated him for it the day after the inauguration in March 1861. Long after her father's death, in a bit of revisionist history, Kate would claim he never wanted the treasury position and accepted it against his inclination.

By early March both Chase and Seward had taken their places in the cabinet along with another of the defeated candidates at the 1860 convention, Edward Bates, the new attorney general. It was to be, as historian Doris Kearns Goodwin has called it, a "team of rivals." And no one would feel the rivalry more than Kate.

CHAPTER 5

# The Belle of Washington

Kate had her own version of what precipitated her famous feud with Mary Lincoln. But her story was pure invention.

On February 13, 1861, en route to Washington with their traveling party, President-elect Lincoln and his wife stopped off in Columbus, where they were honored with a lavish evening military ball. The Chases had already left for Washington, where Chase, still awaiting the official treasury appointment, was attending a peace conference. "Mrs. Lincoln was piqued that I did not remain at Columbus to see her," Kate told a newspaper interviewer three decades later, "and I have always felt that this was the chief reason why she did not like me at Washington."

In her interview Kate said she was absent because she had gone to Cleveland for a celebration of Oliver Hazard Perry's War of 1812 victory over the British in the Battle of Lake Erie. But that ceremony took place in September 1860, before Lincoln was elected. Although it was many years later, Kate could not have forgotten the event in Cleveland or its timing, for that was the fateful day on which she met her future husband. Her rivalry with Mary Lincoln did not stem from any snub in Ohio but rather would develop later when they met for the first time in person, in the nation's capital, as competing political hostesses.

"I shall be glad to see you any time, Miss Chase," Mary Lincoln told Kate at the end of the first White House state dinner on March 28, 1861.

The twenty-year-old Kate drew herself up to her full height, towering above the First Lady, and answered, "Mrs. Lincoln, I shall be glad to have you call on me at any time." The story may sound apocryphal, except that it was related by Mrs. Charles Walker, an intimate friend of the Chase family who counted currency in the Treasury Department and lived for a time in the Chase household during the first Lincoln administration. Speaking after Kate's death, Mrs. Walker had little reason to make up such an incident. A sympathetic friend, she recalled that Kate "exhibited toward me a tenderness that I never knew her to feel for any other woman." However, as Mrs. Walker also recalled, Kate "could be arrogant . . . toward women whom she never loved." She never loved Mary Lincoln, and the same was true of Mrs. Lincoln's feelings toward Kate.

The competition between the women became evident at the first White House levee, or public reception, on the evening of March 8. It was the last public event in Washington where Northern and Southern representatives appeared together on polite terms. After hostilities broke out, the Southern ladies who had long dominated high society in Washington left in a mass exodus. The departure of the Southern aristocracy left a vacuum that Northern and Republican newcomers were eager to fill and created an opening for new social queens in what was America's closest parallel to the royal courts of Europe. As First Lady, Kentucky native Mary Lincoln was now "the titular head of official society," but it was Kate Chase, the young westerner from Ohio, who would become its "sovereign in fact."

At that initial levee the stout Mary Lincoln appeared in a low-cut dress ill-befitting a woman of her figure, along with a heavy headdress of flowers and gold bracelets that "rattled as she tossed her head and shook hands." The First Lady remained the center of attention until a dazzling, auburn-haired young woman entered the receiving line, accompanied by the dignified treasury secretary and the handsome Charles Sumner. Kate was dressed simply in white silk with only a few natural flowers in her hair and no fancy jewelry. But all eyes were on her. Mrs. Daniel Chester French, wife of the sculptor of the Lincoln Memorial statue, would later recall the effect this willowy creature had whenever she appeared at a public gala. Kate Chase was

> more of a professional beauty than had at that time ever been seen in America, with a beauty and a regal carriage which we called "queenly,"

> but which no real queen ever has. . . . She was tall and slim—the universal art of being slim had not been discovered in those days—with an unusually long white neck, and a slow and deliberate way of turning it when she glanced about her. When she appeared, people dropped back in order to watch her.

Mary Lincoln was jealous of the younger woman, whose father, Mrs. Lincoln knew, thought that he, and not Mr. Lincoln, belonged in the White House. Mary Lincoln also suspected, not without reason, that Kate coveted her position as First Lady. It only fed Mary's suspicions when her cousin and confidante, Elizabeth Todd Grimsley, admitted that during the levee she had allowed Kate to cross-examine her about the Lincolns' life in Springfield, on everything from what the president liked for dinner to the style of furniture and entertaining they preferred. Kate could also read with interest the newspaper gossip about Mary Lincoln's expensive shopping trips to New York, where the president's wife, to his great embarrassment and public outrage, spent far in excess of her budget on luxurious clothing for herself and refurbishings for the Executive Mansion.

Kate knew that, as a major cabinet secretary, Chase would be expected to entertain numerous functionaries, and she spent a fortune too furnishing their rented brick three-story mansion in downtown Washington with the most elegant décor. Her father constantly cautioned her to avoid extravagance, but there was more than a little hypocrisy in that admonition, as it was he who always felt the need, in pursuit of political advancement, to put on a show, even if it meant living beyond his means.

The Chase household at the northwest corner of Sixth and E Streets, NW, ten blocks from the White House, became the gathering place for the radical faction of the Republican Party, which distrusted the more conservative Seward and disparaged the wishy-washiness (in their view) of President Lincoln on emancipation and other issues. Kate saw that entertainments at her father's home could serve a political purpose in a way that Mary Lincoln's White House affairs could not. Mrs. Lincoln held regular Tuesday evening levees and Saturday afternoon "at homes" that, by virtue of her husband's office, were open to the public. But cabinet members' parties were by invitation only, and Kate turned the private Chase gatherings to her father's political advantage—a rival court much envied by Mrs. Lincoln. In addition to hosting nearly daily breakfasts for the high and mighty, she set up a series of Wednesday "matinée dansantes"—candlelit afternoon dances, followed by dinner and a reception for her father. Kate directed the servants, controlled the guest list and seating arrangements, and made sure the men best positioned to advance "Chase in '64" were placed near him. Even though Chase neither smoked nor drank, alcohol and tobacco were always on hand for those who did.

Kate was expert in working a room—a careful listener who sized people up quickly for their ability to be useful, knew just what to say to whom, and retained everything. "She had a wonderful memory, and could repeat word for word, conversations on any subject that she had heard or read," recalled her friend Mrs. Walker. Others remarked on the breadth of her conversational skills. Kate's daughter Portia told an interviewer years later that "I never spoke with anyone who had such a truly wide and varied knowledge as my mother, or who carried it so gracefully and made it so attractive and entertaining." Her mother's entertainments, Portia recalled, were expertly choreographed and her hospitality "marked by an originality which gave it piquancy and flavor."

Versed in the art of diplomacy, Kate conversed easily with European foreign ministers, including the British ambassador, Lord Lyons, who had romantic designs on her. Kate's personal influence on the forty-four-year-old bachelor helped diffuse the strained relations between the United States and Great Britain, whose elites tended to sympathize with the cotton-producing South. Kate was also a voracious newspaper reader and courted powerful editors such as Horace Greeley. To gather intelligence on the "enemy," she befriended Lincoln's irreverent, foppish young private secretary, Brown University graduate John Hay, inviting him home for dinner and attending plays and social events with him (and leading him on). For his part, Hay carried back to his boss, the president, the latest gossip from the radical nest at the Chase home. In many ways Kate and Hay were alike: affable, somewhat devious, chameleon-like personalities who could straddle different political camps, expressing sympathy for different points of view and gaining the confidence of their partners in conversation. Like the cultivated, well-mannered Hay, Kate put those in her presence at ease. She exhibited a rare combination of cordiality and aloofness. But her sociability hid a fierce resolve: she did not like to lose an argument, and, according to the powerful men who loved to mingle with her, "in conversation she never came out second."

The Chase father-and-daughter team made a striking couple whenever they appeared together in public. Reporter William Howard Russell of the *Times* of London, a guest at the first state dinner, considered Treasury Secretary Chase "one of the most intelligent and distinguished persons in the whole assemblage,—tall, of a good presence, with a well-formed head, fine forehead, and a face indicating energy and power." He found Kate, one of only a handful of women among the thirty guests, to be "very attractive, agreeable, and sprightly." She was already so closely associated with her father that she laughingly told Russell that office seekers were pestering her with demands to see the treasury secretary.

During the predinner mingling Lincoln had been regaling Russell and others with one homespun anecdote after the other, each time moving on to the next group of listeners after eliciting an outburst of laughter. But just before the formal state dinner was over, Lincoln convened his cabinet to discuss the serious matter of what to do about Fort Sumter, then under siege. A majority of the cabinet, including Chase, who had previously waffled on the question, now supported Lincoln's plan to supply fresh food and water to the men holding the fort, even at the risk of war. In a letter to Lincoln the next day Chase wrote that if war was to come, it was better to let it start with Southern aggression, a view Lincoln himself held. Few were surprised when, a few days later, the Confederate authorities ordered the bombardment of the fort before the Union vessels, with their provisions, could enter the harbor. Union commander Robert Anderson surrendered the fort and sailed with his men to New York.

Shortly after the first state dinner Kate went to New York with Nettie and was there when Sumter was fired upon. The city was swept up in a surge of patriotism, as 250,000 citizens—the largest gathering in America to that time—attended a mass rally in Union Square. They cheered the sight of the tattered American flag, waving from Washington's equestrian statue, which Major Anderson had brought with him from Sumter. Kate and Nettie joined the handkerchief-waving crowd who watched the first waves of Northern troops parade down Broadway to the ship that would carry them south for battle. The two sisters then attended a packed sermon by Henry Ward Beecher at Brooklyn's Plymouth Church, where the congregation cheered the impassioned oration and sang the National Anthem to the accompaniment of a thunderous organ.

Although thrilled at the goings-on in New York, Kate and Nettie were anxious to get back to Washington to be with their father. But they had no direct communication from the capital, the railroad lines through Baltimore having been captured by the Confederate army. Major Anderson, who also needed to get to Washington to make his report to headquarters, recognized the Chase girls' plight and offered to take them with him. Against the advice of their friends in New York, Kate and Nettie undertook the dangerous journey under Anderson's escort. After reaching Philadelphia by train, their party went to Perryville, Maryland, where they set sail on a steamer for Annapolis. During the voyage they eluded a hostile ship that fired at least two booming cannon shots in their wake. From Annapolis they took a train over a route hastily repaired by Union troops and arrived in Washington on a chilly spring morning.

When they had first seen the capital back in February, Nettie thought it a place of squalor, where cows and pigs roamed at liberty through the muddy streets, spoiling the grandiosity of the impressive federal buildings. Now, in April, they found it a changed place—a vast military camp where the streets swarmed with soldiers and white tents were everywhere, arranged in symmetrical rows. Before long, the streets would also flow with the blood of soldiers returning on stretchers.

Unlike Mary Lincoln, who regularly visited the wounded, Kate shied away from the blood and gore of the military hospitals. But she was one of several women who helped convince the surgeon general to employ more female nurses in hospitals that cared for the fallen. She also frequented the army camps and became the most popular young woman among the Union generals. In one well-known Matthew Brady photograph she is seated in front of a tent, in her stylish dress and bonnet, parasol in hand, as the officers hover about her.

One of the officers she met, or, rather, became reacquainted with, was William Sprague.

CHAPTER 6

# The Boy Governor

He was ten years older and, at five feet five, an inch or two shorter than twenty-year-old Kate. A year earlier he had been elected as the nation's youngest governor after spending more than $100,000 of family money to secure the office. John Hay considered him a "small, insignificant youth, who bought his place" but said he was "certainly all right now" because he was the first Union governor to offer President Lincoln troops in defense of the capital. The day after Fort Sumter fell, even before Lincoln's call for seventy-five thousand volunteers, William Sprague tendered more than a thousand soldiers he would personally accompany to Washington. Within days, as Lincoln paced the floor waiting for reinforcements to arrive, Rhode Island's "boy governor" was making his way south with a regiment he had financed himself. They arrived in late April as the first fully armed and equipped soldiers in the Union army. Looking splendid in their uniforms, they paraded past the White House reviewing stand to cheers of gratitude from the crowd. They were sworn in before President Lincoln, who raised a flag from the White House roof in their honor. At their head was Governor Sprague, riding a white horse and wearing a black felt, yellow-plumed hat and matching yellow sash. After taking up temporary quarters in the Patent Office, they soon settled into "Camp Sprague" on a hillside in northeastern Washington. Around the campfires at night they would sing,

*Of all the true host that New England can boast*
*From down by the sea unto highland,*
*No State is more true, or willing to do,*
*Than dear little Yankee Rhode Island*
*Loyal and true Little Rhody!*
*Bully for you, Little Rhody!*
*Governor Sprague was not very vague*
*When he said, "Shoulder Arms, Little Rhody!"*

* * *

*Governor Sprague is a very good egg,*
*And worthy to lead Little Rhody!*

By virtue of his swift action, Sprague earned Abraham Lincoln's eternal gratitude and became a favorite of the president and Mrs. Lincoln. Another person whose affection for him grew was Kate Chase. Visiting the Rhode Island troops, as she often did in those early days of the war, she could not help but be impressed by William Sprague.

She was taken with him when they first met in Cleveland the previous September at a hotel dance following the dedication of a monument to Rhode Island native Commodore Oliver Hazard Perry. Despite his slight stature, Sprague cut a dashing figure with his longish, unkempt hair and drooping black mustache. He charmed Kate by keeping her on the dance floor, talking politics with her, and flattering her father. "It was a case of instant and mutual infatuation," recalled Richard Parsons, a close friend and political supporter of Salmon Chase who drove Kate to the ball and introduced the couple. When it was getting late that night and Parsons and his wife wanted to go home, Kate came over to them with Sprague and persuaded them to stay longer. Years later Sprague would wax nostalgic about the night, reminding Kate that he could still picture her "in that celebrated dress." She wore it several times afterward to test his memory, believing he did not recognize it because he said nothing. But he did remember. "You became my gaze and the gaze of all observers," he later wrote her, "and then left the [hotel] taking with you my admiration and my appreciation but more than all my *pulsations*. I remember well how I was possessed that night and the following day. I can recall the sensations better than if it was yesterday." Sprague, who was handsomely dressed that night in black, attended by his military guard, would remind Kate that she had been equally captivated by him. As he wrote, "you were then taking a good deal more interest in me than mere friendship."

It did nothing to diminish Kate's interest in him that Sprague was reportedly worth around $10 million. He ran the largest calico printing textile mill in the world, as head of a family business begun in Cranston, Rhode Island, in the early 1800s. The path he traveled from his birth in Cranston in 1830 to the army camps in Washington in 1861 bore little resemblance to the one Kate Chase had followed from Cincinnati to the same place. Yet in many ways it was just as impressive.

The second and youngest son of Amasa and Fanny Morgan Sprague, William Sprague grew up immersed in business and military matters, not politics. His uncle William Sprague III had been a Whig governor of Rhode Island, a US representative, and a US senator. (He was sometimes referred to as the "Old Governor" to distinguish him from his nephew William Sprague IV.) For the Spragues, however, elective office was a means of furthering their business interests—not, as for Salmon Chase, something to pursue in service of some higher principle. Old Governor Sprague's Whiggism stemmed from that party's support for a high protective tariff benefitting textile and other manufacturers. William Sprague IV would similarly come to treat his political offices as instruments for advancing the interests of the manufacturing class.

Although he did not receive a classical education and never attended college, Sprague was reasonably well schooled for his day. After attending a local Cranston common school followed by the Providence Conference Seminary in East Greenwich, Rhode Island, he received a brief liberal education at the Baptist-founded Smithfield Seminary in North Scituate, Rhode Island. For about two years, until he was fifteen or sixteen, William attended the Irving Institute in Tarrytown, New York, whose curriculum emphasized courses required by the academy at West Point. That suited William, whose greatest yen was for all things military. At age twelve he had organized a company of forty boys to take part in the defense of Providence, then under attack at the outset of what became known as the Dorr Rebellion. He marched his young recruits toward the hill where the insurrectionists were to meet the defending state government troops in battle. Young Sprague's march was cut short when state militiamen overtook the boys and sent them back home. But he kept up his interest in the military arts, joining the Providence Marine Artillery Company at age eighteen and turning the ragtag bunch of ceremonial parade marchers into an efficient armed unit. He worked his way up to lieutenant, then captain, and, finally, colonel of the company.

At the same time, he advanced to the position of bookkeeper at the Providence headquarters of the great textile manufacturing firm of A. & W. Sprague. The company was named for his father, Amasa, and uncle, William, after they took over the business when their father, William Sprague II, died in 1836. The Spragues owned several cotton mills and print works in Rhode Island, the most profitable enterprise being the print factory in the "Spragueville" section of Cranston, which printed colorful calico patterns onto cloth.

A classic company town, Spragueville was populated by the mill and print shop workers, mostly foreign immigrants, who relied on the company that employed them, owned the tenements they lived in, and ran the company store where they shopped. Despite the paternalistic system, owners and employees worked side by side and often ate around the same table. The owners also expected their sons to learn the textile business from the ground up. Accordingly, young William IV started as a teenager, clerking in the company store in Cranston. He was soon transferred to the counting room in Providence, about five miles away, where he opened the office, made the fires, cleaned the lamps, and swept the floors. He later became responsible for keeping accounts amounting to hundreds of thousands of dollars. By age twenty-two he was accepted as an active partner in the business. And he did it all without the guidance of a father.

On December 31, 1843, Amasa Sprague, his wife, Fanny, and four children, including thirteen-year-old William, had just finished their New Year's Eve dinner on a cold, snowy Sunday afternoon when Amasa left the family mansion in Cranston, supposedly to check on some livestock at his farm about a mile away. He never made it there. A servant in the Sprague home discovered blood in the snow under a bridge and traced it to Amasa's body, lying face down a few yards away. The coroner concluded he had been shot in the right wrist then struck on both sides of head with the butt end of a musket that fractured his skull. The evidence suggested a murder of passion, for a gold watch and sixty dollars in cash were left on the body untouched and his head was "shockingly mangled, the brain being bared in one or two places." In a scene that would forever haunt him, young William Sprague gazed upon the brutally beaten corpse of his father, a burly man in life, when it was brought back home and laid on the floor in a front parlor of the mansion.

Suspicions focused immediately on an Irish immigrant, Nicholas Gordon, who had publicly blamed Amasa Sprague for the loss of his liquor license. The prosecution theory was that John and William Gordon, the brothers of Nicholas, had carried out the actual murder at his behest. Although the circumstantial evidence was weak and the eyewitness testimony questionable, John Gordon was convicted and hanged.* To this day the crime remains unsolved.

Whoever the murderer was, Amasa's death hastened William's development in the family business, which he entered full time at around age sixteen. He came under the influence of his uncle, William III, preferring the expansionist agenda he advocated over the conservative course Amasa Sprague had favored. William III was a reticent, mirthless man who let his considerable achievements speak for themselves. Amasa Sprague, by contrast, was emotionally uneven and easily provoked. He was popular with women, cared little about his dress, and disdained snobbery. William Sprague IV would mimic his uncle's ambition and his father's personality.

After the Old Governor died in 1856, it seemed that his son Byron and nephews Amasa and William would have their hands full just maintaining the existing mills and print works. That would have been fine with Byron, a hard-living playboy who had little interest in the business and who eventually sold his shares in the company to his two cousins. Likewise, young William's brother Amasa was more interested in raising racehorses. But twenty-six-year-old William Sprague IV was more industrious. After weathering a severe national economic depression in 1857, he took a business valued at $3 million at his uncle's death to one that, at its height, had assets of $19 million. Its 12,000 employees turned out 75,000 pieces of calico a week on their 280,000 spindles in Rhode Island, Connecticut, and

---

*William Gordon was acquitted, and Nicholas was twice tried to a hung jury before being released. No Irishmen served on any of the juries trying the Gordons, and the feeling that John's conviction was the result of anti-immigrant prejudice was so strong that the state legislature soon abolished the death penalty. In 2011 Rhode Island governor Lincoln Chafee granted a posthumous pardon to John Gordon, who to this day remains the last person executed in the Ocean State.

Maine. He expanded the Spragues' holdings to unrelated businesses, from timberlands and sawmills in Maine to water power in South Carolina to real estate in Kansas, Texas, and Florida. In Providence the Spragues controlled five banks and had large stockholdings in a railroad, a steamship line, a sheet iron company, a stove foundry, a mowing machine company, and a horseshoe and horseshoe nail company. "Rhode Island," it would be written, "fairly groaned with the weight of the Spragues' property."

For all their money, though, the Spragues were never accepted by the elite of Rhode Island society. They were considered déclassé—working men who lacked the social manners, the Brown University educations, and the European travel of the blue bloods of Providence. The Spragues, in turn, fancied themselves champions of the masses—people who took care of their family of employees living in the tenements of Spragueville within sight of the owners' mansion. In later years, as a US senator, William Sprague IV would brand himself a populist hero of the common man and enemy of continental European morals.

William, in fact, did visit Europe, in 1859, not for the art or culture but ostensibly to add to his military expertise. He toured the battlefields of the Napoleonic wars, studied army equipment, and met the Italian nationalist Garibaldi, contributing substantial funds to his cause. His friends claimed he went abroad for his health, impaired by the cares of the business he was working overtime to enlarge. But, according to another story, his family hurried him off to Europe after he impregnated a young neighbor girl named Mary Eliza Viall. Mary, who was about a year younger than Kate, came from a respectable family. Her father was a prosperous cotton broker in Providence who did business with the Spragues, and her sister married a pastor. When William refused to marry Mary, her family set up a hasty marriage with a young army officer named Anderson who soon abandoned her for parts unknown. She supposedly bore a son she named Hamlet, but if so, it is not known what became of him. Sprague apparently believed at the time that he was the father but came to question his paternity a few years later. Mary went to Paris, where she became a cultured woman, bleached her hair blonde, jettisoned her hoopskirt, and came back a free-love advocate. She literally worshipped William Sprague and would carry on an affair with him for years, as became clear when she self-published a thinly veiled autobiographical novel, *The Merchant's Wife*, in 1876. In it she described her enduring love for her "Lancelot," William

Sprague (named "Hamlet" in the novel), a man she believed loved her too much to marry her.

Whatever scandal the pregnancy created locally had blown over by the time Sprague returned from Europe in January 1860, for he received a hero's welcome in a military parade through the streets of Providence. While he was away, influential Rhode Island politicians, with the blessing of Fanny Sprague, settled upon her son as the best candidate to put up for governor against the Republican nominee, abolitionist Seth Padelford. A faction of more conservative Republicans united with Democrats to nominate Sprague on a pro-Union fusion ticket to defeat Padelford. Sprague was reluctant to run; his nature, he later said, was always to hide himself from the public gaze, and he admitted having no political knowledge. He refused the nomination for a week before accepting when he was told "it was of national importance that the radical element should be suppressed." But critics disparaged him as a political cipher. Even a sympathetic *New York Times* correspondent predicted that Sprague would likely "initiate no new policy, suggest no novel ideas, or carry out any grand enterprise."

Sprague's politics, then and later, might be described as eclectic or, less charitably, muddled. But in fairness to him, so were Rhode Island's politics in those years. "Of all the States in the Union Rhode Island can boast of the most complicated political combinations, the most wonderful political parties, and the most erratic political leaders," observed the *New York Times.*

In his political career Sprague would support Lincoln's Emancipation Proclamation, consistently favor voting rights for African Americans, and reliably vote with the radical Republicans on civil rights and Reconstruction matters. But in the 1860 governor's election the abolitionists assailed him as a reactionary sympathizer with slaveholders. Partly this feeling rested on the theory that Yankee textile producers who needed Southern cotton, the "lords of the loom," had formed an unholy alliance with Southern "lords of the lash." Indeed, Sprague's narrow victory over Padelford, following a vicious, mudslinging campaign on both sides, was celebrated as far away as Savannah, Georgia, where the citizens fired a hundred-gun salute in Sprague's honor. But although Sprague had good reason, from a selfish standpoint, to sympathize with the South, he saw, as a Boston newspaper observed after Fort Sumter, that when his country was in peril and its flag shot down, there was "but one course for the patriotic citizen, and that is to rally to its support, and put down rebellion."

And so the dashing boy governor and soldier with whom Kate had reconnected in the spring of 1861 was acceptable enough politically to the daughter of the antislavery, pro-Union, Republican Salmon Chase. Moreover, given Kate's acute political antenna, she would have quickly ascertained whether Sprague was pro-slaveholder and would have rejected him as a suitor for that reason alone. It is inconceivable she would have formed and maintained a deep romantic interest in someone who did not share the basic liberal outlook on race and other matters of her and her father.

Kate's romance with Sprague progressed with remarkable swiftness. They were constantly in each other's company. While on her way to see her young hero at his temporary quarters at the Patent Office, Kate intercepted a bouquet of flowers Mary Lincoln had sent in gratitude for Sprague's recruiting efforts and presented them to him herself. On another occasion they sailed down the Potomac River, and Sprague stole a "hesitating kiss" from Kate, who responded with a "glowing, blushing face." Sprague later told Kate he remembered it all: "The step forward from the Cleveland meeting, and the enhanced poetical sensation. For it was poetry if there ever is such in life."

As early as the end of May 1861—barely a month after they met again in Washington—newspapers began reporting that Sprague and Kate were engaged to be married. The governor was so popular with the ladies that the names of other alleged fiancées had been floating around, including that of the daughter of War Secretary Simon Cameron. But the *New York Times* insisted Kate was the one.

The courtship was interrupted in July when Sprague led his men into battle at Bull Run in Manassas, Virginia. Ever since being sent home at age twelve with his company of boys in the Dorr Rebellion, Sprague had been waiting for a chance to see actual battle, and now it had come. The Rhode Islanders were officially under the command of Colonel Ambrose Burnside, but Sprague gallantly entered the fray, remaining at the front with the artillery when Burnside's exhausted men fell to the rear. Sprague said he "wanted to feel the enemy," and so he did, absorbing the full blast of Confederate reinforcements "not twenty paces off" as he prepared to mount a charge, only to see his men scatter. Trying to rally his troops, he had his horse shot out from under him. He shouted, "I am not dead; forward, boys of Rhode Island!"

But the Rhode Islanders had to retreat to Washington at the end of that afternoon, in panic and despair, with the rest of the routed Union army. Among the Rhode Islanders killed was Major Sullivan Ballou, a close friend of Sprague who became famous for the eloquent letter he wrote his wife a few days before the battle, portending his possible death.

With the local hospitals unable to accommodate the wounded stragglers returning from Bull Run, the Chase family opened their home to as many overflow patients as they could handle. As Nettie later recalled, "one after another the poor sufferers were brought into the house until we had eight or ten men to nurse back into health and strength again." Thankfully for Kate, Governor Sprague returned safely to Willard's Hotel in Washington, where he slept until two in the morning. It was to be his first and last battlefield encounter of the war, which he mostly spent in Rhode Island tending to business. He turned down a commission as brigadier general, peeved at not having been offered the major generalship to which he felt entitled as a governor reelected in April on the Union ticket. Lincoln would have liked to accommodate Sprague, but the commission had already been promised to Massachusetts lawyer Benjamin Butler, a Democrat. Nonetheless, Sprague kept up a cordial correspondence with Lincoln, offering recommendations from time to time that Lincoln took seriously and raising additional troops whenever called upon. He also corresponded directly with Mary Lincoln, once offering what she praised as his earnest suggestions for a cabinet shakeup.

He and Kate resumed seeing each other almost immediately after Bull Run. Six days after the battle they joined a party of dignitaries, including the president and cabinet members, in a steamer down the Potomac to shoot at some earthworks thrown up by the Confederates to block the river. The young couple appeared to be enjoying themselves as Kate was allowed to fire a big gun several times.

Then in late summer, without telling her father, Kate went to Providence to see Governor Sprague. Salmon Chase was not pleased. He told her she should not have made such a trip if Sprague was only a friend and that if there was more to their relationship, then he ought to know it. Although Chase admired Sprague's politics, Chase all but told his daughter he objected to the idea that she might marry him. Chase was not eager to see Kate married off, he told her, but he added that she should not assume from his disapproval of one suitor that he would disapprove of all. Indeed, he said he would be happy to see her marry a "good man—a gentleman—and a Christian gentleman—who would be to you the affectionate protector you need." He was not convinced William Sprague was such a man.

Kate's sister Nettie, however, expressing the romantic notions of a fourteen-year-old girl, wrote Kate from boarding school in Philadelphia in September 1861 to say she hoped Kate would marry Sprague. She playfully stated that although she could not give her consent until she was older, perhaps the young governor would tire of waiting. Nettie recognized that if the couple did not act soon, then one or the other would find someone else.

Indeed, Sprague had no shortage of other women to choose from, and Kate did not lack for suitors either. Just days before Nettie's letter Kate attracted much attention at a grand review of artillery and cavalry on a field east of the Capitol, where she galloped around on a large bay horse with a military-style riding habit. Many years later another Union solider remembered her as a "magnificent creature" who rode into camp one day on horseback "and created no end of stir among us chaps. She was one of the few women I have ever known who seemed born to the saddle; and she walked as divinely as she rode."

In many ways her union with Sprague was a logical one. Both were "catches": Kate, the young, beautiful, Northern belle, and Sprague, the rich, handsome governor and war commander. They complemented each other: Kate had class but not money; Sprague money but not class. The young couple also shared an important bond: Kate was motherless, and Sprague had lost his father when he was a boy. And just as Salmon Chase had been a stern and demanding single parent, so had Fanny Sprague. As Sprague would later write, his mother tried, without success, to instill "habits of order" in him that were not in his nature.

For Kate, Sprague held the allure of the "bad boy." He was everything her solemn, abstemious father was not. He smoked and drank and had little regard for the strictures of polite society. With his money and romantic nature he offered her the prospect of a more adventurous life than the static, ornamental existence her father envisioned for her. Her father loved and idolized her, but, ever the perfectionist, he expected too much of her. Sprague, by contrast, adored her without qualification. Kate found it refreshing—and thrilling—to be loved by someone who, at least at the time, considered her perfect just as she was.

In due course Salmon Chase would come to accept the relationship, either because he realized Kate's feelings for Sprague were not going away or because he warmed to the idea of having a multimillionaire for a son-in-law. Though not poor, Chase had never been a wealthy man, and his $8,000 salary as treasury secretary was consumed by mounting expenses: $1,800 in annual rent at the Sixth and E Street mansion, elegant furnishings and frequent open houses, wages for half a dozen servants, Kate's extensive wardrobe, and out-of-town schooling for Nettie, who followed in Kate's footsteps to Maria Eastman's school near Philadelphia and transferred, at age fifteen, to a competitor of the Haines School in New York City. Chase also faced doctors' bills for the girls' frequent illnesses: when Nettie contracted scarlet fever in Philadelphia in early 1862 Kate went immediately to her bedside and came down with a severe cold. Chase, ever mindful of the history of death in his family, was distraught over the prospect of losing his only surviving children to the same illness that had claimed the young life of his first child. He wrote Kate in Philadelphia to counsel the use of a homeopathic, natural-remedy treatment, telling her he would never forget "how futile was allopathic [traditional medical] practice in the case of my own dear child, whose name you bear." To Chase's relief, both his daughters recovered, although every time either of them came down with so much as a cough he would fear the worst.

If Kate followed her father's advice on medicine, she was less obedient when it came to his warnings against overspending. When she went east to shop for furnishings for their Washington home, he asked her to look for carpets and furniture in Philadelphia first before going to New York. But under escort from Governor Sprague, she had already gone on to Manhattan, where she opened an account at A. T. Stewart's fashionable department store (Mary Lincoln's favorite) and ordered carpeting from there. Bypassing her father, she telegraphed one of the servants at their Washington home to have some dresses and other articles from Stewart's sent directly to her. Shortly afterward Chase wrote to remind her that she was still his daughter and he expected her to yield gracefully to his admonitions. "You will easily remember instances in which you have tried me pretty severely by not doing so," he scolded.

Chase was working long hours at this time, burdened with the job of financing a war that was lasting longer than anyone had assumed and was costing more than anyone might have imagined. At the outset of the war the nation's finances were in disrepair and, with military spending exceeding $1.5 million a day by early 1862, the treasury secretary was desperate. "Chase has no money and he tells me he can raise no more," lamented President Lincoln at the time, asking out loud, "What shall I do?" Although Chase entered the Treasury with little experience himself in high finance, Lincoln, who knew even less of such matters, preferred to delegate them to Chase, telling him, "You understand these things: I do not."

To keep the army afloat Chase had to put aside some of his long-held views, such as his aversion to the use of paper currency and his opposition to deficit spending. Despite fears it would lead to inflation, he pushed legislation that made paper money—so-called greenbacks—legally binding tender for the payment of debts. The unprecedented notes were backed only by the credit of the federal government rather than the traditional gold coin. "Gentlemen," he told a group of Wall Street bankers, "the war must go on until this rebellion is put down, if we have to put out paper until it takes $1000 to buy a breakfast." He would come to enjoy the nickname "Old Greenbacks," conferred on him due less to his advocacy of the idea than to the fact that cannily, for political purposes, he had put his face on the one-dollar bill. As Kate told a newspaperman many years later, some of her friends also tried to have her picture put on one of the bank notes, and though it would have made a more attractive visage than her father's, she said that as soon as she heard of the idea she "positively forbade" it.

In the same interview Kate extolled her father's war efforts as "a success as great as the surrender of the Confederate army" at Appomattox. "The world will never know the strain that [he] had to undergo at that time," she recalled. "My father lived at the department, and he slept with his ear at the telegraph. An order would come that millions must be had at once, and it was his business to raise the money." His success in doing so, she asserted, "will be one of the wonders of history."

Chase came to support other measures, such as a federal income tax and a national banking system, that went against his small-government economic philosophy. And he embraced creative solutions for raising money, notably the nationwide marketing scheme by financier Jay Cooke to sell war bonds to average citizens by appealing to their patriotism, presaging the "buy bonds" campaigns of the First and Second World Wars. Cooke made a fortune in commissions after Chase selected him as the exclusive agent for selling millions of dollars of government loan issues that previously were undersubscribed. A devout Christian and abolitionist from Sandusky, Ohio, Cooke became an intimate friend of the treasury secretary and his family, entertaining Chase on fishing trips to Cooke's Lake Erie island retreat, "Gibraltar," and hosting him, Kate, and Nettie many times at his estate near Philadelphia.

Although it exposed him to charges of preferential treatment, Chase was not above accepting financial help from Cooke and other friends he favored with government business and patronage. Near the outset of the war Chase borrowed several thousand dollars from Hiram Barney, a loyal political supporter Chase had rewarded with the plum job of port collector at the New York Custom House. Chase's personal financial dependency on Cooke eventually became more extensive. It started out innocently enough: in the fall of 1861, while Kate was visiting Cooke in Philadelphia, Chase wrote her to say she needed a new carriage but that he could not afford an expensive one. A short time later Cooke shipped a gift to Chase—a modest carriage the treasury secretary was tempted to accept but felt compelled to decline. Later he changed his mind and decided that Kate, described by Cooke as "a glorious girl," could accept the gift, although he sent it back after determining that it was too light for their purposes. But before long another gift came Kate's way. In Philadelphia she ordered some expensive bookshelves, the bill for which Cooke found and paid himself. Kate thanked him afterward with a mild reprimand that she would need to be careful in the future about leaving her bills around his house.

Although he broke no laws, over time Chase allowed the line between his public and private dealings with Cooke to blur. He used Cooke as his personal broker and investment adviser, borrowed money from him, and became a shareholder in his railroad company. Still, Chase turned down many more gifts than he accepted, including a check for a profit of $4,200 Cooke once sent him for the sale of some stock Chase had bought but not yet paid for. "In order to be able to render most efficient service to our country it is essential for me to *be* as well as *seem* right and to *seem* right as well as *be* right," he explained to Cooke. In an era when self-dealing and outright theft by high government officials were far from uncommon, Chase never dipped his own fingers in the Treasury till. He had once lamented to Kate how unfair it was that someone who worked as ceaselessly for the public as he did had to bear so many of his own expenses. "Not that I am pinched or what I *call* poor," he wrote her another time, but he could not afford to be extravagant because he was "determined to be honest."

Cynics might observe that any temptation Chase had to use his position for personal gain receded once it became clear his daughter was going to marry one of the richest men in the country. That would be unfair, however, both because Chase was an honest public official and because the courtship of Kate and William Sprague, even as it proceeded apace, was fraught with uncertainty. Despite being a match on paper and for all that brought them together, other equally powerful factors made them a total mismatch. Kate was calm and deliberate in thought and in speech, whereas Sprague was erratic and impulsive. As he explained in declining to speak to a library association in late 1861, he was a man of action, not words. In letters to Kate he would later confess to a mind that was "sadly disconnected." Much of it was undoubtedly due to his drinking, but he also had "very limited mental capacity," Civil War journalist Henry Villard observed. Sprague was a far cry from the men Kate grew up with—giants such as Daniel Webster, Henry Clay, and Charles Sumner (not to mention her father).

To Mary Viall, though, the girl Sprague apparently had gotten pregnant, it was Sprague who deserved better. In her *roman à clef* she described him as a "handsome cavalier" while painting Kate—the "statesman's daughter" and "merchant's wife"—as soulless. "You discover tact, but not tenderness," she wrote of Kate. "Pity, without sympathy; a certain kind of sentiment devoid of feeling; a romantic temperament, but not poetic; a sensuous nature free from ideality or emotion." Kate's manners were "too mechanical, stereotyped, and stilted. There were no outbursts of naturalness. . . . There's a certain stateliness, which is not royal; an electrical power which does not magnetize."

Like many, Viall could not see beneath the controlled exterior of Kate to an inner core that, as her diary revealed, was more emotional and romantic than Kate let on. Just after her wedding, when Sprague took her into his arms, Kate had felt a "sense of ineffable rest, joy, and completeness. It was like a glimpse of Heaven for purity and peace. All strife ended, all regret silenced. . . . Every thought, every desire, every feeling merged with the one longing to make him happy. Not a reserve in my heart, not a hidden corner he might not scan, the first, the only man that had found a lodgment there!"

And so, although the engagement talk was premature and they would even break off relations for a time, they would be drawn back together. There was something almost inevitable about it. Years later, recalling their first meeting in Cleveland, Kate would describe her attraction to William Sprague in a terse two words: "My fate."

CHAPTER 7

# Mrs. Lincoln's Rival

Was Jim Garfield the cause of their breakup? The future president, from Mentor, Ohio, moved in with Kate and her father in September 1862 and immediately started giving chase to Kate. Within weeks she stopped seeing William Sprague.

Thirty-year-old Brigadier General James A. Garfield was large, handsome, and boyish in appearance. Outwardly he was a warmer man than Salmon Chase—an effusive backslapper with a buoyant personality. But underneath he was a sensitive soul who, prone to self-doubt, accused himself of "vacillation of purpose." In other respects the former classics teacher and lay preacher had several traits in common with Chase: scholarly, pious, and self-righteous. Both men hated slavery, felt the Southern rebels needed to be crushed, and had a low opinion of Abraham Lincoln. Most importantly, they shared a high regard for Salmon P. Chase.

Chase adopted the young man as his protégé, got him a military command, and invited him to stay in his home when Garfield arrived in Washington in the fall of 1862 in search of another military assignment. The treasury secretary gave him the opportunity to sit around the breakfast and dinner table with the leading men of the day and tutored him in economics as they played chess in the evenings. Garfield was an eager listener and agreed with virtually everything his mentor had to say.

So did Kate, of course, and she was happy to flirt with Jim Garfield, a man after her father's own heart. She had insisted the young fellow Ohioan stay with them at the Sixth and E Street house. Garfield thought Kate the most impressive woman connected to any of Lincoln's cabinet members and appeared smitten with her. During his six-week stay they bantered easily and took long horseback rides together in Washington's Rock Creek Park. They visited the army camps together and sang the German *lieder* around the piano with Carl Schurz, now a brigadier general in Franz Sigel's German immigrant corps. Kate must have charmed General Sigel too, for soon afterward he sent her a friendly note with an ornament stolen by one of his scouts from a Confederate watch guard's hat.

Kate and Garfield made a great couple. There was only one problem: he was married—unhappily, at the time, to cold, sober Lucretia "Crete" Garfield, his former star Greek pupil, but married nonetheless. Garfield, who wore his heart on his sleeve, may well have confided in Kate about his marital dissatisfaction. It is not known whether he made any pass at Kate, but he clearly was on the prowl at the time, for he began a secret extramarital affair toward the end of his stay with the Chases with *New-York Tribune* reporter Lucia Gilbert Calhoun, a widow one year younger than Kate. Garfield had written his wife in October, two weeks after entering the Chase household, to report that although Kate had good form, good sense, and "pretty good culture," her beautiful face was marred by a slightly pug nose. But he was probably trying to conceal from Crete his attraction to Kate. Garfield had just received a letter from his wife saying she had learned that "you and Miss Kate are taking dinners out, visiting camps etc. . . . Is Miss Kate a very charming, interesting young lady? I may be *jealous* if she is." Under the circumstances Garfield was hardly about to go overboard in his praise of Kate. Still, Crete Garfield would long suspect that her husband had flirted—or worse—with Kate Chase.

Even if nothing happened between him and Kate, Garfield's extended stay had to have aroused strong feelings of jealousy on the part of William Sprague. Sprague was not the kind of man who would have kept those feelings to himself. And Kate was not the kind of woman who would have reacted well to his accusations.

Meanwhile, in Washington, as the two of them sat and talked with Salmon Chase night after night, Kate and Garfield heard her father's litany of complaints about the Lincoln administration: that the president, though well meaning, was weak and incompetent; that he was too slow to move on emancipation and the arming of black troops; that the war was not being vigorously prosecuted; that the wrong generals were in command; that the army was infested with too many proslavery officers; that he (Chase) was insufficiently recognized for his Herculean efforts to finance the war; and that although he was expected to fund the army, he was kept in the dark on military matters. If only his advice on this or that general or military maneuver had been followed, Chase maintained, the war would have been won already. Instead, as he claimed in a letter to Kate, the administration had "trifled with our opportunities—mismanaged our force—and kid gloved rebellion." And his favorite refrain, repeated ad nauseam in private correspondence, was that there was no real "cabinet" but, instead, a bunch of department heads who met only sporadically and were expected to run their respective machines "as if [they] were the Heads of Factories supplying shoes or cloth."

Just as, in her father's opinion, Kate could do little right at Miss Haines's boarding school, neither, in his view, could Lincoln as president. Some of Chase's points may have been valid, but the manner of attack—petty, peevish, and self-pitying, and all behind the president's back—marked him as borderline disloyal to the very administration in which he served.

Not that Chase had any personal complaint with Lincoln, he was careful to point out. Within his own treasury department Chase was given free reign and always received from the president "a cordial support . . . manifesting in me all the confidence I can possibly claim." But Chase could never quite outgrow the idea that he, not Lincoln, should have been the Republican nominee in 1860 and that in time the country would come to recognize its mistake and right the wrong.

Given the steady stream of negative comments about Lincoln that passed from the mouth of Chase *père* to *fille*, it is hardly surprising that Kate also denigrated the president in private. Through John Hay and others, Lincoln was well aware of Chase's criticisms and came to learn that Kate concurred in them. Nonetheless he went out of his way to extend cordial treatment to "Miss Kate," as he called her. Early in the war, when she visited the White House, he took her aside to point out through a spyglass the Confederate tents across the Potomac. She was one of half a dozen women Lincoln invited to the White House to meet a delegation of Native American tribes. And, according to one oft-repeated story first recounted by Elizabeth Keckley, Mary Lincoln's African American dressmaker, Mrs. Lincoln once forbade her husband in advance of a White House reception even to talk to "Miss C" [Kate] or "Miss D" [Stephen Douglas's widow Adele], two of the "silly women" flatterers Mary detested. Lincoln responded that he had to talk to someone and could not just "stand around like a simpleton, and say nothing," adding that Kate, in particular, was "too young and handsome to practice deceit." He ignored his wife's edict and spoke to whomever he liked, including Kate, whose lively conversation he quite enjoyed.

Lincoln adopted a higher-minded attitude toward his enemies than did his wife, Mary, but no amount of diplomacy could mask the hostility between Mrs. Lincoln and Kate. The irony is that, age and physical appearance aside, Kate and Mary Lincoln were not dissimilar in background and outlook. Both were intelligent, educated, and cultured women who knew their politics, had independent streaks, and resisted the conventional constraints imposed on women in their day. Though raised in a slaveholding home, Mary Lincoln was not the Confederate sympathizer (or, worse, spy) some accused her of being, and during the war she was as opposed to slavery as Kate or Salmon Chase were. Indeed, Mrs. Lincoln became devoted friends with the Chases' favorite abolitionist, Senator Charles Sumner. Sumner had a habit of strolling into breakfast at the Chases', lingering afterward to sit on the sofa talking things over with the treasury secretary, then wandering over to the White House to discuss theater or history with Mrs. Lincoln, often in French, before escorting her to the opera in the evening. The genuine fondness Mary Lincoln and Sumner developed for each other helped thaw the sometimes chilly relationship between the radical Sumner and the more politically moderate president.

Both Kate and Mrs. Lincoln felt the sting of criticism for their shopping habits. As one Ohio newspaper reported, "The Lincoln-Chase contest has extended into the women's department. Mrs. Lincoln has got a new French rig with all the posies, costing $4,000. Miss Kate Chase 'sees her and goes her one better,' by ordering a nice little $6,000 arrangement, including a $3,000 love of a shawl. Go it, greenbacks, while it is yet today." Both were taken to task for their ambition and the political influence they exerted on the powerful men in their lives. They had another common bond: each of them had lost her mother at an early age (Kate at five, Mary Todd at six), and each had been raised by a politically important but emotionally distant father. Both women came to Washington as outsiders, not being members of the Southern aristocracy who had ruled capital society for decades. For these reasons, as has been recently argued, Kate and Mrs. Lincoln were potentially more "kindred spirits than rivals" and might have found ways to help each other out had they stood together in the new Republican administration.

But the political rivalry between President Lincoln and Secretary Chase made any sort of real communion between Mary Lincoln and Kate Chase impossible. Mary Lincoln constantly warned her husband that Chase was scheming against him, which was true, as Chase had an extensive network of treasury agents throughout the country working to advance his political cause. Mrs. Lincoln's "hostility to Mr. Chase was very bitter," her dressmaker, Elizabeth Keckley, recalled. As Keckley confirmed, Mrs. Lincoln also feared that any political advancement by Chase would build up his daughter's social position. And so, just as there could be only one president, Kate and Mrs. Lincoln knew there could be only one Queen of Washington.

In early 1862, tired of the public receptions she was forced to hold for walk-ins as well as the smaller, more formal state dinners for cabinet members and other dignitaries, Mrs. Lincoln decided to throw a private gala, paid for out of Lincoln's own pocket. Like Kate's dinner dances, it would be by invitation only, but on a grander scale. Finally, Mrs. Lincoln's party, held for five hundred guests in the East Room, was the hottest ticket in town. Half of Washington was "jubilant at being invited" and the other half "furious for being left out in the cold." The guests included Generals George McClellan and Irvin McDowell, John Frémont and his celebrated wife, Jessie, and virtually the entire European diplomatic corps in their colorful sashes and medals. The event featured a sumptuous midnight feast and Japanese bowls of champagne punch as well as elaborate floral displays and decorations, including water fountain nymphs made of nougat and sugar confections in the shapes of a Union fort, a Chinese pagoda, and the Goddess of Liberty.

As for the contest between Mary Lincoln and Kate, the evening was something of a wash. Despite grumbling in some quarters that such merrymaking was in poor taste in the middle of a war, many hailed the party as perhaps the most brilliant of its kind ever held in the capital. Mrs. Lincoln's typically ostentatious dress and adornments drew mostly positive reviews, even if some, including her husband, raised their eyebrows at her extremely low-cut dress. Just as typically, Kate, attired in a mauve-colored silk gown that perfectly set off her auburn hair, attracted more attention than any other female guest. *Frank Leslie's Illustrated Newspaper*, the most widely read journal of its kind in the North, called her "La belle des belles."

As if to steal back some thunder, Kate held a soirée of her own the very next night, to which she invited the Hutchinson Family Singers, the most popular vocal group in mid-nineteenth-century America. With a rural folk style that foreshadowed the protest singers of the 1950s and 1960s, the Hutchinson Family's music promoted such causes as abolitionism, temperance, and women's rights. The Lincolns were fans of the Hutchinsons, and Salmon Chase was a big supporter, dating back to the 1840s, when they supplied the campaign theme song for his Liberty Party. Some people considered them controversial, though, and just weeks before being invited to the Chase home they were banned from appearing at Union Army camps on the order of General-in-Chief McClellan, an opponent of emancipation. Some of his offended soldiers at a concert in Fairfax, Virginia, hissed when they heard the following lines from the Hutchinsons' musical rendition of John Greenleaf Whittier's abolitionist poem "We Wait Beneath the Furnace Blast":

*What gives the wheat-fields blades of steel?*
*What points the rebel cannon?*

* * *

*What breaks the oath of the men o' the South?*
*What whets the knife for the Union's life?—*
*Hark to the answer: SLAVERY!*

When the Hutchinsons sang for the antislavery guests at the Chase mansion the day after Mary Lincoln's gala, the song for which they were expelled from the camps was enthusiastically encored. Kate had shown that she knew how to stage a political rally. And although her gathering was a more intimate affair than Mrs. Lincoln's ball, it just as effectively accomplished its purpose—reminding influential radicals of her father's commitment to them.

Although the success of Mary Lincoln's ball helped reestablish her primacy, in the minds of some, over her rival Kate Chase, the competition would soon be over, though not as a result of either's triumph. The only damper on Mrs. Lincoln's party had been the illness of her eleven-year-old son, Willie, who lay upstairs with a high fever, causing the worried Lincolns to spend much of the evening by his bedside. Kate, recently returned from tending to Nettie's scarlet fever at Jay Cooke's home in Philadelphia, extended a few sympathetic words to Mrs. Lincoln that night. But Willie quickly faded and died two weeks later of typhoid fever, probably contracted from drinking contaminated Washington water. Willie had been his father's personal favorite, the son most like him—smart, humorous, kindly—and when Lincoln emerged from the room where Willie died he said to his senior secretary, John Nicolay, "Well Nicolay, my boy is gone—he is actually gone," then burst into tears.

Lincoln would summon the strength to carry on with his monumental duties, but Willie's death marked the end of Mary Lincoln's career as a society hostess. Overcome with grief, she did not attend his public funeral and never recovered from the loss. She spent months locked up in her room, weeping and convulsing, and began attending séances to try to summon Willie's spirit. After his death she would never throw another large party in the White House, leaving Kate as the unchallenged first hostess of the capital. Mrs. Lincoln would have some further scuffles with Kate, but she had lost her taste for battle in the entertainment wars.

So many stories of the Kate Chase–Mary Lincoln hostility have been passed down through the years that assessing their veracity is difficult. A particularly suspect tale is contained in a 1953 biography of Kate by Ishbel Ross, who authored a later biography of Mary Lincoln. According to Ross, Kate and her father happened to be driving up to the White House in their carriage one day when they saw Mrs. Lincoln shaking hands with an African American teacher, Rebecca Orville, who was seeking help in launching a school for black children. Sensing an opportunity to embarrass the First Lady, according to Ross, Kate "made veiled observations at the next Cabinet dinner about making too much of the Negro." As Ross concluded, Kate's "animosity to the President's wife outweighed her humanity" on this occasion.

There is good reason to doubt this story, which contains no attribution by Ross (and is not repeated in her 1973 biography of Mrs. Lincoln). Kate's precise views on racial issues are not documented, but it is reasonable to assume they would have closely tracked her father's. Although Kate was probably not a pure abolitionist, she certainly opposed slavery and supported greater rights for black Americans. A few years later, when African Americans started to be elected to office during Reconstruction, a conservative Ohio newspaper said her "equality notions are well known" and predicted she would feel "highly honored" to dance "with her delicate waist encircled by the steady arm of the colored Senator from Louisiana or Mississippi." She probably was not entirely free of the racial prejudices most white persons held at the time, including Northern Republicans. Even Salmon Chase could make reference to "an old negress, grimy black, fat and squat and *odorous*" to whom he gave money to help buy her slave son's freedom. And in a letter to Kate during a postwar visit to a Virginia school for former slaves, he complimented the "little darkey" children on their orderliness. It would be surprising if Kate never made any similar private comment about African Americans that, to modern ears, would sound unenlightened. That said, and as much as Kate disliked Mary Lincoln, her alleged comment that the First Lady was "making too much of the Negro" does not ring true.

A further clue to Kate's racial attitudes can be found in her relations with the Chase domestic servants she supervised, most of whom were free black citizens. Despite their omnipresence in the Chases' lives, most of these servants are nearly invisible in the family letters and diaries. What evidence there is, though, suggests that Kate was much beloved by her African American servants, some of whom would serve as pallbearers at her funeral and one of whom would describe her as a "saint." She was a stern but fair employer, capable of imposing extreme discipline. According to another story, when a coachman (of unspecified race) declined to help the butler at one of her evening receptions because it was not his job, she kept him sitting outside in his carriage for hours in the cold. That is the sort of punishment that would have appealed to Salmon Chase's Uncle Philander, the Episcopal bishop.

Many of the more colorful negative stories about Kate, especially those recounted long after the fact, are probably made up. But they gained acceptance over the years because they fed the narrative of Kate as a cunning, sharp-edged woman beneath the graceful exterior. Indeed, reflecting the common perception, when MGM planned a Hollywood movie about Kate in 1940, it chose that queen of harridans, Joan Crawford, to play her. (The film was never made.)

That would seem like miscasting, for Kate was more queen than harridan. But she was a political woman who, no different from most male politicians, was capable of launching caustic and backstabbing attacks on her foes. And nowhere was that capacity more in evidence during the Civil War than with regard to military personnel matters. At a private gathering in May 1862 she was described as "bitter as gall" that Lincoln was dragging his feet on replacing General McClellan, whose anti-emancipation stance made him anathema to the Chases. Later, during an evening John Hay spent at the Chases', Kate complained to him about Lincoln's firing of Ohio General William Rosecrans after the North's calamitous defeat at the Battle of Chickamauga. "Pretty Katie spoke a little spitefully about Rosecrans' removal," Hay noted in his diary. "Her father's old game."

Throughout the war both Kate and her father promoted the cause of generals, many of them Ohioans, such as Rosecrans, who could be counted on to support Salmon Chase's political and military aims. Ironically, when McClellan received his first major promotion in 1861 to major general, Chase wrote him to take credit, saying that, as a result, "the country was indebted to me—may I say it without too much vanity?" But Chase and other radicals, particularly War Secretary Edwin Stanton, would turn on "Little Mac" when he proved to be insufficiently antislavery in attitude and failed to press the war with speed and force. Chase kept up his drumbeat of criticism of "McClellanism" in letters to Kate, and even Nettie joined in the chorus. "Why don't he *move*?" she wrote her father.

After Elizabeth Blair Lee, sister of Lincoln's most conservative cabinet member, Montgomery Blair, heard Kate's attack on McClellan, she privately disparaged Kate as another "Wendell Phillips," the radical abolitionist. "Lizzie" Blair Lee, who really *was* a racist ("Contact with the African degenerates our white race," she averred), made no defense of McClellan in Kate's presence because she believed he needed none. But Lizzie admitted she was "not so nonresistant on the darkey question."

She told Kate that "if Congress did not deliver us of the freed ones we would dispose of them as the Yankees had the Pequo[t]s," a reference to the 1637 burning massacre of several hundred Pequots, including women and children, by New England colonists and their Native American allies. If Kate said anything in response to this chilling statement, it was not recorded. The exchange does illustrate, though, that Kate's peers viewed her as antislavery. Kate's disagreement with Elizabeth Blair Lee mirrored the split within Lincoln's cabinet between the conservatives, led by Montgomery Blair, who saw antislavery efforts as interfering with the struggle to maintain the Union, and the radicals, championed by Chase and Stanton, who viewed emancipation as essential to winning the war. Each group supported those military leaders who echoed their political views, as Lincoln, increasingly in close consultation with the moderate William Seward, tried to mediate between them.

Kate's kind of general was Ben Butler, the "Beast" of New Orleans, who, in May 1862, ordered that Southern women who insulted and harassed his Union soldiers be treated as prostitutes. Kate wished he were in Washington "to keep the secession women quiet," and she sympathized with the radical Butler, as did her father, when Lincoln replaced him with a more politically moderate commander, Nathaniel Banks. Kate also shared her father's opinion that General Irvin McDowell of Ohio received a raw deal from Lincoln when he was demoted after losing the First Battle of Bull Run (and again after losing the Second Battle of Bull Run). Chase was instrumental in securing McDowell's original command as brigadier general heading the Army of Northeastern Virginia, and he admired the Columbus native for his strong antislavery views, his erudition, and his abstemious ways—"He never drinks or smokes or chews or indulges in any kind of license," Chase pointed out. Elizabeth Blair Lee had already made known her disapproval of McDowell, writing that "Miss Kate's father has now got Genl McBowels as Frank [Blair, her brother] calls him mounted behind him and they are trying the abolition nag together—full tilt versus the other Mc[Clellan] and his Commander in Chief [Lincoln]." But Kate adored the Ohio general, and she befriended his wife, Helen, who helped Kate with her 1862 New Year's Day reception.

Kate also surely admired William Sprague for his public statements in the summer of 1862, while their relationship was still on, that it was time to stop pussyfooting around with the rebels. In words similar to those Chase had written to Kate, Sprague declared that "no white-gloved handling" of the enemy would work. "Strike him in his vital parts," the Rhode Island governor wrote. "And if the agents who are employed to do this are not up to the mark . . . [l]et new men and new agents occupy their places." Although Sprague himself saw no further battlefield action after First Bull Run, he did return to that site in 1862 to reclaim the bodies of Rhode Island's Union dead, including his friend Major Ballou, only to be told that Ballou's corpse had been exhumed and decapitated by vengeful Confederate soldiers. Sprague was outraged to the point at which, according to a still widely held belief in Rhode Island, he declared war on the state of Georgia.

Sprague further endeared himself to Kate and her father by ordering the enlistment of a Rhode Island regiment of black troops in 1862. The project was abandoned when the African American recruits, who wanted to be "accepted as citizens and soldiers, in short, as men," received no assurance they would be able to serve in battle and not merely as laborers. They would get that assurance the following summer, and despite sneers by a Democratic Providence newspaper that Lincoln and Sprague were on a "wild goose chase," a company of black soldiers was raised and went to New Orleans to take up garrison duty. Sprague later boasted to Chase that the black Rhode Islanders who manned guns at Little Washington, Virginia, were the bravest and most determined men their commander had ever seen.

Lincoln thought highly enough of Sprague to send him on a secret mission in July 1862 to Corinth, Mississippi, to see General Henry Halleck, head of the Union's western command. By that time Sprague had been reelected, without opposition, to a third term as governor, and then elected by the Rhode Island legislature as a US senator to take office the following year. In the letter of introduction Sprague brought with him Lincoln explained to Halleck that Sprague was there to ask the general to send part of his force east or come himself. "Please give my friend Governor Sprague a full and fair hearing," Lincoln wrote. But Sprague hardly needed to travel a thousand miles to convey Lincoln's request for troops. In reality the president wanted Sprague to sound Halleck out on becoming supreme commander of the entire army. Halleck was unconvinced but, nonetheless, received a telegram from Secretary Stanton the next day appointing him to the elevated position.

At the time of Halleck's appointment, Kate had gone to Ohio to see relatives and escape the summer heat of Washington. In August 1862 she went to visit Helen McDowell, the general's wife, at Buttermilk Falls in upstate New York. Kate brought along Nettie, who was about to enter boarding school in New York City. Nettie enjoyed the visit, but the quiet country setting bored Kate, who was more accustomed to the glamour and sophistication of Washington and Manhattan. "Our hours do not suit her and the cooking does not agree with her," Mrs. McDowell wrote Chase. Kate jumped at the chance to leave the McDowell farm to go to the nearby spa resort town of Saratoga Springs, where fashionable women in parasols could parade down the main thoroughfare, which was lined with opulent hotels and grand piazzas. Having figured out by then that if she did not ask her father's permission to do something or go somewhere he could not say no, Kate left it to Mrs. McDowell to inform him of her departure. In the meantime Chase, who was often left to wonder as to Kate's whereabouts, found life at home "very dull" without her.

Kate slowly made her way back to Washington, awaiting the outcome of Lee's invasion of Maryland in September 1862, which also threatened the capital. From West Point she wrote Hiram Barney, her father's Custom House appointee in New York, to say she had been enlivened by her stay at Saratoga but was hearing so much bad news on the war front that it almost made her despair of the future. "However," she added, "I try to keep up a good heart, and only long to be of some use, in the humble sphere *women* are allowed to fill, in great crises like the present." But on her return she did not shy from involvement in military matters. She wrote to Lincoln to lobby for the promotion of Julius Stahel, a German colleague of her friend Carl Schurz, to major general; a month later Stahel received the appointment. Accompanying her father, she also took a basket of grapes and peaches to General Joe Hooker, who was laid up with a foot injury suffered at Antietam, so the two Chases could sound him out on his views of the military situation. Hooker was severely critical of McClellan and impressed Chase and Kate as a man who would make a suitable replacement for him.

Although McClellan had stopped Lee at Antietam, Chase pooh-poohed the accomplishment, saying he should have destroyed the Confederate army. Halleck, at Lincoln's request, then asked Chase what financial measures needed to be taken, and the treasury secretary told him to replace

McClellan, open the Mississippi River, and advance the army into East Tennessee. "The first was not done; the second was not done; the third was not done, and today the Treasury is almost thirty six millions behind, and almost without resources," Chase complained to Ben Butler, adding, "Was there ever anything like it?"

Lincoln agreed that McClellan had missed a golden opportunity to crush Lee's army, but the president chose to claim Antietam as the victory he had been waiting for to issue his preliminary Emancipation Proclamation. William Sprague, together with other loyal Northern governors attending a highly watched conference in Altoona, Pennsylvania, unequivocally endorsed the edict, providing Lincoln with much-needed political support—and causing many Rhode Islanders to denounce Sprague and hiss him in the streets back home. But, ironically, Chase was more guarded in his approval. He said on the one hand that it was *too* sweeping, arguing that emancipation was best accomplished piecemeal by military commanders in the field (many of whom he had cultivated friendly political relationships with). Yet on the other hand he also complained that the proclamation was subject to too many exceptions.

Chase had been agitating for months for action on the emancipation front, but now that it came, he was politician enough to realize Lincoln had stolen his thunder on the issue. He did take pride in one suggestion he made that Lincoln adopted in the final proclamation—adding the words "the gracious favor of Almighty God" at the end. And to make sure Chase received appropriate credit, on September 24, 1862, the evening after the preliminary proclamation was issued, Kate organized a reception at their home. A group of serenaders moved from the White House to the Chase mansion and demanded a speech from the treasury secretary. After they left, John Hay stayed and drank wine inside with "a few old fogies" who listened as Chase mocked the "insanity" of the slaveholder class. Hay wrote in his diary that everyone "gleefully and merrily called each other and themselves abolitionists, and seemed to enjoy the novel sensation of appropriating that horrible name."

It was only three days after this reception that James Garfield had accepted the Chases' invitation to stay with them. He remained more than six weeks, until mid-November, when he moved into bachelor quarters with his army staff, telling his wife that the Chases' prolonged hospitality had become embarrassing to him. Or perhaps he had embarrassed himself with some overture to Kate. In any event, not long after he left, Kate and Sprague were back on again. It is unclear when the courtship resumed and when "the blank," as Sprague later referred to it, ended. But by May 1863 they were corresponding again, and on May 24 they were seen together at the Blair family home in Silver Spring, Maryland. Elizabeth Blair Lee saw Kate "turn a *restless* eye upon us all" when she overheard Sprague agreeing with Francis Preston Blair Sr., Elizabeth's father, in his criticism of General Hooker, one of Kate's favorites. The next day Sprague wrote Chase to say that Hooker was drunk during his recent loss at the Battle of Chancellorsville, was drunk every day, and was "wholly undependable."

Although no one at the May 24 Blair gathering knew it at the time, Sprague and Kate had just recently become engaged. On May 18 Sprague wrote Hiram Barney, who had been championing his cause, to say that "the Governor and Miss Katy have consented to take me into their fold" and to thank Barney for having "fought my battles." Word hit the newspapers the first week of June that Kate Chase, daughter of the treasury secretary, and William Sprague, Rhode Island's junior Republican senator, were to be married.

On May 31 Chase, who had been asked by his recently departed houseguest Garfield to "remember me kindly to Miss Kate," broke the news to his protégé and expressed hope that Garfield could attend the wedding that fall. When told the answer was no, Chase asked Garfield, "Why can't you be here?" Why, indeed. When the wedding took place in November Garfield was in the Washington area and even gave a speech the following week, at Chase's invitation, in nearby Baltimore. But for the actual wedding, an event the entire nation's capital clamored to attend, Jim Garfield, as close to a son as Salmon Chase ever had, would be a no-show.

CHAPTER 8

# Wedding of the Decade

James Garfield was not the only man disappointed to learn that Kate Chase was marrying William Sprague. "She is to be married on November 12th which disgusts me with life," her erstwhile suitor, John Hay, wrote to a friend. He thought Kate "only a little lovelier than all other women" because she was so busy making her father the next president. Still, he considered her "a great woman" with a "great future." Curmudgeonly Gideon Welles, Lincoln's navy secretary, who frequently tussled with Kate's father in the cabinet, was characteristically cynical about the union. The engaged couple called on him on May 19, 1863, to tell him the news, prompting him to record in his diary: "I have been skeptical as to a match, but this means something. She is beautiful, or, more properly perhaps, interesting and impressive. He is rich and holds the position of Senator. Few young men have such advantages as he, and Miss Kate has talents and ambition sufficient for both."

When November 12, 1863, came, Kate would have an earthly crown in the form of a diamond and pearl tiara worth $100,000 in today's money and a royal wedding to usher her into married life. But it was to be a roller-coaster ride getting there. And although, given Sprague's wealth, the question of "for richer or poorer" seemed academic, it was far from clear whether her marriage would be for better or for worse.

"In America," wrote French historian Alexis de Tocqueville in his famous 1840 book on his travels to the United States, "the independence of woman is irrecoverably lost in the bonds of matrimony." If an unmarried woman was less constrained in America than elsewhere, de Tocqueville thought, then an American wife was subject to greater strictures. "The former makes her father's house an abode of freedom and pleasure; the latter lives in the home of her husband as if it were a cloister." As if writing with Kate Chase in mind, he also observed that "the women of America, who often exhibit a masculine strength of understanding and a manly energy, generally preserve great delicacy of personal appearance and always retain the manners of women, although they sometimes show that they have the hearts and minds of men."

Kate would later express the same sentiments, retrospectively, in her diary. Five years into her marriage she reflected back on her thinking going into her betrothal. She had then been "in the full flush of social influence and triumph," she wrote, a woman "whose career had been curiously independent and successful." Surrounded by male flatterers, she was accustomed to issuing commands and being obeyed. But she had given it all up for "one long dream of happiness and love." Twenty-three at the time, the average age of marriage for Yankee brides, she decided it was time to settle down.

But if blissful domesticity was her goal, any number of red flags suggested that achieving it could be problematic. In the months preceding her wedding, in almost daily and sometimes twice-daily correspondence with Kate directly or through her father (who routinely showed her Sprague's letters), Sprague revealed himself to be a man of wild mood swings and enormous self-doubt. He veered from desperate expressions of love to confessions of weakness and "childish" and "unmanly" behavior. Writing to his future father-in-law, he alluded to his "infirmities of nature," his resort to "improper remedies to assuage the disease," and his "eccentric" life to that point. He attributed his perceived improprieties to alcohol and warned Kate that he became cross and ugly when he laid off chewing cigars, an admittedly "disgusting habit" he hoped not to subject her to. He later reported to Kate that he was getting on well with his health, having limited his drinking to cold water. "Don't influence me to smoke," he added, "for if I do then comes the cutting of tobacco, then follows brandies and whiskies. Then dyspepsia and an unhappy life. Look out for this won't you my love. You won't have tobacco smoke about, or whiskey or brandy, then we will have no war." But he begged Kate to let him "indulge in the luxuries which are soon to be mine," a clear reference to physical intimacy, even as he took note of Kate's objection to premarital relations. But it appears from her later diary that, despite her father's warning to do nothing that would diminish Sprague's respect for her in the slightest, she gave in at least once before the wedding, for she wrote a few years later that he was then holding her premarriage "weakness" and "sin" against her.

They quarreled a number of times during the engagement period. Kate's first meeting with his family in Rhode Island did not go well, and he accused her of unspecified strange behavior for which she needed to apologize to his mother. "I trust we may never undergo another such crisis of great discomfort and discouragement," he wrote her, further cautioning that they must be "careful of each other's temper. We must not be such cowards as to allow it to control us."

Sprague was well aware of Kate's independent streak. "You know she is very tenacious of everything," he told her father. Just after their engagement the husband-in-waiting reminded Kate that she was no longer her own person and that she had his happiness to consider as well. Three weeks before the wedding he added that they must resolve to fail, if fail they must, for reasons other than their differences—differences she needed to accept. "I shall expect this sacrifice of you," he wrote. "Thus ends the lecture." But he went on to fret about her delay, for which she gave no reason, in allowing the invitation cards to go out. She had already rejected his preference for a wedding date in September rather than November, and now she seemed to be getting cold feet. It threatened to push his fragile psyche toward the edge. "Must I wait for your explanation?" he demanded. "Are you to put off the time? Are you to continue the torture? Must I be forced to forgo that which absorbs all my thoughts and unfits me to live or breathe?" He took to wallowing: "I am so lonely. I am so heartsick. . . . I shall soon become desperate and will then I hope have an antidote for that which is consuming me. Darling good night. Say something to help me, or do something to change the current of my thoughts." Shifting to self-abasement, he asked, "Is this the reserved, cold uncommunicative man which you have tied yourself to? Forgive the childishness of it all and I will be different bye and bye." But he closed, as usual, with terms of endearment: "My darling Bridy good night. Angels guard you."

Kate must have responded with strong words of reassurance, for several days later he thanked her effusively for her latest letter. "*To get such a letter.* Well! *I don't know what I shall do,*" he rejoiced. None of Kate's letters from the engagement period have survived, so it is impossible to know whether she was suffering from normal prewedding jitters or was beginning to have second thoughts. Cancelation was unthinkable; she had spent thousands on her wedding trousseau, flowers, catering, and invitations, and Sprague spent many thousands more on her wedding gifts and jewelry. Plus, the newspaper society columns had been abuzz for weeks about their upcoming nuptials, with some writers giddy with enthusiasm and others disgusted with the cost and ostentation of such an affair in the middle of a war ("sickening twaddle," a Kansas newspaper called all the stories). Then there was the embarrassment that further postponement would cause to the politically minded, reputation-conscious Salmon P. Chase.

It had been a rough several months for her father, beginning with the famous Cabinet Crisis of December 1862. In conjunction with the radicals in Congress, he had engineered a coup to force the removal of his chief cabinet rival, Seward, and create a governing council, purged of moderates and conservatives, that would determine national policy by consensus. Chase would set himself up as first among equals and the effective premier, with Lincoln marginalized as chief executive. But Lincoln outwitted Chase, forcing him to air any grievances he had in an open cabinet meeting attended by the conspiring radicals. Surprised at being put on the spot, Chase lost his nerve, pulled his punches, and forfeited the confidence and support of his coconspirators. Humiliated, he offered to resign (as had Seward, when he learned of the attempted coup), but Lincoln, who needed both men in the cabinet to maintain balance, accepted neither of their resignations. "I can ride on now," Lincoln exulted to a private visitor, explaining, "I've got a pumpkin in each end of my bag." It was the first of several resignations Chase would offer during his tenure, and it was the beginning of the end of any real influence he had within the administration.

Adding to Chase's public woes was his private discomfort about giving Kate up. He put on a brave front, advancing the old cliché in a letter to Garfield that he was not losing a daughter but gaining a son. "I expect to *love* the Governor," he wrote Kate. "Why should I not? Will he not be my only son?" He praised Sprague's letters, calling even the most bizarre of them "delightful." He extolled Sprague to Kate, saying, "I love him now for his love to you as much as I have always honored him for his courage and patriotism." Still, he had his doubts the wedding would come off. He told Jay Cooke the couple were to be married in the fall "if they both live and don't change their minds."

Partly because Sprague saw Chase as a missing father figure and partly because he knew how highly Kate thought of him, Sprague went out of his way to praise his future father-in-law to Kate. "To get the esteem of one like your father is a great satisfaction to me," he told her not long after their engagement. "We must be guided by his better judgment and his affectionate interest." Sprague was in awe of Chase and cognizant of the many ways in which he failed to compare favorably with him. "Writing is not my trade as you must have discovered," he admitted to Chase. He was glad to read the treasury secretary's well-penned letters to him but cautioned, "I cannot promise you compensation in kind."

But at times Sprague was frustrated with Chase's overprotectiveness, as when he refused to let Kate go to Rhode Island immediately after the engagement to be with her fiancé. Sprague argued that the invigorating ocean air would be better for Kate than that summer's record-breaking heat in Washington, but Chase's concern was more for her chastity than her comfort. (He did allow the couple in late June to visit the McDowell country home in upstate New York, under the watchful eye of Mrs. McDowell.) Chase also forbade Kate from performing a boat christening in New York in early July because he thought it would appear too festive after the great loss of life at Gettysburg. Sprague grumbled privately to Hiram Barney that it was an "old womanly view."

Before Kate's own hesitation later that summer, Sprague thought it was Chase who was having second thoughts about the marriage. "I have written your father, I think *three* letters" requesting answers to questions about the wedding, he told Kate, and had received no reply. He speculated that Chase had heard some attacks on his character and was looking for an excuse to withdraw his consent to their marriage. Kate evidently prevailed upon her father to be more responsive, for Sprague soon reported that he had received three letters from him. "I am afraid it rather chokes him to write but I am none the less grateful," Sprague told her. Chase eventually agreed to join Kate and Nettie in late July on a visit to the Sprague family in Providence, leaving his daughters to spend August at the seashore in nearby Narragansett, where the Spragues had a summer home. Kate and Nettie were chaperoned by Sprague's mother, Fanny, whom Chase met for the first time on his visit. Chase found the family matriarch to be a "lady of such true sense and genuine dignity" and wrote Sprague afterward to say that although Kate had "known almost nothing of a mother's care," now she would find a mother of her own in Fanny Sprague.

After Chase returned to Washington he vented his frustration over Kate's habitual silence as to her whereabouts. He blew up when he received a letter from Sprague saying that, the night before Nettie was to begin her second year of boarding school in New York, Kate and Nettie had left Providence for Boston and that he, Sprague, knew nothing of their further movements. "You and Sister or one of you try my patience a good deal," Chase wrote to Nettie. When Kate told Sprague of her father's anger with her, her fiancé chivalrously wrote Chase to accept the blame for keeping her away too long.

Kate relished the freedom of movement she had during her last throes of life as a single woman. In this she was like other unmarried, well-to-do American women at midcentury, who traveled alone "as free as a butterfly until marriage." Sprague accepted Kate's mobility during this time in a way that Chase, from an older generation, did not.

The gulf between Chase and his prospective son-in-law, however, was more than just generational. Not only were they as unlike as two men can be, but the younger man had so much more money than the older one. That reality created some awkwardness over their prospective living arrangements. Shortly after the engagement the proud treasury secretary told his future son-in-law he would not feel easy about any household arrangement in which Sprague was not the head. Chase suggested that the married couple move into the rented mansion at Sixth and E and that he move out, to someplace closer to the White House, which would give him better access to the president. But Kate wanted him to stay.

Sprague told Chase he recognized "the delicate link which has so long united father and daughter." He also understood Kate's desire to continue living under the same roof as the only birth parent she had ever known. Kate broke the logjam with a compromise: the three of them would live together, the Spragues to pay for food and Chase for the servants, with stabling costs split half and half. Everyone would have private quarters after an extensive remodeling that Kate would direct. And that she did. While Kate was off traveling, Chase stood by helplessly as a steady stream of carpenters and painters worked about the house. "What *they* are doing I do not know," he wrote to Nettie, "for I was not consulted in their employment and have not thought it best *to* enquire." He constantly expressed concern to Kate that the renovation costs had to be considerable, which he thought was a waste of money given that the house was only a rental. But Sprague mooted the issue by buying the townhouse for $30,000 from the landlord. He also purchased a second carriage for them that his father-in-law told him they didn't need. For Sprague it was little more than pocket change.

Paying for the wedding was still the responsibility of the bride's father, and Chase was exasperated with the bills Kate was running up. She told him she needed a thousand dollars for what she'd ordered from Europe and would need more for what she planned to buy in New York. Chase protested that he knew nothing about ladies' expenses and asked her to figure out what she actually needed for an attractive bridal outfit, not what she could spend. He ended up shelling out more than $4,000, an enormous sum for a wedding in those days, and overdrew his checking account by some $150.

Chase's longstanding money woes would soon be ameliorated by the arrival of Sprague as a son-in-law. Still, he was uneasy about the prospective union. He was not the most observant of men, but he had seen enough to realize that "some inequalities of temper" existed between the young couple. He rejoiced in Kate's happiness, but, "with trembling," he wrote her, "few lives are so unclouded as yours has been hitherto; and I fear the dark days." He also worried she might be too materialistic. What he wanted more than anything, he told her, was for her and her husband to become good Christians in heart and deed. Curiously, though not a churchgoer, Sprague expressed similar thoughts, telling Kate she found excessive pleasure in "all the fine 'things' that the great Father has permitted us to enjoy." He hoped that in time she would find favor with his own "old fashioned ways" and would come "to appreciate the gloss from the reality."

Sensing some of Chase's concerns about the marriage, Sprague told him he did not expect all would run smoothly between himself and Kate but that it would be the object of his life to see that Kate "receives no detriment in my hands." He thanked Chase "from the bottom of my heart for the treasure you have reared and given to me." Then, ten days before the wedding, anticipating Kate's possible chafing at the strictures of marriage, he promised her she would have "all the liberty, all the freedom that your heart desires." He gave her a last-minute pep talk: "This is indeed our month, and to think of our always being lovers."

They had one last hurdle to overcome before the wedding. Throughout the summer they had been receiving anonymous letters raising ugly stories about their respective pasts as part of what Sprague described to Kate as a systematic effort to sever their connection. When another such unsigned note came to him three weeks before the wedding, Sprague commented to Kate, "Your Ohio friends are getting desperate." But his practice on receiving the notes, which he urged Kate to follow, was to read only as far as necessary to determine their nature and then immediately toss them out. Kate and Sprague faced plenty of challenges in making it to their wedding, but at least this one did not prove to be serious.

By the time the great day finally arrived, any negative thoughts were set aside and Kate was in full bridal mode. She had been receiving a steady stream of wedding presents, their value estimated at between $60,000 and $100,000. Sprague's gift was a $6,500 jewelry set he bought at Tiffany's, including a diamond and pearl crown and matching earrings. "I wish not to be extravagant, but let me indulge only once," he told Kate after letting her know the price. "You know I am but gratifying my own desires, when I contribute to your pleasure. I have earned the right to do this." He also ceded almost all the invitations to Kate, asking for only twenty for himself in addition to his family, compared to more than four hundred Kate sent out for the reception. He admitted he had few close friends and was reluctant to invite anyone he did not know well.

Kate was swept up in the flutter and flurry of a big wedding and enjoyed all the attention she was getting. She was serenaded at home the night before the wedding by the 17th Infantry Band, joined by John Hay. Her excitement is evident from a short note she wrote later that night, preserved by her descendants and seen by no one else for almost 150 years. It read, simply, "Kate Chase, 11th November, 1863, Midnight. *My wedding eve.*" Despite all the disappointments she would suffer, she kept that note as well as her wedding box. Inside it were various gifts, such as a game counter, a little Bible, and the white wedding gloves and shoes that covered the tiny hands and feet of this otherwise tall, lissome woman. As the clock struck midnight, passing to November 12, Kate may also have thought of the late mother she never really knew, whose forty-second birthday it would have been that day.

The Thursday evening wedding ceremony took place in the front parlor of the Chase mansion, attended by fifty guests, mostly chosen by Secretary Chase, including almost every cabinet member as well as various senators, military men, and diplomats. Carriages lined the street for blocks outside and stalled all traffic except for pedestrians seeking a glimpse of the celebrated couple. President Lincoln came alone, without Mary, who pleaded for him to stay home. He kissed the bride and gave her a gift—a small fan. Along with her brilliant jewelry and a white lace veil, Kate wore a white velvet dress around her twenty-inch waist. Sprague dressed in a black coat and pantaloons and white satin vest. Neither bride nor groom had a close enough personal friend to attend them: Kate's bridesmaids were her sister, Nettie, her cousin Alice, and a niece of Sprague's, while Sprague's groomsmen were three military men in dress uniform.

At 8:30 p.m., after the Episcopal service concluded, the parlor doors were flung open and another five hundred guests poured into the back room for a dinner of meats, oysters, wine, and champagne, followed by cigars for the men. The Marine Band played the "Kate Chase Wedding March," specially written for the occasion by popular composer Frederick Kroell. Kate led off the quadrille with Richard Parsons, the family friend who had introduced her to Sprague in Cleveland. The celebration continued into the wee hours, and the whole affair was pronounced a brilliant success, a much-needed diversion for war-weary Washingtonians. One disappointed guest was Betty Blair, daughter of Montgomery Blair, the only absent cabinet member. She thought the wedding "a great display of elegance and riches, but the young people were not acquaintances, consequently the gayety was very lame." A more discordant note was struck by the *New York World*, which sneered at the wealth heaped on the latter-day "Aladdin" and his "princess" while a group of working women on New York's Lower East Side protested their starvation, two-dollars-a-week wages. The antislavery ideology championed by Salmon Chase called for labor to be free; it would be years before any consensus that it needed to be fair. And the fact that the Sprague textile empire was built in part on child labor, including that of girls as young as ten, using cotton picked by Southern slaves, seems never to have troubled him, Kate, or her father. In the late 1840s, agreeing with his friend Charles Sumner, Chase had derided Northern textile men as "Lords of the Loom" who were in league with Southern plantation owners. Now his daughter was married to one of those lords.

As for Kate, she was about to enter a rarified world as the wife of one of the very richest men in the country. She had always had servants around to take care of life's most difficult and menial chores, but from now on not only would she never have to work, cook, or clean house, but she need never worry about money again. That realization may have hit home with her, for the first time, in her bridal chamber at the end of the long evening. Among the visitors saying their good nights was John Hay. He found her looking "tired out and languid" but noticed she "had lost all her old severity and formal stiffness of manner, and seemed to think she had *arrived*."

Hay was the last date of Kate's life as a single woman, having accompanied her to Ford's Theatre three weeks earlier to see the actress Maggie Mitchell in *The Pearl of Savoy*. Hay wrote in his diary that "the statuesque Kate" (a reference to her manner, not her height) "cried like a baby" at the melodramatic story of an Alpine peasant girl who goes insane after her beloved father disowns her, mistakenly thinking she had compromised her virtue before marrying a rich nobleman. The story ends happily when her father takes her back, she regains her reason, and she marries her marquis. Kate may have shed her tears in sorrow at the reminder that she would no longer be known as Salmon Chase's daughter or out of joy over her impending nuptials to her own marquis.

Of course she had to have doubts about her new husband, from whom she had been receiving letters for months testifying to a highly erratic, even disturbed personality. Regardless of whether she had heard the story of Sprague's impregnation of Mary Viall, Kate—an avid follower of newspaper gossip—must have been aware of the rumors of his prior womanizing. It might have been continuing even then: at the wedding reception Francis Preston Blair, patriarch of the Maryland political family, upbraided Sprague for recently being seen with one of the young man's old flames.

Kate was no starry-eyed naïf. She had known Sprague for more than three years, had traveled with him several times, at length, in the rough conditions of the day, and was privy to his innermost thoughts. As someone who was so astute at sizing up people, Kate must have had a very good idea of the man she was marrying. Many have said she married Sprague only for his money, but her diary reveals her to have been a woman in love. Moreover, for her to marry Sprague, there had to be something more to the man than the paper cutout figure of a millionaire governor on a white horse. She was not that superficial. Sprague was not the most forward-thinking of men, but for Kate, a fundamentally liberal person, to marry him—or anyone else—there had to be an inner decency and liberality to him she could see, even if few others could.

Perhaps when they married Kate thought she might change him, smoothing over the rough edges. Or his insecurities and vulnerability, which rendered him so unlike her morally certain father, appealed to her and challenged her. Or she had decided she would live with the bad along with the good and hope for the best. For whatever set of reasons—and for better or for worse—she was now Kate Chase Sprague.

# PART 2

# MRS. SPRAGUE

CHAPTER 9

# "Imagine My Disappointment"

The marriage got off to an inauspicious start. When the newlyweds arrived at Sprague's house on Young Orchard Avenue near Brown University, Kate was horrified to find a huge "Welcome" sign draped across the gateway arch and a gaudy homecoming display of red, white, and blue flags and streamers hanging from the front porch. She retired to her room, citing fatigue, but emerged after the "horse fair" decorations were taken down. She appeared at a large reception thrown by the Spragues, but Providence's old-line families, who considered the Spragues beneath their station, declined to show. Kate was not used to being on the receiving end of such social snubs.

The married couple soon left Rhode Island on their honeymoon, stopping off at Niagara Falls before heading to Ohio, where Kate showed off her new wardrobe and jewelry to her relatives. The first signs of postmarital friction did not take long to emerge. After they left Ohio, Sprague returned to Providence to tend to business, and Kate was writing her new husband from Washington to say how much she missed him. "The sunshine has all gone from our beautiful home," she wrote. "Paradise is no paradise without a God and my Eden is indeed deserted. . . . Oh darling, I hope these separations will not come *very* often. They are so hard to bear." He was, she said, "the one absorbing thought of my life." Her father was driving her crazy at home by delegating responsibility to her for deciding matters of furnishings, then criticizing her decisions afterward. "To you, darling," she appealed to Sprague, "and to you only, do I turn now for help in all trouble and sympathy in all joy." But as Kate ramped up the floridity and frequency of her letters to match Sprague's prewedding missives, her new husband, who now had his "treasure," wrote less often. "Forgotten so soon!" she chided him. She was bitterly disappointed when he said his business duties prevented them from spending their first Christmas and New Year's together. He responded by saying he needed her sympathy and hoped she would not become an added burden as he worked long hours trying to keep things running at the family business in Rhode Island. When he mentioned he hadn't received any letters from her lately she shot back angrily, saying it was the mail's fault, not hers—that she had been writing him every day and that, by contrast, all she received from him was a brief note with a couple of sheets of business papers. "Imagine my disappointment," she told him. She called him "the absent one." He was dismissive and accused her of insensitivity over the fact that it was the twentieth anniversary of his father's murder. Yet they generally closed their letters on a cheerful, affectionate note. All this drama, and they had been married just seven weeks.

One path Sprague knew he had to Kate's heart was through politics. The card he always had to play was the financial backing he could bring to Salmon Chase's presidential ambitions. Buoyed by the enthusiastic reception he had received in the Midwest during the 1863 fall campaigns and egged on by newspaper editors such as Horace Greeley, Chase was gearing up to challenge Abraham Lincoln for the 1864 Republican nomination. The very day of Kate's wedding, a Kansas newspaper carried a story headlined "The Next Presidency: The Strife for the Succession—'Honest Old Abe' vs. Secretary Chase." Chase cooperated in producing a campaign biography for young readers, entitled *The Ferry Boy and the Financier*, intended to humanize him—no small task. Unable to conjure up many warm, personal anecdotes to supply the writer, Chase asked his last surviving sister, Helen Walbridge, to rack her brains for some helpful ones. Always, though, he professed only half-interest in the nation's highest office. Just after the wedding Chase wrote his new son-in-law to say that if he were "controlled merely by personal sentiments," he would prefer the reelection of Lincoln (a laughable claim) but that he thought "a man of different qualities from those the President has will be needed for the next four years." Chase was "not anxious to be regarded as that man," he wrote Sprague (another disingenuous statement), but was willing to be considered if others thought he was best for the job. It was a not-so-subtle appeal for support, and Sprague took the hint. He soon wrote Kate to say it was "necessary to have some plan concocted to defeat [Lincoln's] too well laid plan" for reelection.

Kate, of course, was delighted her husband was on board for a Chase presidential run. Indeed, in the same letter in which her father fished for Sprague's support Chase said that Kate was "maybe a little too anxious about my political future. She must not be so." But he did nothing to stop the politicking she did for him during the winter of 1863–1864, when she raised her hostessing to a new level. An invitation to her receptions continued to be the most desired in Washington, and any politician from the hinterlands became the object of her attention, provided he was likely to control delegates to the Republican convention in June.

Mary Lincoln kept imploring her husband to do something about the growing Chase movement. In January 1864 she went so far as to cross Kate and Sprague off the list of invitees to the year's first state dinner. Lincoln's senior secretary, John Nicolay, concerned about how the snub would look, took the matter up with the president, who countermanded Mary's action and ordered "Rhode Island" and "Ohio" reinstated to the guest list. Then there "arose such a rampage as hasn't been seen in the House for a year," Nicolay wrote to John Hay. But Lincoln did not need Mary to tell him about Chase's activities; he knew that the treasury secretary was, as Hay recorded in his diary, "at work night and day, laying pipe" for the coming election. Lincoln told his young secretary that he supposed Chase would, "like the bluebottle fly, lay his eggs in every rotten spot he can find." Yet Lincoln respected his rival's ability and told Hay he hoped the country would never do worse than to have Chase as its leader.

In December 1863, just a month after the wedding, a Chase-for-President committee was formed, funded mostly by Sprague with assistance from Chase's banker friend Jay Cooke. It was headed by Samuel Pomeroy, an unscrupulous Kansas senator seeking aid for his railroad interests. Other committee members included new Ohio congressman James Garfield, Ohio senator John Sherman (brother of the general), and Whitelaw Reid, an influential Ohio newspaper editor who had disappointed Chase by backing Lincoln in 1860 but who now had flipped his support to the treasury secretary.

In February 1864 the Chase committee produced a confidential pamphlet, which would become known as the "Pomeroy Circular," attacking Lincoln and recommending Chase replace him on the ticket. The document was leaked to the press and created a huge backlash, galvanizing support for Lincoln and seriously damaging Chase's prospects for the nomination. The embarrassed treasury secretary implausibly claimed he had no knowledge of the circular in advance but nevertheless offered up another resignation to Lincoln. The president again declined it, saying he perceived no reason for a change. Chase also announced his withdrawal from the presidential contest, although those who knew him suspected it was only a temporary move. Indeed, after his public disclaimer, his private criticism of Lincoln only intensified, and he continued to supply material for his campaign biography while his agents in the Treasury Department kept working behind the scenes to advance his candidacy. There was nothing improper, per se, in Chase seeking the nomination, but the ham-fisted way in which the Chase forces went about their business made him seem disloyal to the administration he was appointed to serve.

No document links Kate specifically to the Pomeroy Circular. But no doubt she had knowledge of the committee's overall efforts and supported them. She was, after all, the daughter of the committee's candidate and the wife of its chief financier, and she had close ties to committee members Cooke, Garfield, and Reid. According to Lincoln biographer Carl Sandburg, Kate worked for the Chase committee "modestly and without ostentation, quiet as a church mouse, yet fertile of resource and quick of wit."

In the meantime the rift between Kate and Sprague over his absence during the holidays blew over, one of the many times they would patch up their differences after quarreling. "Kate seems very happy," Chase wrote his sister Helen the day after New Year's. "She and her husband seem to love each other dearly. He is a noble fellow, and I love him almost as much as she does." Kate and Sprague soon attended a grand army ball in Washington, at which one young captain recalled having had "the distinguished honor of dancing once with the queenly beauty, Mrs. Sprague."

Sprague returned to Providence after the ball, and Kate was soon writing to again say how much she missed him. "Don't neglect me dear, as you did before," she pleaded, "for a day without some tidings of you seems so very long." She had come down with a severe cold and would spend much of the spring and summer of 1864 trying to recover. In a pattern that would repeat itself throughout their marriage, in which the sickness of one or the other brought them closer together, Sprague tended to her and, as Chase told Nettie, "was all devotion"; indeed, Chase reported, for Kate "to be so petted" made her think it almost worthwhile to be sick. With the thaw in their relations, Chase advised Kate to start showing interest in her husband's business, to "go out among the workmen, see what is being done and why." But Sprague never gave her access to that realm. His business was *his* business, and it was the only arena in which he could claim superiority over Kate.

Meanwhile, throughout the first half of 1864 Chase's relations with Lincoln continued to deteriorate. The breaking point came in June 1864, when Chase impulsively submitted another resignation—by this time his fourth—after Lincoln refused to make a patronage appointment Chase wanted. Chase anticipated that, per past practice, Lincoln would refuse the offer and was shocked to receive a terse note from the president saying their official relations had reached a point of mutual embarrassment and that his offer of resignation was accepted. Lincoln confided to John Hay that he could stand Chase's antics no longer. Chase was oblivious to it all. He wrote in his diary that although he felt Lincoln had caused him "a good deal of embarrassment," he "could not imagine" what he had done to incur the president's displeasure. The only explanation he could come up with was that he was "too earnest, too anti-slavery, and, say, too radical" for Lincoln's tastes. "The truth is," Chase offered in further explanation to Whitelaw Reid, "I have never been able to make a joke out of this war." He wrote Kate to say that if she felt him wronged, she should not let anyone *think* she thought so, because people never sympathize with complainers. Whereupon he continued in the following weeks to feel sorry for himself and complain about how badly he had been treated.

Out of a post and with Lincoln having been renominated at the June convention in Baltimore, Chase went east to see friends, do some summer fishing, and visit the Spragues in Narragansett, where he found Kate and her husband arguing again. He had a talk afterward with Kate, and at some point Sprague chastised Kate for telling her father of their squabbles. "I hope you . . . will not hereafter refer any of our differences to your father," he wrote her, "as that can only bring on a difference which cannot be healed." But Sprague need not have worried about Chase, who invariably advised Kate, after her frequent fights with her husband, that she needed to learn to submit.

Kate was worried about her father for a different reason. She feared the funk he was in after his resignation might encourage him to resume his courtship with any number of women who had been pursuing him for years. Among them were Washington socialite Adele Cutts Douglas, the beautiful widow of Stephen Douglas; Susan Walker, a strong-minded, countess-like woman from Baltimore who was active in the abolitionist and other reform movements; and Charlotte Eastman, a Massachusetts widow of a former congressman. Kate was so opposed to her father remarrying that when things began trending romantic between him and this or that eligible woman, she would sometimes intercept their letters to him, prompting Chase to direct the women to communicate with him directly at his treasury office. If they ventured to visit the Chase household, they received a chilly reception from his oldest daughter. Kate especially disliked Mrs. Eastman, who seemed to be her father's favorite and to whom he was more than once rumored to be engaged. Chase had earlier hoped the two women could "wipe out all past disagreeable remembrances on both sides," but to no avail. In August 1863 he wrote Mrs. Eastman to say he was "so sorry that you and Katie—one so dear to me as a friend and the other as a daughter don't exactly *jee* [get along]." He paid numerous visits to Mrs. Eastman on his eastern trip in the summer of 1864, but he did not tell Kate about them.

As the war dragged on in stalemate during the summer of 1864 Chase's White House dreams were given new life. With "Grant the Butcher" continuing to run up tens of thousands of Union casualties in his battles with Lee's army, the president's reelection prospects declined by the day. Radical Republicans, convinced Lincoln could not win, plotted to replace him on the ticket at a new convention to be held in September. Both Horace Greeley and Whitelaw Reid told Chase he stood a good chance of getting the nod. As the summer bloodshed wore on, it seemed that only military success could now put a stop to the dump-Lincoln movement. Chase, who remained open to the nomination, had been denigrating Grant's efforts in Virginia as more costly than they were worth and had predicted that General Sherman, advancing on Georgia, would meet his "Moscow," a reference to Napoleon's disastrous invasion of Russia.

And then came a series of events that changed the course of history, both for the nation and for the Chase-Sprague clan, forever. In early September Sherman captured Atlanta, which, combined with General Phil Sheridan's recent success in the Shenandoah Valley and Rear Admiral David Farragut's victory at the Battle of Mobile Bay, all but ensured Lincoln's reelection and the North's eventual triumph in the war. As a result, the radicals' plot against the president collapsed. Then, in October, Roger Taney, the aging Southern Supreme Court chief justice and author of the infamous Dred Scott opinion, died after a long illness. And finally, in December, Abraham Lincoln, the sixteenth president, appointed Salmon P. Chase as the sixth chief justice of the Supreme Court of the United States.

He had not wanted to do so. Although Chase was no longer a presidential threat by the time of Taney's death, Lincoln was concerned that even as a Supreme Court justice, Chase would not stop running for president in the future. He also had not forgotten what Chase—and Kate—had said about him behind his back. "He talked feelingly of the many hard things Mrs. Sprague, Mr. Chase's daughter," had said of him, a supporter of Chase was quoted as saying. Lacking any other options at the time, Chase badly wanted the appointment, as did present and former cabinet members Stanton, Bates, and Montgomery Blair, who were far more loyal to Lincoln. Charles Sumner and other radicals lobbied hard for Chase, but Lincoln remained coy. "I feel that I do not know him," Chase wrote to Kate of his cordial but distant treatment by the president at a pair of meetings in September attended by others. Lincoln, as one-time Ohio governor Joseph Foraker later said, was "enough like other men to enjoy, no doubt, the discomfiture Chase had brought on himself." But Lincoln was "enough unlike other men to magnanimously overlook his weaknesses and offenses when public duty so required." He knew Chase was the best man for the job, and he believed that, as chief justice, the former treasury secretary would uphold wartime measures such as the Legal Tender Act and keep the rights of freed slaves secure. Lincoln said he would despise himself if, out of personal pique, he failed to do the right thing. According to Lincoln's bodyguard William Crook, who later served eleven other presidents, Lincoln also said, "I ought not to blame Chase for the things his daughter said about me." And so he made the appointment. On the evening of December 6, 1864, Chase arrived home at Sixth and E and was greeted by Kate with the news. He thanked the president profusely and, nine days later, was sworn in during a ceremony in which both Kate and Nettie appeared, "gorgeously dressed."

It has always been a point of controversy just how Kate felt about her father's Supreme Court appointment. For many years the story persisted that she was enraged by what she saw as Lincoln's effort to put her father out to pasture in a judicial position that ended his chances at ever becoming president. "And you, too, Mr. Sumner?" she is reputed to have cried, shaking her finger at the senator she so admired. "You, too, in this business of shelving Papa? But never mind! I will defeat you all!" That particular story is almost certainly apocryphal, for Kate would not have opposed an appointment her father clearly wanted. An outburst of that sort also would not have been in character, for whatever private grievances she harbored, Kate was always unflappable in public. What's more, as she probably knew, Chase had no intention of letting his Supreme Court position stop him from running for president again. Indeed, Chase reportedly confided to an intimate friend just days after he was sworn in that he viewed the position as an "experiment" and that he might find it in his interest to resign in two or three years—a clear reference to the 1868 presidential contest.

But there may be something to the story of Kate's displeasure after all. According to journalist Donn Piatt, a longtime friend of Chase, when Chase was being considered for chief justice Lincoln raised the subject of Kate's possible opposition. Lincoln reportedly asked one of the sitting justices, Stephen J. Field, "how Mrs. Sprague would like the appointment of her father; that he had heard the remark attributed to her that her father 'was not to be set aside by a place on the bench.'" To that, Field made no reply.

So Chase became chief justice. And Kate became pregnant. But pregnancy did not necessarily mean things would change between Kate and her husband. Sprague forgot their first anniversary, and they spent Christmas and New Year's apart for the second year in a row, as he again pleaded business obligations. He said he appreciated all her loving notes, that she shouldn't have to do all the courting, and promised to do his part in the future. But shortly afterward, back in Washington, more trouble arose between them. They failed to show for breakfast with Chase, which made him "very uneasy." At a dinner for guests three days earlier she had become suddenly indisposed and left the room, not returning until dinner was over and the company had gone into the parlor, putting a damper on the evening. Four months pregnant, she might have been suffering from lingering morning sickness, but just as likely she was having a tough time with her spouse.

A January White House reception brought more unpleasantness with Mary Lincoln. In their effort to speak to the president, Kate and her father inadvertently cut in line ahead of Mrs. Lincoln, and when they apologized later, as Chase wrote, "she either misunderstood or chose to appear very ungracious." In February Mrs. Lincoln invited a friend to the theater, saying she presumed the woman would not "'trip the light fantastic' [dance nimbly] at Mrs. Sprague's *matinee or ball.*" Mary Lincoln was able to watch in triumph when, on March 4, her husband was sworn in for his second term by his erstwhile rival, now chief justice, Salmon P. Chase. Although Kate would have preferred her father to be taking the oath himself, she was proud to see him decked out in the new judicial robe she placed on him the night before with the help of Frederick Douglass. She hosted a matinee reception that day, and despite her pregnancy, she attended the inaugural ball that night, though she stayed off the dance floor.

In mid-March Sprague returned to Providence, leaving his expecting wife in Washington. The following month, on Palm Sunday, Lee surrendered to Grant at Appomattox. Five days later, on April 14, 1865, John Wilkes Booth, who had been playing a comedy a few blocks away at Ford's Theatre on Kate's wedding day, made another visit to that venue.

CHAPTER 10

# "Our Accomplished Countrywoman"

Kate and Nettie, both dressed in black, were two of only seven women allowed into the funeral service that took place in the crowded, candlelit East Room of the White House. William Sprague, who rushed back from Rhode Island, was there with them, as was Kate's father, who had sworn in the new president, Andrew Johnson, hours after Lincoln's death. One newspaper correspondent contrasted the gaiety and laughter once seen in the room with the pall then cast upon it: "Now only a very few, brave enough to look upon death, were wearing funeral weeds. The pleasant face of Mrs. Kate Sprague looks out from these; but such scenes gain little additional power by beauty's presence."

What thoughts must have passed through the minds of Kate and her father as the mourners gazed upon the open coffin of the man, so revered by the multitudes, who had been the chief impediment to Chase's presidential dreams the past five years. The question had to cross both of their minds as to what impact the president's assassination would have on Chase's political future; indeed, Chase would lose no time before he began laying the groundwork for his next campaign. In the first week of May 1865, less than a month after the assassination, Chase took off on a land-and-sea tour of the defeated South, during which he wrote a series of lengthy letters to President Johnson, peppering him with his observations on conditions and attitudes in the former Confederate states and lobbying him with his advice on Reconstruction policy. With Kate in her final two months of pregnancy, he took seventeen-year-old Nettie, who practiced her illustrations and got seasick on the boat trips, yet cheerfully soldiered on. Along with them came several others, including journalist Whitelaw Reid, who wrote a book about their experience.

Everywhere he went Chase was warmly greeted by ex-slaves who constituted a huge potential voting block for him if they were granted the franchise. He wrote Johnson to say the conquered rebels would willingly extend voting rights to African Americans if the president made that a condition of reconciliation. But Chase misjudged Lincoln's successor, who turned out to be a virulent racist who sought restoration of white supremacy in the South and vetoed all major civil rights legislation passed by the Republican Congress.

For once Kate was on the political sidelines as she prepared to give birth, but Chase kept her abreast of his journey, privately painting for her a less rosy picture of Southern racial attitudes than he was reporting to Johnson and confiding to her his great disappointment with the new president. He also surprised her with the news that when he arrived in Fernandina, Florida, he found that its newly elected mayor was none other than Adolphus Mot, her old French tutor from Columbus.

Upon Chase's return to Cincinnati in June, he was greeted with a telegram from Sprague announcing that Kate had just given birth at Narragansett to a baby boy, "bright, black haired and handsome." The newborn William Sprague V would always go by "Willie." Kate wanted to name him after the baby's famous grandfather, but Chase insisted that because William was "the name of one to whom *your first duties* belong," it should be borne by his first son. "So please consider that 'case' 'adjudged,'" he wrote Kate. Willie's birth was regarded as a national event, and descriptions of the baby's wardrobe, birthday gifts, and "even the clever speeches of the little prattler were published far and wide."

Chase left Washington for Rhode Island soon after the birth to see his new grandson, pronouncing him everything that had been advertised. He also found Kate to be in better health and more attractive than in years. While there, Chase visited the Sprague offices in Providence and the textile print works in Cranston, commenting on how comfortable conditions had been made for the working masses. Chase wished only, he told Kate, that his son-in-law would spend less time on business and more time on the reading and study necessary to qualify him for his Senate office. When Kate asked her father for advice on what to get her husband for his thirty-fifth birthday that September, Chase suggested a beginner's collection on American history, starting with the best books written about Rhode Island. It was as if to suggest that Sprague, a US senator and former Rhode Island governor, knew little of the nation's or even his native state's history.

But Sprague's mind was more on his textile empire than his Senate duties. While Chase was touring the South that year for political reasons, Sprague was invading the conquered region to expand and diversify his business interests. Taking advantage of the weakened Southern economy, Sprague leased or bought up cotton plantations and other properties at government tax auctions, placing many of his operations under the supervision of ex-Confederates. The irony was not lost on one South Carolina newspaper, which commented that Sprague was "actually employing ex-rebel generals to manage extensive saw mills he owns in Florida, while sitting in the Senate and voting once a week that the ex-rebels are virtually little better than cut-throats, and not to be trusted."

Like many Northern businessmen who had no desire for permanent residence, Sprague preferred leasing plantations rather than buying them because, with cotton prices skyrocketing and labor cheap, a small investment could produce a large profit without the risk of long-term ownership. The former owners, in turn, were happy to lease their plantations to these "New Masters," as it gave them a steady income without the headaches of overseeing the newly freed slaves, who resented their old rebel masters. "Let them that freed the negroes work with them," was the attitude of the old plantation class. But some Yankee textile makers, lacking confidence in the ex-slaves' work ethic, decided to use their white, mostly immigrant workers to raise the cotton they needed. Sprague sent a crew of a hundred Germans to his leased plantations along the Mississippi River, later adding some Dutch, Danish, and Swiss employees. But he soon discovered that the ex-slaves who had worked the fields for years were more productive than foreign immigrants from the company town of Spragueville. As one of Sprague's plantation superintendents complained, the white workers, being accustomed to better working conditions in New England, were harder to provide for than their black counterparts. They ate "at least one third to one half more than the negro, and do not accomplish more than two thirds as much work." The immigrants also were hampered by language barriers and, though they knew how to spin cotton, were inexperienced at growing it. And so Sprague and other Northern businessmen turned back to employing African American freedmen, sometimes alongside the white hands, and hiring Southern overseers who knew the business.

Although Chase would have preferred that cotton lands be placed directly under the ownership of the freedmen rather than Northern speculators, such as his son-in-law, Sprague's experiments with freed slave labor constituted progress of sorts. Sprague also endeared himself to the chief justice by agreeing to support black suffrage. Chase told Kate he was proud of Sprague and that she should be too, as he was "independent, and manly as well as intelligent; and real manliness and intelligence are rare qualities in these days." He was speaking of the same man who, two years earlier, had confessed to "childishness" and "infirmities of nature."

In the meantime the birth of Willie held out hope for bringing Kate and her husband closer together than they had been since the wedding. Back in Washington in late 1865 Kate seemed more content than she had been for years. Resuming her receptions, she sent for her baby Willie at one of them and looked "the picture of happiness with him in her arms," an observation confirmed by a surviving family photograph. Her retinue of nurses and servants allowed her to take full part in Washington's first postwar social season, a giddy series of events in the winter of 1865–1866 over which she presided as America's queen. Washington that winter had gone wild, and Kate was among the regulars who partied late into the night. At the French Ambassador's ball she attended in February 1866, the first cotillion did not get going until five in the morning. The dancing went on until a sumptuous breakfast was served, after which the men left for their offices and the women for their morning receptions, still wearing their ball costumes. Some called it the most magnificent social event ever held in the capital, but according to society columnist Emily Edson Briggs (better known as "Olivia"), the final word on all such matters, the ambassador's ball was no more impressive than the parties given by "our accomplished countrywoman, Mrs. Senator Sprague."

She drew out the taciturn among her guests and made even the dullest of them momentarily shine while continuing to play hostess to people already in the limelight. Among those attending one of her dinner parties in March 1866 were her old friend James Garfield, a rising Republican star and now reconciled with his wife, and cavalry commander George Armstrong Custer, yet another Ohio-born military man marked by Salmon Chase for promotion.

By this time Kate was one of the most famous women in America. In an age long before television or other electronic mass media, she was the focus of regular news coverage not only in the large city papers but also in places like St. Johnsbury, Vermont; Ebensburg, Pennsylvania; and Oskaloosa, Kansas. Often the small-town papers carried snippets of stories written by a new wave of eastern female society reporters, such as Olivia and "Miss Grundy" (Maria Austine Snead), who came to prominence after the war and for whom Kate became a favorite subject. The public fascination with her lay not in any particular works or deeds but in her entire persona. Yet she was no mere celebrity (a word not yet in general use) but instead someone admired widely for her talents.

The happiness Kate appeared to enjoy after Willie's birth was marred by the inevitable resumption of strained relations with her mercurial husband. Senator Sprague, who had gone back to Providence, was not there the night of the Garfield-Custer reception, and he rarely accompanied Kate to any of the lavish social events she attended. One affair he did show up for—a state dinner given by President Johnson—ended in complete embarrassment. As the story goes, he got to drinking too much, and someone at his table warned him that "a pair of bright eyes" was looking at him. "Damn them, they can't see me," he countered, proceeding to refill his glass. "Yes, they can see you," Kate jumped in, "and they are heartily ashamed of you." True or not, the story captures the back and forth the couple engaged in over Sprague's alcoholism.

Kate needed to get away. She later wrote in her diary that she felt absence might help their relationship, and it was a strategy she would adopt many times in the coming years. Even though she was in Washington and her husband mostly in Rhode Island, she needed even greater distance—an entire ocean—between them. And so she decided to go to Europe that summer with Nettie, Willie, and the boy's nurse. She would dazzle many foreigners and develop a lifelong attachment to the Continent. But for her and her husband it would be the summer of their discontent.

CHAPTER 11

# "More Unfitness Day by Day"

Sprague had tears in his eyes as he watched Kate's party board the Cunard Line's *Australasian* in New York harbor in early April 1866. But it was Kate who soon had to be crying, at least silently, over the series of letters he sent her while she was away for what turned out to be the next eight months. Although Kate's own letters from this period have not survived, given the content of her husband's correspondence, her reaction is not hard to imagine.

Ten days after she sailed he wrote her from Washington to say he had "taken to whiskey since you left." He was "depressed past weakness," the result of yielding to influences that possessed him. He tried to soften the blow with some political talk, reporting pridefully on Congress having overridden Johnson's veto of the Civil Rights bill. Then he got to the real point of his letter. "Expect to hear of my doing all sorts of things during your absence," he forewarned her. "You know I am fond of the ladies and you must not blame me for indulging in that fondness. I know you will not if you reflect but will rather commend me for it." He claimed to be still madly in love with her and, as compensation, told her to travel wherever she wanted and to spend as much money as she wished. The letter's wild ride continued with his audacious proposed remedy for his depression: "I must I think get some young woman to live with me. Do you consent?" he asked. Even more baldly, he reasoned that if he were permitted "to try to love a little" in Kate's absence, it would strengthen his love for her upon her return. He closed with what can be read as either a lighthearted or cruel dig, attempting to place the onus on her: "Are you not sorry you have deserted me?"

Sprague was living alone with Chase at the Sixth Street house in Washington, and together they formed an odd couple. They entertained dinner guests on a regular basis and often took horseback rides together around the capital, but Sprague found his father-in-law bashful around him. The two men eagerly devoured every letter Kate and Nettie sent, but Sprague accused Kate of forgetting all about him. Figuring she was always interested in politics, he fed her a steady diet of tidbits about the latest developments, including his assessment that the climate was favorable for Ulysses S. Grant for the next presidency (hardly a welcome piece of news to Kate). Sprague also reported on his growing disgust with Andrew Johnson, "a slave to passions and prejudice and to hate."

Sprague's greatest contempt, though, was reserved for himself. In a letter on April 30 he revealed that he felt "more unfitness day by day." He wandered the streets in search of peace of mind but found none. One day he would report that he was getting control of his drinking, the next he would admit to a relapse. He was afraid his "physical infirmities" and "weakness" had placed him in "very false and uncomfortable positions." He wrote in May to say that his mind was "sadly disconnected. . . . When writing I lose my connection, the same as I do when talking, hence my great trouble—I cannot remember." The press was commenting on his drinking, one newspaper calling upon him to pass a constitutional amendment to stop him from using his "shirt collar as a funnel." He had to admit to Kate that the stories were on target and that the criticism was warranted. He refused to let her see the newspaper articles, although he showed them to her father, who gave him no satisfaction. "He does not understand such weakness as *mine*," Sprague sighed. Sprague was more and more of the belief that he was unequal to his post and felt he might even have to quit the Senate. He did not want to resign, he told Kate, but was sure that, unless he changed his habits, he would slide downhill fast. He disparaged his tenure in office: "If I cast back one, two or three years, and see how little I have accomplished, it is enough to discourage anyone."

Confessions of drinking, weakness, insecurity—Kate had heard it all before. But talk of resignation was something altogether new and ominous. She had seen her father rashly resign from the cabinet several times, only to pay the price in loss of reputation and influence. Faced with her husband's musings about quitting the Senate, Kate immediately offered to return to America to help rally his spirits. Her offer jolted him into dropping the idea. He wrote four days later to acknowledge his last "doleful letter" and thanked her profusely for her offer to return and care for her "disconsolate one." As he wrote, "However much I wander and stray away I am always brought back with further stronger sentiments of love and affection for my wife. I don't see how I can longer endure the separation."

With talk of resignation having disappeared, Kate stayed in Europe to undertake a traditional "Grand Tour" traveled by the upper classes. She visited London, where she met Queen Victoria and the reformer John Bright; toured the Scottish Highlands with Nettie; and visited a baroness in Bonn. They traversed the Black Forest and the Swiss Alps and took in the spas of Baden-Baden. Everywhere Kate went she studied the art, architecture, and interiors, taking notes for the opulent mansion she planned to build in Rhode Island and buying up china, silver, and objects to furnish it with. And, of course, there was fashion. In Paris she ordered dozens of gowns from the famous dressmaker Worth, who kept her measurements on file and pronounced hers the best figure for showcasing his designs of any client he had worked with. She was received by Empress Eugénie, the attractive, calculating wife of Napoleon III and the queen to whom Kate was most often compared. No doubt Kate addressed the monarch in French.

From Europe Kate and Nettie engaged in a sort of letter-writing contest, in which their father judged the respective merits of each daughter's correspondence. Kate won on composition, spelling, and penmanship; Nettie on interest, creativity, and humor. Nettie's letters and landscape sketches were, as Chase put it, "a real treat." He acknowledged to Nettie that "Katie seems to think that I *criticize* too much" but explained it was only because he did not want either of them to feel satisfied "as long as any degree of perfection" remained unattained. And in a rare display of praise he admitted to Kate that both she and Nettie were every bit as qualified to take part in public affairs as he was at their age. That, he said, made him begin to see a good deal of sense in the lighthearted remark he once made, when asked his opinion on women's rights, that he was for putting everything in their hands and letting them govern.

From Kate's forlorn husband, meanwhile, the eccentricities continued to pour forth. He reminded Kate in June that in her last letter she had, as he construed it, given him "encouragement to admire beautiful women." Whatever she said, it is doubtful she granted him any such dispensation. In any event, her husband didn't view things as a two-way street, telling her, "I don't think I can be so liberal with you." He was convinced that no woman of both beauty and intellect, such as Kate, would reciprocate any overtures from him, but the same was not true with her. She would admire impressive men and they her, which was unacceptable to Sprague. He wanted it made clear he did not favor some sort of open marriage. She had sent him some note paper with a playful suggestion that he use it to write love letters to other women, but he failed to see the joke. "Dearie, do you give me this liberty that you may enjoy similar liberty?" he asked. He tried to reassure her of his faithfulness, saying he was glad he was no longer pleased "with the rustle of other women's dresses." But in a subsequent letter he tried to arouse her jealousy, telling of his having spotted a buxom woman on the street—developed, as he put it, nearly as much as Kate—and that he had deliberately stepped in her path so he could obtain a full view.

A few weeks after Willie's first birthday in June 1866, Sprague wrote him a long letter intended for Kate's consumption. "Mama and Papa are young yet," he wrote his son. "They want to form their plans of life so that they can work together." He continued by saying that little children were sent into the world "to teach their fathers and mothers to love one another, to keep fresh the marriage vows, to keep green their affection and to cultivate all virtues and to dissipate all vices, to teach each to be patient with one another, to live for one another and to let nothing come between them."

Soon, after lamenting to Kate his "poor show" in opposing a proposed cut in the tariff, owing to a "very sluggish" mind, Sprague resumed his talk of quitting the Senate. She once more talked him out of resigning, and a week later he thanked her for forestalling such a "cowardly act." He also credited her with improving his attention to his appearance. She was right, he told her, in advising him that "neatness in dress brings neatness and discipline of mind." He suddenly imagined that his Senate colleagues saw great improvement in him and that he now commanded their respect. In truth, his fellow senators never held him in high regard, but Kate had accomplished her mission. "Dearie I thank you for your letter," he wrote on July 19. "It will give me strength to reach after good and great things." Buoyed by all of this, he even gave thought to studying law and sounded out Chase on the idea. The chief justice responded that it would tax Sprague's time and patience and would demand a year of diligent reading, but he offered to read along with Sprague and help him as far as he could. It is doubtful that Chase, who knew his son-in-law's capacities by now, thought Sprague would follow through on the idea, and he did not.

Sprague was not the only member of Kate's family whose mindset she had to worry about while she was touring Europe. In midsummer her father traveled east to visit his native New Hampshire and his Dartmouth alma mater, then spent many days on the North Shore of Massachusetts in the company of Charlotte Eastman. Kate had done her best to discourage the relationship in the past, but now she had ample reason to be worried. Just before her father left the beach house of a friend where he and Mrs. Eastman were staying, he went knocking on her door at night, only to receive no answer. The following night she left him the key to her chambers, and he tiptoed up to the door and unlocked it. Finding when he pulled on it that the door, though yielding a little, was barred, he gave up and returned to his room. When she saw him the next morning "Lottie," as he called her, bent over and kissed him and said she had wanted him and "would have yielded" if he had come in. She showed him the bar she had put across the door and tied with her garter, saying it would have given way if pulled. They sat side by side that morning on a couch in his room, grieving at his scheduled departure.

Any concerns Kate had that her fifty-eight-year-old father might do something rash, such as propose marriage, only intensified after Chase wrote her in September, while she was in Paris, to report the "most astonishing piece of news"—that the old bachelor Charles Sumner was to be married at age fifty-five to a woman half his age. Within days fresh rumors surfaced that Chase was to marry Charlotte Eastman. Chase wrote his former treasury clerk and sometime-secretary Jacob Schuckers authorizing him to deny any such report until he heard from Chase directly that he had decided to marry again. It was not that he absolutely renounced the idea, Chase told Schuckers; indeed, he said he knew of no more suitable marriage partner than Charlotte Eastman. "But I am still and still likely to remain a widower," he wrote. "Ought there not to be a law against grandfathers being married to any but grandmothers?!" To Nettie he confided that "but for the looks of the thing in an old gentleman like me, and the feelings of Katie, and I daresay yours too, and some other considerations, who knows that I might not have been tempted" to marry the widow Eastman. It was, Chase admitted, "rather solitary this life that I lead." But he ultimately may have been dissuaded as well by the quick breakdown of Sumner's marriage, which ended in separation after less than a year when his young bride began seeing another man. Kate would end up witnessing much of Sumner's suffering, and his painful experience gave her valuable ammunition in opposing any temptation Chase had to take a similar route.

If Kate was concerned about her father's interest in other women, she witnessed an even more alarming resurfacing of Sprague's paranoia about her and other men. He wrote her on September 17, 1866, a few weeks before he planned to go to Europe to bring her and Willie home, to say he found her last letter "a little wanting in your usual fervor." He speculated that she had been dazzled by the glitter of Paris and that, surrounded by temptations, she might be in danger of succumbing to them. Had she forgotten her "lord at home?" he asked. "Do you need his presence to keep you in the faith? I think you are undergoing serious temptations and if you survive and surmount them, how glorious will be the conquest." These were curious statements coming from a man who had previously signaled his own intention to be unfaithful.

While Sprague was in transit to Europe, rumors of an impending divorce began to surface. One paper in late October said the couple had separated "in consequence of gross immoralities on his part." Chase was mortified by the stories and again turned to Schuckers, asking him to work the newspapers to print a denial without mentioning Kate's name in any way. Within days the *Providence Journal* referred to "the shameful libel upon Senator Sprague," which it called "an utter falsehood" and "without one iota of foundation. There is not, in the country, a man happier, or who deserves to be happier, in his domestic relations" than William Sprague, the paper asserted—dutifully leaving out any mention of Kate. But her name came up in other papers, prompting the *New-York Tribune*, published by Chase's friend Horace Greeley, to issue an equally stout refutation. On October 31 the *Tribune* called the stories "infamous calumnies" spread by Democratic newspapers trying to strike back at Sprague for his gallant wartime service. "He has been as true to the country since peace as he was during war, and while not a conspicuous or noisy Senator, votes always right," the *Tribune* declared.

By mid-October Sprague had met up in Germany with Kate, Willie, and the boy's nurse, and on December 10, 1866, the family reunited with Chase in Washington. Kate's father, who had not seen her in eight months, the longest separation of their lives, was joyful at her return. He did not much care for Kate's new curled hair look, though, and he was chagrined that Nettie chose to remain in Dresden, Germany, for another year to study art, as he thought it at best a hobby and not a realistic vocation for a young woman.

Although Kate's own thoughts at the time are not recorded, years later, after facing a scandal of her own, she would identify 1866 as the year her marriage began to constitute a constant burden on her. She would allege that sometime in 1866 her husband committed adultery in Rhode Island with Maggie English, the nurse who accompanied Kate and Willie to Europe. At the same time, according to Kate, her husband was continuing his long-standing affair with Mary Viall. In the years to come the difficult times would alternate with periods of real affection and reconciliation. And three more children would follow. But it is safe to say Kate knew by the time she got back from Europe, if not before, that the marriage had failed of its promise. She would endure even greater indignities in the coming years.

In the meantime Kate would channel her energies into other areas, like building a home to rival the royal castles she had seen in Europe, making her return to politics, and raising her children. And eventually, after her father was gone, letting a new man into her life.

CHAPTER 12

# "I Am Told That She Actually Controls the Entire Affair"

They called it Canonchet, after a Native American chief who camped on the property two centuries earlier while fighting the English colonists in King Philip's War. In 1866 Sprague completed purchase of the three hundred-plus-acre Robinson family farm in Narragansett with a view toward turning the site, with its panoramic ocean view, into a summer home. Over the next few years they constructed a four-story Victorian Gothic mansion and spent $650,000 to $1 million to finish it (although the grand ballroom was never completed). Different sources numbered it as having anywhere from sixty to ninety rooms. To some, its many piazzas, turrets, mansarded towers, and belvederes gave the rambling structure an air of magnificence, whereas others thought it an ugly pile. The residence featured a sauna, a bowling alley, an octagonal glass-domed main salon, multiple libraries, and a hand-carved staircase imported from Italy variously estimated at between $10,000 and $50,000 in cost.

The interior, a maze of crisscrossing halls, was stocked with purchases from Kate's trips to Europe: French Barbizon paintings, Aubusson carpets, Chinese vases, a full-length Venetian mirror, and the finest tapestries, period furniture, and objets d'art. Kate brought back a mantelpiece originally from Marie Antoinette's palace at Versailles.

She threw herself into the whole construction project, directing the workmen here and there, sometimes changing her mind about a room after they had already completed it. It was important to her that it be done right, for Kate envisioned Canonchet as the grandest villa in America, a salon that would attract the most powerful men in the nation. Indeed, with a telegraph office, a blue room in imitation of the one in the president's mansion, an apartment for Chief Justice Chase, and a guest room set aside for Horace Greeley, Canonchet was fit to serve as a future summer White House.

After Kate and Sprague returned to America from Europe in December 1866 they were apart again at Christmas, but Kate swallowed her pride and went to Providence to be with her husband for New Year's. "I am glad you went," her father wrote her. "Your first duty is to your husband. . . . I hope that henceforth you will find less and less enjoyment in the society-whirl and more and more in making *home* attractive to husband and child." As always, Chase looked for ways to praise his son-in-law. In a letter to Nettie he complimented "a little speech" Sprague had given in the Senate expressing support for women's suffrage. Chase also glossed over Sprague's shortcomings, as in his report to Nettie, six weeks later, that Sprague was still suffering from "a great deal from dyspepsia" (a euphemism for inebriation). The night before, Chase recounted, Sprague was feeling so bad that he couldn't even come downstairs.

Still, Chase told Nettie that "no woman could have a kinder or more indulgent husband than he has been to Katie. Sometimes I fear she do[es]n't feel it quite enough though I know that she loves him truly and is proud of him." Too often Chase turned a blind eye to Sprague's limitations as a man and husband. But Chase evidently saw positive qualities in Sprague that Kate, with her combative nature, did not always fully credit. Chase understood that it takes two to tangle and that both parties bore responsibility for the sorry state of relations between them.

The now eighteen-month-old Willie ("that baby of babies," his grandfather called him) was the glue holding his parents together. As Chase told Nettie, Sprague "takes more to *the* boy than to anything or anybody else," and Kate dressed up the toddler "*en prince*" (as a prince) and regarded him as "*facile princeps*" (easily first in her attention). She also kept up her interest in the social scene, throwing regular Saturday afternoon receptions at the Sixth and E Street townhouse and attending any dancing party that came along. Often she stayed out until three or four in the morning, a schedule Sprague thought was impairing her health. But Washington was still celebrating the end of the war, and Kate could not resist taking part in the carnival atmosphere. John Hay, back in Washington after serving as secretary of the US legation at Paris, where Kate and Nettie had visited him the prior summer, recalled attending a ball thrown by Kate in February 1867 at which the women powdered their hair in the French style. The still-single Hay danced with the hostess and gushed in his diary that he had "never seen so beautiful and picturesque a roomful" of women.

Kate and Hay remained good friends, and he joined her and Nettie for a walk about the capital one sunny winter morning in 1867. They shopped and rode in street cars, Kate and Nettie paying his fare because some Irish toughs at Willard's Hotel had stolen all his money, which, he said, "like an idiot, I had left lying on my table." The two women took him that afternoon to meet President Johnson's daughters, with whom Kate got along well because they posed no social threat. Johnson's wife was an invalid, so the unofficial duties of First Lady fell to his eldest daughter, who described her family as "plain people from the mountains of Tennessee, called here for a short time by a national calamity" and hoped not too much was expected of them. Kate would have no Mary Lincoln–like rivalry with the Johnson women.

Hay continued to value Kate's political instincts. In that same February of 1867, after William Seward, who had stayed on as Johnson's secretary of state, offered Hay a position as his private secretary, Hay asked Kate's advice on whether he should take the job. Kate "slept on it and said no," so Hay turned down the offer and soon returned to Europe as secretary of legation at Vienna, continuing a diplomatic career that one day would make him among the most influential secretaries of state in American history.

Right after the ball she threw in February Kate was off to Philadelphia to attend the ostentatious housewarming party for Jay Cooke's newly built mansion, Ogontz. The following week she was back in Washington for a reception thrown by Treasury Secretary Hugh McCulloch, an affair one correspondent lambasted as being full of "costly dressing, distortions, ornaments, puff, twists, wheels, rivulets, waterfalls, scalp knots, or what nots." Chase believed Kate was overdoing her quest for luxury, and he wrote Nettie to say, "Oh how I hope you will retain your simplicity of tastes!"

He need not have worried about Nettie on that score. "There could not possibly have been sisters more unlike each other than were the Chase sisters," declared Mary Logan, the politically active wife of an Illinois officeholder. They differed not only in appearance but also in personality and talents. "Nettie, though of plainer face, was one of the most gentle, modest, retiring, and lovable characters that one could possibly imagine," Logan wrote. Viewing them side by side, a Washington reporter observed that Kate "has the look of a French lady, being slight and dashing; her sister has a staider look, like a Holland maiden." John Hay described Nettie as "large and blonde and, barring the irregular profile, like a Flemish Venus." Nettie was not unattractive, but she could never hope to compete with Kate in the looks department nor could she match Kate as a political guru or socialite. Yet if Nettie was jealous of her more celebrated older sister, she would not say so, for Kate had done much for her over the years. Nettie also had some positive attributes Kate did not—a self-deprecating sense of humor and a fully developed creative side.

In April 1867, barely four months after returning from her first trip to Europe, Kate went back for another extended stay and to fetch Nettie from her art studies. She took Willie and his nurse, Maggie; her French maid; and two of her husband's second cousins, Susie Hoyt and her brother Will. They met up with Nettie in Paris, and Kate brought her sister back to the States that fall. While they were away both Chase and Sprague forgot Kate's birthday in August, with Chase blaming his son-in-law for mixing up the dates of Kate's and Nettie's births. But Chase was already confused. The prior year he forgot Kate's birthday as well, confessing to her afterward that he was "not quite certain which was on the 19th of August and which on the 13th of September." The answer was neither: Kate was born on August 13 and Nettie on September 19.

Visions of the presidency may have distracted Chase. He privately made clear to operatives that he was open to another presidential run and asked them to put out feelers about his prospects. As early as September 1866 he said he thought he understood the country's needs and would like to try his hand at running things from the White House. He wrote Nettie in July 1867 to say that "it does look now that, if there were no military names before the public [a clear reference to General Ulysses S. Grant] the choice of the people might fall upon me."

Chase invariably claimed he would be content to stay on the Supreme Court if the main prize never became his, and he paid lip service to the notion that as chief justice, he had to remain above the political fray. But in truth he was bored with what he called the "irksome" drudgery of Supreme Court work and was anxious to cast aside his judicial robes. He was also starting to question radical Republican Party orthodoxy. Chase opposed federal military occupation of the South and other Republican congressional measures he viewed as draconian. He resisted putting ex-Confederate president Jefferson Davis on trial for treason. Chase was willing to extend full amnesty to Southern rebels and end military rule as long as the former Confederate states agreed to extend voting rights to black males.

He continued to receive material financial aid from his son-in-law. In the summer of 1867 Sprague "came to the rescue" of the southern branch of the Union League, an organization dedicated to the spread of Republicanism among loyal whites and black freedmen. In exchange for two hundred dollars a month and a lump sum donation of a few thousand dollars, Sprague secured a commitment from the organization's president to support Chase for the Republican nomination. Sprague's motives were not unrelated to his growing business interests in the South; it could not hurt to spread a few political dollars around Dixie on behalf of a father-in-law seen as a possible future occupant of the White House. Chase acknowledged Sprague's efforts, writing him in August 1867 to report that the public mood was favorable to his candidacy and that what was needed most was execution.

After her return from Europe in the fall of 1867 Kate's political juices got flowing again. It was rumored that she arranged for any Washington correspondents who kept the Chase movement before the public eye to be paid $100 a week out of the Sprague coffers. The story may have been exaggerated, but the practice of buying off journalists for favorable coverage was not uncommon in those days.

In January 1868 Kate was plotting her father's nomination on the Republican ticket and was described as "the most splendid woman at the present time amid the Republican politicians and courtiers of Washington." But at a reception she threw on the night of February 22 she astonished her visitors by saying "unreservedly that she thought President Johnson was right in his entire controversy with Congress" and that she intended to use all her influence to help the *Democratic* Party. She was referring to the showdown between the Democratic President Johnson and the Republicans in Congress over Reconstruction and the limits of executive versus congressional power. Two days after Kate's reception Johnson was impeached by the House for firing Secretary of War Stanton in violation of the Tenure of Office Act, which forbade the president from removing any cabinet member without Senate approval. Though no fan of Johnson, Kate's father believed the president had not only the right but the duty to disregard the law if he believed it unconstitutional. Kate agreed, telling her guests that night that "the time had now come to act to save the Constitution."

Johnson's impeachment trial in the Senate began on March 5, 1868, with Salmon Chase, as chief justice, presiding. Men Kate had known and admired for much of her life, including Charles Sumner, James Garfield, Carl Schurz, and chief trial prosecutor Ben Butler, were pressing for conviction of the president. Kate knew that her husband, who had described his contempt for Johnson in their correspondence, was likely to vote with his Republican colleagues to convict as well. But there was someone else whose opinion counted for more than all the others combined. Chief Justice Chase privately told Kate that he was in favor of acquittal. And although his conduct of the impeachment proceedings was regarded by independent observers as fair and impartial, his procedural and evidentiary rulings mostly favored Johnson's defense, to such an extent that Republicans such as Sumner and Garfield viewed him as a traitor to the cause.

Dating back to the Cincinnati race riots in the 1840s, Chase had always detested mob justice, and he saw the rush to remove Johnson in a similar vein. "To me the whole business seems wrong," he told his old abolitionist friend Gerrit Smith. But he also had personal reasons for taking that position. He did not relish the prospect of seeing his old enemy, radical Republican Ben Wade, ascend to the presidency upon a conviction of Johnson. With the position of vice president left vacant since Lincoln's assassination, Wade, as president *pro tempore* of the Senate, was next in line of succession. Chase had never forgiven Wade for having, in Chase's view, denied him the 1860 presidential nomination by splitting the Ohio delegation at the convention that chose Lincoln.

The most serious accusation that has dogged Chase down through the years is that he opposed impeachment to bolster a planned run for president as a Democrat. By the start of the impeachment trial Grant was the all-but-certain Republican nominee, so to have a shot at the presidency, Chase would need to switch parties. The radical Republicans accused Chase of "coquetting with the Democrats," and they charged the Democrats with using flattery to induce him to steer his actions at trial in Johnson's favor.

Kate too was suspected of siding with Johnson for reasons of personal ambition. Jane Swisshelm, a dyed-in-the-wool abolitionist Republican journalist (and friend of Mary Lincoln), accused Kate of influencing her father to side with Johnson so she could retain her title as sovereign queen of Washington. Swisshelm pointed out that as long as Johnson stayed in the White House, Kate would have no effective challenge to the highest social position in the nation's capital from his wife or daughters. By contrast, Swisshelm wrote, Ben Wade's wife, Caroline, was self-confident enough to maintain her claim to First Ladyship if her husband became president. Kate reacted indignantly to the article, but Swisshelm said she was a legitimate subject of public comment and challenged anyone to contradict what she had written.

Other papers either attacked or defended Kate depending on their point of view—North or South, Republican or Democrat. A Georgia newspaper, extolling her powers of persuasion, asked, "Can it be that by winning her talented father over to the sound doctrines of the Democratic party, Mrs. Sprague has pointed out the road to prosperity and political reconciliation for this now distracted Republic? I am told that she actually controls the entire affair." But a Republican Massachusetts paper responded sarcastically that apparently "no reward is thought too great for this Joan of Arc of the dinner table. . . . She artfully mingles coaxing and confectionery, and supports the weak by the joint tonic of her conversation and her coffee." The paper thought it much better to "have 'woman's rights' in earnest, and give that sex the open responsibility of the ballot, than reduce it to the necessity of these indirect and underhanded schemings."

Kate fed the rumors of her ambition by attending every session of the impeachment trial. She made the twenty-minute daily walk with her father from Sixth and E Street to the Capitol and, each afternoon, watched his dignified entrance into the Senate chamber. Chase presided from the podium, clad in his flowing black judicial robe, while Kate, seated at the front of the gallery reserved for senators' wives, was much noticed in her luxurious gowns and matching accessories. Society journalist Olivia observed Kate in "a Parisian suit of royal purple velvet, perfect in all its appointments." As she wrote, "Paris has Eugénie; Washington has Mrs. Senator Sprague, the acknowledged queen of fashion and good taste." Known for her purple prose, Olivia described Kate's costume as "just as perfect as the lily or the rose. She is a lilac blossom today." Was she a "woman or a flower?" the columnist asked, then answered her own question: "She is a flower of immortality."

With the outcome of the trial in doubt and likely to come down to a single senator or two, there was intense speculation as to how William Sprague of Rhode Island would vote. Sprague was one of a handful of senators who had not publicly committed to voting one way or the other. In a little-noticed interview with Garfield in April he asserted that Johnson was "dangerous" and "ought to be removed," but he said little on the Senate floor itself (often he was thought to be drunk).

Many assumed Sprague would ultimately follow the wishes of his wife and father-in-law and vote for acquittal. At the time of Sprague's marriage, one Brooklyn newspaper predicted he would vote "just as Papa Chase tells him." During the trial Kate reportedly gave her husband a good working over, and he was described as more afraid of his spirited wife than he was of radical Republican threats of reprisal. One paper called him "hen pecked," and it was even rumored Kate would leave him if he voted to convict. Horace Greeley's *New-York Tribune* reported that the chief justice also did his best to sway the vote of Sprague and several other senators. Chase denied the charge, telling Greeley that "Sprague was not influenced by me, nor did I seek to influence him" or any other senator.

In the end Sprague voted for conviction, but it did not matter. On May 16, 1868, the thirty-five to nineteen vote to convict fell one short of the necessary two-thirds majority. By the time the tense, dramatic roll call made it to Sprague, it was already clear that the effort to remove the president would fail.

Sprague made no speeches and gave no interviews explaining his vote. One newspaper said he voted "guilty" to demonstrate his independence from his wife and father-in-law. Others have asserted that Sprague feared

Secretary of War Stanton, who possessed a secret report of possibly treasonous conduct by Sprague during the war with respect to cotton trading and was prepared to use it against him if he did not vote to convict. The theory is a tenuous one, as there is no evidence that Stanton ever threatened Sprague about the matter or that Sprague even knew at the time of impeachment that Stanton was holding some sort of confidential report. (That fact was not revealed until 1870, after Stanton's death.)

The likeliest explanation for Sprague's vote is also the simplest one: politics. Sprague was up for reelection (which he would win in June), and his fortunes were tied to the radical Republicans, who controlled the party machinery in the Rhode Island legislature. Rhode Island was also heavily Republican in those years, and impeachment was the ultimate test of party loyalty. A vote for acquittal would have been political suicide. Already on record as anti-Johnson, Sprague needed no pressure from Stanton to vote for conviction. Kate may not have liked her husband's vote, but she would have understood the political reality that dictated it.

Despite Kate's intense interest in the outcome, she abruptly left Washington for Narragansett in early May, shortly before the final Senate vote, prompting speculation that she was enraged at her husband for not bowing to her political will. But although Kate and Sprague may have argued over impeachment, the tenor of a letter from Chase to Kate right after her departure suggests that something more personal than politics had come between the married couple. "I never saw him so much affected as by the difference that occurred between you just before you went away," her father wrote Kate on May 10. "He was almost unmanned—moved to tears." But in attempting to effect a reconciliation, Chase again sympathized with Sprague. "I see now in your husband something of that which I blame on myself," he wrote Kate. Chase admitted that he had too often failed to show his fatherly love for his oldest daughter. "But I know how strong my love really was," he assured her, "and I know how strong his [Sprague's] is." He reminded Kate it was her duty to submit to her husband. She must, he told her, "*love away all his reserve.*" Finally he told her she did not appreciate how good a spouse she had. She needed to consider "how generous, self-sacrificing and indulgent a husband he has been to you. How few husbands would consent to such absences, and be at once so liberal and thoughtful. If he were only a true Christian he would be nearly perfect." It is doubtful that Kate agreed with that assessment.

After the impeachment trial ended and the Republicans nominated Grant, Kate's thoughts turned to her father's presidential prospects. Increasingly friends and supporters were urging Chase to run as a Democrat. Kate also pushed that idea, with one Georgia newspaper reporting that she was "pulling the wires with great effect." The case she was making, the paper explained, was that as an antislavery man and former radical Republican, her father could help split the black vote in the South and the radical vote in the North that would otherwise go entirely to Grant. As the treasury secretary who financed the war, Chase could also help neutralize Grant's advantage as a war hero and make the contest, as Kate would later put it, "an even one." And his pro-Johnson conduct of the impeachment trial, his support for amnesty for Southern rebels, and his opposition to military occupation in the South placed him in good stead with Democrats as well as moderate Republicans. In words that would not have pleased Chase but reflected the thinking of conservative Democrats, editor James Gordon Bennett Jr. of the *New York Herald* wrote that Grant was the "slave of the nigger supremacy faction," whereas Chase was admirably fending off "the radical desperadoes" who viewed Reconstruction as "a programme for revenge."

Many Democrats, however, viewed Chase as an opportunist. He had been a Henry Clay National Republican in 1832, a Harrison Whig in 1836, an out-and-out Whig in 1840, a Liberty Party member in 1844, a Free Soiler in 1848, a Democrat in 1851, a Liberty Party man once more in 1852, a Republican in 1856, and then, when he had no chance against Grant, suddenly a Democrat again in 1868. As one-time Ohio governor Joseph B. Foraker later remarked, "It is probably safe to say that [Chase] had membership in more political parties . . . with less mutual obligation arising therefrom than any other public man America has produced." One Democrat put it bluntly in May 1868: "I can perceive no other reason for the selection of the founder of the Republican Party than his supposed availability."

Chase tried his best to allay those concerns, stressing in letters to friends that he was and had always been a Democrat at heart. He favored the old Democratic principles on finance and was an advocate of small government in the Jefferson-Jackson tradition. Unlike his son-in-law, he supported free trade and low tariffs, and despite having promoted greenbacks during the war, he was philosophically a "hard money" man who preferred paper backed by coin, making him attractive to Wall Street Democrats such as August Belmont and Samuel Tilden. The only issue that previously separated him from the Democratic Party, he said, was slavery. But his support for equal rights for African Americans—in particular, his endorsement of universal suffrage (meaning full voting rights for white and black *men*)—was a serious obstacle to his nomination. The postwar Democratic Party saw the principle of black suffrage as conflicting with its professed devotion to "states' rights."

To address the conundrum, Chase came up with what he considered an elegant formulation. He urged Democrats to endorse universal suffrage in principle while leaving its application to the states. It was a clever but disingenuous position because, as Chase knew, no Southern state, left to its own devices, was going to extend the vote to black Americans. The author of the definitive history of the 1868 election called it a "compromise subterfuge." But with this declaration of principles, Chase's chances for the Democratic nomination markedly improved. He would leave himself now in the hands of Kate and a few of his "most discreet friends."

Unfortunately the men Kate was given to deal with were a ragtag, unimpressive bunch. The most prominent of them at the time and Chase's floor manager at the convention was John Dash Van Buren, a minor Democratic politician, financial journalist, and distant relative of former president Martin Van Buren. His primary value to Chase lay in his close relationship with Tilden and with ex-New York governor Horatio Seymour. Democrat and Wall Street financier John Cisco was a former career federal bureaucrat and Chase loyalist, but he suffered from fatigue and ill health. From there it went downhill. Alexander Long was a seedy politician and ex-Ohio Democratic congressman who was nearly expelled from the House during the war for making seditious antiwar speeches. His motives were also suspect, as his support for Chase derived as much as anything from a vindictive desire to deny the nomination to his fellow Ohioan, George Pendleton. James C. Kennedy, another Democrat, was a medical doctor and former small-county Ohio state legislator with no national political experience. Jacob Schuckers, Chase's occasional private secretary, had no practical political experience and was blinded by idolatry for Chase. Sixty-four-year-old Hamilton Smith's only qualification was that he was a former Dartmouth classmate and occasional business partner of Chase. Amasa Sprague was Kate's brother-in-law, with whom she did not get along. Nominally the business partner of his brother William, Amasa's main occupation was raising horses.

For better or worse these were the men Kate had to work with at the convention in July. But she knew she was the person best qualified to turn them into an operation that might succeed in securing the nomination for her father. And so, just before the Fourth of July, she went to the Democratic National Convention in New York, leaving her husband and Willie at the seaside in Narragansett. And it was at New York's Tammany Hall, on Wednesday, July 8, during the twelfth ballot, that she rose to join the tumultuous ovation for Salmon P. Chase, whose name had just been placed in nomination by the one-half vote from the California delegation.

CHAPTER 13

# "You Have Been Most Cruelly Deceived"

The ovation for Chase went on for ten minutes before a Kentucky delegate moved to clear the galleries. But the temporary chair said he had "no power to suppress cheers, only hissing and bad conduct."

The balloting continued that Wednesday for six more rounds, through the eighteenth, after which it stood Hancock 144.5 and Hendricks 87, with Pendleton, the one-time frontrunner, fading to 56.5 and now out of it. To stop Hancock's momentum, Seymour, the convention chair, called an adjournment until ten o'clock the following morning. Chase's token one-half vote had not increased during ballots thirteen through eighteen, but that did not mean much. The *New York Herald* predicted that either Hancock or Chase would be nominated when voting resumed, its front-page headline reading "Seymour in Favor of Chase" and "The Star of the Chief Justice in the Ascendant."

Chase's fate now was in the hands of the New York delegation, led by Tilden, as well as a group of Ohio Democrats, some supportive of Chase, others violently opposed. A core group of New Yorkers and Ohioans met late into the night on Wednesday, July 8, at Delmonico's restaurant in lower Manhattan to plot strategy. Tilden, the coy politico Kate had been trying to pin down for days, was there, but his sidekick Van Buren, who was instrumental in securing Seymour's support of Chase, was not. Neither was Seymour; he was out buttonholing the New York delegation to go for Chase in the morning. Kate was not invited to Delmonico's; it would be an evening of brandy and cigars.

At a meeting of the New Yorkers the next morning Seymour and Van Buren convinced the delegation to cast its thirty-three ballots as a unit for Chase, at least after Hendricks, to whom New York had been committed, began to lose support. On his way to the convention that morning Seymour read to one of the New Yorkers a prepared speech he planned to make in seconding Chase's nomination. According to one of Chase's backers, Seymour fully expected the chief justice to be nominated once balloting resumed.

At the opening of proceedings on Thursday, July 9, Pendleton withdrew. Starting with the nineteenth ballot and continuing through the twenty-first, Hendricks unexpectedly began to surge, pulling to within three votes of Hancock. Chase received four votes from Massachusetts, prompting loud applause, followed by a few hisses. The New York delegation continued to give all thirty-three of its votes to Hendricks, but savvy observers knew that New York was voting for him only until its true favorite candidate emerged. As the *New-York Tribune* reported, "Many thought this was to be Chase."

On the next ballot, the twenty-second, the roll call reached New York. This was the moment Kate was waiting for, when Seymour would step forward, announce that his delegation was switching its support to Chase, and start a stampede that would nominate her father. But for the time being New York stuck with Hendricks. The next state called was Ohio. Its spokesman, General George McCook, a known enemy of Chase, stood up and mounted a chair. "Mr. Chairman, I rise at the unanimous request and demand of the delegation from Ohio, and with the consent and approval of every public man in the State, including the Hon. George H. Pendleton, to again place in nomination, against his inclination, but no longer against his honor, the name of HORATIO SEYMOUR, of New York." Rousing cheers and applause broke out and continued as McCook said that, as much as Seymour did not want the nomination, the overwhelming desire of the convention was that he be their candidate.

Kate was horrified at this development, but all was not lost, for the delegates had yet to hear from Seymour himself. He sheepishly stepped forward to express his gratitude but to emphasize he had "*meant* it" when he earlier said his honor prevented him from accepting a nomination. "Gentlemen, I thank you, and may God bless you for your kindness to me; but your candidate I cannot be."

It appeared the danger had passed. Another hopeful sign for Chase followed when Ohio delegate Clement Vallandigham rose to speak. Vallandigham was a notorious Copperhead who was exiled to the Confederacy for treasonous wartime activities, and Chase had campaigned against him when Vallandigham ran for governor of Ohio in 1863. But now that Pendleton was out of the running, Vallandigham favored Chase, who welcomed his rather embarrassing support. That support, however, did not materialize at this crucial moment. After hearing Seymour's refusal, Vallandigham declared that the convention could not take "no" for an answer. In times of crisis such as these, he avowed, "every personal consideration must be yielded to the public good. . . . Ohio cannot—Ohio will not accept his declination, and her twenty-one votes shall stand recorded in his name." As if on cue, New York senator Francis Kernan seconded the nomination and, one by one, every other delegation began switching its votes to Seymour who, unable to bear watching the scene unfolding before him, left the podium. At half past noon he was chosen by acclamation. Adding insult to Chase's injury, the convention swiftly nominated, as Seymour's vice presidential running mate, longtime Chase foe Francis P. Blair Jr., the brother of Elizabeth Blair Lee and an outspoken opponent of black suffrage.

Just like that, it was over. When Chase, reached at home in Washington and playing croquet at the time, learned the results of the convention, his first words were, "Does Mrs. Sprague know? And how does she bear it?"

The answer was: not well. The day after the convention ended, as she lingered in New York, she wrote her father a letter full of passion and fury:

> *My dearest Father,*
>
> *You have been most cruelly deceived and shamefully used by the man whom you trusted implicitly [Van Buren], and the Country must suffer for his duplicity. I would not write you yesterday, in the excitement of the result of the action of the Convention, and until I had carefully gone over in my mind all the circumstances that had come under my knowledge of the action of Mr. Van Buren. When I*

*get comfortably settled at Narragansett, I will write out a full and detailed history of my knowledge of this matter that cannot fail to convince you of his bad faith. Nothing more would be needed, than that since the result of the Nomination was announced Mr. Van Buren, though constantly at the Manhattan Club next door, has not been near me, and has passed both Mr. Kennedy and Mr. Schuckers this morning without a recognition.*

She went on to assert that Van Buren had placed a block in the way of her father's nomination by advising him, in a telegraph, to "answer no questions in regard to the Platform." She told her father that if she had received a letter from him before 3:30 p.m. Wednesday unequivocally endorsing the platform, he definitely would have been nominated on the wave of enthusiasm created at that hour by the one-half vote from the California delegation. But she had not received her letter, nor would Van Buren or any of her father's other backers step forward to take responsibility for speaking for the chief justice. And so the moment of golden opportunity had passed. "Mr. Tilden and Mr. Kernan have done this work," she continued, "and Mr. Van Buren has been *their tool*—This is my honest belief; but I will mite it out carefully—So dear Father in the future, be guided by the advice of some of those who are devoted to you, but who are more suspicious than your own noble heart will allow you to be. . . . Your name is a watch word with the people, and they have been outraged and deceived."

She closed by referring to life on her home front:

*I am perfectly well, and go to the Country to kiss Willie and see the Governor. I may return, and think I shall, to Washington with the Governor, then I hope we can capture you and take [you] to Narragansett. Mr. Cisco, is as true as tried steel, Mr. Long has gone home broken hearted. You can form no conception of the depression here.*

Kate's letter reflects her sincere belief that Chase had a good chance of being nominated and would have been but for the treachery and deception of Van Buren and Tilden. But her assessment was flawed. The essence of her charge against Van Buren was that he failed to let Chase's support for the platform be announced to the convention before the one-half vote for him set off a tumultuous ovation. But that was on Wednesday, July 8, and the delegates were not ready at that point to go for Chase, as Pendleton held a substantial lead and Hancock and Hendricks were both still very much in the running. Attending her first convention, Kate overestimated the significance of an excited gallery reaction, which does not necessarily translate into ballot success. Actually Kate's original game plan was a sound one—to hold her father's name back until the right moment, which seemed poised to occur on Thursday, July 9. It was not the lack of a letter in Kate's hands on Wednesday afternoon that prevented her father's nomination.

Van Buren was not conspiring against Chase. It was Van Buren who worked closely with Chase to formulate a fifteen-point statement of principles, acceptable to Seymour and Tilden, that kept Chase in the running on the eve of the convention. And it was Van Buren who helped secure Seymour's endorsement of Chase and urged the New York delegation on the morning of Thursday, July 9, to vote for the chief justice. When Seymour was nominated on Thursday, during his absence from the podium Van Buren urged him to return to the speaker's chair to "throw back the nomination" and, as Van Buren later wrote, "in my earnestness I went beyond civility to one who was my guest." As for Van Buren's hesitation on the platform language, he was merely carrying out the spirit of Chase's instructions. The day before the convention Chase rashly supplied some notes and a letter to Alexander Long to be presented to the convention at the appropriate time, essentially committing to endorse the party's platform and its eventual nominee whoever he might be. But Chase quickly retracted this blank check and made Van Buren promise not to allow any pledge to be made in his name that he would later regret. They both agreed that, if anything, Van Buren should err on the side of caution. It was Kate and others, such as Long, who were pressing her father to go further and faster in endorsing the platform than he was prepared to go. She did not want him to dishonor himself, but she also did not want to see him lose the best chance he ever had for a presidential nomination due to quibbles over semantics. Van Buren cannot be blamed for paying closer attention to Chase's quibbles.

Chase himself exonerated Van Buren of any blame for his loss, writing him afterward to say, "I know you would not deceive." Indeed, Van

Buren's problem was not that he was treacherous but that he was powerless. He had no influence over the Ohio delegation, which, at the crucial moment on Thursday, turned the convention to Seymour rather than to its native son Chase. Nor did Van Buren control Tilden, the true powerbroker at the convention. Although Tilden at one time was receptive to a Chase candidacy, he had cooled to the idea by the time of the convention, his preference being for Seymour and, failing that, Hendricks. Tilden likely was influenced by a leading New York Democrat who wrote him before the convention to say that "Chase is out of the question. . . . We will use him well, but must not think of nominating him."

Chase came to believe he would have been nominated on the twenty-second or twenty-third ballot if the Ohio and New York delegations had not conspired to force the nomination on the reluctant Seymour. Tilden maintained that he was as surprised as anyone by Ohio's nomination of Seymour, but it is likely he at least knew of the plan and tacitly approved it at the dinner at Delmonico's the night before, from which Seymour and Van Buren were absent. Yet it is hard to accuse Tilden of betraying Chase. Tilden had never promised Chase anything, much less endorsed him. In fact, Van Buren had warned Chase a week before the convention not to count on Tilden's support. On July 2 he was even clearer, telling Chase that Tilden was "setting back against you" (hardly something Van Buren would have revealed if he was secretly in league with Tilden against Chase). Neither Chase nor Kate had any right to feel betrayed by Tilden. But that would not stop Kate from forever holding Tilden responsible for her father's defeat.

The 1868 Democratic Convention was the closest Chase ever came to being nominated for president. But in reality the vast majority of voting delegates did not want Chase as their nominee. As one newspaper editor wrote a week after the convention, Chase "was on every man's tongue, but in no man's heart." Despite his recent conversion—or, as Chase would have it, reversion—to Democratic Party principles, he was too closely associated in the minds of the negrophobic rank-and-file, with radical Republicanism and abolitionism to be their candidate.

If Kate overestimated the chances that her father *could* have won the 1868 Democratic nomination, she was on firmer ground in contending he *should* have been nominated if the Democrats were to have any chance of defeating Grant. Seymour predictably went down to defeat in November, and Ulysses Grant succeeded Andrew Johnson as president. Seymour proved such a weak candidate that, in October, Chase's followers instigated a movement to replace Seymour on the ticket with the chief justice. Tilden poured cold water on the idea, and it went nowhere.

After the convention Chase told supporters he had not really sought the nomination and that, not having compromised his principles, he now could honorably give up politics for good and return to the Supreme Court, his reputation intact. He was fooling himself. In embracing the Democrats, who, in 1868, opposed the most important cause he had stood for his entire life—equal rights for the black man—Chase created a stain on his legacy in the minds of many who had long admired him. Frederick Douglass, who had once been welcomed to Chase's dinner table when such invitations from white to black men were unusual and who had fitted the chief justice in his new judicial robes the night before Lincoln's Second Inaugural, said Chase had descended from a higher point and fallen further than "any of his predecessors in treachery." A similar comment came from preacher Henry Ward Beecher, an old Chase friend from Cincinnati, whose father, Lyman, had married Chase to his first wife and whose sister based a character in *Uncle Tom's Cabin* on an escaped slave Chase defended in court. Beecher was quoted just after the 1868 convention as saying that Chase's switch to the party of bigotry proved that his "ambition was consuming the better elements of his nature." Chase's banker friend Jay Cooke called it "disgusting," a "terrible blunder," and attributed it to Chase's "overweening desire" for the presidency.

Chase bears ultimate responsibility for his decision to seek the Democratic nomination, a decision that, as one of his eulogists would lament, caused him to be shorn of much of the respect that belonged to him as chief justice. But Kate gave him every encouragement to take the path he did. And it was she who pushed him to endorse the racially inflammatory platform he found distasteful—not because she was a racist but because she wanted him to win. She understood, in a way her father never did, that to gain the prize, one had to reach for the brass ring. And in the end Chase was prepared to accept the Democrats' nomination and their platform if the votes were there for him. The unfortunate fact is that he trimmed his sails *and* suffered an embarrassing defeat—the worst of both worlds.

Kate came to realize this and, years later, offered a revisionist account of what happened at the 1868 convention. In a lengthy newspaper interview in 1893, one of the few she ever gave, she said that when a delegation of men came to her during the convention and asked her to authorize them to assure the delegates that her father would accept the platform, she refused. She claimed to have told them that her father would never accept the platform and that he confirmed that to her after the convention. That, of course, is exactly the opposite of what actually occurred: Kate was among those urging her father to go along with the platform, she blamed Van Buren for standing in the way, and Chase ended up saying the platform was good enough for him to run on. When he asked the messenger who brought news of his defeat how his daughter was bearing it—before going back to his game of croquet—Chase was being philosophical about his fate in a way he feared his daughter might not. He had told her during the convention that she was "acting too much the politician," and although that statement ignored his own blinding ambition, it accurately reflected Kate's. "Mrs. Sprague's disappointment was very great," one of Chase's Supreme Court clerks would later recall. "I think that she was really more disappointed by the failure of the presidential dream than her father was, for he was still a leading figure in the world—the head of one department of the Government, but she was only the wife of William Sprague."

She was actually much more than that, but that she still was. And as difficult as things were between them of late, they were about to get a whole lot worse.

CHAPTER 14

# "I Almost Hate This Man"

Kate had never enjoyed a close, long-lasting friendship with any other woman. Her only real confidante was a diary she kept in her youth but that she had given up several years before her marriage. "Well my old friend," she wrote to herself in November 1868, "it is long since when I have appealed *to you* for relief as I used to in the old days when I was alone, and trouble overtook me. So I come back to you for that silent sympathy that even a listener may give." She promised not to spare her "Confessor" any of her thoughts and desires and committed to reveal her own faults and shortcomings to help "relieve this weary disappointment that seems often more than I can bear."

In a total of three diary entries recorded in November and December 1868—each almost a short story in itself, with elements of memoir—Kate would reflect her kaleidoscope of emotions, from extreme self-reproach to long-suppressed bitterness and anger over her husband's treatment of her. This woman of such poise and self-possession revealed an inner turmoil that seemed ready to erupt—and that one day would in a desperate, public plea for sympathy following the harrowing events of the summer of 1879. But that was a decade off. For now she needed some way to give vent to her true feelings, and her diary was the only place she was able to do so.

Relations between her and her husband had been rocky since the end of the July 1868 convention. In August Sprague summarily fired Kate's coachman for having drunkenly driven Kate's horse too hard, requiring that it be destroyed. Kate complained that her husband had acted too rashly. As usual, her father counseled her that "there can be but one head to a family" and that it was her wifely duty to acquiesce cheerfully and affectionately in her husband's decisions.

The couple came together again in September when Kate found a satisfying occupation in tending to a broken leg Sprague had suffered in a horse riding accident. But the reconciliation was short lived. As Kate wrote in her diary on November 4, they had a blowup earlier that day over his accusation, within hearing of his workers and son, that she had contrived to obtain some money from him. Stung by his criticism of what she called "a simple act of carelessness," her pride caused her to refuse to take even a single cent from him. He appeared to her "small, and mean." Though he gave generously when he did give to her, he lorded her dependency over her, begrudging every dollar given. She recognized that her own spending habits were "great in the other extreme" and that it was right he impose some check on her, but she despaired of his "littleness of soul." She attributed it to his having been "reared in a pinched prejudiced narrow atmosphere" that valued money as an end in itself. She had a different view: "Money as a possession I despise," she wrote, but "money as a means for usefulness, for good and for happiness, I respect."

How often she wished, she said, that her husband was a man of greater intellect, even if less wealthy. "Sometimes I have almost worshipped him," she wrote, and then some act or word would make him appear so petty as to make her wonder at the discrepancy. Quickly she added, "But there, I judge him hastily perhaps." She acknowledged that in the past she too often tried to get what she wanted from him by "harsh and cruel words." So much of what she suffered, she admitted, was the result of her "own mistaken course." Better, she now thought, to have led by example: "My *life*, its consistency and gentleness should have been my most powerful argument. Alas, often disheartened and disappointed, I have yielded to angry impulses and forgotten myself and my womanhood in a way that it mortifies and distresses me to remember. But my punishment has come, and God knows it is heavy."

If she could not bring herself to submit cheerfully, as her father advised, she at least resolved to keep silent, "remembering it is far better to feel the smart, than the remorse of having inflicted it." She was giving voice to sentiments similar to those she expressed around the time of her marriage after reading the memoirs of famed actress and antislavery activist Fanny Kemble. Like Kate, Kemble was a high-spirited woman of intellect, and she divorced her plantation-owning husband, a man not unlike Sprague. "What a lifetime of misery she brought upon herself and friends by her ungoverned and capricious temper," Kate had said of Fanny at the time. Yet even with all of Fanny Kemble's faults, Kate had written, "I feel for Mrs. K."

Kate returned to pouring out her own woes in her diary. Sprague had lately taken to accusing her of unfaithfulness, claiming to know things about her, "which if true," she wrote, "would make me unworthy to be a wife—any man's wife!" As evidence for his suspicions he reminded her of her long-ago "weakness" and "sin" in surrendering to his request for premarital sex. "Is no joy, no substance left in life for us?" she asked.

Evidently not, as she recorded a week later. She went to his office in Providence, a place she found distasteful, just before their fifth anniversary, forgotten by him, as he had forgotten every anniversary since their marriage. She went in search of "some little token of remembrance" but found none. After keeping her waiting in an outer office while he talked with an employee in full view of her, Sprague sauntered indifferently into the room, "looking shabby and unkempt." When she asked cheerfully, with her heart in her throat, whether he was coming home that week, he responded that he had thought of no such thing. Shuffling through the papers on his desk, he asked impatiently whether she wanted anything of him and, after a careless good-bye, allowed her to find her way out into the rain. He was, she concluded, "a coarse, dirty boor." She found it "a matter of wonder that I feel so hard and bitter that I almost hate this man at times who calls himself my husband, and yet has so little title to the name." He had no idea how she felt either. "William thinks I have not suffered!" she exclaimed. "He does not know and I would not have him dream of the hours and hours of agony, chagrin and disappointment" the last five years had brought. Normally she had no difficulty speaking her mind, but she was too proud to admit, other than to herself, just how miserable she was.

She may have feared blowing up the marriage and all that that would cost her—in money, reputation, and social standing. But Sprague's wealth and position were only part of what attracted her to him in the first place. More importantly, he was exciting, even dangerous. She was drawn to him out of reaction against her proper upbringing by an emotionally cold father and stern boardinghouse headmistresses. Sprague's dashing nature and passionate entreaties had been a powerful magnet. It was, as she labeled it late in life, her "fate" to have met him that first time in Cleveland. There was no shortage of warning signs in their nearly three-year-long, on-and-off courtship: the many quarrels, his confessions of childish and eccentric behavior, his obvious drinking problem. Surely when she married him she also was aware of his limited intellect. But due to forces deep within her, Kate blocked most of it out. She had not appreciated how combustible their combination was. Once lit, the fires could not be controlled, and now they had become a way of life—the loving, the fighting, the making up, the coming back for more. She appeared to comprehend the pattern but was at a loss as to how to change it. And at this point, at least, she was not prepared to end it.

Sprague kept no diary, so his innermost feelings about their marriage are unrecorded. Undoubtedly he was cognizant of the conventional wisdom that, as journalist Henry Villard would write, Kate was "far superior to him in every way." But Sprague knew he was marrying a woman of substance, someone with a laser-like thinking ability he could not hope to match. After their marriage he came to value brains as well as beauty, having written Kate, when she was in Europe in 1866, to say that "beautiful and intellectual women both, by my new education, are now necessary to my full appreciation." His longtime mistress Mary Viall was a fiercely independent modern woman, and his strong matriarch of a mother was also larger than life. But much as he may have thought he wanted a strong woman for a wife, he misjudged himself. Mesmerized by Kate's beauty and charisma, he could not see that she was too much for him. He would later compare Kate to Fanny Sprague; both of them, he said, were always reminding him of his shortcomings and nagging him toward better behavior.

Sprague would have agreed with an English counterpart who, in an essay in 1868, the year of Kate's diary, complained that modern women "interfere and restrict and pay out just so much rope, and measure off just so much gamboling ground, as they think fit." A woman would get her own way in large matters more easily if she would leave men more liberty.

in small ones, this writer thought. Another essayist in the same book—edited, coincidentally, by Lucia Gilbert Calhoun, James Garfield's one-time mistress—said that although the accomplished man did not want a "vapid, flippant, frivolous, empty soul" for a mate, "he probably has no inclination for a bluestocking, nor for a lady with aggressive views on points of theology, nor for one who can beat him in political discussion. Strong intellectual power he can most heartily dispense with." Accomplished though he was in his own right, Sprague was too insecure a man to be married to Kate Chase.

Kate's last diary entry was on December 27, 1868. She had spent much of December on a southern business trip with her husband, during which he bought a water power plant in South Carolina and a nine thousand–acre plantation on Cumberland Island off the Georgia coast. He and Kate intended to turn the island's dilapidated Dungeness estate into a winter residence, and she described the trip in her diary as a "long and pleasant sojourn."

Then, on Christmas, she opened her husband's present to her, expecting to find a beautiful Tiffany jewel they had seen while shopping in New York not long before. His manner had been kinder that day, and when he asked whether she would like to have it, she, in a mood of discouragement and indifference, said no, that it was too costly, and that a gift of money for Christmas would suffice. She actually wanted the jewel badly but thought it would seem too much like begging to say so. She woke on Christmas morning, though, full of glad anticipation that her husband had disregarded her statement and gone ahead and bought the Tiffany item. She opened her present to find a gift of money that, though liberal in amount, "was a bitter disappointment." She tried hard to conceal her reaction, for if she said anything negative, "he would think me very ungrateful and it would only add another to the contemptuous taunts he hurls at me when angry." But he recognized the awkwardness of his gift, asking her not to tell anyone about it. She had taken the time to find actual gifts for his family, and now she was unable to answer their repeated question, "What was your husband's Christmas gift?"

Her sadness was compounded by the fact that, for the first time in her life, her father neglected to buy her a Christmas present and seemed "entirely gone" from her. She had acted selflessly to please everyone else and now was "almost ready to abandon all effort for the future." But after "a long, fierce battle with myself" that day, she determined that she would "force back the old bitterness of spirit" and would not—would never again—"display upon provocation the very qualities I protest that I despise." Whatever aggravation she might feel, her husband would "not again witness my humiliations."

There her diary ends, the rest of the book's pages remaining blank. She would never return to it again, having finished commiserating with the one person she could trust—herself. Her diary would stay hidden from public view until nearly a century later, when a great-granddaughter, after reading it, believed it to be of historical interest and donated it to Brown University and the library named for John Hay, a man Kate may have regretted not marrying instead. There it can be found today, just a few blocks away from the site of the Sprague business office that Kate left, on the eve of her fifth wedding anniversary, to go out into the rain.

CHAPTER 15

# "She's Capable of Hitting Him"

Within a month after ending her diary Kate was pregnant again. She told almost no one for months—not her father, not even Nettie. It is not known when or how Sprague learned of the pregnancy. In later years, according to Kate, he would vaguely assert that his daughters were not his, but there is no record that he denied paternity at this time, in 1869. He did, however, continue to make veiled accusations of infidelity against Kate that would test her diary vow not to allow any provocation by him to get her goat.

In January 1869 the Grant administration was preparing to take office, and new faces, many of them military men and their wives, settled into Washington. Julia Grant, wife of the president, and Julia Fish, whose husband, Hamilton, was secretary of state, were the highest-ranking women in official society. But both of them were considerably older than Kate, and neither posed any challenge to "Mrs. Senator Sprague's" title as social queen. ("Her reign is undisputed," said one writer.) Shortly after Grant's inauguration, however, Mr. Senator Sprague would put his wife's continued high standing at risk.

Although Salmon Chase's political star had fallen after his unsuccessful bid for the Democratic presidential nomination, Sprague saw his own as rising. Reelected to a second Senate term, he decided it was time to make his presence known in that body. Insecure in his post, intimidated by the

Senate's heralded orators and statesmen, Sprague usually sat quietly at his desk, sunk down in his chair, with his drooping mustache and disheveled look, as if in a stupor. When he did speak up no one paid much attention. A story would later be told that as he left the Senate floor one day he asked Kate, who was watching from the gallery, what he might do for her, to which she responded, "Nothing, but go in there and make a speech,—and that, you *can't* do." On the Ides of March 1869 he took to the Senate floor to try to prove her wrong, and in a series of bizarre speeches over the next month he proceeded to stab her—and many others—in the back.

He began in his usual quiet, careless manner of delivery but had not proceeded far before he startled the chamber by declaring that the Senate was composed of too many lawyers. He went on to attack his father-in-law's Supreme Court, the Constitution's framers, Wall Street bankers and monopolists, journalists, and half the population of Rhode Island. Among his home-state targets were not only his business and political rivals, including the state's other Republican senator, Henry B. Anthony, but also Civil War general Ambrose Burnside, his former superior officer. Sprague accused Burnside of cowardice at the First Battle of Bull Run and, for good measure, labeled the Rhode Islanders who retreated there as cowards as well. Sprague suggested the war had been fought not for virtuous purposes but to protect the capitalist class and enhance the power of despotic Northern politicians, a charge conservatives seized upon as an indictment of the radical Republicans by one of their own. It was as if a volcano had erupted; a *Chicago Tribune* correspondent reported that Sprague looked his colleagues squarely in the face, his manner "aggressive and spirited, like one long restive under the chafing of invisible woes."

Sprague's speeches were rambling and often incoherent, veering off into extended discussions of English history and civilization, the superiority of the Dutch system of government, and the evils of the Spanish Inquisition. A Montana paper called them "highly eccentric verbal pyrotechnics." In the middle of it all Sprague introduced a petition for women's suffrage, explaining that because the American people had so little influence over their government anyway—less than "any other people in the world"—he could see no harm in giving women the vote. At times his speeches produced laughter and derision throughout the chamber, as when one of his fellow senators suggested that if Sprague were a little more of a lawyer, he might not be so puzzled about legislation that he called indecipherable. Undaunted, Sprague looked up at the visitors in the gallery who were laughing at him and said that although they might be educated, they were thoughtless and frivolous. The times were serious, he said; the nation was on the brink of financial disaster, and America was losing its virtue as the rich strove to become richer and the poor sought to imitate the rich. Anticipating what he knew everyone was thinking, he denied he was speaking under the influence of "wine or whiskey, or any other stimulant." Nor was he crazy, he insisted; he had simply been studying "our exact situation" for the past three years. He was hesitant to speak at first, admitting that in his prior six years in the Senate he "would rather have stormed a triple line of presented bayonets" than stand on the floor to advocate his views. But as the size of the galleries increased to hear him, he warmed to the exercise, convinced he had "aroused the attention of the country to their affairs." He had thousands of copies of his speeches printed and distributed. In his own euphoric mind he had become Daniel Webster.

His most sinister accusations were reserved for American women in general and, by implication, his wife in particular. It was widely known that Kate had been to Europe twice in the past few years, and it was assumed he was referring to her when he spoke of "Americans who travel abroad and mix and mingle in that filth and come home here to inculcate the immoralities that they have seen upon their own society." He asked rhetorically, "Where is there a father who leaves his house with any security? . . . Where is there a husband who closes his doors with satisfaction?" He questioned whether the fashionable gowns the women in the gallery wore clothed "any more virtue and integrity than do garments of a less gaudy and a less luxuriant quality." Those present thought they spied Sprague looking up at Kate, adorned in a black cashmere shawl and headdress with a red carnation that relieved "the pallor of her icily-beautiful face." One who apparently came to see the show was Mary Viall, who described the scene in her barely fictionalized novel, *The Merchant's Wife*:

> It was like a hot cannonball hissing into the Chamber. . . . Fathers, brothers, husbands were outraged . . . and there was a general imaginary leaping of swords from their scabbards, to the defense of the American women,—to the defense of the insulted queen of the Capitol . . . [her]

> face now bolt upright on the stem is reddening fast, and begins to look like the face of any other angry red-faced woman. . . . For almost the first time in her life the Statesman's daughter has dropped her mask.

According to Viall, Kate then grabbed her shawl and scurried up the aisle from her front-row seat, whereupon "an eye-witness from the corridor laughingly remarked, 'I believe, 'pon honor, she's capable of hitting him with the coral stick of her parasol.'"

Humiliated, Kate fled Washington before her husband's final speech on April 8, joining Nettie in Aiken, South Carolina, a resort area Kate had visited with Sprague on his southern business trip in December. For a change, her father offered words of comfort, acknowledging that she had been "sorely tried" by her husband's "unkind words and unkind acts," and he expressed sympathy "that out of this great trial may come true peace for you." But his advice was still the same: turn the other cheek. "You have both erred greatly," he told her, and each "*ought* to do all that is possible towards reconciliation." But if her husband did not, then she must. "Humble your pride—yield even when you know you have the right on your side," he counseled. "Overcome your own temper, and be transparently truthful." Chase told Kate that "much of your trial is as you acknowledge brought upon you and continued by yourself." Finally he said he was glad she had forgotten to put a stamp on a letter to a man he knew, causing the post office to return the envelope to Chase. "I don't want to have you write anything to anybody of the Male Variety of the human Species," he told her.

Chase was desperate to head off any possibility of divorce, and the only party he had any influence over was Kate. Rather clumsily he alluded to questions Sprague had raised about her marital faithfulness. He told her in late April 1869 that he hoped it was not true what Nettie had written him—that Charles Leary, a wealthy socialite who summered in Newport, had been her houseguest in Aiken and had escorted her to a nearby city. Just that morning, Chase added, he had received an anonymous, libelous note from New York about Kate and Sprague that he immediately destroyed. He reminded her to "avoid all possibility of occasion for evil eyes and evil tongues."

Kate took great umbrage at her father's cautionary note, for which he apologized in his next letter, saying his warning had not been "in distrust."

But in the same letter Chase reminded Kate of a recent incident in which Sprague went into her bedroom in search of some missing papers. Sprague had found, inside Kate's trunk, a sealed package of letters to her from Colonel John Schuyler Crosby, a twenty-nine-year-old aide to General Phil Sheridan. Kate then entered Sprague's room while he was asleep to search his pockets for the letters so she could retrieve them. One wonders just what sort of marriage Chase thought he was trying to save.

In late October 1869, in Narragansett, twenty-nine-year-old Kate bore her second child, a daughter. Chase recorded her name as "Esbelle"—possibly from the French "tu es belle" ("you are beautiful") or a play on the name of his third wife ("S. Belle"). But the girl would always go by "Ethel." Was she Sprague's? Ethel most likely would have been conceived in January, not long after Kate's sorrowful diary entries. But there is no evidence that Ethel was some other man's child. Nothing more is known of the nature of Kate's relationship with Leary, although there is some indication she remained friends with Crosby for many years after. Crosby—a wealthy and aristocratic soldier, big-game hunter, and world traveler who consorted with the likes of Wild Bill Cody—was just the sort of larger-than-life figure who would have appealed to Kate. But he could not have been Ethel's father: he had been out West fighting Indians, with Sheridan and Custer, from at least early November 1868 until mid-March 1869.

Kate and Sprague, however, were together in January on a combination business/vacation trip that appears to have had, as one purpose, a restoration of affections between them. From at least January 18 to January 25 they were at a logging camp in the Maine woods near some sawmills Sprague owned. There, roughing it in the bush, they listened to backwoodsmen tell campfire stories of bear hunting while they feasted on trout caught by Sprague. Kate rode a sled out to see the felling of trees, and her colorful apparel scared a team of oxen so much that they became agitated and ran off snorting and tossing their heads. But she braved the rigors with great fortitude and found the cold, snowy atmosphere exhilarating. It may have been then and there that Ethel was conceived. Although Ethel did not look much like Kate, she did resemble Sprague. As no other clear candidate for her paternity has ever emerged, it is reasonable to assume she was Sprague's child.

Kate would always deny Sprague's accusations of infidelity and would later contend that he was the one who was unfaithful during this period and, indeed, throughout their marriage. His affair with Mary Viall may have been continuing around the time of his Senate speeches, and there is some indication that Sprague, self-confessedly "fond of the ladies," was looking for others. In May 1869 he fired a servant at the house at Sixth and E and replaced her with what Chase called "a very fine looking Englishwoman." With Kate gone, Chase asked his son-in-law whether it was not "a little risky to bring such a woman into the house while there are no other women here?" Kate later alleged that Sprague had an affair with this woman, "Harriet Brown, in the year 1869, at Washington."

Sprague's behavior by this time had become too much even for his housemate Salmon Chase. After Sprague brought the new servant woman into the house, Chase decided he could not live with him any longer. The two men, despite their wildly different personalities, had gotten along well enough over the years. But Chase no longer felt his son-in-law "loving me and trusting me." Sprague was reserved and uncommunicative and less cordial than before and had long since stopped treating Chase like a father figure. With the explanation that Nettie, now twenty-two, felt it was time to try her hand at running her father's household, Chase wrote Kate in Rhode Island on October 1, shortly before Ethel's birth, to say that he and Nettie were moving out of the mansion at Sixth and E and into a rented apartment near Eighteenth and I Streets in Washington. Soon afterward Chase also purchased a large brick house and fifty acres on the northeastern outskirts of the District of Columbia. Built high on a knoll overlooking the city, the Federal-style manor sat three miles from the Capitol building, with a panoramic view of its dome. The densely wooded, hilly property was reminiscent of the Clifton suburb of Cincinnati where Kate lived as a child and was near the camping ground where Kate visited Sprague's Rhode Island troops at the start of the war. The rundown farm estate, which Chase would refurbish and Kate would turn into another of her salons, was to be known as "Edgewood."

Chase would never again write to Kate to take sides with Sprague or give her marital advice. It had to have crushed him to realize that all his advice to her to "submit" had accomplished nothing. Salmon Chase would go to his grave knowing that his beloved daughter had not found happiness in her marriage.

As for Sprague, he had suffered much ridicule over his Senate speeches earlier in the year but had gained a new measure of respect in certain quarters. For all his incoherence, he had struck a chord with his harangue against nearly every powerful institution in the country, his attacks on the concentration of wealth, and his message of "power to the people." He received hundreds of admiring letters from across the country and read many of them into the congressional record. Even Chase, who told Nettie that "I don't exactly comprehend his views," acknowledged that Sprague's speeches in favor of the masses had done more for his reputation than anything else in his career. Chase also told Kate that all the attention paid to her husband's speeches ought to have made her happy, "for, if I am not mistaken, you have been always ambitious for him."

Much of what Sprague advocated was in his own self-interest—lower taxes and tariffs on manufacturers and easier credit and inflated currency to help business borrowers like himself. His proposals, the journalist Olivia scoffed, "can be summed up in exactly three words: 'Make more greenbacks.'" But his comments on the corruption of Gilded Age politicians were on target, and he would prove prophetic in warning that excessive debt, high interest rates, and financial speculation portended a national economic crisis. Several newspapers and commentators said his ideas, though oddly expressed, made a lot of sense. One Washington correspondent likened Sprague to "the inspired Cassandra, foretelling ruin and disaster." One of Sprague's proposals, to create a new Financial Council to regulate interest rates and the money supply, would come to fruition more than forty years later with the creation of the Federal Reserve. Sprague had a decent grasp of fundamental economic principles; his problem was a lack of focus, an inability to organize his thoughts and articulate them coherently and persuasively.

He did himself no favors with his outward appearance. A New York correspondent, upon paying a visit to the Sixth Street mansion one afternoon, found Sprague in his dressing gown, looking old beyond his years, his hair worn "somewhat long and with extreme carelessness as though the comb that nature provides in the fingers had been the only one he ever made use of." Yet the writer insisted that Sprague showed no "trace of the malady called craziness" and praised him for cultivating the inside of his head rather than lavishing attention on the outside. Sprague was also serenaded by several hundred members of the Working Men's Association of the District of Columbia, a self-styled labor union, who gathered by torchlight with a brass band in front of the house at Sixth and E. Sprague favored the crowd with a twenty-minute speech as the chief justice stood admiringly by his side. There was even talk of Sprague-for-President. Sprague had no desire to become a Democrat, he said, but neither did he feel bound to the Republicans, as he thought "both as parties are rotten." A Minnesota politician—ironically, a leader in the state's temperance movement—asked Sprague whether he was willing to form a new political party, whether "a Sprague Party or a Chase Party or a Chase Sprague Party." It was one campaign Kate had no interest in running, and the idea never went anywhere.

After the last of his formal Senate speeches, Sprague continued lashing out at some of his colleagues. He called two fellow Republicans "pukes" and one of them a "mutton head." He nearly provoked a duel with a Republican North Carolina senator by calling him a "mongrel puppy dog" controlled by the big "mastiff" guard dogs of the Senate, meaning the radical leadership. Only the intervention of Senators Sumner and John Sherman as mediators averted further confrontation. One senator urged that "Little Spraguey be spanked and put to bed." The incident earned Sprague a sharp rebuke from Kate, writing from South Carolina, which further angered him. But Kate's father thought the "dog and pup" story turned out well and had a good effect on Sprague, who promised to refrain from further name-calling. In fact his tongue was silenced thereafter, for Sprague made no more Senate speeches of any consequence.

After all the shouting was over, Sprague had lost all influence as a senator. He was now a man without a party, having destroyed his standing with the Republican leadership. More importantly, he had damaged his relations with the most powerful business, political, and newspaper interests in his native Rhode Island, and this would come back to haunt him in later years. In only the first year of his second six-year term, William Sprague was done with the Senate. As he soon learned, though, the Senate was not necessarily done with him.

CHAPTER 16

# Some Dared Call It Treason

With the rift in her marriage and two young children to raise, Kate spent less time in the Washington social scene of 1869–1870, prompting Mary Lincoln, writing from Europe, to inquire of a friend, "I do not see Mrs. Sprague's name among the gay notices of the winter. Is she in Washington—or South?" In the same letter Mrs. Lincoln, who always had a soft spot in her heart for the "boy governor" Sprague, referred to him as "truly kind-hearted."

Kate would have begged to differ. She was doing her best to avoid her husband—when he was in Rhode Island she was generally in Washington, and when both were in Rhode Island she would be at Canonchet and he would stay up at Providence. As her father noted in a letter to Nettie, written from Canonchet in October 1870, "the Governor, as long as Katie was absent, was very constant in his attendance, coming down every night" from Providence.

Chase was at Canonchet recuperating from a moderate stroke he had suffered that summer. It left him barely able to speak at first and his hand unable to write, requiring him to dictate all letters to a private secretary. The strain of Supreme Court work, exacerbated by Kate's marital woes, had taken its toll. A particularly acrimonious case was *Hepburn v. Griswold*, decided earlier that year, in which the court ruled that the Civil War legislation authorizing "greenbacks" as legal tender was unconstitutional.

Although Treasury Secretary Chase had strongly supported the measure, Chief Justice Chase, writing for a majority of the court, said the law was not justified by wartime necessity. It seemed like a total about-face, but in principle Chase had never liked the printing of paper money. Much to his consternation, a year later a court containing new Grant appointees overruled the *Hepburn* decision.

Back in Washington after his convalescence (which Kate called a "most laborious and trying" time for her), Chase lived, as his secretary Eugene Didier recalled, "a solitary existence, passed in his library or in the Supreme Court, paying few visits, and receiving few visitors." Conversation at the dinner table was "of a very quiet character," with Nettie taking the lead. "The Chief Justice was a great thinker, but not a great talker," Didier remembered. "Unlike Falstaff, he was neither witty himself, nor the cause of wit in other men; like Poe, he never laughed, and seldom smiled; a joke was foreign to his nature. . . . He seemed oppressed by the burden of life, or crushed by disappointed ambition." Once or twice during the Washington season he would give dinner parties, always solemn affairs, "too dignified for laughter, and not pathetic enough for tears."

Nettie, once described by her boarding school headmistresses as lacking discipline—full of talent and intelligence but erratic and needing to better apply herself—had come into her own as a charming and accomplished young woman and hostess. The still-single John Hay, who from time to time Kate and Nettie tried to set up with other women, thought Nettie had "more art and culture than the *ainée*," or older Chase daughter. Society columnist "Miss Grundy," who had long admired Kate, wrote in 1870 that Nettie was "more universally liked than is her more haughty sister." Miss Grundy and others were also impressed with Nettie's recently released book of Mother Goose rhyme illustrations. A few years later Nettie published another children's picture book, *Janet et ses Amis* ("Janet and her Friends"), written entirely in French.

In late 1870 twenty-three-year-old Nettie, who at age sixteen had foreseen for herself a future of "old maidism and forty cats," was engaged to be married to William Sprague Hoyt, a younger cousin of William Sprague one generation removed. John Hay, who would serve as a groomsman for Hoyt, gave one of his characteristically sardonic remarks about the affianced couple. Nettie was "a very nice girl and no end of talent," whereas

Hoyt was "a very nice fellow—and no end of cash." Will Hoyt was the son of a wealthy New York merchant whose dry goods business, Hoyt, Spragues & Co., was the principal commission agent for selling the printed textiles of A. & W. Sprague Manufacturing Co., the firm run by Kate's husband. Nettie and Will Hoyt would have four children, including an eminent New York jurist and a championship woman golfer, but their marriage and finances would crumble when Will Hoyt turned out to possess many of the same demons as his older cousin.

That was many years off, though. In late 1870 Nettie and Will were happily engaged, in contrast to Kate and her husband, who remained at odds with each other. Then Sprague ran into even more trouble. Thomas Jenckes, a Rhode Island congressman running for reelection, dropped a bombshell at a campaign rally in Providence: William Sprague, the valiant warrior of Bull Run, was, it turns out, a traitor. "In the darkest days of the war," Jenckes charged, Sprague had "violated the Articles of War of the United States in holding commerce with the enemy, and aiding them with money and munitions of war." He was referring to what would become known as the "Texas Adventure."

Jenckes's motives were open to challenge: a political enemy of Sprague, he was running for office against one of Sprague's friends. But his information appeared solid. He read to his audience from a military investigative report provided in late March 1865 to then secretary of war Edwin Stanton describing Sprague's alleged involvement in an illegal plot to smuggle arms and other supplies into rebel Texas in exchange for cotton. Stanton, since deceased, had never acted on the report.

Sprague had been called many things before, but no one had questioned his patriotism. He now had to answer these explosive charges himself. He denied their truth, denounced their biased source, and called for an investigation to clear his name. A Senate select committee was formed to look into the matter. But what did it all have to do with Salmon Chase or his daughter Kate? It turns out there were connections aplenty.

* * *

The question of what to do about Southern cotton during the war had never been a clear one for the North. New England still needed cotton, and the livelihood of many Union loyalists in the Southern and Border States depended on trade with their Confederate neighbors. Northern military leaders, such as Grant and Sherman, advocated a strict prohibition on all rebel trade. As president, Lincoln was inclined to be more liberal in allowing trade with the enemy, believing it more important to supply cotton to Northern industry than to deny arms and munitions to the South—arms the South was obtaining anyway by running the Union blockade. Chase, whose Treasury Department was responsible for issuing trading permits with the South, tended toward Lincoln's view and favored restrictions as moderate as possible.

William Sprague was especially interested in securing trading privileges. When Secretary Chase liberalized the Treasury Department policy to allow private parties to get cotton out of military-occupied districts by posting bonds as security, Sprague (reflecting the anti-Semitism common at the time) asked him whether permits would be "given to *anyone* who furnishes proper bondage thus letting in the *Jews* and Gentiles in the general rush?" Like Chase, Sprague was all in favor of a more lenient permit policy, but he was not anxious to have any competition.

Chase was constantly besieged by requests for privileges and exemptions, most of which, under a confusing welter of regulations, he felt compelled to deny. But his treasury agents often accepted bribes, both to enrich themselves and to advance Chase's campaign to challenge Lincoln for reelection. Although Chase did little to probe the irregularities, he did not personally profit from them. Thus, he was livid when, in 1864, Frank Blair Jr., son of the Maryland patriarch, launched a vicious attack on Chase from the floor of Congress, accusing him of corruption in the Treasury Department and, specifically, of granting illegal cotton trading permits to his son-in-law. The attack had the effect of uniting Chase, Sprague, and Kate in their outrage. In a speech Chase edited for him, Sprague took to the Senate floor to defend his father-in-law against the charges, adding that he, Sprague, had neither asked for nor received any special privileges from Secretary Chase to buy cotton. That he had received none was true; that he had sought none, as both Chase and Sprague knew, was false.

On October 14, 1862, while he was still seeing Kate, Sprague wrote the treasury secretary to introduce one Harris Hoyt (no relation to Nettie's fiancé) as "a union man of Texas" with a plan. As explained by Sprague, Hoyt proposed to go to rebel Texas in a boat loaded with "a few goods" that he would exchange with his Union friends for cotton. Sprague reminded Secretary Chase of the importance of getting cotton out of the South and asked for his help in securing the necessary clearance.

A shadowy figure and smooth-talking con man, Harris Hoyt was at best a sort of double agent with ties to both unionists and rebels and, at worst, a secret Confederate sympathizer. But he was no dummy. He knew that Salmon Chase was someone who could get him a trading permit, he knew who Chase's oldest daughter was, and he knew that her beau, William Sprague, who presumably had influence with the treasury secretary, both needed cotton and had the money to pay for it.

But Chase declined to issue a permit. Coincidentally or not, this was around the same time Kate and Sprague had broken off relations, during the period of James Garfield's stay at the Chase home in Washington in the fall of 1862. Undeterred, Hoyt and his co-adventurers, largely financed with Sprague's money, decided they would run the Union blockade. They smuggled some cargo—including guns and ammunition—into Texas, and emerged with several hundred bales of cotton. In November 1864, however, the Union blockade captured one of their schooners while it was on its way to New York with cotton. Hoyt and several others were arrested, including Sprague's cousin Byron, and it looked as if Senator Sprague might be next.

But Sprague was never charged. Hoyt was given immunity in exchange for a confidential statement that implicated Sprague, but the statement mysteriously disappeared from the file. The charges against the others were dropped for lack of evidence. A military report concluded that Hoyt lacked credibility and that Sprague was a victim of "mistaken information" and "unjust suspicion." The Senate special committee, finding "nothing in the papers implicating Senator Sprague," closed its book on the matter in March 1871. Sprague was in the clear.

Sprague had to suspect that the Texas Adventure was not entirely clean. He certainly knew that trading without a permit was against the rules of war. But he kept himself far enough removed from the day-to-day operations that he was able to maintain plausible deniability on the more serious charge of treason.

What Sprague may have discussed privately with Kate or her father about the matter is unrecorded. In a highly fictionalized scene in Gore Vidal's novel *Lincoln* and in the television miniseries of the same title, Kate explodes in rage when she learns of Sprague's involvement in the venture and tells him he deserves to be hanged. But in reality it was in neither Kate's nor Chase's interests to have Sprague convicted of treason. Chief Justice Chase, who valued his reputation for integrity, had no desire to return public focus to the issue of cotton permits and the corruption that existed in the Treasury Department during his tenure. Despite Kate's estrangement from Sprague, no woman would want to be known as the wife of a traitor or to have him branded one for posterity in the eyes of his children. Her husband could do her no good financially sitting in a jail. Kate and her father also may have felt conflicted, for it was Southern cotton that fed the business that paid for Kate's expensive lifestyle and helped fund her father's presidential runs. No, Salmon Chase and his oldest daughter would have nothing to say on the question of the Texas Adventure and the doings of Harris Hoyt. They turned their attention, instead, to happier thoughts, like the upcoming wedding of Nettie to a different Mr. Hoyt.

CHAPTER 17

# End of an Era

Kate was determined that her younger sister would have her moment to shine. Their relationship had always been a warm if not extremely close one—not surprising for half-sisters seven years apart, in which the older one was considered the more beautiful and enchanting and the younger one plainer, if sweeter and more playful. From an early age Nettie looked up to Kate and praised her—telling Kate that her *carte de visite* photograph did not do her justice, while lamenting that she, Nettie, was told she looked like her "noble" father. Her sole parent being that busy, important man, Nettie turned to Kate for advice and permission on various matters—to take gymnastics, to invite visitors to her boarding school—and Kate played the surrogate mother, telling her, as Chase had so often told Kate, that her spelling needed to be made "perfect." Nettie would feel hurt and distressed when Kate admonished her for bad behavior, and their father would intervene, talking with Nettie "quietly and affectionately" while advising Kate to "be *very* kind to her and very considerate for her. Let your *thought* supply her thoughtlessness." But if Kate felt put upon in the role of the good mother, she never said so. Likewise, if Nettie, having observed Kate spending freely on clothing, resented the fact that her father gave Kate control over her younger sister's allowance ("Katie thinks $300 a year will suffice for Nettie's clothing," Chase told Nettie's boarding school proprietress), then Nettie didn't make her feelings known either.

Just as Kate saw no need to enter into a popularity contest with her sister, Nettie never tried to compete with Kate in areas in which it would have been futile: political hostessing, fine jewelry and gowns, interior decorating. Kate was still at a point in her life when public appearance and recognition were important, as evidenced by the ostentation and conspicuous consumption on display at Canonchet. Nettie, by contrast, channeled her creative impulses into the quieter endeavors of sketching and drawing. But like any bride-to-be, she looked forward to at least one big public splash in her life.

And so although Kate's wedding, the social event of the war era, could hardly be surpassed, she generously took over planning an extravaganza for Nettie, hosting several bridal parties and making all the arrangements for the wedding. Sprague footed the bill for the reception at the house on Sixth and E, even though he had no official role in the wedding and disappeared into the background.

The whole affair came off brilliantly, as would any social event Kate choreographed, but not without ruffling some feathers. Kate had been married in her home, but Nettie was more overtly religious and chose to hold the ceremony in her regular place of worship, St. John's Episcopal Church on Lafayette Square in Washington, across from the White House—the "Church of the Presidents." The wedding was set for March 23, 1871, prompting the local Episcopal rector to object because it was during Lent, in violation of High Church doctrine. He agreed to let the event go forward on the selected date only after Chase secured an Ohio Low Church bishop—Charles McIlvaine, who had married Chase and his third wife—to officiate. But the St. John's rector ended up feeling sandbagged by certain "objectionable features of the ceremony," which he found out about too late to stop, that he said were "entirely attributable to the selfishness of the Chases." They "abused my generosity in the most inexcusable way," he told the Episcopal bishop of Maryland, whose jurisdiction the church fell under.

The reception, which the family controlled, drew nothing but accolades. The several hundred guests included the president (now, Ulysses Grant), cabinet and Supreme Court members, senators and foreign dignitaries, as well as ladies fashionably attired in their Easter bonnets. The Marine Band, which played at Kate's reception, entertained here as well.

Nettie, no doubt under the guiding eye of Kate, shone in a filmy white gown, adorned with natural orange blossoms. But it was inevitable that Kate drew the most attention. In her green silk dress and pink silk train, point lace overdress and shawl, reported gossip columnist Miss Grundy, Kate looked "if possible, more regal and more graceful than ever."

The proud father, haggard and shrunken from his illness, summoned the energy to give Nettie away and stand behind her, alongside Kate, during the ceremony. But he had not recovered from the shocking snub his son-in-law directed at him (and, by extension, Kate) the previous month. Faced with a proposal to raise the salaries of the chief justice and associate justices of the Supreme Court to a more livable wage, Senator Sprague cast the deciding vote against it. "Why would he not help us in this emergency?" asked Richard Parsons, now the Supreme Court marshal, in a letter to Chase. If Sprague had merely absented himself the day of the vote or abstained, the measure would have passed.

Sprague's shabby treatment of a father-in-law who had defended him against the indefensible for so many years revealed the depths to which his marriage to Kate had descended. Still, the couple kept up appearances in public, showing up together one night that August, at ten o'clock, for the gala opening of Narragansett's Tower Hill House, an elegant new hotel outside town.

That same summer of 1871 Chase's quest for health took him to the mineral springs of Michigan and Wisconsin. Kate wrote him from Narragansett in late August, first to say how pleased she was that Nettie had remembered her thirty-first birthday earlier that month. "I fear I am a good deal of a child about such things yet," she admitted. She also reported on her young children: Ethel, nearly two, was now talking ("I want Grandpa Chase to pum, (read come)—I hurrah for Bubnor Sprague, and I hurrah for Chase") and had several Mother Goose melodies and popular songs down pat. Six-year-old Willie was prizing a miniature French machine gun given him by Nettie and, following in his father's military footsteps, had it cocked and ready to fire each morning as Kate woke up. But as usual, Kate's thoughts turned to politics. She enclosed a *New York Herald* article "advocating a Mutual friend of ours for the next Presidency." She added that "if you meet him in your travels, advise him . . . to devote all his energies for a while to getting quite well, that he may yet live a long while to gladden the hearts of his children and if need be serve his

Country." Difficult as it may have been to believe, in light of the fiasco of 1868, she was urging him to start thinking about the 1872 presidential contest.

Just as surprising in some ways was the birth, in early February 1872, of Kate's third child, a girl she named Katherine and called Kitty, the nickname borne by Chase's beloved first wife. Unlike Ethel, Kitty inherited her mother's beauty. Unfortunately she was tubercular and, it became clear with time, had a mental disability that left her forever childlike. In an era in which developmentally challenged children were often hidden away, Kitty was never photographed alone (she was captured once or twice, from a distance, with others).

That Kate still harbored presidential hopes for her father became clear in April 1872, when she hosted a reception for him at the Sixth Street townhouse, the purpose being to convince eminent politicians and opinion makers that he was physically up to another run for office. It was an elaborately catered and decorative affair, with refreshments served outside under a pavilion on a warm spring night. Chase stood next to Kate in a receiving line, greeting the various guests, trying hard not to slur his speech or reveal his trembling hands. Kate made sure the guests were told that the chief justice, per his custom, had walked in from Edgewood, more than two miles out of town. Some people were fooled by the pretense, but most were not. Carl Schurz, their old family friend, shook his head at Chase's "futile efforts to appear youthfully vigorous and agile," which he found "pathetically evident." Still, Chase clung to his same old line: he would not actively seek the presidency and did not even want a nomination, but he would accept one if the country concluded that his duty demanded it. No doubt he hoped to receive that summons.

But no groundswell for him emerged in 1872. Instead, another aging giant, Chase's old ally Horace Greeley, was nominated by the Liberal Republicans, a hodgepodge of intellectuals, journalists, free traders, and self-described reformers who had bolted from the regular Republican Party, united by their disillusionment with what they regarded as the corrupt Grant administration. William Sprague, recognizing there was still advantage to him if his father-in-law became president, poured money into the effort to secure the Liberal Party nomination for Chase and sent some of his friends and workers to the convention in Cincinnati to assist in that cause. But neither Sprague's money nor the hometown advantage was enough to make a difference, and the Liberals nominated Greeley. Chase entertained some hope that the Democrats would turn to him, but they nominated Greeley as well, ending Chase's two-decades-long quest for the presidency.

Some have argued that Chase was not distinctively ambitious for his era, but the assessments by Chase's contemporaries belie that assertion. Not only his rival Lincoln but also his close friends and supporters, from Henry Ward Beecher to Jay Cooke to Carl Schurz, commented on his maniacal desire for the presidency. Schurz said Chase "continued to nurse that one ambition so that it became the curse of his life to his last day. It sometimes painfully distorted his judgment of things and men" and made him "depreciate all the honors and powers bestowed upon him." No other politician of his era switched parties so frequently or ran for president as often as Chase did—four times actively, in each election from 1856 to 1868, and at least tacitly in 1872. No other chief justice of the Supreme Court sought the presidency, as Chase did twice, while sitting on the bench. Although it is arguable that Chase's ambition was mostly in service of principles he strongly believed in, his contemporaries were not wrong to view him as someone who uniquely hungered for the nation's highest office.

Kate wanted that prize for him as well, and there were those, like Chase's friend Roeliff Brinkerhoff, who thought his infatuation with the idea "arose more from a desire to gratify the ambition of his daughter rather than his own." Had Chase been elected president, Kate would have become not only the First Lady but also, effectively, the nation's first female White House chief of staff. Another contemporary source asserted that it was "her, not so much his, wild ambition" to make Chase president. But to ask whether Kate lit her father's burning fires of ambition or whether it was the other way around posits a false choice. The reality is that both Kate and her father craved a Chase presidency, not only for themselves but also for each other.

In 1872, as in 1868, the man who bested Chase for the nomination proved to be a weak general election candidate. Horace Greeley had become merely eccentric in his old age, and an advocate of such unorthodox causes as vegetarianism, spiritualism, and human manure scientific farming. The one-time abolitionist now decried African Americans as "an easy, worthless race, taking no thought for the morrow" and supported a return to white rule in the South. Ostensibly a supporter of women's rights, Greeley opposed giving women the vote. Regular Republicans could see that Grant was the greater proponent of equal rights and protections for the black man, and Grant's platform was more woman-friendly than Greeley's. But like many of Greeley's longtime friends, such as Sumner, Schurz, and Whitelaw Reid, Kate and her father had a blind spot when it came to Grant, who, in their view, lacked any redeeming qualities as president.

To Kate, Greeley's policy views mattered less than his close personal connection to the family. And so, when her father was passed over for president, she joined him in supporting Greeley. In an illustration in Frank Leslie's popular newspaper from April 1872, she can be seen at the head of the dining table at Canonchet, entertaining lavishly, as always, and talking animatedly with Horace Greeley seated next to her. But it was a hopeless cause; Greeley lost the election that November to Grant in a landslide. Three weeks after the vote, Greeley died, before the Electoral College even met. Chase was one of the pallbearers at his funeral.

Not long after Greeley's death Chase's own health began to further deteriorate. Toward the close of the Supreme Court term, in March and April 1873, he became noticeably weaker. On the last day the court was in session he gave his place as presiding justice to a colleague and sat the whole day, resting his head on his hand. On May 3 he left Washington for New York City to visit Nettie, after which he planned to see Kate in Rhode Island and relatives in Boston before traveling to Colorado to spend part of the summer. On the evening of May 6, at the home of Nettie and Will Hoyt on West Thirty-Third Street, he suffered a massive stroke and was discovered unconscious in bed the next morning. Kate and William Sprague rushed to be at his side, joining Nettie, her husband, and Chase's friend Hiram Barney.

On the morning of May 7, 1873, surrounded by his family, Salmon Chase died at the age of sixty-five. His funeral service in Washington was attended by President Grant, James Garfield, Roscoe Conkling, and numerous other dignitaries. The pallbearers included not only his old friend General Irvin McDowell but also Lincoln's conservative cabinet member Montgomery Blair, a one-time adversary. Chase's body lay in state in the Supreme Court room in the Capitol, on the same catafalque that had been used for Abraham Lincoln's funeral eight years earlier.

Chase was extolled at his funeral as well as in other memorials in later years as a great American. Which he was. As treasury secretary during the great sectional conflict, he stood together with Hamilton, one eulogist said, as one of the two "great financiers in our history." His guidance of the Supreme Court through the difficult Reconstruction years was steady and wise. But his greatest legacy was as a man who did more than any other statesman of his time, excepting only Lincoln, to bring about the emancipation of the slaves and an end to the great original stain upon the nation's character. He enlisted in the antislavery movement when it was unpopular, predicting that one day multitudes would "join the advancing host of Liberty." As much as anyone, Salmon Chase led that advancing host.

He was, perhaps, to the modern mind, not a great father. Although he dearly loved his two daughters, he constantly reproached them, particularly Kate, and seemed clueless about the basis for her marital despair. Yet rarely did Kate herself utter so much as a single negative word about her father. She started a biography of him once (although she abandoned the project), and undoubtedly it would have been entirely positive. Indeed, when competing biographers were vying to complete the first book about the late chief justice, she chose to cooperate only with the one—Chase's one-time secretary Jacob Schuckers—she knew would produce an unblemished portrait of his subject. No, Kate would never criticize her father, for she was too much like him. To tarnish him would have been to diminish herself.

She spent the rest of her life doing her best to preserve and extend her father's legacy and reputation. She would live to see his statue placed on the lawn of the Ohio Statehouse in Columbus and a marble bust of him, by sculptor Thomas Jones, grace the old Supreme Court chamber in the Capitol. Four years after his death she saw a new bank (with which he had no affiliation) named in his honor; it eventually became the Chase Manhattan Bank, for years the world's largest. She was not around, however, to see his face make the ten thousand dollar bill, the largest denomination of US currency ever in general circulation.

There would be times when she dwelt on the past. Three years after her father's death, writing from Edgewood to John Nicolay, she confessed to feeling the "distress of returning to this house so full of memories of my dear father." Some have said all meaning for her dissolved with her father's passing. Journalist Donn Piatt, Chase's longtime friend, went so far as to claim that "she seemed to die in his death." But clearly she did not view it that way. She was lonelier now and, at times, would be lonelier still. Yet in one sense the death of her father and the figurative death of her marriage liberated her to become her own person in a way she had never been and to begin living her life on her own terms.

Those terms would change, however, not long after her father died, and not for the better, when the financial comforts to which she was so accustomed suddenly were put at risk.

CHAPTER 18

# End of an Empire

With the income generated by the world's greatest textile empire, there was nothing Kate could not afford to buy. Her wardrobe included an $18,000 French silk dress she ordered from Paris not long after Nettie's wedding. She thought nothing of contributing a thousand-dollar floral ornament to Grant's second inaugural ball in March 1873. When the Episcopal parish of Narragansett sought money to build a church, to be known as St. Peter's by-the-Sea, Kate issued a blank check to cover any deficit in the construction budget. At the theater she always sat in the premium boxes. Even if her husband admonished her for her extravagance, her mother-in-law encouraged it, reportedly placing $250,000 in the bank for each of Kate's children when they were born, with $50,000 for Kate herself. Few women in America were better off financially than Kate Chase.

And then suddenly, on "Black Thursday" in September 1873, it all came crashing down. At that time Jay Cooke, the man who had spearheaded Treasury Secretary Chase's effort to finance the Civil War, was running the most powerful bank in the country, due to expansive postwar investment in railroads. On the morning of September 18, 1873, he was entertaining President Grant at his Ogontz estate just outside Philadelphia, where Kate, Nettie, and their father had often stayed. When he sat down to breakfast with the cigar-chomping president, Cooke could boast of a financial institution more trusted than the Bank of England itself. But by eleven that morning, as he was driving Grant to the train station, Cooke's bank had gone bust. The speculative railroad bubble burst, and Cooke's firm was driven into bankruptcy overnight. Tears ran down his cheeks when he learned that his New York office had closed its doors, followed quickly by the Philadelphia and Washington branches. It was a classic run on the banks, with the failure of Cooke's empire setting off a chain reaction throughout the financial world. The Panic of 1873, which turned into one of the worst economic depressions in US history, was on. Stocks plummeted, numerous businesses failed, and hundreds of thousands were thrown out of work and into poverty.

Among the casualties was William Sprague's company, A. & W. Sprague Manufacturing. By October 30 its imminent collapse was being predicted, after it was announced that the closely connected Hoyt, Spragues & Co. (the commission firm run by Nettie's side of the family), had gone belly up. Unlike the Hoyt firm, which was clearly under water, A. & W. Sprague's problem was not its book value; it was never bankrupt in the classic sense, as its assets always exceeded its liabilities by several million dollars. Rather, it was technically insolvent because, with the downturn in business and, unable to borrow money, it could not pay its debts as they became due. Virtually a conglomerate as a result of William Sprague's acquisitiveness, the company had twelve thousand employee mouths to feed and was severely overextended, with investments in timber and sawmills, manufacturing equipment, railway and steamship lines, myriad real estate holdings, and even the infant oil industry. But the underlying business had considerable value. The real problem was that the banks had cut off Sprague's credit.

Both overspeculation and tight government fiscal policies had caused the national economic crash: the nation's business and population had expanded, but the supply of money had not kept pace. Ironically, Sprague had warned against all of this in his 1869 Senate speeches, but in continuing to extend himself, he failed to heed his own advice or plan accordingly. Nor did he receive any credit, even figuratively speaking, for having predicted the whole thing four years earlier. Wall Street money lenders remembered his populist attacks on them and were not inclined to do him any favors. He was also largely friendless in Rhode Island, having burned his bridges with the state's politicians, businessmen, and largest newspaper, the *Providence Journal*. But Sprague the businessman was too valuable to the state's workers and economy for the money men to let him cease operations. Creditors were unwilling to keep him in place as before; they had heard the stories of his (and his wife's) spending, and they could see with their own eyes the extravagance on display at Canonchet. To keep Sprague afloat, however, the banks agreed to place his company in a trusteeship and installed Zechariah Chafee, a financial man of great intelligence but no experience in the textile business, to run the company's affairs. Under the terms of the trust, Sprague mortgaged away almost all his property and gave promissory notes to his creditors at 7.3 percent interest to be repaid in three years, when it was assumed (wrongly, as it turned out) the depression would be over. Because the creditors had lost confidence in Sprague, he stepped down as president, and his brother Amasa, though no businessman, was installed as a temporary replacement. William Sprague became essentially an employee of Chafee on salary, part of which was to go to Kate as an allowance for her and her children, now including Portia, her last child, born just as Sprague's business collapsed.* The good times were over.

So were the friendly family relations between the Spragues and Hoyts. Within a year of the crash Will Hoyt, Nettie's husband, and Charles Francklyn (who had married Will Hoyt's sister Susie) filed suits against various members of the Sprague family, including William, his brother, Amasa, his mother, Fanny, and Mary Sprague, widow of William Sprague III, the "Old Governor." The Hoyts alleged they had been defrauded many years earlier when, before they had reached the age of maturity, the Spragues had conspired to deny them the full benefits of the family textile business. Besides having been brought almost ten years too late, the suits were dubious on the merits. They depended on the claim that Mary Sprague—Will and Susie Hoyt's own grandmother and their guardian

---

*When listing her children, Kate sometimes named Kitty last, creating the impression that she was the youngest. Indeed, most prior biographers have incorrectly cited Kitty as Kate's third daughter and last child, when in fact Kitty was the third child, and Portia, born in November 1873, Kate's fourth and final child. Portia was named in honor of her late grandfather, in a variation on his middle name, Portland. Of all three daughters, Portia most combined the looks of both her mother and her father.

for inheritance matters—should have cashed them out of their beneficial share of the Sprague partnership, either after Mary's husband, William III (Sprague's uncle), died in 1856 or in 1865, when the partnership was converted to a corporation. Instead, not unreasonably and certainly not fraudulently, Mary reinvested everything, including her own money, in the still-thriving business that no one ever expected to fail. The lawsuits were a long shot, but the Hoyts continued to pursue their claims for more than a decade, all the way to the US Supreme Court, losing at every stage. The effect was to create a permanent rift between the two families and the two Chase half-sisters, Nettie and Kate, who rarely spoke to each other afterward.

The strain became worse when Kate and Nettie, cobeneficiaries under their father's will, disagreed over what to do with Edgewood. Kate wanted to keep her father's beloved estate and continue living there; Nettie, valuing cash in hand over nostalgia, wanted it sold and the proceeds split. After some acrimonious exchanges and a fallen-through deal, Kate ended up paying Nettie $16,000 (plus interest) to buy her out of her share of the property. The Hoyts insisted, however, that the furniture and other items be sold. And so Salmon Chase's personal possessions were put up for auction, except for certain sentimental pieces Kate retained. The spectacle of curiosity seekers tramping through Edgewood's library, bedrooms, and parlors was more than the absent Kate could bear to watch.

She had gone to Europe again to get away from it all. There she could also educate her children for less than it would cost in the United States. As she explained to a banking adviser, her "little people like so many Locusts" had eaten up her subsistence, forcing her to overstep her allowance. She also thought stern German tutelage would be good for nine-year-old Willie, who showed a tendency toward unruly behavior and slovenly appearance. She did not want him to turn into his father.

Sprague was at a low point in his life, depressed over the diminishing prospects of a business that, more than politics or military dabbling, was the source of his self-esteem. He took no part and showed no interest in the business being run by the trustee Chafee, who, as time wore on, came to observe such eccentric speech and conduct by Sprague that he thought him "of unbalanced intellect, and unfit for the management of any business." By contrast, the press saw Kate as bearing her altered fortunes "with the strength of intellect" and as one of those women who seemed "created on purpose to diminish their husbands"—not so much by superior achievement as by force of personality. In the public mind Sprague could never live up to the reputation of his celebrated wife.

In his last days in the Senate, which he left in March 1875, Sprague was a lonely figure. In December 1874, defying the wishes of President Grant, he was the sole Republican to vote against the "Resumption Act," which returned the country to the gold standard and sought to remove greenbacks from circulation by providing for their redemption by the government in coin. After that vote he withdrew from the Republican caucus, bitterly accusing it of being under the control of the money power, but he would not join the Democrats either, as the same power, he said, dominated both parties.

Although three thousand miles away, Kate continued to stand by her husband and champion his cause. From Europe she wrote a remarkable series of letters to various third parties extolling the virtues, talents, and integrity of one William Sprague. In January 1875, in the course of a letter to General William Tecumseh Sherman touching on Reconstruction politics, she called her husband "a brave, independent, public spirited, deep thinking man" whose ideas for restoring the nation's financial health were at least "worthy of a hearing." Her husband, she said, took "a very comprehensive view of the situation," and no man was more familiar than he "through *actual* knowledge and experience (dearly bought) with the crushing incubus under which the Industrial Masses of our American people, are at present staggering." To her husband's brother Amasa, Kate described William Sprague as a man with "a rare fund of strength and wisdom" and urged Amasa to work with him to try to rebuild the business.

As for herself, Kate wrote Amasa, she was sacrificing by living alone with her children in a strange land, contributing cheerfully to the effort and "hoping to relieve my husband of care and expense, that he may have his mind and time for his work." She also wrote Will Hoyt, Nettie's husband, to try to persuade him to drop his futile, costly lawsuit, saying that instead of litigating to place his own interests ahead of the hordes of creditors, he should join forces with her husband to keep them at bay. Sprague was "peculiar and difficult to approach," she admitted to her brother-in-law, "but he is honest and he is capable. Trust him instead of suspecting him . . . your only hope lies in him."

Kate's *coup de grace* was a letter to her husband, written in December 1875 from her modest little apartment at 18, Rue Duphot in Paris near the Madeleine Church. In her letter she tried to lift her husband's spirits at a critical moment, as it then appeared that trustee Chafee would have difficulty making the January interest payment to creditors. "Why is this not the *golden moment* for *you* to seize the dilemma by the horns, and strike your blow?" she asked. "How does a program like this strike you: *You* to call in advance of a crisis (foreseeing it, and showing the moral courage to proclaim it, which few men would have) a meeting of your Creditors. . . . Offer to assume the *entire* management of the Interests of the A. & W. Sprague Manufacg. Co. with the full co-operation of the Hoyt faction, if it can be obtained. . . . Rest assured that the Hoyts are taking advantage of and misconceive your apathy, and that your Creditors will do the same unless you anticipate them." If he would do this—if he would get himself up off the canvas to fight—she would "go home at once to help you bear it with heart and soul. . . . You may make me General Inspector of the Factories, or the head of a Corps to gather up the waste, and fragments that nothing be lost, everything to be of use. . . . Faithfully always your wife."

What was going on here? William Sprague—"brave," "deep thinking," a "rare fund of strength and wisdom?" Did she mean it, or was it just a matter of self-interest, a desperate attempt to regain financial comfort and security? And, most perplexing of all, was she in fact hoping for yet another marital reconciliation? Had absence again made her heart grow fonder?

The answer, it seems, is that for all of Sprague's faults, Kate saw through to an inner soul she considered good and decent as well as a vulnerability behind the unseemly outbursts that made him attractive to her. When his mind was not clouded by drink or when it was in a state of equilibrium between the extremes of depression and euphoria, he was an agreeable fellow. Never mind that such moments might be rare. Then, too, Sprague appeared more tolerable to Kate when he was an ocean away, and the couple had no opportunity to act out their anger with one another. Of course there was self-interest in her letters, and the intoxicating effect of untold wealth, now withheld from her, influenced her efforts. But her genuine feelings for a man she had once "almost worshipped" were not entirely extinguished. As for the women he dallied with, maybe the domestic servants had resisted his advances before quitting or being fired. And hopefully the long-running affair with Mary Viall was long over.

But it was not, as became apparent in 1876, with the release of Viall's self-published book, *The Merchant's Wife, or, He Blundered: A Political Romance of Our Own Day and Other Miscellanies*. The merchant, of course, was Sprague, compared by the author to Napoleon, "with the same eccentricity of manner and of dress: that belief in a destiny: that antagonism for the lawyers." Alluding to his estrangement from the Senate, Viall wrote that "no more than would the Commons listen to Disraeli, would the Republican Peers listen to him." His eyes were now "great fires burned out, never to be rekindled," a result of "that more unfortunate blunder of his life"—marrying the beautiful "statesman's daughter," whose only real love was for her father and whose only goal, the author maintained, was to make him president and herself First Lady. "The expression of the fair, chiseled face does not change," Mary Viall said of her rival, "*fine*, half smiling, somewhat calculating." It was clear that Viall had seen Kate up close, and the details of the author's descriptions of the interior of the fictionalized Canonchet—the domed octagonal room, the Venetian mirror, the "malachite clock in the form of a pelican"—made plain that she had been a guest there more than once. She had also seen his daughters "Elsie and Pauline" (Ethel and Portia): "Pauline resembles Mamma even more than Elsie; in whom he used to fancy to discover traces of himself."

The writer still loved her businessman-turned-senator, lamenting that she was "willing never to have been his wife, *but to give him up to another*—she had not dreamed of that." Still, would not "true love sacrifice itself for the beloved?" she asked, then quickly answered: "*She* forgave him." She was also confident he still loved her. "Can you understand that a man may love a woman too well to marry her?" she asked. She knew they would be "reunited one day."

Mary Viall saw in Sprague some of the finer qualities that Kate also did, but that could not have lessened the humiliation Kate felt over the publication of this barely disguised autobiography. And when her husband ignored her offer to come home to help him take up cudgels against the world, Kate stayed in Europe, not returning until October 1876, in the middle of a presidential election. Obviously Sprague was still attached to his not-so-secret admirer. But Kate now had her own admirer, and she would soon attach herself to him.

CHAPTER 19

# "Intended by Their Creator for Each Other"

If her husband could engage in multiple, serial infidelities, then surely Kate was entitled to at least one affair of her own. With her revered father dead and herself stuck in a loveless marriage, Kate had felt a need for a new, great man in her life. She found him in New York senator Roscoe Conkling, a man who, ironically, turned down President's Grant's offer to succeed her father as chief justice after his death in 1873. With the exception of her father and Sprague, Roscoe Conkling was to be the most influential man in Kate's life.

"Lord Roscoe" was the undisputed political boss of the Republican Party in New York and head of that state's well-oiled patronage machine. A close affiliate of Ulysses Grant, Conkling was the most powerful man in the Senate and among the most controversial politicians of the post–Civil War era. He was vain and arrogant, and he never forgot nor forgave an enemy. He was also, for the better part of a decade, Kate's lover.

Conkling and Kate had much in common. Son of a prominent upstate New York federal judge, Conkling, like Kate, grew up in a political atmosphere, in a home visited by some of the foremost figures of the day, such as John Quincy Adams, Martin Van Buren, and William Seward. Like Kate, he received private schooling in New York City as a teenager. After passing up a university education to read for the law, he studied literature and was fond of quoting Byron and Shakespeare. He was Episcopalian, the faith in which Kate was raised, but, like Kate, he was not especially religious.

If similar to Kate, Conkling was almost the opposite of William Sprague. Where Sprague was short and stooped, Conkling was around six feet three and stood ramrod straight. Sprague's dark, drooping mustache and features gave him a haggard look, whereas the sandy-haired Conkling was an Apollo-like figure, with broad shoulders, a tight waist, and muscular chest. In an era when most men paid little attention to their physiques, he was a fitness freak, adopting a regimen of vigorous exercise, especially boxing. To women, he exuded sexuality, and more than one male colleague called him among the handsomest men of his time.

His most distinctive physical feature was a golden corkscrew forelock that came to a curl on his broad forehead, above his flashing eyes and pointed beard. But he was even better known for his flamboyant attire. Sprague often exasperated Kate with his slovenly dress, but Conkling was the picture of sartorial splendor. He bore himself like a proud peacock, favoring bold colors and gaudy patterns in clothing. A "veritable bird of paradise" among a sea of black-clad colleagues, Conkling was known to sport green trousers, scarlet coats, striped shirts, and yellow shoes. He walked, as his bitter enemy James G. Blaine observed, with a "turkey gobbler strut." In all ways he cut a very different figure from the small, insignificant William Sprague that John Hay had commented on years before.

The differences went beyond appearance. Unlike Sprague, Conkling indulged in neither alcohol nor tobacco. Whereas Sprague rarely gave speeches and usually embarrassed himself when he did, Conkling was an orator of matchless skill. He spoke slowly and theatrically, enunciating every word of the lengthy perorations he committed to memory during long walks in the country. He delivered them in dramatic fashion, one foot placed slightly ahead of the other, his head thrown back, his thumb hooked in his vest pocket. His speeches were filled with literary quotations and classical allusions. The Senate galleries would fill up, particularly with women, just to hear him declaim. Highly perfumed and bedecked in their satin, lace, and velvet, they watched him through their looking glasses and sent flowers to his desk, making the scene reminiscent of an opera box on opening night.

About the only thing Conkling and Sprague had in common was an eye for the ladies. The subject of numerous, widespread rumors of philandering, Conkling was only nominally married to Horatio Seymour's sister Julia, a quiet, retiring woman who had little interest in politics. Governor Seymour had opposed the marriage, and Julia soon regretted not taking his advice. The couple was estranged early on, and by the time he took up with Kate, Conkling had been living apart from Julia for many years. While Conkling was in Washington, his wife usually stayed in Utica with their young daughter, Bessie, an only child born a year into the marriage. Even when he ventured home, Conkling preferred boarding alone in fashionable Bagg's Hotel in downtown Utica rather than at the family mansion at 3 Rutger Place, in a residential section up the hill almost a mile away.

As for what attracted Conkling to Kate, it was simple enough. For starters, she was ten years younger than Conkling's wife, a woman two years his senior who, though not unattractive, was no great beauty. Just as Conkling was everything Sprague was not, Kate was the opposite of Julia—strong, spirited, and politically savvy. As one of Conkling's biographers has written, "Even to be invited to one of Kate Chase Sprague's functions was a heart-thumping honor; to have the attention of the hostess for more than a few minutes was to be established in Washington society; while to be credited with being her lover . . . was a distinction reserved for one man." A senator's son, upon seeing them together at a Washington reception, said that, judging by their appearances, "these two people were intended by their Creator for each other."

It is impossible to know when their physical relationship began. Running in the same Republican social circles, they had known each other since the Civil War and had ample opportunities to fraternize with each other. Both of them attended Grant's inaugural balls and the weddings of Kate's sister Nettie and Grant's daughter Nellie. Conkling was also among the mourners at Salmon Chase's funeral.

A number of sources contend the affair blossomed shortly after Chase's death in 1873, if not earlier. More likely it was a few years later. One of Kate's Ohio acquaintances claimed Conkling had been hanging around her for years and was infatuated with her long before anything developed between them. An 1879 newspaper account maintained that the affair began in 1875 or early 1876, coinciding with the end of Conkling's extramarital affair with another government official's wife. Another source said their relationship began after a dinner party Kate hosted at Edgewood in early 1878. According to this unnamed guest, Kate looked her finest that night—in a regal dress, her hair recently dyed reddish, her face and eyebrows freshly made up. From that moment forward Conkling threw caution to the wind and pursued her openly.

Many of these stories were recalled only after the affair burst upon the nation's front pages in the summer of 1879. But articles linking Kate and Conkling appeared in the press as early as February 1878, which suggests the relationship had begun some time before that, although probably not as early as 1873. The best evidence is that the affair started after Kate's return from Europe in late 1876 or in early 1877, around the time of the famed Hayes-Tilden presidential election dispute. Their relationship, it turns out, may even have affected the outcome of that controversial election.

On election night in November 1876 it appeared that the Democrat Tilden had won, but if nineteen disputed electoral votes in the South all went to the Republican candidate, Ohio governor Rutherford Hayes, he could still eke out a victory. Both parties charged the other with fraud, and there was talk of renewed civil war. Outgoing President Grant, although a Republican, wanted the deadlock broken in a nonpartisan way to reduce the risk of bloodshed. He supported a bill to create an independent electoral commission to resolve the controversy, and, to push it through Congress, he tasked his man Conkling, who, like Grant, privately believed Tilden had legitimately won.

Tilden, of course, was Kate's *bête noire* from 1868, the man she accused of conspiring to deny her father the nomination at the New York convention that summer. But Conkling had come to distrust his fellow Republican Hayes. After seeking the 1876 Republican presidential nomination himself, Conkling had thrown his support to Hayes at the convention to prevent the nomination from going to Conkling's arch-enemy Blaine. But Conkling turned against Hayes when the candidate pledged to abolish the political spoils system and aligned himself with civil service reformers such as Carl Schurz, who threatened the New York senator's vaunted Republican patronage machine. Conkling was virulently opposed to any movement with the "reform" label, and nothing got his dander up more than talk of what he referred to as "snivel service" reform. Claiming illness,

Conkling barely lifted a finger for Hayes during the general election campaign, and although he was careful not to support Tilden publicly, it was clear that Conkling opposed certifying Hayes as the winner. Tilden too had a reputation as a reformer (he helped break up the Boss Tweed Ring in New York City), but the corruption he ferreted out was at Democratic Tammany Hall, which was fine with Conkling. Unlike the do-gooder Hayes, Tilden was at least a man Conkling could do business with.

The initial composition of the electoral commission favored the Democrats. It was to have fifteen members: five congressional Republicans, five Democrats, and five Supreme Court justices—two Republicans and two Democrats each, who in turn would choose a fifth from their court brethren. It was widely assumed the fifth justice would be David Davis, who was nominally independent but was expected to side with the Democrats. Partisan Republicans such as James Garfield squawked at the idea. Neutral observers were urging Conkling to do the right thing and support the impartial commission. The *New-York Tribune* reported in January 1877 that no one knew anything about what Conkling would or would not do. That wasn't true: Kate Chase knew.

"Senator Conkling will support the Commission with a speech," she whispered in the ear of Billy Hudson, a journalist she had met at the 1868 convention, when he was a cub reporter who fell under her spell. It was now eight years later, and Hudson, a political writer for the *Brooklyn Eagle,* had gone to the train station in Washington to see off a friend to New York. "From one of the trains that had just arrived a stately lady swept across the room," he recalled. He recognized Kate, and she him, greeting him with the kind of knowing, playful manner that reporters find so winning in a good politician. "Why, it is my pink-cheeked reporter!" she exclaimed. "But where are the pink cheeks? All gone in hard work, late hours and—dissipation? Ah, I know the habits of you boys."

As she was about to leave, she turned and asked whether Hudson was in Washington to cover the electoral dispute. When he said he was, she hesitated momentarily and said she would give him a scoop if he promised not to tell anyone. He swore himself to secrecy, after which she revealed to him Conkling's plans.

Recounting this incident thirty years after it happened, Hudson, who was a bit of a storyteller, might not have remembered all the details perfectly. For one thing, Kate's apparent enthusiasm for the electoral commission, which favored the Democrats as originally conceived, would have been inconsistent with her hatred of Tilden. But if the gist of what Hudson wrote is true—that Kate possessed some sort of inside information about Conkling's political intentions—it suggests that by that time a very close relationship between them had already developed.

They went ahead with their affair, knowing the knives would be out for them. Kate had always been dogged by stories that she was an opportunist in love, marrying the rich Governor Sprague to finance her plans to make her father president. And Conkling was loathed by just about everyone. According to Gideon Welles, he was an "egotistical coxcomb." Another man who knew Conkling well called him "vain as a peacock, and a czar in arrogance." His boxing training and ace poker playing reflected his pugilistic nature—he relished doing battle with his enemies, who were "pursued, sought out, slaughtered." He was prone to cruel invective, and, as the wife of a close ally noted, Conkling's "powers of sarcasm never soared so high as when feeling that his antagonist was wounded in some vital spot."

Kate, who was often accused of arrogance and haughtiness, brushed aside any such criticism of Conkling. Indeed, having been forced to deal with Sprague's weaknesses and insecurities for so many years, Kate found Conkling's style and swagger appealing. He was, as one writer later put it, filled "with a spirit not unlike her own in its intense self-confidence and its disdain of ordinary men."

Much as she admired him, though, she was not above trying to use him for her own purposes, as witnessed by the denouement to the Hayes-Tilden imbroglio. Just as Kate predicted, Roscoe Conkling did give a speech supporting the electoral commission. On January 24 and 25, 1877, Conkling held the Senate spellbound as he made the case for an independent body to decide the election. The commission bill, he argued, would "once again proclaim to the world that America is great enough, and wise enough, to do all things decently and in order." The bill passed the Senate and cleared significant Republican opposition in the House, with enough Grant and Conkling loyalists joining the Democrats to approve the measure. To many, it was Conkling's finest hour.

But not to all. Partisan Republicans mourned the bill as a guarantee of Tilden's election. But then fate intervened to save the Hayes forces. David Davis, the independent Supreme Court justice everyone assumed would side with the Democrats, unexpectedly resigned from the court to take a US Senate seat to which he had just been elected by the Illinois legislature. James Garfield rejoiced that it was an act of God. With Davis gone, the four other justices on the commission chose Joseph Bradley—the most independent remaining member of the court but, importantly, a Republican—as the fifth court representative. What had looked like an eight-to-seven advantage for Tilden had turned into an eight-to-seven majority for Hayes.

Bradley supported the Republicans in a series of straight party-line votes. The commission declared Hayes the winner, but the Democrats refused to accept the results and began a filibuster to delay the final vote count beyond the March 4 inauguration date, when the Democratic-controlled House might be able to decide the outcome. The Tilden forces pinned their hopes on a showdown Senate vote on whether to accept the commission's certification of the Louisiana vote in Hayes's favor. Knowing where Conkling's sympathies lay, Tilden's friends secured a commitment from him to support the Democrats when the crucial Louisiana question came before the Senate. It was rumored that Conkling would give another great speech, this time opposing the action of the commission he was so instrumental in creating. He had convinced enough Senate Republicans to go along with him in overriding the commission's decision, which the Senate was permitted to do.

It was at this point that Kate, according to many accounts, worked on Conkling to drop his efforts on behalf of Tilden and to switch his support to Hayes. When the day scheduled for a final Senate vote on the Louisiana question came, on February 19, Conkling was nowhere to be found. Absent his support, the case for Tilden collapsed and the Democrats lost what they considered their last hope for a Republican revolt. Tilden's friends felt deceived by Lord Roscoe, saying he failed to keep faith with them.

What had happened to Conkling? It turned out that the day the critical Senate vote on Louisiana was to take place he conveniently absented himself by taking a train to Baltimore, supposedly to visit friends. In his memoirs reporter Billy Hudson said that Republican leaders, fearing the effect of another Conkling speech in favor of the Democrats and aware of Kate's relationship with him, got her to summon Conkling to join her at a friend's house in Baltimore. Conkling went to see Kate, the story goes, and Hayes—the man Conkling would refer to as "Ruther-*fraud*" or "His Fraudulency"—was seated as president. Kate's own motivation, it was said, was to avenge her late father, whom she remained convinced was denied the Democratic nomination in 1868 through Tilden's scheming. Writing many years later, Alexander McClure, a Republican newspaper editor at the time of the electoral dispute and later a presidential historian, said it had been an "open secret that Conkling resolved his doubts as urged by Mrs. Sprague." Another memoirist, who knew several presidents, quoted Kate as saying afterward, "I got even with Mr. Tilden for defeating my father."

Although the story, with its elements of a Greek or Shakespearean revenge tragedy, practically begs for acceptance, its truth remains uncertain. Conkling's biographer scoffs at it as "utter fantasy," arguing that it was not Conkling's absence from the Louisiana vote that ended the Democrats' challenge to Hayes's election but rather a deal by which Hayes promised to withdraw federal troops from the South. The problem with that argument is timing: the deal was brokered at a meeting at Wormley's Hotel in Washington on February 26, a full week *after* the critical Louisiana vote on February 19 that Conkling missed. Two of Kate's biographers, adopting a different argument, dismiss the idea that party loyalist Conkling ever would have supported a Democrat, even against a Republican he hated. But that overlooks the fact that prior to the February 19 vote Conkling had *already taken* many actions designed to help Tilden secure the presidency. Something—or someone—caused Conkling to change his mind about supporting Tilden, and the theory that it was Kate cannot be so easily dismissed. Indeed, as Conkling said to Kate from time to time in reference to some political problem, "I know your bright mind will solve this quicker than mine."

One of Kate's most fervent supporters, George Hoadly, a former law partner of Salmon Chase, claimed insight into Conkling's thinking and behavior during the election dispute. A Democrat, Hoadly argued Tilden's cause to the electoral commission and would later serve as governor of Ohio. It was "perfectly true," Hoadly wrote, that Conkling organized a bolt from the Republicans and secured enough senators to support reversal of the Louisiana certification at the critical February 19 vote. Conkling would have made Tilden president, Hoadly averred, had he been in the Senate instead of in Baltimore that day. According to Hoadly,

Conkling changed his mind at the last minute only because Republican Party leaders, at a 2 a.m. meeting, told him his political future would be ruined if he did not support Hayes. Deciding he had no choice, Conkling took the earliest train to Baltimore, where he spent the day. So much for the argument that Conkling would never have supported a Democrat; he was more than prepared to do so and backed off for reasons of self-preservation, not out of party loyalty.

Hoadly disputed that Kate kept Conkling away from the Senate on the crucial day, but he did not and could not deny that they had been lovers at the time, and he admitted he was unaware of Kate's whereabouts during the electoral dispute (she was in Washington). The sole basis he gave for doubting that Kate took action to influence Conkling was that neither Conkling nor Kate ever told him so. But that is hardly surprising. Hoadly never spoke directly to Conkling about his absence from the Louisiana vote, and even if he had, Conkling would not have revealed it was Kate who kept him away from the Senate that day. As for Kate, she knew of Hoadly's great fondness for Tilden, which is precisely why she would *not* have told him of any conspiratorial role she played in denying Tilden the presidency.

One thing can be said with certainty about Kate's behavior during the electoral dispute: it was driven by shrewd political considerations and personal relationships. Kate's actions during this period were no more those of a Republican "party woman" than Conkling's were of a "party man." The two of them shared the basic ideology of Republicanism, but ideology was a secondary consideration. For both of them all politics was personal, and obtaining and maintaining personal political power were of paramount concern. It was another reason they were made for each other. And henceforth, for the next several years, they would be inseparable, linked together in politics and love.

CHAPTER 20

# "Mrs. Conkling Is Not Here This Winter"

In June 1877 Kate and Roscoe Conkling both went to Europe, separately and alone. They returned to the States, separately again, in August. A few months after they were back they began appearing together in public for the first time.

Kate's trip was, as usual, an attempt to escape a strife-riven home life. In February 1877 she and Sprague had a frightful confrontation at Canonchet; Kate would later allege that her drunken husband tried to throw her out of an upstairs window. She left after the incident and took her three daughters back to Edgewood in Washington.

Another reason she went to Europe that summer was to see her son, Willie, who remained in school in Germany. "Your Mama thinks of you a hundred times a day," she wrote him in February before her trip. Just as her diary revealed a more feminine side she rarely showed the world, her letters to Willie evidenced sweetly maternal instincts her harshest critics did not know existed. She told him of his little sisters' longing for their "beau boy" and described them in their white fur coats "looking like little Polar bear's cubs" as they sledded down the hill. But her correspondence had another object.

Aside from the pleasantries, she began to sound like Salmon Chase, offering up didactic lectures sprinkled with bits of praise. Just as her father had once criticized her handwriting, she now took her son to task for his, even though his was much more readable than hers (just as hers was more legible than her father's). She told him he needed to pursue his Latin and German with greater diligence. Further mimicking her father, who once returned one of Nettie's letters, requesting she send it back after making his corrections, Kate similarly wrote to Willie, "I shall send you a list of words that you misspell which I want you to return to me with the correct spelling written opposite *on my list*." And just as her father had cautioned Kate against extravagance, always reminding her he was not a wealthy man, Kate admonished Willie not to "throw away money on useless things" because it was too hard to come by. Like father like daughter.

Kate, who had often told Sprague to spiff up his slovenly look, likewise urged Willie to develop habits of neatness and order. She quoted Shakespeare to him: "'The apparel oft bespeaks the man,'" and told him that "others respect a man in proportion to the respect which he shows for himself." Kate was trying to make Willie the Un-William. Good habits, she told her son, could be acquired only while he was young. If he did so, then he would feel their benefit all his life, and without them he would be a trial to himself and everyone around him. She was speaking from personal experience.

Sprague had ceded virtually all care of his young daughters to Kate, but he worked hard to keep Willie close to him. In one of his few letters to Willie during this period he thanked the boy for the many letters he had continued to write, even though Sprague never answered them. He praised Willie's communiqués, saying, "Indeed, at your age, I could not write and express myself as well as you do now, by a good deal." Sprague further sought to curry favor with Willie by denigrating Kate. He compared her to his own "rigid" mother, Fanny Sprague, saying that both women were "constantly reminding us of defects and worrying us into obedience." He told Willie that before Kate "bribes you away from me," he wanted to offer the boy a proposition: "Make me a part of your family by joining me when you come home." Sprague was launching the opening salvo in what, for the next few years, would be a struggle between him and Kate to win Willie's loyalty and companionship.

Roscoe Conkling too had home front troubles he sought relief from by going to Europe. He remained estranged from his wife, and the stress from the electoral dispute and a recent bout with malaria left him exhausted and haggard looking. His fears about Rutherford Hayes were also proving well founded. Hayes's actions since his inauguration in March 1877 showed he intended to make good on his campaign pledge to end the spoils system. The new president enraged Conkling by appointing to his cabinet Kate's old friend Carl Schurz, a champion of civil service reform who had gotten into shouting matches with Conkling on the Senate floor. Even worse, Hayes ordered an investigation into alleged corruption in the New York Custom House, which collected the lion's share of the nation's customs duties, and eventually fired Conkling's protégé Chester Alan Arthur, the New York port collector, creating a permanent rift between the president and Conkling.

Ironically, while Kate was away in Europe for the summer, she sublet Edgewood to the widower Schurz and another Hayes cabinet member. It may seem strange that, if Conkling had been spending private time with Kate at Edgewood, she would have rented out the same house, while they were both away in Europe, to one of Conkling's biggest enemies. But unlike Conkling, Kate was able to maintain friendly relations with persons whose political interests might not square with hers. Rather than argue with Schurz, she could tease him about civil service reform, as when he came out to Edgewood one Sunday morning to proudly read her his first draft of a civil service bill. "He had not read many minutes when I laughed aloud," she later recalled. "'What is the matter?'" he asked, frowning. "I said, 'That law is impossible in this Republic. It will never be enforced.'" And before leaving for Europe she wrote President Hayes a warm letter of recommendation for a former clerk in Chase's Treasury Department with close ties to Schurz. Much more than the petulant Conkling, Kate understood how the Washington political game was played—how today's enemy might be tomorrow's friend. It did not pay to burn bridges the way Lord Roscoe did. Although Kate was certainly capable of plotting to undermine her opponents behind the scenes, she was always gracious and civil to them in person. Conkling, by contrast, although comfortable in front of a crowd, shunned contact with individuals and disdained small talk. His nephew called him a "very nervous man" who "could not bear to have his person or even his chair touched by others." Kate may have worked on Conkling, though without much success, to improve his people skills. And if he tried to make an issue over her letting her house out to Schurz, Kate would have told him he was being petty and ridiculous. Besides, she was going to Europe and needed the income.

* * *

After his trip abroad, Roscoe Conkling arrived back in New York to a hero's welcome. He was serenaded at his hotel in New York and, four days later, in what may have been the supreme moment of his life, was given a torchlight parade through the streets of his home town of Utica. Hotels, stores, and residences were brilliantly illuminated, and Chinese lanterns strung from tree to tree, forming "a starry canopy." Arriving at his gray stone mansion at Rutger Place, which he found ablaze with light from foundation to rooftop, he told a cheering crowd that the further he went in Europe, "the more it seemed to me there was no country like America, no state like New York, no county like Oneida, no city like Utica." A summer in Europe with Kate had reenergized him. The thrilling new romance seemed to rejuvenate her as well. In a photograph taken that year in Washington she appears in a Worth costume, looking younger than her thirty-seven years. She is wearing a bracelet with an inscription in German that reads, "I lock you into my heart and throw the key into the Rhine and now you must always be within me." The giver is not identified, but Conkling is a logical candidate, for upon his return from Europe that summer he extolled the people and "land of the Rhine." The bracelet was one of the few mementoes Kate kept her entire life. Even if Conkling did not speak German, Kate did, and a foreign-language inscription would have been a clever way of conveying a romantic message to her while masking his identity from others. In any event, Kate's European trip had filled her with renewed confidence and panache, as is evident in another photograph from around that same time, taken in New York, showing her in black top hat, clutching a riding stick. In this image her customary half-smile, always verging equally on a grin and a frown, seems slightly closer than usual to the former.

In January 1878 Kate was back at Edgewood giving weekly receptions as in days past. A month later stories started appearing in the press for the first time linking her with Conkling. They surprised people by showing up together at a ceremony in the Capitol for the unveiling of Francis Carpenter's famous painting depicting Lincoln's first reading of the Emancipation Proclamation, in which Salmon Chase is looking over the president's shoulder. After others' speeches, Conkling and Kate came forward to shake hands with the artist, and, as slyly noted by one female journalist, Kate's proximity to the senator "gave a new light and color to his face." Stories began cropping up about them passing notes between each other in the Senate, locking themselves behind closed committee room doors while Conkling's secretary stood guard outside, and leaving their carriages outside each other's residences at night.

Kate made it a point to be present in the Senate gallery whenever Conkling was scheduled to speak. A newspaper from Kate's home town of Cincinnati later added color to the description of the pair's method of communication in that chamber:

> Mr. Conkling would write Mrs. Sprague a note, fold it up deliberately, and place it with a blank piece of paper and a small envelope inside of a large official envelope, when a . . . messenger would appear without even being summoned, and the package would be handed him. Then he would disappear. After a while he would be seen to enter the gallery and to hand the large envelope to Mrs. Sprague. . . . Mrs. Sprague was never in a hurry. It was her custom to place the envelope upon her lap and let it remain there for some moments as if it was some trivial matter. Then, after a proper time, she would open the envelope, read the enclosure, and then the blank piece of paper would be used for writing the answer.

Her reply would be duly delivered by the same messenger to Conkling on the Senate floor. As he read the note "a deep flush of pleasure" would pass over his face before he looked up at Kate, who was eagerly watching him from the gallery.

One longtime Washington social observer said they were spotted together so often that it was generally supposed she was his mistress. The gossip writer Miss Grundy expressed dismay that "Senator Conkling and the fair lady have, in effect, snapped their fingers contemptuously in the face of public opinion, as if to say, '*We* are too lofty to be affected by aught *you* can say of us.'" As far away as Idaho a newspaper noted that "the scandal-mongers of Washington are linking the names of Senator Conkling and Mrs. Kate Chase Sprague in a very free way."

Around the same time, in June 1878, Conkling represented Kate in an ejectment suit she brought against a tenant farmer for nonpayment of rent on her Edgewood property. The man alleged that, per agreement with Kate, his rent was to be paid in eggs, butter, and poultry and that he had already supplied her to the tune of $300. All he was asking, he said, was to be able to stay until September 1878, when he could realize from the crops he had planted. One Washington correspondent saw this as a David and Goliath fight that pitted a poor farmer against "a selfish politician who espoused the cause of a woman who remorselessly crushes everything which opposes her will." The law at the time heavily favored landlords, and within two weeks a judge ruled she could evict the man.

If Conkling was performing special favors for Kate, others thought he was getting more than fair recompense. Miss Grundy saw their partnership as proof of the adage that behind every great man is a great woman. As she wrote, Conkling was planning to challenge James G. Blaine for the presidency in 1880 and was anxious to have the politically astute Kate working for him. Another society writer concurred that Kate was just the right woman for Conkling. "Mrs. Sprague is a born diplomat," the journalist wrote, and could do for Conkling that which "in his vanity and arrogance he would overlook, or thrust haughtily aside."

Further evidence of their relationship is found in a letter Kate wrote from Edgewood to Willie in Germany in March 1878. She told her son of an experiment with the newly invented telephone she had participated in during a recent visit to Rhode Island. Situated in Cranston, she "heard distinctly every word of a conversation" taking place between some people in Providence and another nearby town. "Then *I* spoke to Providence and they answered me and recognized my voice," she marveled, although "they did not know where I was." She then slipped in the fact that Senator Conkling had dined with her and the girls the day before and entertained them with an account of a demonstration of the phonograph he had recently seen in New York. Clearly, by the spring of 1878, she and Conkling were seeing quite a bit of each other.

She was also seeing less and less of her husband. Evidently Fanny Sprague tried to encourage some sort of reconciliation, for she paid a rare visit to Edgewood that summer. Likely at her mother-in-law's urging, upon Willie's return from Europe in late July Kate went back to Canonchet. Her stay there would be brief. Around the end of the summer of 1878 Sprague was arrested in what Kate would later describe as a "disgraceful orgy" with Mary Viall at Nantasket Beach in Massachusetts. According to newspaper accounts, the two of them were drunk and disorderly and were evicted from the seaside hotel where Viall was staying. Having been embarrassed by the publication of Viall's book two years earlier, Kate, humiliated again, headed back to Edgewood, where she felt more secure. Willie remained with Sprague in Rhode Island and was sent to an agricultural academy in Maryland in early 1879. To Kate's dismay, her son's behavior regressed, as he took to smoking, sloppy appearance, and an interest in guns.

Her relationship with Conkling, though, continued to progress. In March 1879 she sent Willie a box of writing materials "liberally furnished, owing to Mr. Conkling's kindness, who made the selection and filled it himself." She drew comfort from Roscoe Conkling, a man so unlike her husband and yet, in many ways, as much maligned. She saw a side of him others did not, someone who did not fit the characterization of a man who, as James Garfield once said, was "inspired more by his hates than his loves." For all the enmity Conkling could display, he was capable of genuine acts of compassion, as in 1875, when he was the only person to escort former slave Blanche Bruce, the first African American elected to a full Senate term, up the aisle to take the oath. When the senior senator from Mississippi, who by custom should have performed the honors, refused (hiding behind a newspaper), Bruce started up the aisle alone. Conkling stepped forward and said, "Excuse me, Mr. Bruce, I did not until this moment see that you were without an escort, permit me. My name is Conkling." Conkling thereafter became Bruce's mentor in the Senate, procuring committee assignments for him, and when Bruce's only son was born in 1879, the grateful protégé named him Roscoe Conkling Bruce.

Conkling also was popular with the congressional pages, who hung at his elbow, anxious to serve, without his need to clap his hands to summon them. Asked why they were so willing to do his bidding, one boy explained, "He never said a cross word to a page in his life. He says: 'My little man, will you do this kindness for me?' Then we all run!" People did not understand Conkling, Kate knew, just as they had so many misconceptions about her. No, she would not even consider ending things with Roscoe Conkling.

By early 1879 their affair was the worst-kept secret in Washington. "Mrs. Conkling is not here this winter," one paper wrote, "and the gossips say it is because her imperious lord has been too devoted in his attentions to Mrs. Kate Sprague." Conkling was seen taking Kate in his carriage to the opera, where they occupied a box where "all the Washington peasantry" could gaze up at them. Donn Piatt, the Washington gossip columnist, called their affair "the most open and defiant social transaction" ever seen in the capital.

On April 30, 1879, just as these stories were appearing in the papers, Conkling's daughter, Bessie, was getting married in Utica. But Conkling did not attend the wedding. The *New York Times* reported that he opposed the marriage because the groom, Walter Oakman, though "a worthy gentleman," possessed little wealth. According to Conkling's biographer, Conkling disapproved of Oakman's past, when he worked as a common laborer to learn the family railroad business. But these explanations do not ring true: Oakman was a graduate of the University of Pennsylvania, an accomplished mechanical engineer, a man of classical interests who had traveled the world, and, at the time of the wedding, local superintendent of the Delaware, Lackawanna, and Western Railroad. (He would later become chairman of the Guaranty Trust Company of New York and a director of several other large corporations.) There had to be more to it than the fact that Oakman had gotten his clothes dirty while working in his youth. It is more likely that Conkling's affair with Kate caused some blowup in the Conkling household. Sure enough, it was later reported that Conkling boycotted the wedding because his wife refused to invite Kate, and his daughter sided with her mother. Conkling's escalating involvement with Kate probably did have much to do with his absence from the wedding.

At this same time, Conkling was also using his influence to provide Kate with questionable government favors. She owed $3,700 in property taxes on Edgewood left unpaid since her father's death in 1873. To bail her out, Conkling championed what one newspaper called an "unjust bill" to exempt Edgewood from all past and future taxation as long as it was in the possession of any child of the late chief justice. The ostensible public purpose of the bill was to honor Salmon Chase's memory, but it was obviously designed solely for the benefit of Kate. Popularly known as "the Mrs. Sprague bill," it was first introduced in the House in mid-1878 and pushed, without success, by James Garfield. It was Conkling who got the bill passed by the Senate in February 1879, although the Democratic-controlled House limited the exemption to taxes up to June 1880.

Then came the famous "fainting incident." During the special session of Congress that began in March 1879 the Democrats controlled both houses for the first time since before the Civil War. They spent the spring attaching to various appropriations bills a series of riders designed to overturn the federal election laws guarding against vote fraud. The Republicans charged the Democrats with trying to facilitate the same kind of violence and intimidation southern whites had used against black voters in the 1876 presidential election. When the Democrats proposed another rider, this time to prevent the use of federal military force to police any election, Conkling led the opposition. In typically histrionic language he charged that it would embolden "all the thugs and shoulder-hitters and repeaters, all the carriers of slung-shot, dirks, and bludgeons, all the fraternity of the bucket-shops, the rat-pits, the hells and the slums, all the graduates of the nurseries of modern so-called democracy, all those who employ and incite them" to commit skullduggery at the polls.

The issue came to a head on June 18, 1879, with Kate watching from the gallery. At six o'clock that evening, with Senate Democrats pressing to cut off debate and vote on the measure, Conkling moved for an adjournment. A stormy scene followed for several hours, with Republicans filibustering and the Democrats resisting. There matters stood just before midnight, when Conkling launched into a half-hour speech accusing the Democrats of bad faith. Mississippi senator Lucius Q. C. Lamar, an ex-Confederate general, took offense and, trembling with anger, pronounced Conkling's statement "a falsehood, which I repel with all the unmitigated contempt that I feel for the author of it." Conkling slowly rose from his seat and, glaring at Lamar, said that if he had heard him right, then but for the fact that they were standing in the Senate, with its rules and proprieties, "I would denounce him as a blackguard, as a coward, and a liar." There followed applause and hisses from the gallery, a demand for quiet from the presiding officer, and dead silence as the entire chamber anxiously awaited Lamar's response. Lamar stood again and said he had been understood correctly and meant to say "just precisely the words, and all that they imported." He apologized—not to Conkling but to the Senate—for his harsh language, which was "such as no good man would deserve and no brave man would wear." In southern code Conkling had just been challenged to a duel. It was reported afterward that, upon watching this exchange, Kate turned ghostly pale and nearly fainted.

At three in the morning the filibusterers were still speaking, to a nearly empty chamber, with a skeleton crew of Senators, including Conkling, holding the floor. Kate was still there, virtually alone in the gallery. Everyone present was tired and cranky. Two nights later, after the acrimony had subsided, the bill passed, and President Hayes, who could not understand what all the fuss was about, signed it.

There was no duel. Because Conkling was the insulted party, the ball was in his court, and he brushed off the whole idea as a silly southern plantation tradition. Lamar's backers claimed a moral victory over someone afraid to fight. One person who pronounced himself delighted was Conkling's foe Blaine, who called it "exceedingly rich! I don't think I ever saw Conkling's wattles quite so red."

Kate would later deny that she had almost fainted, saying she had not shown anything more than concern for a "warm personal friend." She claimed she hardly even noticed the hostile exchange until after it was over. Perhaps the fainting reports were exaggerated, but it strains credulity to believe that, having stuck around until three in the morning, Kate was anything but glued to the drama unfolding before her.

The cumulative impact of all these stories was taking its toll on Julia Conkling, for in June 1879 the Utica press reported she was about to institute divorce proceedings. The rumor was insistently denied, but talk of the Conklings' troubled marriage would resume in the coming months. Another person seething over the stories was William Sprague. He had to admit that Conkling, his former colleague, was a brilliant senator, he told one friend, but he thought ill of him as a man. He had formed an intense hatred of Conkling and made his animosity clear in bars, hotel parlors, and other public places in Providence. If he ever caught him with his wife, there was certain to be trouble.

CHAPTER 21

# "The Now Notorious Outbreak"

Roscoe Conkling had no intention of being in the same room with William Sprague when the senator landed at Narragansett Pier on Tuesday, August 5, 1879, to spend a few days with Kate at Canonchet. Conkling had waited patiently across the bay at a friend's villa in Newport until he received confirmation that Sprague was to be absent for a few days, then met Kate at the landing with luggage in hand. Kate's husband was not expected back from a business trip to Maine until at least Saturday, August 9.

The beautiful seaside resort was one where anyone would be happy to spend a week in August. Until Kate started building her magnificent chateau a decade before, the place was just a sleepy little village with a few shacks and a single shabby hotel. Now it was one of the finest summer retreats in the country, with its matchless beach and first-class hotels and boardinghouses, twenty in number, whose sweeping verandas lined Ocean Road. After the railroad was extended directly to the Pier in 1876, society types began flocking there, attracted by the music and dining halls, the nightly dress balls and parties, and the pure, invigorating ocean breezes.

Just a few weeks earlier Kate had come there with her three girls, with trustee Chafee's permission, to gain relief from Washington's summer heat and, she hoped, to help her husband adjust his affairs with his creditors to guarantee sufficient financial support for her and her daughters. In late July the girls, accompanied by a nursemaid, were sketched by a local artist as they played on the beach. Little could they anticipate the storm that would arise some three weeks later.

Conkling stayed at Canonchet from Tuesday through Thursday night, August 7, along with some other guests of Kate's—Mr. and Mrs. Throop Martin of Auburn, New York, and two of their daughters. During his visit Conkling was seen openly promenading around Narragansett in a carriage with Kate. He sat down to breakfast with her on Friday, August 8, a warm, lazy day in Narragansett, and began reading the newspapers. They gave every indication this summer day would be as uneventful as any other. The lead story in the *Providence Journal* concerned a Christian camp meeting in Hyannis, Massachusetts. Another front-page article celebrated the local baseball club's eleven-inning victory over the "light weights" of Troy, New York. The paper was filled with ads for boat excursions leaving from Narragansett Pier for Martha's Vineyard and Block Island. Gilbert and Sullivan's *HMS Pinafore* was being performed on a nearby lake. Nothing much newsworthy ever took place around Narragansett during vacation season. But all that would change on this day: the peace and quiet would not last, things would go horribly wrong, and threats of violence in the halls of Canonchet and streets of the nearby village would shatter Kate's world and jeopardize, it seemed, her very life.

The prelude to the blowup began in June, two days after Kate's alleged fainting spell in the Senate gallery over Conkling's row with Senator Lamar. At that time she had hired a German professor, George Linck, to tutor Willie in Rhode Island that summer for fifty dollars a month. After meeting Linck in New York on July 1 with Willie in tow, she sent the two of them off to Canonchet while she returned to Washington, hoping to bring the girls with her to Rhode Island in another week or so.

Kate kept getting delayed in going to Canonchet, whereas Linck was running into trouble with his pupil's father. Sprague objected to the idea of a tutor that summer, explaining that Willie needed a break from schooling and that his creditors would not look favorably on his incurring such an expense. Sprague ordered Linck off his property, but Kate told him to stay put until she could get there to straighten things out. After the second time Sprague told Linck to get out, the professor packed his bags and left Canonchet, forever, he thought. He was glad to be gone—the bespectacled, bearded professor, a self-important man of forty-six, considered himself in "the prime of life" and disparaged Sprague (now bearded himself) as "mixed up and muddled" in conversation.

In mid-July, however, Linck agreed to Kate's request to join her and her girls at Watch Hill, another seaside resort town in Rhode Island, where she would stay until Canonchet was ready to receive her. Sprague showed up at Watch Hill unexpectedly on July 19 and, seemingly intoxicated, blew up when he saw the teacher. "If I find you again near my children or place, I will surely kill you, that I will, and take my word for it," Linck claimed he heard Sprague say. Kate took the children to Canonchet two days later and persuaded Linck to stay close by at a boardinghouse on Silver Lake, a couple of miles from the mansion, and await further developments. Two weeks later, around 1 p.m. on Friday, August 8, Kate's coachman showed up at Linck's boardinghouse and told him Kate wanted to see him at Canonchet "on important business." Against his better judgment, Linck yielded once more and drove off with the coachman for Canonchet.

As if on cue, within moments after being dropped off at the entrance, Linck was met on the front steps by Kate, who whispered to him, "The Governor has just arrived." Linck replied, simply, "Thank you for the information." Following Kate's advice, he jumped back in the buggy and prepared to take his leave once more.

Precisely what happened next and during the next few hours—indeed, over the course of the next thirty days as the story continued to play itself out—can never be known for certain. It would combine elements of melodrama, tragedy, and farce. The truth about the events themselves would become less important than what people thought and said about them. As in the Kurosawa film *Rashomon*, with each retelling the story changed, as the major participants, witnesses, and newspapers all produced their own contradictory versions, most of which were impossible to reconcile. All that can be said for certain is that in the end, the reputations of three national figures would be badly damaged, with consequences not only for themselves but also for the course of American politics.

As Linck would tell it, in the first and longest of a series of formal statements he gave to the press, when he stepped back into the buggy to leave Canonchet he heard footsteps approaching that turned out to be Sprague's. Sprague peered inside the buggy, glared hard at the teacher,

A future "queen": The oldest known image of Kate Chase, this portrait shows her, even as a young girl, with a *Mona Lisa* smile. (*Courtesy of Aura Carr*)

Kate's father, Salmon P. Chase. An Ohio governor, senator, Lincoln's treasury secretary, and finally Supreme Court chief justice, he was, as one man put it, "light without heat." (*National Archives*)

Henrietta Haines (*right*), the stern headmistress of the exclusive boarding school Kate attended in New York from 1850 to 1854, where she learned her famous social skills. (*University of Michigan Special Collections Library*)

The soon-to-be "Belle of Columbus" (*below*): Kate around age 14. (*Library of Congress*)

A portrait of Salmon Chase around 1857 as governor of Ohio, flanked by his younger daughter, Nettie (*left*), and sixteen-year-old Kate. (*Courtesy of Franklin Hoyt Moore*)

The "boy governor," William Sprague, the Rhode Island multimillionaire Kate married in the social event of the Civil War. (*Carte de visite, photographer unknown*)

The "Belle of the North": Kate with the staff of General John Abercrombie (seated to her left), early in the Civil War. (*National Archives, photo by Matthew Brady*)

Kate, an accomplished equestrian, with military-style riding habit, around 1862. A Union soldier remembered her as a "magnificent creature" who rode into camp one day on horseback "and created no end of stir among us chaps." (*New York Public Library*)

William and Kate Chase Sprague at the time of their wedding in November 1863. President Lincoln attended the ceremony; his wife, Mary—Kate's jealous rival—did not. (*National Archives*)

Some other men in Kate's life: admirers included (*clockwise from upper left*): Charles Sumner, John Hay, James Garfield, and Carl Schurz. (*Center photo courtesy of Aura Carr; Sumner, Garfield, and Schurz: Library of Congress; Hay: New York Public Library. Photo design by Ken Graff*)

Kate (*above right*) with her half-sister Nettie, in the late 1860s. (*Cincinnati Museum Center-Cincinnati Historical Society Library*)

Kate's son Willie (*right*), who would later add to the family tragedy. (*Cranston Historical Society*)

William Sprague as a senator from Rhode Island, after his marriage to Kate had begun falling apart. He lacked the respect of his colleagues and admitted to a mind that was "sadly disconnected." (*National Archives*)

Kate (*below*), at the height of her virtual royalty, posing as Mary Queen of Scots. (*University of Michigan Special Collections Library*)

Canonchet, the Spragues' opulent seaside mansion in Narragansett, Rhode Island, and site of the infamous "shotgun" incident. (*Courtesy of Aura Carr*)

Janet "Nettie" Chase (*left*), Kate's half-sister, around the time of her wedding in 1871. (*Cincinnati Museum Center-Cincinnati Historical Society Library*)

A rare close-up photo of Kate (*above*), taken at age twenty-eight, around the time of the 1868 Democratic Convention, where she managed her father's presidential campaign. (*Cranston Historical Society*)

Kate (*above*) engages Horace Greeley in conversation while entertaining at Canonchet. (*Frank Leslie's Illustrated Newspaper*, April 24, 1872)

Chief Justice Salmon Chase, not long before his death in 1873. (*Library of Congress*)

New York senator Roscoe Conkling, "the Adonis of the Senate" and Kate's longtime lover. (*National Archives*)

In this photograph (*right*), taken in New York around 1877, during her affair with Conkling, Kate seems filled with renewed confidence and panache. (*Courtesy of Ann Donaldson*)

Kate's three daughters with their governess at Edgewood, Kate's home in Washington, around 1880. This is the only known photograph of Kitty *(far left)*. At far right is Ethel, and next to her, Portia. (*Courtesy of Ann Donaldson*)

Roscoe Conkling, flanked by his "Stalwart" henchmen Thomas Platt (*left*) and Chester Arthur, accosts President-elect James Garfield in March 1881 over patronage appointments. Kate would embroil herself in the war between Conkling and Garfield, which ended in tragedy with Garfield's assassination a few months later (*New York Public Library*)

Kate, sometime in her forties, wearing the "306" pin given to her by Conkling to commemorate the Stalwart delegates who stuck with Ulysses Grant at the 1880 convention. (*Courtesy of Ann Donaldson*)

Kate's daughter Ethel (*below*), early in her acting career. (*New York Public Library*)

Kate's daughter Portia (*above*), in 1899 at Canonchet, where she reconciled with her father. (*Courtesy of Aura Carr*)

Ex-governor William Sprague, near age seventy, on Narragansett beach. The restored portrait now hangs in Rhode Island's State Capitol. (*Williamstown Art Conservation Center*)

Kate, in later years, still wearing Conkling's "306" pin. (*Courtesy of Ann Donaldson*)

One of the last photos of Kate, taken around 1898, at Edgewood with her daughter Ethel and her only grandchild, Chase Donaldson. (*Courtesy of Aura Carr*)

An American queen: Kate in a statuette sculpted in Paris, showing her in the gown she wore when presented at the French royal court. (*Courtesy of Aura Carr; photo by Ken Graff*)

and shook Linck's arm in a menacing manner. Linck braced himself for a struggle that did not come, as Sprague turned around and raced back inside the house without saying a word. Linck was not sure what this move implied but "was not prepared to be shot down by an infuriated madman." He had Perry the coachman drop him off at a bar at the pier, less than a mile from the mansion. Linck had not yet received the beer he ordered when he saw Sprague speeding up the road in a buggy. The professor ducked into the kitchen in back, and a few minutes later the landlady's daughter threw open the door to report that Sprague had rushed in wildly, with gun in hand, looking for him. She told Sprague the professor had gone into the village, whereupon Sprague jumped back in his buggy and drove off at a furious pace. The girl then hailed a carriage for Linck, and he was driven away, "out of harm's way," as Linck put it.

Linck's account, printed in Monday's August 11 *Providence Journal*, was similar in one principal respect to the initial, sketchy newspaper reports that started trickling out of Narragansett Pier on Sunday the tenth. The original brief dispatches attributed the dangerous confrontation entirely to Sprague's animosity toward Linck. The *New York Sun* said there was "scarcely anything in the occurrence which places it beyond an ordinary private family matter."

The original newspaper dispatches also included, in passing, a curious piece of information Linck had omitted. The Sunday *New York Times* reported that Senator Roscoe Conkling happened to be present Friday at Canonchet, having stopped off there "on some legal business" on his way to Providence. The *Sun* added that Conkling had seen nothing of the altercation between Sprague and Linck, as he was in the library at the time. Upon hearing ladies screaming, Conkling escorted them safely out of the house and helped Mr. Martin, an invalid, into a departing carriage. Conkling then walked into the village and was overtaken by Sprague, who was driving to the pier, presumably in search of Linck. Conkling asked the Governor why he was acting "like a wild man," and Sprague replied that it was none of his business. Conkling took the train to Providence, where he spent Friday night as a guest of Rhode Island senator Henry B. Anthony, and on Saturday evening went to New York, where he checked into the Fifth Avenue Hotel. "The report that Senator Conkling had a personal encounter with ex-Senator Sprague, and was shot by him, has no foundation whatever," the *Sun* assured its readers.

Other papers, though, had begun to sense that something didn't ring quite true. The *Washington Post* thought the story "too thin." Both the *New York Times* and the *Cincinnati Enquirer* found it strange that Linck's lengthy statement failed to mention Conkling, even though the senator had tried to intervene with Sprague on the professor's behalf. The newspapers had good reason to be suspicious: the *Providence Journal*, which put out the first dispatches via the Associated Press and printed Linck's statement, was published by Senator Anthony, a close friend of Conkling and longtime political enemy of Sprague. A copublisher of the newspaper, managing editor George Danielson, was also Conkling's good friend. Meanwhile, the *New York Sun*'s editor, Charles Dana, was an admirer and former business partner of Conkling, who had helped Dana take over control of the *Sun* in 1868. It sounded like Conkling's powerful friends were perpetrating a cover-up.

The original story took on even less credibility when it turned out that Conkling had helped write it himself at the *Providence Journal*'s offices on Friday evening. Even more suspicious was the fact, which soon came out, that Linck went to the *Journal*'s offices on Saturday, at Conkling's request, to prepare his formal statement. Before Linck left for Providence, Kate called on him at his lakeside boardinghouse and had a conversation with him. Over the weekend Kate went to Providence as well and took up residence with her girls at the Narragansett Hotel, the city's finest. On early Monday morning the *Journal*'s managing editor, Danielson, sent her a proof of Linck's statement to revise, and she made numerous substantive changes to build up the allegations of Sprague's misconduct.

The cover story quickly unraveled. "No German Teacher Concerned," declared a headline in the *New York World*. The *Cincinnati Enquirer*'s story appeared under the headline, "Sprague's Shotgun," with the subheading, "All the Circumstances Point It Toward My Lord Roscoe." Some papers made light of the mix-up, with the *St. Paul Daily Globe* referring jokingly to "Professor Conkling, that distinguished teacher of German" for the Sprague family. "Sprague-enze Deutsch, Herr Conkling?" the paper asked, adding its belief that "Conkling is the missing Link."

Having exposed the original story as phony, the press turned its attention to trying to figure out what actually did happen. Neither Sprague nor Kate was making any statements, and the Conkling camp had retreated to silence. The newspapers, therefore, began piecing together a chronology based on eyewitness accounts. For the next week the story would be front-page news all over the country. Reporters from New York and elsewhere came to town to interview locals in search of the latest scoop, and Narragansett Pier residents crammed the railroad depot at noon every day to await the arrival of the New York train and a supply of New York papers, which were sold out within minutes.

As best as could be reconstructed, on Sunday, August 3, while still in Narragansett, Sprague heard that Conkling was just across the bay in Newport visiting his friend Levi P. Morton, a Republican congressman and banker who owned a villa there. Sprague told friends he doubted Conkling would dare to come over to the Pier, "for I will not have him." He said he was heading over to Newport on unrelated business and that if he ran into Conkling, there would be a "tall row." He was overheard to say that the custom of dueling needed to be revived in the United States, as some things could be settled only in that manner. In fact, he just missed Conkling at Newport, as Sprague entered the post office minutes after Conkling and Morton picked up their mail and left. Sprague then went up to Portland, Maine, where he said he had other business, and was not expected to return to Narragansett until the following Saturday.

Carrying a trunk and large valise, Conkling arrived at Narragansett Pier on Tuesday, August 5. He stayed at Canonchet through Thursday night and planned to remain at least through Friday. But unbeknownst to Kate or Conkling, after they retired for the night on Thursday, Sprague returned unexpectedly from Maine around 3 a.m. and went unseen to his apartments in a wing of the cavernous mansion remote from the rooms his wife and her guests occupied. (Many years later Sprague would claim he returned from Maine after a butler, per prior instruction, tipped him off to Conkling's presence.) Unable to sleep, he got up early Friday and went to a restaurant in town called "The Studio," where he played billiards. Reports conflicted as to whether Sprague was inebriated on this fateful day. Kate's friends said he was, although witnesses in town insisted he was not, one of them describing him as "sober but dreadfully in earnest." But clearly he got himself worked up after hearing villagers talking about how Roscoe Conkling was at Canonchet and had been there at least a couple of days. Sprague raced back to the mansion, not much more than a five-minute ride away, and around 2 p.m. he had some sort of confrontation, first with Linck out front, then with Conkling. According to Perry the coachman, Sprague met Conkling on the piazza. Conkling rose to his feet and, calm and dignified, bowed to the Governor and retreated a little. Sprague may have asked Conkling whether he was armed, to which the answer was no. With great vehemence Sprague then ordered Conkling to leave, took out his watch, and said he had exactly twenty minutes to get out (five minutes according to other stories, thirty seconds according to another account). Some reports said Conkling left immediately and without argument, the coachman said he seemed hesitant to leave, and another report said Conkling refused to go until Sprague ordered him out again and ran upstairs to get a gun. (The story that Conkling carried an invalid to his carriage was debunked as nonsense.) Conkling left without his luggage and walked slowly down the path leading downhill to the Ocean Road, about three hundred yards from the mansion, then another few hundred yards to the pier, where he waited at Billington's café to catch the 5:30 p.m. train to Providence.

Sprague, still in a lather, drove his carriage into town in search of Conkling and found him standing in front of Billington's. Druggist W. C. Clarke, from outside his shop five hundred feet away, could see that something exciting was going on. Conkling crossed the street, and Sprague jumped from his carriage and followed him, gesticulating violently. A. H. Wood, the café manager, together with his waiter boy, watched and listened to the confrontation from the front window. Sprague shouted, "Have you not gone yet, G—d— you?" The senator said something in a low tone of voice that Wood couldn't hear, but Sprague responded loudly, "I will accept no apology for what you've done." Conkling then said, "You will think better of all this tomorrow," to which Sprague replied, "No sir; no sir; I want this distinctly understood. Go away from here at once. You say you are not armed. Then go, for, by God, if you don't I'll blow your brains out; and further, never cross my path again. If you do, be armed. I shall be armed, and if you cross my way I shall kill you." Wood and the waiter boy then watched Conkling cross the street to reenter the café, and Sprague drove off.

Inside Billington's, Conkling was pale but quiet. He asked the trembling waiter boy to bring him some milk and crackers, which he ate with no show of emotion. The next train to leave the Pier was not for another two hours, so Conkling aimlessly strolled the beach, poking holes in the sand with his umbrella. He returned to the café, and Kate soon arrived by carriage to speak with him before she went to Tower Hill House, a couple of miles from Canonchet, where she and the girls would spend the night. Conkling made the short walk to the depot, where his luggage had been delivered in the interim. He took the train to Providence and stayed the night with Senator Anthony after they worked with Danielson to put out the original dispatch from the *Journal's* office.

After Conkling left, Sprague was seen conversing quietly in the street with several persons, making no reference to the incident, and seeming "less irritable than usual." Interviewed a few days later, he confirmed he had ordered Conkling from his house. "For what reason, may I ask?" the reporter inquired. "Because he has tried to destroy my household in Washington and now he seeks to do it here," Sprague replied. When pressed for further explanation Sprague curtly responded that if his interviewer had read the Washington newspapers the past winter he would know why.

For those in the press who had previously remained mum about Conkling's affair with Kate, the Canonchet shotgun incident was treated as license to bring it all into the open. The only wonder, the *Brooklyn Eagle* declared, was that the affair had not blown up sooner. Many papers resurrected old gossip implicating both Conkling and Kate in scandals. According to one such story, Conkling had broken up a marriage between a New York state official and his wife. As another legend went, the youthful Conkling, prior to his marriage, sired an illegitimate, look-alike son who still frequented the Utica area. And the story of Kate's dalliance, at age sixteen in Columbus, with the married Dick Nevins was given fresh circulation.

Meanwhile William Sprague, who had been ridiculed by the press ten years earlier for his Senate speeches, now drew, if not accolades, at least understanding nods. The *New York Times* observed that although Sprague had never been regarded very warmly, people were "decided in their opinion that if he has erred, he has also been greatly provoked." Conkling was castigated both for invading another man's home and for trying to shift the blame to the hapless Linck. As one paper put it, Sprague's actions were not "so flagrant and vital as that committed by Senator Conkling in giving to the public an unmanly and untruthful account of the affair." Back in Kate's native Ohio the *Cincinnati Enquirer* declared that Sprague "has the sympathy of the majority of the people," with "the weight of expression being over the wonder that the Ex-Senator did not long ago do what he a day or two [ago] attempted to do."

The flood of stories about Kate and Conkling's relationship and the total backfiring of the Linck cover story was causing considerable embarrassment to both of them. A counterattack needed to be mounted. To defend their reputations, they would have to destroy William Sprague's. The time had come for Mrs. Sprague to make a statement. It came in the form of an ostensibly private letter to a friend in Boston that found its way into print in the *Providence Journal.* Her eagerly awaited version of events—written on her thirty-ninth birthday—was Kate's first public comment during her entire marriage on the sad state of affairs between her and her husband, and it made front pages all over the country.

"As you must have surmised," she began, "Governor Sprague's dissolute life and dissipated habits long ago interrupted our marital relations, though I have striven hard through untold humiliation and pain to hide from the world, for my children's sakes, the true conditions of a blighted, miserable domestic life." She referred to Sprague's arrest on a Massachusetts beach the prior year with Mary Viall and spoke of his rupture with trustee Chafee, which had turned off the spigot of money being paid to her for support. The Governor's "causeless and shameful persecution of the children's teacher is literally true," she wrote. Sprague's real animus, she claimed, sprang from his unwillingness to be restrained in his home by the constant presence of a gentleman. Sprague had further frightened away the guests in her house with his threats of "murder to be done."

The attempt to implicate Conkling in the matter, Kate declared, was "absurd." She averred that "Mr. Conkling was of course, as unconscious as I, that Gov. Sprague sought occasion to enact the tragic role of the injured husband." To the contrary, she claimed, she invited the senator to Canonchet to see her husband and offer advice on how the impasse with Chafee might be broken so that support of her children could resume. "Mr. Conkling stopped at Canonchet for this purpose, and was awaiting Gov. Sprague's return to seek an interview with him, when the now notorious outbreak occurred," she explained. "If any hostile words were exchanged between Mr. Conkling and Gov. Sprague at Canonchet, they alone know what they were, for no one else heard them," she added. "What transpired in the village I do not know beyond what is reported in the sensational accounts given in the newspapers."

Kate's statement was full of holes, starting with the preposterous claim that Sprague was on friendly speaking terms with Conkling. She did not explain why, if Conkling merely wanted to provide a bit of legal advice to her husband, the senator waited until Sprague was expected to be absent for several days, then moved in with a full trunk of luggage for an extended stay. Most absurd of all was her suggestion that her husband should not have been upset to learn that, while he was away, his wife was sleeping under the same roof as the man rumored to be her illicit lover.

Though she had scored some easy points off Sprague, Kate had damaged herself in the process. It was bad enough for a woman to resort to the newspapers to air such dirty laundry; it was worse if her story was palpably untrue. "The design of the statement was supposed to be to excite sympathy for Mrs. Sprague," the *New York Times* noted, but "if that was the purpose, it has failed completely." Kate's statement was "incoherent, abrupt, and more aggressive than would have been expected from a lady. . . . She is sharply criticized for publishing it at all, as public sympathy throughout the State has turned against her."

Some have assumed that the Conkling forces put Kate up to issuing her statement, against her better judgment, in order to protect the senator's political reputation. But Kate had an agenda of her own, which was to begin laying the groundwork for an eventual divorce suit against Sprague. The statement she gave was so hostile and broad based in its attack on Sprague's actions and character as to leave no doubt she was choosing to burn any remaining bridges. As a Cincinnati paper put it, "we presume legal proceedings are now unavoidable."

Just as Kate was putting her statement out, Linck was starting to backpedal from his. The day after Kate's public letter, Linck said that his initial draft statement was taken out of his hands and revised by Kate to the point that it was "no longer his property." Linck later revealed that Kate had "talked to him rather severely for not censuring the Governor's conduct in a stronger way." She ended up so distorting and mutilating his statement that he disavowed it, saying he could no longer recognize it. Much if not most of the professor's hyped-up story now had to be discounted as unreliable.

Linck had become a pathetic figure, a laughingstock, and an unpaid one to boot. Probably he hoped that if he went along with Conkling and Kate, he would be taken care of financially. But he had no idea he was dealing with two people who would drop him once he was no longer of use to them. He wrote to the *New York Sun* saying he had made his initial statement "not to be made a cat's paw of," but that is exactly what had happened. His original statement was "found ridiculous by Mrs. Sprague," he said, and she even taunted him for his cowardice in dealing with Sprague. What's more, Kate—whom he referred to as "This lady"—had repudiated all responsibility for paying him, saying her husband should be the one to do so. Linck now believed Sprague's objection to his employment was understandable and that it stemmed from "his wife's persistency to carry her point" about Willie's need for summer school. Linck thought Kate might even have effected a reconciliation with her husband had her "proud spirit" not gotten in the way. He still blamed Sprague "for his senseless frenzy toward me, and for that only" but said he would not prosecute him for assault.

In the meantime, for almost a week, from Saturday the ninth until Thursday the fourteenth, Kate had been living in seclusion at the Narragansett Hotel in Providence. She huddled with lawyers and vowed she would "never sleep under the same roof with Mr. Sprague again." An ill-advised summit meeting between her and Sprague was set up for Narragansett Pier, where she went by train on August 14. She was accompanied by her daughters and their nurse; a Providence lawyer, Robert Thompson; and Emma Fosdick, an old Cincinnati friend now living in Connecticut. The purpose of her trip, the *New York Sun* reported, was to arrange for collecting what belonged to her at Canonchet before she returned to Washington. She arrived at Narragansett on the afternoon train and went with the girls and Fosdick to the nearby cottage of her friend Mr. Hale, the local railroad conductor. She met there with Sprague in the presence of Thompson, Fosdick, and Mrs. Hale, the conductor's wife, while the children were attended to in a different room. At some point Kate's cousin, Ralston Skinner, who was staying at a nearby hotel, was also summoned and joined the gathering.

"This is your work, madame," Sprague began the meeting, to which she made no reply. It then degenerated into a "stormy and painful" interview. By this time Sprague had seen Kate's inflammatory public letter, which he called a "tissue of falsehoods." He accused her of poisoning the minds of his children against him and charged her with infidelity, which she indignantly denied. Kate in return accused him of "general brutality when under the influence of alcohol." Referring to her allegations of nonsupport, he asked, "Where is that $5,000 you got recently? I suppose you have squandered all that." He taunted her about Conkling, saying, "Your man got away pretty quick that time, didn't he?" According to one of Kate's friends, she bore these remarks for the most part in silence, although she reacted strongly when Sprague told her she belonged in an insane asylum. Finally he asked whether she was planning to return to Canonchet. "I fear for my life if I do," she replied. "I never harmed anyone," he said, "and you are safe." According to the *Sun*, Kate then accused him of—and he did not deny—recently pointing a loaded pistol at her head. The *World*, however, reported that he merely acknowledged having a loaded gun on the day he threatened Conkling. The *World*'s less dramatic version is more plausible than the Conkling-friendly *Sun*'s, as it is unlikely Sprague would have admitted, in front of Kate's friends, that he had threatened her with a gun, as this would only have given her ammunition to use against him in a divorce suit.

Sprague then repeated his demands for surrender of the children, but Kate resisted, at which point Thompson and Skinner (who was also a lawyer) were brought into the conversation. They advised her that Sprague was on strong legal grounds and, accordingly, the children were fetched and delivered up to him. Although he had spent precious little time with the three girls, Sprague was quoted as saying that he was "deeply wrapped up" in them and found their presence "soothing and comforting."

By the end of the meeting at the Hale house it was getting dark. Sprague took the girls and their nurse back to Canonchet in his carriage, and Kate stayed behind. But after their departure she was greatly agitated and decided to follow them to Canonchet, where she was driven after nightfall, accompanied by Thompson, Skinner, and Emma Fosdick. Either or both of the two men, at Kate's request, remained in the mansion overnight, but Sprague, having taken a strong dislike to Kate's friend Fosdick, refused to allow her into the house, setting off another argument. That night the house was reported to be closed up and dark.

Public sympathy now began to shift in Kate's favor, with the press describing her as being under a sort of house arrest. The *New York Sun* ran a front-page story on Saturday, August 16, with the headline "Is His Wife a Prisoner?" It told of a report that Kate was being kept at Canonchet by Sprague "in a room under lock and key." According to the newspaper's source, Sprague was opening every telegram or message sent to Kate and had instructed the servants to take no orders from his wife. Sprague reportedly threatened with discharge one sympathetic maid who smuggled in a telegram to Kate, although he later changed his mind.

Now it was Sprague who was on the defensive. He denied that Kate was a prisoner, saying she was free to come and go within the house as she pleased and could leave at any time, so long as she did not take the children. His only interference, he said, was to "prevent her communication with persons whom he regards as hostile to him." Sources described as mutual friends of the Spragues said the imprisonment story was overblown, that Kate had in fact received visitors as well as unopened correspondence freely. Sprague maintained that by keeping his wife composed for a few days and beyond the reach of distressing influences, he might induce her to come to some better understanding with him. Still, he acknowledged he had limited her contact with the outside world, so the prisoner analogy was not so far-fetched.

Sprague apparently concluded that the stories of his imprisonment of Kate were a public relations disaster, because he soon allowed a *New York Sun* reporter into the mansion to interview her. When the correspondent arrived, Sprague greeted him cordially and asked Arthur Watson, a younger relative, to take him to see Kate. The correspondent was escorted up the winding mahogany staircase to the second floor, where a doorway opened into an elegantly furnished suite, half parlor, half library, with a bay window overlooking the lawn. Kate sat in a chair near a table and rose to receive her guest. He found her "extremely pale, but her manner betrayed only the slightest trace of agitation." Once or twice her lips trembled, but in general she spoke calmly and earnestly "with a degree of native eloquence and grace which would make a powerful impression on the most obdurate." She thereupon proceeded to give yet another version of the events of the preceding days.

"I have sent for you," she said to the *Sun*'s reporter, "because I wish to correct some false impressions which have gone abroad in regard to my conduct at Thursday's meeting," the one at the Hale residence two days earlier. She denied making any verbal attacks on her husband and said she had borne "with meekness the unmanly sneers and reproaches that he showered upon me, not responding save when my children's relations to me were touched upon." She continued, "I have my story to tell, and when the truth of this terrible business is known I know that I shall be justified. God knows that I have no reason to fear the truth."

Kate went on: "For thirteen long years my life has been a constant burden and drag upon me," she said. The stated time frame was telling, for it placed the beginning of her domestic hell in 1866, less than three years into the marriage. That was the same year Kate spent eight months in Europe, Sprague wrote his bizarre letters asking her for permission to see other women, and divorce rumors had surfaced and been denied. "For years I have had this thing weighing upon me, and have striven with all my might to stand between my husband's wrong-doing and the public. I have done it for the sake of my children, not for any affection that existed between us; for there has been none for years."

Kate then turned to address the Conkling rumors. Conkling had been dragged into the "whole miserable affair . . . without a particle of reason or excuse." She said she had known him, like so many friends of her father, "from the time I was a child," but that was a dubious claim. There is no evidence Kate ever met Conkling before 1861, at the earliest, when she arrived in Washington at age twenty and Conkling was a freshman congressman. In her father's meticulous diaries and voluminous correspondence, Conkling is not mentioned until 1862, when the treasury secretary recorded his first impression of the young representative as someone "who has not been as cordial to me as I think he should have been." Conkling was no childhood friend of Kate.

"There is not a word of truth in all these atrocious reports," she insisted to the *Sun* reporter. "Conkling never paid me any attention a wife could not honorably receive from her husband's friend, and it is false to say otherwise. Mr. Sprague was simply worked upon by his business troubles, which have been culminating for years, and by his indulgence in strong drink. He regarded everyone, no matter how honorable, who was a friend of mine, as an interloper and an intriguer against him. His jealousy and hatred of that poor German shows the workings of his monomania."

The reporter then asked the question on everyone's mind: "How did Mr. Conkling venture to come to Canonchet under the circumstances?"

"He came," Kate replied, "simply to use his influence with my husband to consent to a certain policy in his management of the estate." She "considered that there would be no impropriety in his visiting us here for that purpose." Perhaps it was true that Conkling at some earlier point offered Sprague some friendly legal or business advice. But Kate was elevating it, implausibly, into the principal explanation for Conkling's sojourn to

Canonchet. Asked two days later to respond to this particular assertion, Sprague disputed it, and the *New York Times* dismissed it entirely.

Kate went on to tell the *Sun*'s correspondent that during his visit Conkling occupied a room on the third floor (her bedroom was on the second). Then, on Friday morning at breakfast, she was told that Sprague had come home suddenly at three in the morning and left again. "I paid no attention to this, however, as his movements are always very erratic. He comes in on you like a ghost in the middle of the night and at the most unseasonable hours, and hurries away in the same disquieting manner." Although Conkling was somewhat startled to learn of Sprague's presence, Kate thought no more of it and busied herself with household affairs while Conkling sat at breakfast reading the newspapers. Kate began reading to her invalid guest, Throop Martin, and just then Sprague came up the staircase. "He walked slowly into the room, Mr. Conkling rising to meet him," she said. "Some words passed between them, which I did not hear, but the tone of which arrested my attention. I rose to my feet. Mr. Conkling walked straight across the room to where I stood and said: 'Mrs. Sprague, your husband is very much excited, and I think it better for all of us if I should withdraw. If my departure puts you in any danger, so say, and I will stay, whatever the consequences.'"

Conkling "spoke in a very calm voice, although I know he must have been very excited," she continued. "I told him not to mind me, but that if Mr. Sprague was in a passion it would be useless to argue with him, and might only lead to violence." According to Kate, Conkling walked out onto the piazza, followed by nine-year-old Ethel, who put her arm around him and said, "'Don't go, Mr. Conkling.'" Kate told her, "'No, Ethel, Mr. Conkling will go, but no one shall hurt either him or us.'" As this scene was unfolding, Kate said, Sprague stood "eyeing us in a sort of desperate way."

And what of the famous shotgun? "Mr. Sprague took his gun with him in the buggy when he went after Mr. Conkling," she said. "I know it was loaded, for Willie, my boy, came to me just afterward and said: 'Mama, papa's gun is loaded with three slugs, and if he shoots anyone he'll kill them sure.'" Fortunately, Kate continued, Sprague had no percussion caps, and although he asked Willie for some, the boy thought it best not to give them to his father. Kate concluded that she had "reason to be grateful that no one was murdered."

That was the last time Kate ever said anything publicly about Sprague threatening to shoot Conkling. When she filed for divorce the following year she made no mention of any shotgun or of Conkling. Ironically, even though Sprague himself admitted—even boasted—that he had threatened to shoot Conkling, Kate's divorce lawyer would later claim that "the story of Conkling and the shot gun is all a lie, that Sprague had no shot gun and therefore did not threaten to shoot Conkling with it." Another self-described representative of Kate insisted that "the yarn that he [Sprague] followed Mr. Conkling with a shotgun is so ridiculously untruthful, and known to be so by a number of people, all at Canonchet at the time, that I have no patience to discuss it. There was absolutely nothing whatever in that story—a downright falsehood, made up out of whole cloth." Apparently neither of them had gone back to read Kate's interview with the *Sun* and her statements about the shotgun.

None of the houseguests, all friends of Kate, were going to contradict anything she said about the incident. But she was telling so many untruths and half-truths during this period that little she said can be accepted at face value. Conkling, after being called out for fabricating the original story, never commented publicly on the entire episode. Sprague, described by the *New York World* as "sensibly silent," remained mostly mute about the key events, leaving it to representatives to make his case in print. For once his infelicity with words served him well.

Having finished her statement of what took place inside the house, Kate said there was "another falsehood that has been extensively circulated, and that is that Mr. Conkling endorsed that statement which attributed the whole affair to my husband's hatred of Mr. Linck. I know from gentlemen who were present when that dispatch was written that Mr. Conkling disapproved of it." That assertion was directly contradicted by what Conkling's friend Danielson, the *Journal*'s managing editor, told the *New York Times*—namely, that the original dispatches were approved by Conkling and based explicitly on information he provided. More significantly, Kate was now admitting that the Linck story—including the professor's own statement that she helped write—was largely invented. By now the *New York Times* regarded the entire Linck tale as "apocryphal," and the *World* commented tersely that Kate's statements in the matter were "not consistent." She had been willing to implicate herself in a series of lies in order to shield her lover from condemnation.

The interview concluded with Kate labeling all insinuations of an affair between her and Conkling as "outrageous slanders" and "monstrous falsehoods." She said she wanted only "the truth, and every particle of the truth, about this matter to be known at the proper time" and vowed that eventually she would "show the true character and origin of the persecution."

Kate did not tell "the whole truth," but it is easy to understand why she chose not to and even to sympathize with her decision. No ironclad evidence proved her affair, and if any amorous letters were written, they were never found or were destroyed. People could believe what they wanted about Kate and Conkling, but they could never know for sure. The easier thing was to just deny it. Her decision was a product of cold calculation—by a mind that was always playing chess and seeing several moves ahead. She thought like a politician, and as journalist Donn Piatt said around this time, "she looks at the world from a man's standpoint."

Just four years earlier famed preacher Henry Ward Beecher was charged with "criminal conversation" with the wife of influential New York newspaper editor Theodore Tilton. Although the evidence of Beecher's adultery was as least as strong as that implicating Kate, Beecher elected to endure an embarrassing public trial rather than admit to an affair. After a hung jury, Beecher emerged with his reputation mostly intact.

If a famous man could get away with brazenly denying the obvious, then, Kate might have reasoned, so could she. She also would have understood the double standard that applied to sex scandals: the dalliances of a man might be winked at, even congratulated; a Senate colleague reputedly called Conkling a "lucky dog" after seeing Kate show up to watch him from the gallery. But in Kate's time a woman adulteress would always bear the scarlet *A*. On her tenth birthday, while Kate was at Miss Haines's school, her father pointed out to her that whenever she did something for which she might be blamed, she was "peculiarly tempted to swerve from the truth in order to conceal or excuse it." Twenty-nine birthdays later, her fear of censure had not gone away.

Kate had other good reasons to maintain her innocence. She would not want her children to know she had committed adultery, even as a technical matter and even if, considering her estrangement from Sprague and his own numerous infidelities, it was understandable and forgivable that she had strayed. Equally important, admitting to marital infidelity could jeopardize her chances of retaining custody of her children. For all these reasons it made sense for Kate to deny the affair.

There were those who believed she was "more sinned against than sinning." The *New York Times* editorialized that the "vain Senator," having clouded her name, "had not the self-respect nor the manliness" to come to her defense. Such comments as these may have seemed patronizing, but they were about the best press she could hope for. It was better to be an object of pity than condemnation.

Meanwhile, Kate's confinement at Canonchet continued. By now she was permitted to take carriage rides about town, always accompanied by a loyal servant of her husband. According to the *Sun*, Sprague set up a strict surveillance system to prevent her from abducting the children. Kate was said by friends to be in constant fear of some sudden outbreak that would threaten her and her daughters' lives.

Shortly after her return to Canonchet it became clear she was contemplating some sort of exodus, for she started sending jewelry, papers, furniture, and expensive artifacts out of the mansion. Sprague knew it was happening but took no action to stop it. There was talk that some of Sprague's creditors wanted to eject Sprague from Canonchet and put Kate in sole charge, but trustee Chafee objected to leaving someone of her spending habits alone in control at the estate. That gambit having failed and unable to get rid of her husband, Kate decided to get away from him.

As the end of August neared, she was ready to make her move. Friends of Kate told the *New York Sun* the last straw came on August 29, when Sprague came home drunk, went to the upstairs room where the nurses were dressing the children, and, seeing Kate there, cried out, "I'll show you who is master here," then dragged her around the room and tried to throw her out the window. Whatever the truth of this story, the incident was not the impetus for her departure, for Kate had already sought and, three days earlier, received her lawyer's blessing for her suggested plan. "Leave and take immediate proceedings to secure possession of your daughters," she was advised.

On Friday, August 29, she was closeted at Canonchet with two or three attorneys who were drawing up an agreement they hoped to induce Sprague to sign. Kate arranged for livery driver Tom Handy, who had been sneaking letters and telegrams to her, to bring a carriage and two wagons to the house after dark that same Friday evening, when Sprague was expected to go sailing. Kate had her bags packed and on the elevators ready to be taken down to the wagons, at which point she would signal one of the children's nurses that everything was ready. But Sprague did not go sailing that evening, so the plan was aborted. A new plan was hatched the next morning, Saturday, when Handy brought Kate's letters and telegrams to her. She hoped Sprague would visit the beach in the afternoon, as he usually did. In the meantime, sensing a conspiracy afoot, Sprague had summoned his friend Dr. Jerome Greene to provide him with some disinterested advice. Greene breakfasted with Sprague and Kate on Saturday morning and thought matters looked smooth enough as they both conversed with him in friendly terms. That afternoon Sprague walked to the beach with a visitor while Kate met with a New York lawyer at a local hotel for some last-minute advice. She returned to Canonchet in late afternoon and went to the rear of the house. Sprague came back from the beach sooner than usual because of his suspicions but fell asleep in a room in the front of the mansion. Now was her chance, and it was not clear when she would have another. She made a decision—to launch the escape plan.

CHAPTER 22

# "The Bird Has Flown"

There was not much time now—they would need to hurry. The Governor was dozing in a front room of the mansion, taking his customary late-afternoon nap after a swim in the bay, but he might rouse at any moment. He had his loyalists among the household staff—Morris the overseer, Ernest the black cook, and that officious, busybody relative of his, Arthur Watson, who had been keeping vigil over Kate and the children during their captivity the past two weeks. One of the help was sure to sound the alarm the moment they noticed the inmates' escape. But Kate had her accomplices as well—Narragansett Pier locals she had taken into her confidence. Tom Handy would meet them with his carriage around back, beyond the stable and barns; Gaius Smith, the railroad depot clerk, made the arrangements with Handy and furnished a trunk for Kate's belongings, and the nurses were dressing the three girls, awaiting the signal from Kate that all was ready. At half past five on this next-to-last day of August 1879, they took their flight.

First Kate, then the girls and their nurses, carrying as many personal items as they could, slipped out the back and hurried along a private lane past the Robinson family cemetery. Tom Handy picked up the girls and two nurses at the prearranged spot. After a feint in the direction of the waterfront village to throw off anyone who might have seen them, he drove them a few hundred yards inland to a place along Tower Hill Road, where

Kate had gone to wait. A second horse-drawn wagon, driven by Richard Brown, joined them there. Kate was helped into the buggy while the girls and nurses were crammed into the four-seat wagon with the belongings they managed to smuggle out with them. With that, they took off over the interior road in the direction of Wickford, about eleven miles north on the water, where they planned to catch a boat for the shore of Massachusetts, from where they would travel overland up into New England and to the safety of friends. As the two vehicles drove as fast as the bumpy Tower Hill Road would allow them, on what would be a two-hour journey, the occupants looked nervously behind them at intervals for any signs of an approaching William Sprague.

Sitting alone in her carriage as it trudged along the Tower Hill Road, Kate knew she was saying her final good-bye to Canonchet. She had spent years turning it into the house of her dreams, but during those same years, as the house grew in grandeur and splendor, the love in her marital life had dissolved. Now all of it was gone. Backward though her thoughts must have drifted, she needed to look forward and to get to Wickford. She knew Sprague would not let them go without giving chase, which is why the passengers kept looking back, fearing to see him in pursuit.

Sprague had been catnapping on a sofa in the mansion, listening to the noise his children were making, when it suddenly ceased. The groggy ex-governor stayed resting on his lounge for about fifteen minutes, then got up and went out on the piazza. It was some time after 5:30 p.m. Workmen informed him that they saw Kate drive away from the house in a buggy. Sprague knew then that she had taken the children. Arthur Watson, who had somehow failed in his surveillance duties, came up to him and said simply, "The bird has flown."

There had been a 5:30 train out of Narragansett Pier, so Watson, along with Ernest the cook, drove hastily to the depot. But Tom Handy's ruse of starting toward the pier had worked; Kate had not gone to the train station, and no clues as to the escapees' whereabouts could be found, either at the depot or in the village hotels. The fugitives had thereby gained valuable time. On their way back to the mansion Watson and Ernest were met by Sprague, who went to the station to telegraph ahead to West Kingston to see whether they had arrived yet at the station there, eight and a half miles away. They had not, so Sprague set off on horseback at a breakneck pace for Kingston Junction, hoping to overtake them somewhere along the way. In the meantime, because no train would leave Narragansett Pier between 5:30 and the last train at 7:30, Willie was sent to wait at the pier station to see whether they showed up there.

When Sprague arrived at West Kingston he found that Kate was not aboard the 5:30 train. Willie went over to Tower Hill House in Wakefield, where Kate had taken the girls the first night after the shotgun incident, but they were not there either. They had disappeared like quicksilver.

Some newspapers speculated that Kate had gone to Newport in a speedy yacht seen hovering about Narragansett Pier all Saturday afternoon. Another report said they were on a steamer to Europe. Others said she was spotted in a carriage outside Providence, bound for Boston, to where a trunk full of her articles had been checked. The press treated it as a mystery and enjoyed the guessing game.

Sprague purported to be unconcerned. In his first wide-ranging interview since the shotgun scandal broke, he said he did not intend to sue for divorce but would take steps to regain his daughters, who were legally, if not physically, as much in his possession as when Kate took them away. But he would not, he said, race all over the country to find them or try to obtain them "surreptitiously." He sent Willie to carry a note to Kate's lawyers, saying he was prepared to forward the girls' clothing and personal effects anywhere Kate's counsel directed. He went on to deny—implausibly—that he had been intoxicated at any time recently.

He also provided his version of the "window" incident. Suspecting that an escape was being planned, he wanted to enter the nursery to check on the children, but Kate refused to allow him admission because the girls were not dressed. That explanation did not satisfy him, and although he was angry and did use harsh language, he did not enter the nursery. He strenuously denied using violence against Kate at that or any other time. He said Kate was well provided with money, and in truth, it did seem she always had plenty of cash on her not only to pay drivers and couriers but also to stay in the most expensive hotels in town.

Where she got her spending money remains something of a mystery; she had nothing from the Sprague estate, and Chafee was not paying Sprague anything, having refused to employ him the past six months because he considered him unreliable. Sprague did claim to have recently transferred $5,000 worth of negotiable paper to Kate that she cashed in, and possibly she was receiving outside help from Conkling or others.

The details of Kate's escape from Canonchet eventually emerged, and the story evoked images of the fabled Underground Railroad. On their way north her party stopped at the Four Chimney House to rest the horses. Then, satisfied they had not been followed, they drove with less anxiety over an unfrequented road to Wickford. There they met some friends and sat down to supper. After supper they went another three miles to a place on the shore called Chapin's, where Handy chartered a small sloop to take them across the bay. At Chapin's, Kate gave three dollars to a young man to take care of driver Richard Brown's horse because it had been driven so hard, and she then sent the buggy back to Narragansett Pier with Brown, promising him a gold watch for his services. It was now after midnight. Kate's party, including Handy, set sail in the sloop for Fall River, Massachusetts, but in midstream Handy advised the captain to change course and land at Bristol, Rhode Island. At Bristol, after an overnight sail, Handy engaged a double team of horses that conveyed the party to Lonsdale, a small village just outside Providence, where they stopped until noon while Kate consulted with her lawyers in the city. At Lonsdale she paid a stable keeper fifty dollars for a fresh team of horses, which drove them to Walpole, Massachusetts, where they rested before being driven on to Boston. Kate bought Handy a new suit of clothes, and he escorted them to Norwich, Connecticut, from where they embarked by boat for Long Island. They ended up in Babylon, New York, at the home of Austin Corbin, a wealthy real estate developer of Coney Island and a distant relation of Kate. Corbin harbored Kate and the three girls for two weeks under the protection of half a dozen workmen who "would have made it very unpleasant for anyone who had dared to molest them." From there they made their way back to Edgewood.

* * *

Whatever happened at Canonchet, Kate's flight from there and her subsequent odyssey were daring and courageous. Thereafter the "Canonchet scandal" receded from the news until late September, when a hearing was held in Rhode Island on Kate's petition to appoint a trustee for her personal property in Narragansett. Her preferred trustee—Robert Thompson, the lawyer who guided her during the shotgun affair—was appointed over the objection of Sprague's lawyers, who suggested Arthur Watson, the Sprague relative who had joined in giving chase after Kate's flight.

All three principals in the shotgun episode were tarnished by it, but the two presumed lovers received the most stinging rebukes. That was especially true in the conservative hinterlands. A Nebraska paper regretted that the scandal had forced upon the public "the salacious history of the two imprudent and perhaps wicked parties, most talked about in this transaction." The paper in Hillsboro, Ohio, where Kate had often visited relatives, criticized the couple for attentions "such as no honorable man ought to have paid to another man's wife, and such as no prudent married woman, with a proper respect for her own and her husband's honor, would have permitted herself to receive from any other man."

The scandal had taken its toll on Kate. Around the time of the trustee hearing a reporter showed up at Edgewood and found her looking washed out. She lamented that she had been "maligned and ground down until I have felt that I was a target at which everybody could fire, and yet without means or method of redress." As she explained,

> The bitterest part of my recent troubles has been that I should be thought a silly, vain woman. Why, I have been trained to look upon dignity and brains as of the highest importance, and I have a high regard for conventionalities, although I believe I have not that reputation. To be so misrepresented, so misunderstood, has given me my greatest pain. I have been charged with all sorts of misdoings, of which I am totally innocent.

She expressed gratitude for the kindness of southern newspapers, which sympathized with her "because I was a woman and defenseless." She offered hope that "the chivalry of the North will grant me the same fairness, and I hope to show that it is not unmerited."

Kate was not accustomed to negative press coverage. She had her detractors over the years, those who considered her cold and ambitious, but by and large the papers wrote about her in positive terms. The rumors of her affair with Conkling, beginning in early 1878 and through the first half of 1879, caused some respectable society types to pull away from her, but the reaction was nothing compared with the ostracism she faced postshotgun.

After the early stories in August nothing more was heard from the Conkling camp, and Conkling himself never issued a statement about the incident. He was lucky, a Cincinnati newspaper opined, "that his career was not terminated by a shot then and there." He spoke publicly at the New York State Republican Convention in Saratoga on September 3 and succeeded in getting his machine stooge, Alonzo Cornell, nominated for governor. But his strategy regarding Canonchet was to ignore it and, seemingly, Kate as well. To many, he had abandoned her in her hour of need, further evidence of his vanity and selfishness. Kate's earlier effort to paint him as a sort of gallant protector seemed ludicrous in retrospect. His nemesis, President Rutherford B. Hayes, gloated in his diary that the "exposure of Conkling's rottenness will do good in one direction. It will weaken his political power, which is bad and only bad." Indeed, from Canonchet forward, Conkling relinquished any serious thought of making another run for the presidency. And the scandal would continue to be an albatross around his neck in Conkling's political struggles with Hayes's successor in office.

In some ways Sprague suffered the least of the three players in the drama, if only because he started from the lowest rung. For years he had been portrayed as an insignificant, ineffectual, chronically drunken character. The shotgun incident did not erase that image, but in chasing Conkling from his home, Sprague was seen by many to have gained back some of his self-respect. It came at a price, though, for, beginning with the shotgun affair, Sprague defined himself in the public eye as a crazed gunman. Almost every subsequent story about his quarrels with this or that adversary pictured him with his double-barrel shotgun, itching to pull the trigger. Certainly Sprague had a short fuse and an inordinate attachment to weaponry. But for all his bravado and alleged death threats, he had scarcely laid a hand on either Conkling or Linck. In fact, apart from First Bull Run, there is no documented instance of him ever discharging a firearm at anyone. Nonetheless the image of shotgun-toting Sprague would become a convenient one to be trotted out from time to time by those seeking to discredit him.

Sprague lost something else as a result of the Canonchet affair. The woman he once called a "treasure" and who, he promised her father, would never receive any detriment at his hands was gone from his life forever. He extended overtures to her through the press—talking and acting, the *New York Times* observed, "as if he believed his wife entirely undeserving of the dreadful innuendoes" printed about her. But if Kate was listening, she was not swayed. It was too late; she would never return to him. The bird had flown.

Every scandal has its ridiculous figure, and in this one it was Professor George Linck. The *New York World* quipped in August that the controversy was not all bad for Linck, for he had become the most widely advertised tutor around. But Linck didn't see it that way, and he ended up suing Kate for $240 he had never been paid. He seemed to have a strong case, as Kate, by her own letters and statements, had confirmed the existence and terms of their contract. But Linck underestimated how tough a customer Kate could be. She defended the suit on the grounds that she made the agreement in her capacity as a married woman and that, under the law, her husband, not she, was legally responsible for the debt. She had successfully used the same defense a few months earlier, when she avoided paying for some professional photographs taken in Washington. It was an ironic position for the daughter of the chief justice who, as the lone dissenter in the famous *Bradwell* case, rejected the view that a woman had no separate legal existence from her husband and was incapable of entering into binding contracts. But in litigation, as in the rest of her life, Kate played to win, not to make a symbolic statement. Linck's counsel pointed out that because Kate had been separated from her husband for six months at the time of the contract, she should be held liable under it as if she were a single woman. "She travels with a retinue of servants and a caravan of baggage and entertains foreign noblemen at her residence," Linck's lawyer pleaded, "but she refuses to pay the just demands of the man whom she engaged to teach her children." The court reserved decision, and the final outcome was never reported on, so it is likely the case eventually settled.

Kate could and would play hardball just as much when it came time to go to court to seek a divorce from William Sprague. Partly it was in her nature to do so, and partly she would be urged on by aggressive lawyers. And much of it would have to do with her love for her children and her tenacious desire to keep custody of them. But more than anything it was because, from the moment she took her final leave from Canonchet that August day, she no longer considered herself to be Kate Chase Sprague. She would go by that moniker, nominally and legally, for almost another two years, but in her mind she was no longer Mrs. Sprague. Instead, she longed to be and saw herself once again as Kate Chase.

# PART 3

# KATE CHASE AGAIN

CHAPTER 23

# "A Dinner with the Queen"

The shotgun affair did not end Kate's love affair with Conkling; their relationship continued and, in some ways, strengthened. But having grown incautious in the months leading up to the notorious episode, the couple now took their liaisons underground while trying to convince the world there had been nothing romantic between them.

Their next public relations effort ended up backfiring. In January 1880 Kate gave a dinner party for Conkling and his wife, Julia, in Washington, with an Associated Press reporter and several prominent guests in attendance. The press saw through the event, condemning it as an obvious ruse to keep up appearances. One correspondent reported that "the suppliant air of Mrs. Sprague was counterbalanced by the rigid reserve of Mrs. Conkling," who, in Washington for the first time in many years, appeared to rebel at this test of devotion. As the reporter noticed, "Mrs. Conkling does not pretend to have the slightest reconciliation with her husband, but went through the performance at his request" and then hurried back to Utica the next day.

Conkling's enemies took for granted that the dinner had been his idea. One story making the rounds was that Conkling first tried without success to persuade his wife to write Kate a letter, for eventual publication, expressing sympathy for her and belief in her honesty, and when Julia balked at the idea, the dinner was arranged as a substitute. In later years, reminiscing with a friend, Rutherford Hayes commented on the "brutality of Conkling in compelling his wife to attend the dinner at Washington at which Mrs. Sprague appeared." But a letter from the now-married John Hay to his wife two days before the dinner casts some doubt on whose idea it was:

> I made up my mind yesterday that I ought to call upon Mrs. Sprague now that she has come into the city and as I did not know when I would have an hour again, I went there last night. She has a little house on Connecticut Avenue, the Diplomatic quarter, and she has saved enough things from the shipwreck of her fortunes to make it very pretty. She seemed really glad to see me, but did not break down in the least. She made only one reference to her troubles and that was when she spoke of "the New England caution which resembles something that begins with 'C'" and she added plaintively, "I much confess I do not understand New England methods." She is still a very handsome woman, but her trouble has left its mark, and I felt ashamed to suspect that she has taken to repairing the ravages of time. I was not to go without a surprise. She asked me to go there Wednesday and dine with Mr. and Mrs. Conkling. I told her I was engaged to some Ohio people, Garfield and Townsend, and she positively asked me to try and get out—and when I said that was impossible she asked me to come in after dinner, which I said I would do if I could. I cannot believe the foul stories, but the fact is, that married people cannot have any intimate friendships outside of their own families without danger of trouble and suffering.

Although the reference to New England caution and methods is ambiguous, Kate clearly was apprehensive about the evening. In any event, she went along with the subterfuge.

Kate tried to put on another show again that April, when she hosted a luncheon at Edgewood for female journalists, among them the influential society columnist Olivia. Kate wanted to demonstrate that the scandal had not diminished her famous hostessing skills. In an article entitled "A Dinner with the Queen of American Aristocracy," Olivia described an elegant table in a perfect dining room that recalled the days of Marie Antoinette. "Flowers alone occupy the center of the table, and these are so artistically arranged that each guest is visible to every other." At high noon Kate took her seat at the head of the table "with her ebony assistant at her right," followed by the guests, called for and seated by the waiter one by one. Multiple courses followed, served on imported royal porcelain: French bouillon, oyster patties, sweetbreads, Virginia mountain lamb, custard, then more meat, vegetables, salads, and champagne. Each arrived in perfect time, set down by "the white-gloved, machine-like Ethiopian, who understands a glance from the Princess's eye and does not have to be regulated by means of the English language." All that was missing to "bring the old millionaire days back," Olivia wrote, was the presence of the "young war governor of Rhode Island." Kate had proved she could still orchestrate anything she put her mind to, but she could not make people forget the events of the prior August.

Nonetheless, her subterranean relationship with Conkling went forward. Kate attended the Republican National Convention that summer in Chicago, where Conkling was managing the effort to nominate Ulysses Grant, four years out of the presidency, to run for a third term. She went incognito, with the sister-in-law of Richard Crowley, an upstate New York congressman and close political ally of Conkling. Crowley and his wife, Julia, were also good friends of Kate and had entertained her at their Lockport home when she and Conkling attended as the star attractions. Kate and Mrs. Crowley's sister received their convention seat tickets courtesy of Chester Arthur, Conkling's right-hand man.

Grant was the favorite going into the convention, followed by Conkling's longtime nemesis, Maine senator James G. Blaine and Ohio senator John Sherman (the general's brother). Grant was poised to sweep to victory after Conkling brought the house down with his electrifying nominating speech. Dramatically climbing up on a reporter's table in front of the platform, arms folded across his chest, he began his oration with a familiar piece of campaign doggerel that set off a lengthy ovation:

*When asked what state he hails from,*
*Our sole reply shall be,*
*He comes from Appomattox,*
*And its famous apple tree.*

But the surprise dark-horse winner, who emerged after thirty-six ballots, was Kate's old friend James Garfield. Conkling, so confident of victory heading into the convention, was shocked and angered that the prize had gone to the man he called "the Trickster of Mentor." Kate surely felt for Conkling, who, with a "funereal" voice, offered a perfunctory motion to make Garfield's nomination unanimous. His only solace was that the Grant supporters—306 of them—followed his command to stay the course and vote for the general through the final ballot. They became known as the "immortal 306," or "Old Guard," as they called themselves at annual reunion dinners. At one such dinner they passed out small breastpins consisting of a miniature silver sword drawn through a set of diamonds that formed the number "306." In photographs taken years later, Kate could be seen wearing her "306" pin, given to her by Conkling. It would be one of a handful of mementoes she kept until her death.

To defeat the Democratic candidate, General Winfield Scott Hancock, Garfield needed the support of Conkling, and to obtain it the Ohioan had to promise Conkling adequate representation in the cabinet and noninterference with Conkling's New York patronage machine. After receiving assurances he considered satisfactory, Conkling campaigned energetically for the Republican ticket. And he took Kate along with him. "Mrs. Sprague has been travelling with the Republican party this fall, Roscoe Conkling is in the same palace car. Comment unnecessary," quipped the *New Haven Register*. They tried unsuccessfully to keep it secret, as another paper reported that Conkling, while in transit to Buffalo to give a speech in nearby Lockport, kept his drawing-room car locked the entire trip and that when the train reached Buffalo "Mrs. Sprague suddenly appeared." At Buffalo, just days before the election, they were spotted together at Pierce's Palace hotel. This particular rendezvous provoked a heated reaction from Sprague, who called it "positive proof of criminality extending over many years."

But Kate no longer cared what her husband thought. Over the summer it was reported, falsely, that their troubles had been smoothed over and that Kate, then living in Washington with her daughters, would return to Narragansett after the resort season to be with her husband and son. Probably because she distrusted Sprague, Kate declined Willie's offer in September to care for Kitty at Narragansett, where her tubercular condition might benefit from the vigorous salt water atmosphere. "Were not your lungs in a bad way once, and was it not the air at Narragansett that helped to cure them?" Willie asked his mother, to which she made no reply.

There would be no reconciliation. On Tuesday, November 2, 1880, James Garfield won what remains the closest presidential election in American history in terms of popular vote. Three days later the *New York Sun* printed a story under the headline "Mrs. Sprague to Sue for Divorce."

CHAPTER 24

# "As Much Alone as Cleopatra"

The divorce case would drag on for a year and a half, but it got off to a rollicking start. Winchester Britton, a New York lawyer Kate retained to file suit, went to Canonchet to serve papers on Sprague seeking return of a piano and part of Kate's wardrobe and found the house barricaded. Sprague was intent on fending off creditors' attempts to take possession and vowed that any man who tried to enter the place would be "shot down like a cur."

Britton left without serving the papers and was lucky he was not shot at. The next man to try was not as fortunate. That same week fifteen-year-old Willie allegedly fired a pistol at Kate's lawyer and personal property trustee, Robert Thompson, who also went to Canonchet to try to retrieve some of Kate's belongings. Thompson retained his law partner to press charges against Willie, who was put on preliminary trial for attempted murder. Witnesses for the prosecution had seen Willie with the weapon and heard it go off near Thompson but had not actually seen the boy shoot it. Willie then took the stand in his own defense. He claimed the pistol was loaded only with powder, not a ball, and that he'd fired it "for fun" at a mark fifty yards away from Thompson. Willie's twelve-year-old accomplice backed up his account, as did two other witnesses. A motley, pro-Sprague crowd of "long-haired bushwhackers," fishermen, farmers, and mill operatives filled the seats at Willie's trial in the little Narragansett

Town Hall courtroom and kept up a constant din throughout. At one point the young men overturned a stove and kicked the coals around like a football. They jeered at Thompson and "enjoyed his discomfiture." After sitting sphinx-like through the proceedings, the trial judge calmly dismissed the charges for lack of evidence, whereupon the crowd cheered lustily. Sprague, there as legal guardian for Willie, was seen weeping during the defense counsel's emotional closing argument. In the boy's moment of peril his father had been at his side while his mother's people were attempting to put him away behind bars. It could not have endeared Kate to Willie.

A month later, in December 1880, Kate filed her divorce petition, and it was a doozy. It alleged three principal grounds: adultery, extreme cruelty, and nonsupport. As to the first, the document was replete with names, dates, and places of Sprague's alleged infidelities stretching almost from the beginning of their marriage in 1863 through 1880. The longest-running affair, allegedly extending from 1864 to 1879, was with Mary Eliza Viall, the author of *The Merchant's Wife*, with whom Sprague had been arrested in 1878 on a Massachusetts beach. The petition further asserted that Sprague had "frequently attempted to have criminal intercourse with the female domestics and guests in the family, causing them to leave the house," and that he had consorted with prostitutes and "other diverse lewd women" in Washington, Providence, Alexandria, Virginia, Philadelphia, and New York City between 1863 and 1878. The "extreme cruelty" detailed in the petition told a story of domestic violence and alleged threats upon Kate's life by Sprague, including his attempt to throw her out a window. She told of how he once lit a bonfire on the lawn of Canonchet and burned bedding and furniture. The petition recalled his menacing behavior toward Professor Linck but did not mention the shotgun incident with Roscoe Conkling, whose name appears nowhere in the document. Kate asserted that Sprague was frequently drunk, repeatedly hurled vile epithets at her, and often denied paternity of his daughters, having falsely accused her of "gross improprieties with other men—sometimes one man, sometimes another." As for financial support, Kate painted a picture of a man who had simply given up and was no longer being paid by the trustee because he refused to work. In addition to requesting a divorce on these grounds, Kate's petition asked for custody of all four children, reasonable alimony, and "permission to resume her maiden name, Katherine Chase."

Sprague filed an answer denying the charges and a countersuit accusing Kate of adultery and "improper intimacy with other men"—he declined to name names, even Conkling's. He alleged Kate had squandered his fortune through "the most lavish, extravagant, and foolish expenditure of money." He charged that she was absent from the household for long periods, "living abroad and at hotels," thus depriving him of the companionship to which he was entitled. As a Kansas newspaper commented, according to Sprague, Kate was "little better than a high-toned strumpet."

There is no evidence Kate engaged in marital infidelity with anyone other than Conkling. Certainly the fact that Sprague alleged it does not make it true. Divorce petitions, affidavits, and testimony have always been notoriously prone to exaggeration if not outright perjury. That was especially true in the era before no-fault divorces, when securing a legal separation required painting one's spouse in the worst possible light. For that reason too not all the allegations in Kate's petition, particularly the more sensational ones, need be accepted at face value. Undoubtedly Sprague was unfaithful to Kate during their marriage, but the specifics are elusive. His advances to the servants may have been rebuffed. One of the women named in the divorce petition, Canonchet housekeeper Elizabeth Rhing McCue, was so enraged that she wrote Kate the day after the petition was filed, demanding a retraction of the "infamous lie" and threatening a libel suit. "I can't believe you made such a statement," the now-married woman wrote. "Have you any conscience left?" She also turned the tables on Kate, reminding her that "I never saw you and the Governor quarrel but once, and that was the evening you came to my room and asked me to come upstairs and witness your quarrel. That same evening I burned that gentleman's picture for you and you burned the bag of letters received from him." Kate's lawyer, Britton, responded to Mrs. McCue with a letter offering to apologize if they had made a false charge, but there is no record of what happened after that.

As for the other women, one of Sprague's representatives, Jerome Greene, a former army surgeon with the Rhode Island artillery, offered explanations designed to muddy the waters. Nurse Maggie English, who accompanied Kate to Europe in 1866 and 1867, was "thought to be dead." The whereabouts of Harriet Brown, the servant Sprague brought into the

Sixth Street home in 1869 (prompting Salmon Chase's departure), were unknown. Prostitute Minnie Wilson was either in St. Louis or dead, and the other lady of the evening, Fannie Adams, was said to inhabit the house of ill repute of Ann Ballou in Providence, who "swears like a pirate that Gov. Sprague was too high-toned to ever step within her doors." That left Mary Viall, who, according to Greene, was confined to an insane asylum "and cannot refute the charges in person." Greene's defense was less than convincing, but it was the best he could do.

Kate's allegations of attempted murder and other physical assaults need to be considered with caution. They appear either for the first time in the divorce petition or are rehashes of accusations made following the shotgun affair, when she was dissembling to the public. Of course, Sprague's adamant denials do not disprove the allegations of domestic physical abuse, which is often quietly endured by the victim and invisible to the outside world. Sprague clearly had an explosive temper and was capable of blustering death threats, even if, as he proved with Conkling and Linck, his bark was worse than his bite. At the very least he was guilty of emotionally abusing his wife. And Kate's decision to flee Canonchet suggests she did fear, if not for her life, then at least for her safety.

Inevitably, as soon as Kate's divorce petition hit the newspapers, it rekindled talk of her affair with Conkling. A Los Angeles paper called Conkling "a breaker, not merely of the laws of man, but also of the law of God." Washington gossip columnist Donn Piatt wrote that "God may have made a more despicable wretch than Roscoe Conkling, but he never did." An Ohio official of high position was quoted as saying, "You have no idea of the feeling in our State against Conkling on account of this Sprague affair. We all feel that he has dragged one of the most honored names in our State, and degraded in the vile slough of his society the fame of one of our social queens."

The timing of these stories was particularly bad for Conkling. In early 1881 he was locked in a bitter political battle with Garfield over appointments in the new administration. Garfield was trying to placate both factions of the Republican Party—the pro-Grant "Stalwarts," or party spoilsmen, commanded by Conkling, and the more moderate "Half-Breeds," led by James G. Blaine. Conkling felt that he and his Stalwarts were due credit for winning the election and were entitled to their rightful bounty of spoils. But the press viewed his political position as severely compromised by the Sprague divorce case. As the *Indianapolis Sentinel* opined, the divorce trial was "likely to effectually squelch Conkling" and eliminate his "strut." A Washington correspondent remarked that in the coming battle over patronage "the chief force likely to be arrayed against the lordly senator will come through the revelations of the Sprague case." Sprague vowed to "follow him and expose him" at trial, and the Governor's friends warned that Willie Sprague would have "an interesting story to tell regarding his mother and Senator Conkling."

With Conkling politically weakened, his foes, notably Kate's friends John Hay and Whitelaw Reid, both of whom were close to Blaine, continually urged Garfield not to bow to pressure from the Stalwart faction. Hay, now writing for the *New-York Tribune*, which Reid had taken over after Horace Greeley's death, savaged Conkling in a series of unsigned editorials. Garfield's wife, Lucretia, advised her husband that the Stalwarts would be a thorn in his side "until you fight them *dead*. You can put every one of them in his political grave if you are [of] a mind to do so and that is the only place where they can be kept peaceable." Herself a victim of marital infidelity, "Crete" Garfield excoriated Conkling as a "peacock" who was "guilty of most selfishly compromising the reputation of Mrs. Sprague and of appearing cruelly neglectful of his own wife." Crete had gotten over whatever suspicions she harbored about her husband's wartime relationship with Kate, and the Garfield and Sprague children had become good friends, attending birthday parties together.

But James Garfield had not changed much; he was still the vacillator of years past. True to his nature, he would tilt toward the Stalwarts one day, then to the Half-Breeds the next. He angered Conkling by appointing Blaine secretary of state and by refusing to appoint Conkling's choice for treasury secretary, Wall Street banker Levi Morton. Garfield virtually promised Morton the post during the campaign, and Conkling felt the president-elect was reneging on that and other commitments made to secure the New Yorker's support in the election. "How willing Garfield was then," Conkling said, when "certain defeat seemed to stare him in the face; how willing he was to concede anything and everything to the Stalwarts if they would only rush to the rescue and save the day!" But complicating matters for Conkling, Morton did not want to accept the treasury position, preferring to run for an open Republican Senate seat in

New York. He was engaged in a three-way contest for that office with two other Conkling machine men: Thomas Platt and Richard Crowley, Kate's upstate New York friend, whose sister-in-law had accompanied her to the Chicago convention. Crowley enjoyed the backing of Vice President–elect Arthur, whereas Conkling, ostensibly neutral, secretly preferred Platt. Conkling's desire to handpick a Stalwart for New York senator and to force Garfield to select Morton for the Treasury were important tests of his political power.

Kate looked for a way to be of assistance. Having helped save Roscoe from himself during the Hayes-Tilden dispute four years earlier, she now took it upon herself to enter the political thicket directly on his behalf. She decided to appeal to his old friend and protégé, Chester Arthur.

"Chet" Arthur was a cool, dapper, raconteur who seemed unqualified to hold the second-highest office in the land. He always had viewed government office as a vehicle for earning money to support his expensive tastes in clothing, fine food, and liquor (which he was good at holding). Something of a dandy with his carefully manicured hands and mutton-chop sideburns, and bearing the look of a "well-fed Briton," he worked short hours and was the "last man to go to bed in any company." He came from refined circles and was "master in all the arts and conventionalities of what is known as 'best society.'" He was just the sort of man to get along well with Kate Chase.

He and Conkling had had a tense encounter at the Chicago convention when Garfield's supporters asked Arthur to run as the Ohioan's vice president. After Garfield's nomination Arthur found Conkling in a room off the platform, sulking. "The Ohio men have offered me the vice presidency," Arthur announced. "Well, sir, you should drop it as you would a red hot shoe from the forge," Conkling responded. Arthur started to say he had come to consult, not to ask his permission, when Conkling cut him off. "What, sir, you think of accepting?" Conkling asked, incredulously. Arthur summoned enough courage to respond: "The office of the Vice President is a greater honor than I ever dreamed of attaining. . . . In a calmer moment you will look at this differently."

"If you wish for my favor and respect you will contemptuously decline it," Conkling retorted. Then, for perhaps the first time in his life, Arthur defied his mentor. "Senator Conkling, I shall accept the nomination and shall carry with me the majority of the delegation."

Although Conkling had since forgiven Arthur, Kate had to approach the vice president–elect somewhat gingerly. She wrote Arthur a "*Strictly Confidential*" letter that made clear she was still the paramour of Conkling and that the two of them favored Platt over the other two Stalwart candidates. What she penned was a piece of political art.

She began with flattery. Their "mutual friend," Conkling, had "brought the other day from New York two exceptionally good lithographs of our Vice President elect. One was brightly festooned at Edgewood and the Senator, *your friend* never passes the table where the likeness stands, that he does not apostrophize it with some hearty expression of real affection, such as is rare in man to man." Then she got down to business. She told Arthur she was personally fond of his choice for senator, Richard Crowley. "But my dear friend," she asked, "consider are you using our good generous but improvident Mr. Crowley for his own best advantage in the long run?" As for the other Stalwart candidate, Levi Morton was "too small a man for the position. New and untried in politics, an apprentice at legislative business. Not a man to decorate the Senate." No, Kate made it clear, the new senator had to be Conkling's man, Tom Platt. Seizing on that advantage, Platt leaked to the press the fact that Kate favored his candidacy, prompting one paper to ask, "Could anything indicate more lamentably the subservience of the splendid Empire State to the love affairs of her autocratic Senator?"

Crowley's wife heard the rumors that Kate was trying to torpedo her husband's Senate chances, but she refused to believe them. She wrote in her memoirs that to suppose that Kate had used her influence against Crowley, a longtime family friend who had defended Kate during the shotgun episode, "would be to think Cleopatra had been changed into an asp, instead of being poisoned by one." Little did Mrs. Crowley know that Kate had, indeed, worked secretly against her husband's interests, and the Crowleys continued to socialize with Kate in New York and Washington.

Absent from Kate's letter to Arthur was any discussion of the Senate candidates' policy positions. In reality, there was not a dime's worth of difference between the three men because all three could be counted on to vote as instructed by Conkling. In elevating personal over substantive considerations Kate was emulating her lover Conkling, for whom the perpetuation of his political machine, rather than any policy issue, was the primary concern. As his biographer has written, Conkling was "never much for ideology . . . so he simply ignored more substantive problems." It was a symptom of the Gilded Age, in which monumental intraparty battles were fought over inconsequential patronage matters.

Kate's letter to Arthur next turned to the subject of cabinet and other patronage appointments. Kate told Arthur he owed greater allegiance to Conkling, his mentor, than to Garfield, the president from Mentor. Conkling had saved the party through his support during the campaign, and now Garfield and Blaine were combining forces to "crush" him, out of "fear and hate," she wrote. Surely in his time of need, she told Arthur, Conkling was entitled to the maximum support, and not embarrassment, from his tried-and-true friends. "If you think me venturesome—perhaps I should say meddlesome—forgive it—it is well meant," she told him. "Do not reply to this unless you can do so without the least constraint. It is entre-nous *strictly* and shall remain so." Kate was proposing that she and Arthur become political confidantes. "You and I are destined to be good friends," she wrote, "and will no doubt as time rolls on discuss many serious questions in confidence. You will always find me straightforward or silent, and you shall elect which it is to be."

Kate's letter may have had some effect. Just as it arrived at Arthur's desk, the Blaine forces tried to strike a deal with him whereby their Senate candidate, lawyer Chauncey Depew, would throw his support to Crowley if he promised to go along with Garfield's appointments of Half-Breeds over Stalwarts. With Kate's reminder of his moral obligation to Conkling ringing in his ears, Arthur turned down the offer on Crowley's behalf, accurately viewing it as a stab in Conkling's back. The Blaine people then offered the same deal to Platt, who had no compunction about accepting it, and he was promptly elected the next day. Conkling was apparently unaware of Platt's promise to the Half-Breeds, for he sent him a letter of congratulations saying New York had chosen a senator who never had to apologize for being a Stalwart.

Kate had never had any use for the Stalwart hero Ulysses Grant, but by the company she kept she was turning into a Stalwart herself. In April 1881, a month after Garfield's inauguration, she gave a Saturday night dinner party at Edgewood where the leading Stalwarts of New York—Conkling, Arthur, and Platt—plotted strategy against Blaine and Garfield. During March and April she was regularly seen in the Senate gallery, often with her daughters, watching Conkling in action. It was a time, long before senators began speaking to an empty chamber with only a C-SPAN camera present, when the galleries were packed with spectators who came to see a show. On one occasion Kate infuriated some cabinet wives whose seats were given to her by Vice President Arthur.

One reporter who spotted Kate in the gallery wrote that she looked "care-worn, and thin, and was dressed in more subdued style than usual." Another Washington correspondent agreed that "she smiles in a mechanical sort of way, has an abstracted air about her, and reminds one of a person who is doing one thing and thinking of half a dozen others." But as usual it fell to the society journalist Olivia to offer the most flowery commentary. She viewed Kate as "cold, stately, and statuesque as a lily, or a bit of marble in human form." In her inimitable style, Olivia embroidered on her description: "The heavily fringed waxen lids fall over the sorrowful eyes—those large, dark almond orbs, such as glorify the Orient. There are faces all around, but she seems as much alone as Cleopatra in her barge floating down the dusky Nile." Referring to Kate and Conkling's affair, Olivia wrote that "history is full of martyred women who have been used to crush obnoxious men." And although Kate's "sunshine friends" had deserted her, "the star does not waver in its course. It is the same haughty Katharine, despoiled of her throne, as true a woman today as when surrounded by her fawning flatterers." Comparing her once more to the French monarch, Olivia concluded her literary peroration with the assertion that "it is the flatterers of the Tuilleries that have changed, and not the Empress Eugénie."

If Kate seemed lost in thought, she had much on her mind. Her divorce action was heating up and turning into a mudslinging battle royal. Both sides had hired high-powered legal teams. Sprague's chief counsel, Roger Pryor, was an ex-Confederate general and congressman who had achieved celebrity status in the "trial of the century" representing Theodore Tilton in his adultery suit against Henry Ward Beecher. Kate's team included Judge George Hoadly, the former law partner of Salmon Chase who had worked with Conkling to secure the presidency for Tilden in the controversial 1876 election. Kate's lead courtroom lawyer and attack dog was Winchester Britton, a former consigliere of the Boss Tweed Ring in Brooklyn. Britton had been removed from his position as district attorney on corruption charges in 1873 and was declared unfit to serve by a citizens committee. Although Britton was returned to office by his constituents, the *New York Times* called his record "indefensible." But his friends praised him as a zealous and skilled litigator.

Kate had to leave courtroom arguments to her lawyers, but she looked for ways to advance her cause in the court of public opinion. At Edgewood she received a visit from Tennessee congressman William Moore and his wife, who happened to be living in the same Washington, DC, hotel as Olive Logan, a well-known author and lecturer. Logan, herself a divorcée who had since remarried, had published a popular book in 1872, *Get Thee Behind Me, Satan!*, in which she cautioned against the dangers of too-hasty marriages and expressed sympathy for women who were driven by circumstance to divorce, which she compared to "removing a cancer with a knife." In an era when divorce was rare, Logan wrote, "When I look around and see the unhappiness which exists between certainly three-fourths of the married people I know, my only wonder is—not that so many people seek divorces, but that so few do." Based on details provided by her neighbors the Moores, Logan wrote a newspaper article extolling the "noble dignity with which [Kate] bears her sorrows." She described Kate's love for her daughters as "absorbing, as is theirs for her," thus providing "the clearest refutation of the terrible charges made against her honor." Kate was so pleased with the article that she called upon Mrs. Moore at her hotel to thank her for supplying Logan with the information. An hour after Kate arrived, Mrs. Moore received "one of the handsomest bouquets of cut flowers that money could buy." They were from Roscoe Conkling.

Kate's lawyers (or Conkling's people), also leaked to the press that Conkling was anxious to take the stand in the Sprague divorce case. The story was pure balderdash; there was no way Roscoe Conkling was going to expose himself to cross-examination about his affair at a highly publicized trial. In fact, he chastised his wife for even talking about the subject privately. Around June of 1881 Julia Conkling complained to friends that the Sprague divorce case was bringing back all the old unwanted publicity about her marriage, whereupon her husband wrote her a stern letter. "Do you not think it better to abstain with acquaintances from discussing family affairs of a private nature?" Conkling asked. "Your habit *was* not to do so, and any modification of it has not I think been for the better." Given that they understood "some affairs quite differently," he wrote, it was unwise for either of them to discuss the matter with others, lest they "get into the predicament of contradicting each other." Julia wrote back indignantly to say that she had studiously avoided comment on their "family difficulties," expressing dismay that Conkling would blame *her*, who had remained so loyal all these years, for others' gossip.

Conkling may have been weakened by the scandal, besieged by the press, and alienated from his wife, but to this inveterate quoter of Shakespeare, the unkindest cut of all came from James Garfield himself. The president named one of Conkling's bitterest enemies, William Robertson, as the port collector for the New York Custom House, the most plum patronage job in the country and a position Conkling considered rightfully his to control. Robertson was a committed Blaine man who had helped swing the 1880 Republican presidential nomination to Garfield when it became clear Blaine could not win. Robertson, whom Conkling hated more than any man alive save, perhaps, Blaine himself, was now being proposed for the same lucrative office from which Chester Arthur was fired in 1877, setting off a bitter dispute between Conkling and then president Hayes. That had been war; this was Armageddon.

Conkling thundered in protest, and Arthur pleaded with Garfield to withdraw Robertson's appointment. To buck him up, John Hay brought Garfield a note from Whitelaw Reid, calling this "the turning point of his whole administration" and warning Garfield that if he gave in, Conkling would effectively become president and Garfield would be a laughingstock. After some customary waffling, Garfield finally showed backbone by refusing to change his mind. He told Hay that Robertson might be carried out of the Senate "head first or feet first" but that "I shall never withdraw him."

Conkling impulsively resigned his Senate seat in protest, thinking he could gain vindication by getting himself quickly reelected by the New York legislature, which he controlled, and returning to the Senate in triumph. He was joined in resignation by Tom Platt, who was in a bind over his earlier promise to support Garfield's appointees. It was a harebrained idea. Upon learning of Conkling's resignation, John Hay predicted that "Roscoe is finished."

Hay proved prophetic, for the resignations boomeranged on Conkling and Platt. The public sided overwhelmingly with the new president, and Albany legislators refused to restore the two men to their former offices. Platt's fate was sealed when he was caught, literally, with his pants down when some of Blaine's supporters raised a stepladder to spy on him and a married woman in Platt's Albany hotel room. The woman's husband was reportedly on his way to the hotel with a shotgun, something Conkling could have told his junior colleague a thing or two about. The story made the newspapers, and on July 1 Platt promptly withdrew from the race.

Conkling would fight on for a few more weeks, buoyed by a pep talk Kate gave him at Edgewood in late June 1881. But after numerous deadlocked ballots in the Albany legislature, Conkling was outpolled by an aging, upstate congressman of no great distinction.

Much of Conkling's defeat was attributable to the public outcry that arose after the life-and-death struggle between Conkling and Garfield proved to be all too literal. On July 2, 1881, less than four months after taking office, Garfield was walking with Secretary of State Blaine across the train station in Washington, preparing to embark on a summer vacation. As the two men strode side by side, Charles Guiteau, a delusional political groupie who'd been stalking both men for weeks for a job, fired two bullets at the president's back. Guiteau seemed confident that the one that struck squarely would prove fatal. On being apprehended by police he declared, "I am a Stalwart and Arthur will be president."

With his Senate career over, rejected by the machine men he once could bend to his will with a glare, Conkling announced he was quitting public life to practice law. For the first time in her adult life Kate's star was not aligned with that of a powerful man.

CHAPTER 25

# Gilded Age Woman

As James Garfield lay clinging to life in the White House, it was not a good time to be a Stalwart. Guiteau may have pulled the trigger, but many thought the motivating force behind the assassination was the insatiable desire of the Conklingites to maintain their spoils machine. It appeared that the diminutive, bearded Guiteau was a grotesque version of Conkling—Roscoe writ small, only loonier. Frustrated by the administration's refusal to give him the major diplomatic post he felt he richly deserved and depressed by Conkling's resignation from the Senate, Guiteau concluded that Garfield had to be removed. "His death was a political necessity," the assassin wrote, in the past tense, even before carrying out his act. "I was with General Grant and the rest of our men in New York during the canvass. . . . I am a Stalwart of the Stalwarts."

After lingering several weeks and victimized by incompetent doctoring, Garfield succumbed to his wounds in September 1881 at a New Jersey seaside resort town where he was taken to recover. In a quirk of history, he died in the summer home of Charles Francklyn and Susan Hoyt Francklyn, coplaintiffs in the lawsuits brought by Nettie's husband, Will Hoyt, against the Sprague family, alleging fraudulent handling of their estate.

It seemed surreal that Garfield's successor was none other than Conkling's henchman Arthur, widely considered to be a political hack who would take orders from Lord Roscoe. As Rutherford B. Hayes lamented in his diary, "Arthur for President! Conkling the power behind the throne, superior to the throne!" But Arthur unexpectedly rose to the occasion, conducting himself with dignity, humility, and grace, and he refused to throw away the public's goodwill by offering Conkling a high position in the new administration. Arthur also elected not to fire Robertson from the Custom House, as Conkling demanded. It all but destroyed the relationship between these two men, who had been fishing buddies, not to mention political soul mates, for many years. Conkling later told Mrs. Richard Crowley that Arthur's "cowardice" in failing to remove Robertson disgusted him more than anything else. But Arthur felt morally bound to continue the policy of the slain president whose office he had assumed. An old political colleague commented that he wasn't good old "Chet Arthur" anymore; he was "the President." In fact, Arthur would go on to support policies, such as civil service reform, that were anathema to the Stalwarts. "For the Vice-Presidency I was indebted to Mr. Conkling," he said, "but for the Presidency of the United States my debt is to the Almighty."

Kate didn't see it that way at all. She still viewed Arthur as Conkling's ex-lieutenant. Less than three weeks after Garfield was laid to rest she embarked on a campaign to have Conkling appointed as Arthur's treasury secretary, a position Conkling badly wanted. She first wrote to former Kansas senator Samuel Pomeroy, whose infamous "Pomeroy Circular" had all but scuttled her father's presidential chances in 1864. In the years since, Pomeroy had distinguished himself as a common bribesman, serving as the fictionalized model for Senator Abner Dilworthy, the corrupt politician in Mark Twain's novel *The Gilded Age*. But Pomeroy was promoting Conkling for Treasury, and Kate decided to enlist in the effort. In a letter dated October 15, 1881, she told Pomeroy that "among those who do their own thinking," who placed "eminent fitness above morbid sentiment" (a derogatory reference to the national mourning over Garfield's death), and who longed for "an administration purer, broader, more national in its character than we have known since the Rebellion, Mr. C stands pre-eminent." According to Kate, Conkling was the *one* man intrepid enough to stand up for the truth. He was "dreaded by the plunderers, hated by the licentious, ridiculed by the sycophants, and ephemera. With the honest, the high minded, his virtues, like his services, plead trumpet tongued for recognition and reaction against the unparalleled injustice which cries 'Crucify him.'" She likened him to her late father, who served when "there were giants" in government. Since then, she told Pomeroy, "high places have been too frequently *occupied* and not *filled*." But Conkling was different—a man of "strong timber" and a bulwark against "the carnival of criers, the masquerade of hypocrisy, the corrupt intrigue which surges about the foundations of our political system and threatens its destruction."

Kate recognized that given her intimate relationship with Conkling, any personal plea by her to Arthur would likely be heavily discounted. But she urged Pomeroy to pass on her letter to the president, which he did, and she hoped Arthur would move at once to perform what she called "this act of poetic justice." Quoting Conkling's favorite, Shakespeare, she emphasized, "'If it were done, when 'tis done, then 'twere well it were done quickly.'"

Quickly enough Kate overcame her inhibitions about approaching the president directly. On October 21, 1881, she addressed a letter to Arthur, written in the ornamental, literary, even poetic style that had become her hallmark. It showcased all of her talents for diplomacy, political advocacy, and cajolery.

"So much gratuitous and doubtless unwelcome advice is thrust upon you that one shrinks from joining the ranks of busy bodies and intruders," she began. But she said she felt compelled to urge in her own "poor way, the vital importance of placing a robust, courageous, clear-headed man at the head of the Treasury." Her way was not so poor, though, for, as Arthur knew, when she spoke, she spoke for Lord Roscoe himself.

She continued by telling the president that "*notwithstanding* the whirlwind of passion, the malignant fury of blinded abuse, that has swept in a craze over the length and breadth of the land; for a host of reasons, unless honor, honesty and patriotism have become empty traditions, Mr. Conkling's association *upon the threshold* of your new administration would become a tower of strength at once a glory and a defense." She advised Arthur that "the greatest opportunities of the Century are yours!" By naming Conkling to the Treasury, Arthur could mend the political fences between the two warring factions of the Republican Party, the Stalwarts and Half-Breeds—the "two great houses of York and of Lancaster," she likened them to. Until that rift was repaired, she maintained, the Republicans, who had barely won the last national election, would never elect another president. The "craze of sentimental hypocrisy," another swipe at what she regarded as the inordinate grief over Garfield's assassination, would not long sustain the party, "and after the Deluge, what then?"

Conkling, she insisted, was misunderstood. She made the extraordinary claim that, far from being a political spoilsman, Conkling was actually "*the victim of Grantism* and the condemned 'machine,' and *not its beneficiary.*" In her opinion Conkling should have taken her advice and "thrown off the old yoke" of party allegiance after the 1880 Chicago convention, asserted his independence, and pursued new third-party movements that would address "the vital issues" of the day (none of which she identified). He would have been better off, she thought, if the Republicans had lost the election, in which case the party would now be supporting him instead of sacrificing him to the ruling faction of Blaine and "Garfield's legatees."

Kate's letter leaves no doubt that she was an intensely political woman. But, as always, her politics were more personal than policy or party driven. She paid lip service to the interests of the Republican Party and no doubt sincerely believed Conkling was the best man for the job, just as she had been convinced that her father was the best man for the presidency. But at bottom she equated what was best for the party with what was best for Roscoe Conkling.*

Kate's letter to Arthur acknowledged that lobbying the president of the United States on behalf of her lover might come across as bold. But she felt obligated to "speak and speak effectively" and not with "half-truths." She did not mince words. She observed that Arthur had questioned Conkling's loyalty stemming from their "old argument" about whether Arthur should have accepted the vice presidential nomination with Garfield in the first place. But like "the true Knight he is," Conkling had campaigned

---

*It is often said that all politics is local; for Kate, all politics was personal. This conclusion derives not from the *absence* of a written record but from the *presence* of numerous writings—the diaries and memoirs of contemporaries who knew her well, such as John Hay, and Kate's own lengthy political letters to her father in 1868, to General Sherman in 1875, and to Samuel Pomeroy and Chester Arthur in 1881—all of which testify to her keen interest in politics but are bereft of any discussion of policy or ideology. Efforts to portray Kate as an ordinary woman preoccupied with love but not especially politically motivated or as an ideologically committed avatar of Republican Party principles miss the mark.

for the ticket "only to be cruelly wounded and to be rewarded with base ingratitude" not only from Garfield but, she made clear, she believed, Arthur as well. She told Arthur he now had the power, indeed the duty, "to make full restitution to vindicate the man who, when you were assailed, never stopped to weigh the chances of the popularity of your defense." Pointedly she told Arthur there was only one way for him to repay his debt to Conkling, and that was to appoint him to the position "already named," secretary of the treasury. Indeed, she avowed, there was no other gift Conkling "would or should accept."

Finally, in case her political discussion failed to persuade the new president, she made a highly personal appeal that played on his feelings of sympathy and guilt. It had been her idea, she revealed, for Conkling to travel from Utica to Washington in early October to plead his case before Arthur, "his trusted friend." During the meeting, as Kate wrote, Conkling "with entire frankness laid bare his heart," but Arthur rebuffed him. "Probably no one but you and I know how ill-judged and unfortunate" the visit had been, she said. "Then I saw him *afterwards* and saw *how he was suffering*. I urged his quitting Washington without delay. Friends who have seen him within a day or two, report him as very ill. It is this, more than all else, that prompts this letter. I do not address it to you as President, but undertake it at the dictate of a sense of obligation to loyalty and friendship." Never one to burn political bridges, however, Kate added a postscript saying that although she was convinced her advice was correct, of course she could be relied on to accept and support the president's course of action, whatever it might be.

Although Kate's letter to Arthur was a forceful and articulate piece of advocacy, she had to realize that, as successor to the martyred Garfield, Arthur was in no position to appoint Conkling to any cabinet position. Her argument that it would somehow help conciliate factions was fanciful; such a move by Arthur would have created a public uproar and increased, not decreased, internecine warfare. Kate's further claim that Conkling was some sort of closet reformer was a large dose of hokum that no one, least of all Chet Arthur, would have swallowed. Conkling's entire career owed itself to "Grantism." He was a committed patronage politician, uninterested in civil service or any other reform movements. His obsession with power blinded him to consideration of any of the "vital issues" of the day, such as growing industrialization and concentration of wealth—issues that William Sprague, in his own clumsy, muddled way, had foreseen. Even the rights of African Americans, which engaged Conkling's attention during the Civil War and its aftermath, faded into the background with time. "He presented no solutions to the racial conflict inherent in America," his biographer has written. "He had his own interests, and these are what he dealt with." Even his biography on the website of the Oneida County Historical Society, in his home town of Utica, concedes that for all his power, "he left practically no legacy of constructive achievement."

Chauncey Depew summed up the man:

> Roscoe Conkling was created by nature for a great career. That he missed it was entirely his own fault. Physically he was the handsomest man of his time. His mental equipment nearly approached genius. . . . But his intolerable egotism deprived him of [the] vision necessary for supreme leadership. With all his oratorical power and his talent in debate, he made little impression upon the country and none upon posterity. . . . The reason was that his wonderful gifts were wholly devoted to partisan discussions and local issues.

In pushing Conkling for Treasury, Kate was probably so blinded by her adoration and love that she abandoned her normally sound political instincts and analysis. Or maybe she was under no illusions at all and simply determined to do what she could for him, however futile, as an act of generosity and devotion to someone who meant so much to her.

There was, however, one position Arthur decided he might reward Conkling with, and that was the ostensibly nonpolitical one of Supreme Court justice. That had been Lincoln's way of dealing with Kate's father's ambitions. She must have relived that moment from 1864 when, in February 1882, Arthur named Conkling to a vacancy on the court. True to form, even though the Senate confirmed the nomination, Conkling brusquely rejected it. He would not be mollified with a bone thrown him by the man he began calling "His Accidency."*

---

*Ironically, Conkling and Arthur would end up together again, as bronze statues facing each other from opposite ends of New York's Madison Square Park, just yards from the site of the Fifth Avenue Hotel, where they had conducted so much political business together.

As Garfield had once observed, Conkling was a man inspired more by his hates than his loves. With Garfield now resting in his grave, Conkling would prove that point once more. He could not resist striking a parting blow he knew Garfield could not answer. In so doing he would enlist the help of Kate Chase in an episode that, like so many others in her life, recalled the turmoil of the Civil War.

CHAPTER 26

# Stalwart Woman

It was almost twenty years since that September day in 1863 when General William Rosecrans's ill-conceived order to his brigadier general left a gaping hole in the center of the Union lines at Chickamauga Creek in Tennessee, allowing Braxton Bragg's Confederate army to smash through and sweep Rosecrans off the battlefield into a panicked retreat to Chattanooga. Rosecrans had seemed "confused and stunned like a duck hit on the head," Lincoln told John Hay. James Garfield, Rosecrans's chief of staff, had been a hero that day, riding to the front in time to watch General George H. Thomas, the "Rock of Chickamauga," hold his ground and prevent the total destruction of the North's Army of the Cumberland. Salmon Chase acquitted himself well in the aftermath of Chickamauga, helping convince a skeptical Lincoln to support Secretary Stanton's bold and ultimately successful plan to reinforce Rosecrans's defeated army with thousands of eastern troops. Kate had spoken bitterly to John Hay of Rosecrans's removal from command, but that was just three weeks before her wedding, and it had been many years since she had concerned herself with thoughts of William H. Rosecrans of Ohio.

Rosecrans did his best to forget the battle that ended his military career. But he was chagrined to see Garfield's campaign biographies extol the candidate's bravery and heroism at Chickamauga at Rosecrans's expense. For years rumors had circulated, then were published in 1879 by

*New York Sun* editor Charles Dana, to the effect that a private letter from Garfield to Salmon Chase had been responsible for Rosecrans's dismissal. When Dana was unable to produce such a letter, Rosecrans asked Garfield for a specific denial, telling him that if the story were true, it set Garfield "in the light of a double dealer and traitor to your chief." Garfield assured Rosecrans that "any charge, whether it comes from Dana or any other liar, to the effect that I was in any sense untrue to you or unfaithful to our friendship, has no particle of truth in it," and he challenged anyone to publish their evidence. Rising to the challenge, in March 1882, six months after Garfield's death, Dana printed a confidential July 27, 1863, letter from Garfield to Salmon Chase. In it Garfield accused Rosecrans, his superior officer, of cowardice and an "almost fatal delay" in attacking Bragg's army during the campaign leading up to Chickamauga. Chase showed the letter to Lincoln after the battle, and, by several accounts, it played a crucial role in Lincoln's decision to relieve Rosecrans of his command—a decision that, unbeknownst to Kate at the time, her father had concurred with.

Though Garfield was now dead, Rosecrans reacted bitterly to the letter's publication, calling it "the blackest treachery" by his former chief of staff. "I had no idea at the time that I was harboring a person capable of such falseness and double dealing or there would have been a court martial at once," Rosecrans bellowed. Many in the press and public agreed, and the saintly reputation of Garfield took a beating. That the letter was written before, not after, the disastrous Chickamauga battle was a detail lost upon the public; Garfield was cast as someone who had betrayed his superior then repeatedly lied about it. As one newspaper reported, "there is much denunciation of Garfield's duplicity."

No one knew how Dana obtained a copy of the letter, but it turned out it came from Salmon Chase's private secretary, Jacob Schuckers, the man Kate favored to write her father's biography and to whom she had supplied Chase's private correspondence. Schuckers admitted giving the letter to Dana, but it was not immediately clear why he had done so.

The press figured out that Kate and Roscoe Conkling were behind it. One newspaper revealed on good authority that Kate had furnished the letter to Conkling, who was holding it as ammunition to use against Garfield before his death. According to the *Washington Herald*, Schuckers's statement that he gave Dana the letter was "equivalent to an admission that Mrs. Sprague gave it out, for Schuckers is merely a custodian for Mrs. Sprague, and has no authority to publish the private papers of the Chief Justice without her permission, nor would he dare to do so. . . . It is still the property of Mrs. Sprague, and Schuckers's statement that he furnished it for publication must be read with the interlineation, 'by direction of Mrs. Kate Chase Sprague.'"

Schuckers denied that Kate had played any role in publishing the July 27 letter, saying he had not seen her in almost ten years. But his belated explanation for why he gave it to Dana—that after holding the letter for almost two decades he suddenly was seized with a desire to set the historical record straight on Garfield—was unconvincing. The controversy had been swirling for several years, yet Schuckers had not seen fit to make the letter public. Schuckers had no known grievance against Garfield, who a few years earlier had supplied a glowing tribute of Salmon Chase for inclusion in Schuckers's biography. Even less credible was Schuckers's contention that he would have given one of Salmon Chase's private letters to the newspapers without an instruction or at least approval from Kate. It is not believable that Schuckers acted alone.

Of all people, Roscoe Conkling had the greatest motive to besmirch the reputation of the late James Garfield. Conkling was a longtime friend and business partner of Charles Dana, whose *Sun* had supplied sympathetic coverage of Conkling—and Kate—during the shotgun episode. Conkling was savvy enough to know that publishing the letter would have the desired effect. In later years the letter would become a historical footnote, with no lasting consequences for any of those connected with it, but at the time it created a stir.

Kate seemingly had nothing against Garfield personally—they were old friends, after all. Garfield was an admirer of Kate's father; and the Sprague and Garfield children were playmates. But her allegiance was now to Roscoe Conkling. She had written Chester Arthur to complain that Garfield was trying to "crush" Conkling, so retaliation did not seem unfair. It may have just come down to the old saying, "the enemy of my friend is my enemy." Kate's father was never one for playing hardball politics, and his constant mantra that he did not want a higher office but would accept one if the people demanded it seemed quaint and naïve. From Conkling Kate learned, if she did not already realize, that in politics one must play to win and that nice guys finish last. Unlike Garfield, an equivocator in the mold of her father, Conkling was a man who did not waffle or waver but rather went after things in a linear fashion, wielding power without apology or hesitation. Even the term "Stalwart" conveyed strength and masculinity in a way that "Half-Breed" did not.

If Kate's cooperation was necessary to diminish Garfield and, thereby, help rehabilitate Roscoe Conkling's reputation, then she would give it, without apology or hesitation. For the rest of her life Kate would also wear that "306" pin, commemorating the delegates who stuck with Grant over Garfield at the 1880 convention, that Conkling had given her. Kate was never a fan of Ulysses Grant. But she was loyal to the New York senator who worshipped him and whom she worshipped in turn. Kate was now someone to whom Roscoe Conkling could pay the highest compliment—she had become, at last, a Stalwart.

CHAPTER 27

# An Unmarried Woman

Just as the Rosecrans-Garfield controversy was heating up, the long-running Sprague divorce case finally began to simmer down. In February 1882 the two sides reached a settlement on the courtroom steps. Sprague withdrew his countersuit, Kate amended hers to expunge all the allegations of adultery and cruelty, and a divorce was granted to Kate on grounds of desertion and nonsupport. Kate obtained custody of her three girls, whereas Willie, now sixteen, remained with his father. The decree contained no provision for alimony but gave Kate the right to apply for it in the future. Finally, and important to Kate, she was given permission to resume her maiden name. She was, once again, Kate Chase.

Despite all the prior bluffing and bravado by both parties, it was in neither of their interests to have the case go to a full-blown public trial. The *Providence Press* credited Kate's lawyer George Hoadly with having quietly resolved a dispute that "threatened to outrival the Beecher-Tilton affair." Reaction outside Rhode Island was more cynical. In an article entitled "Divorce Made Easy," an Oregon newspaper called it a usurpation of the court's function and decried the ease with which parties could, through collusion, avoid airing the messy details. A Minnesota paper commented that the settlement was not intended to settle public opinion on the matter. "While it is generally admitted that Mr. Sprague is an intemperate man," the paper noted, "it is also strongly suspected that Mrs. Sprague is not immaculate." The *Los Angeles Herald* said that in reaching an amicable settlement, "both sides recoiled from their own lives." The verdict would have to be left to history.

That Kate won the case, from a technical standpoint, became clear when Sprague tried to claim later that the divorce was granted to *him* on grounds of Kate's adultery. In applying for a license to remarry in Virginia, Sprague turned the facts on their head, telling a court clerk it was he who had sued first, alleging adultery; that Kate had countersued alleging the same offense; that she eventually dropped the adultery charges; and that on that record he had been granted a divorce. It was a grotesque lie, and when a Virginia newspaper printed Sprague's account, Kate's lawyers promptly wrote a letter to the editor making clear that Kate had filed first and that the legal grounds were based on Sprague's conduct, not hers.

Kate's divorce has been described as a "partisan act" reflecting the "centrality of Republican politics in her life." According to this argument, Republican free labor and antislavery ideology promoted divorce as a means to emancipate women from the tyranny of marriage, an institution that Elizabeth Cady Stanton and other reform advocates compared to slavery.

But just as Kate's political life was driven more by the personal than by the ideological, so too were the actions she took in her marital life. She liberated herself from Sprague not because she was trying to make a statement or strike a blow for divorce reform or against male patriarchal authority. Kate was no flag waver. She ended her marriage because circumstances had made her situation intolerable and she was in a position to do something about it. Unlike most women, Kate had the motive, means, and opportunity to get out. But with all that, she still needed the vision and courage to change her life. She had both. Kate's divorce was a personal, not a partisan, act.

Kate would never remarry, not that she would have lacked for opportunities. A few months after her divorce was finalized, a Washington journalist reported that she retained much of her former beauty. If "an expression of sadness is occasionally detected in her countenance, and heard in her silvery voice, it is but momentary," the writer observed. She remained outwardly cheerful, cordially greeting any friend who approached her and never alluding to her domestic troubles.

She might have entertained some hope that Conkling would likewise divorce and marry her. After he left Washington following his final Senate defeat in July 1881, he took up residence in Manhattan, where he set up a lucrative private law practice, while his wife Julia continued to live in Utica.

Following her divorce in May 1882, Kate returned to Edgewood, then spent the winter of 1882–1883 in New York, postponing a planned trip to Europe so she could be near Conkling. But they appear to have decided around this time that their intimate relationship would not continue. In early 1883 Kate made known that she would sail to Europe that summer and spend the next several years there with her children. That same summer Conkling took a trip to Yellowstone with his wife, although there was no restoration of affection between them.

If Kate and Conkling did intend to end their romance, their parting was an amicable one. While Kate was in Europe, Conkling sent her a package of unknown contents at Edgewood and followed up to make sure it arrived. A few months earlier, when they were both in New York, he sent Kate a short note, dated January 7, 1883, which quoted, fittingly, from his favorite, Shakespeare, "To be thus, is nothing; but to be safely thus." It is Macbeth brooding to himself about his murder of King Duncan. Macbeth is now king, and Duncan safely in his grave, but Macbeth's position as king is not as secure as he imagined it to be, as his friend Banquo still poses a threat. To be king is nothing if Macbeth must live in constant fear of losing his throne.

It is not clear what Conkling meant to convey by this cryptic quotation. It has the feel of wistfulness and of commiseration or self-pity. Perhaps he was referring only to himself, as someone who reached the pinnacle of political power before being brought down by his enemies. But he may have intended it as a sort of parting communiqué to Kate and an allusion to the love and happiness they had found in each other but that could not survive the envy and scorn and prurient interest of lesser people. Unfortunately there was too much truth in his allusion, for the attacks by "scorpion tongues" on the reputations of these two people had achieved their goal. Roscoe Conkling and Kate Chase would be forever linked in any discussion of powerful but scandalous lovers in American political history.

Although divorce was a rare and stigmatizing event in Kate's day, it was not, per se, a disqualifier of success for talented, educated, upper-class women. The actress-writer Fanny Kemble, the author-lecturer Olive

Logan, and the journalist-social activist Victoria Woodhull, divorcées all, enjoyed considerable acclaim despite the dissolution of their marriages. But Kate's divorce—coming as it did to a woman whose renown derived from her place in society and following as it did upon a sensational sex scandal—did far greater and lasting damage to her social standing. And yet it liberated her to achieve a greater degree of authenticity. Now that Kate's queenly throne was gone she was free to embark on a new chapter in her life—one less burdened by the need for public approval or concern over public opprobrium. Her former French teacher at the Haines School, the notorious suspected murderess Henriette Deluzy-Desportes, had found a new life by coming to America from France just as nine-year-old Kate was beginning school there. More than thirty years later Kate would now cross the Atlantic in the other direction in search of her own new beginning.

CHAPTER 28

# An Independent Woman

In July 1883 Kate and her daughters sailed to Europe, where they would spend most of the next four years. After roaming the Continent, they wintered in Germany before taking up residence on the fashionable Avenue du Bois de Boulogne in Paris, where Kate gave weekly receptions heavily attended by American expatriates. But she soon tired of that scene and resettled herself and the girls in the quiet little village of Avon, adjoining Fontainebleau, about forty miles outside Paris. In that middle-class neighborhood, as virtually the only American resident, she found peace and seclusion at the edge of the large green forest surrounding the royal French palace once home to Napoleon and Catherine de' Medici. She placed Ethel and Portia in Mademoiselle Caroline Dussaut's boarding school for girls on the Avenue du Chemin de Fer. The exclusive school, known as Les Ruches ("The Beehives"), advertised itself as "offering high French culture to foreign young women." Kate took an apartment on the same street as the school, employing a live-in German instructor and an English domestic. To the French census takers Kate listed herself as age thirty-six (shaving off almost ten years) and a "rentière," or person of independent means.

Educating her children had been Kate's highest priority ever since their birth. As she explained to an American correspondent, "France is superlatively the best place to educate girls in all practical ways. My little girls are in a village, not learning about dress and the frivolities of fashion, but living a perfect home life, learning the truths of nature with the great Fontainebleau at the very door from which to draw fresh inspirations, and in which to walk and run and drive. And then I have advantages in France that with my limited means I could not enjoy" in the United States. One journalist during this period saw in her countenance "an expression of pensiveness, almost of sadness" that deepened and enhanced her charm. She possessed "a quiet, serene dignity which nobody feels inclined to invade. She is one of the most affable, yet at the same time least familiar, of women. She is, in the loftiest sense, a politician, and if she had been of the other sex she would have been certain of an extraordinary following."

She was "very punctilious in disowning the name of Sprague" and promptly reminded those who so addressed her that her name was Kate Chase. Besides, there was now a new Mrs. Sprague. Shortly before Kate left for Europe, her ex-husband, now fifty-two, married Dora Inez Weed Calvert, a twenty-something divorcée from West Virginia. The "wild yet beautiful" Inez, the name she went by, was an aspiring opera singer of no great talent. She and Sprague lived at Canonchet with Inez's younger sister, Avice, and Sprague's son, Willie. The group was there asserting squatter's rights, for the previous year trustee Chafee had sold the mansion for $62,250 to Francis D. Moulton, a wealthy New Yorker who, coincidentally, had been a key witness in the Tilton-Beecher case. But when Chafee and Moulton met at Canonchet to complete the delivery, they were denied admission by Sprague's rifle-toting sentinels, one of whom was young Willie.

Sprague's reputation for bellicosity did not help him in his futile attempt to regain the Rhode Island governorship in 1883, but litigation over title to the property (and outsiders' fears of shotgun barrels) enabled him to continue living at Canonchet with his new wife. Attempting to erase any traces of Kate, Inez converted the interior to a musical theme, redecorating it with gaudy, brightly colored frescoes of mermaids, dolphins, and Cupids. To help pay for the facelift, the Spragues auctioned off numerous household possessions, some of which belonged to Kate, and later a collection of modern paintings, many of them French landscapes Kate had brought back from Europe many years earlier. Needless to say, none of the sale proceeds were given to her. The Spragues' possession of Canonchet became official when Moulton died in 1886 and his widow effectively sold the property back to them at the original $62,500 purchase price. As much as Sprague had castigated Kate for her extravagance with Canonchet, he loved the place as much as she had.

In the meantime Willie Sprague, who had become something of a lost soul, was seen roaming around Narragansett barefoot and poorly clad. Then, in July 1885, the twenty-year-old Willie, described as "a chip off the old block," married Inez Sprague's seventeen-year-old sister, Avice. As a result, Willie became his father's brother-in-law and his stepmother became his sister-in-law. The soap opera did not end there. Sixteen months later Avice bore a daughter, Inez, but no one seemed to regard the baby as Willie's. The real father may have been Gerrit Smith Wheaton, a rich, forty-eight-year-old Standard Oil man from Cleveland who had competed with Willie for Avice's hand. But according to Chase family lore, William Sprague Sr., the ex-governor, was in fact the father (and uncle) of Inez, not her grandfather. Convinced that *he* at least was not the father, Willie shortly thereafter deserted Canonchet for a nomadic life, began to distance himself from his father, and, in time, came to regard the two Weed sisters as "detestable parasites."

Kate was fortunate to be in Europe while all this messiness was taking place. She came back to America, briefly, in early 1884 to attend the inauguration of George Hoadly, her divorce lawyer, as Ohio's new Democratic governor. She also met with her friend the president, Chester Arthur, who came out to Edgewood to plot how he might gain the Republican nomination over a challenge from James G. Blaine. Arthur did not believe Blaine would enter the field against him and claimed to have some assurances to that effect. But Kate told him she was sure Blaine was ready to make the race. "Blaine will be nominated," she said, "but he will not be elected." She proved prophetic, for Arthur was not renominated, and Blaine lost the election to Grover Cleveland, the first Democratic president since before the Civil War. Internal divisions had finally cost the Republicans the White House, just as Kate had predicted to Arthur in 1881.

Back in France, Kate took up painting and generally avoided going into Paris, not wishing to mingle with the American colony there. She wanted, she said, "to be retired and secluded." She had simpler tastes and fewer regal gowns, and she began selling off clothes and jewelry—including her wedding tiara—to help with expenses. Had the turbulence she left behind in America tempered her fiery spirit? Had she come to reject the "frivolities of fashion" that for so long commanded her interest? She was quoted as saying that she no longer enjoyed "gayety in fashionable life" and was interested only in educating her girls to become good women. "The glitter and transient pleasures of social life are but vanishing joys," she said. "They soon pass and leave nothing." This thinking was partly a necessary adjustment to her altered circumstances, but it also reflected a realization that for happiness and peace of mind, she needed to look more to her interior than her exterior self.

One correspondent remarked on her "buoyancy" and "indomitable nature" that, after all these years, left "the same ingenious smile upon her face." Another found her, if less vivacious and beautiful than in younger years, still in possession of "that queenly air before which beauty pales. She keeps quiet and avoids notice, but she is the same Kate Chase through it all." Yet something *had* changed; she was more contemplative than before. In a rare interview Kate talked wistfully of her early years:

> I was so young when I was thrown upon my own resources. I never had the guidance of an experienced woman relative, and none of the advantages most women have in being surrounded by mother and sister and aunt. I was taken from school at the age of fourteen years and placed at the head of my father's house. But the great men I met there and companionship of my father was a liberal education to me. Why, . . . I never had an hour to spend for my own entertainment. I never planned a day's fun for myself in my life.

If she had it to do over, she said, she would try to get more enjoyment out of life.

While in France, she had one more rendezvous with Roscoe Conkling, who made a sudden trip to Europe in mid-1885, supposedly for health reasons. What transpired between them is not known except that Kate again helped him discredit one of his enemies by obtaining an old letter written to her father, just as she had done with the famous Garfield-Chase letter concerning General Rosecrans. This time the author was Murat Halstead, a powerful and acerbic Ohio newspaper editor guilty of the twin crimes, in Conkling's view, of opposing Grant's reelection in 1872 and supporting Hayes in 1876. Many years earlier, in 1863 (but before Vicksburg), Halstead had privately written his friend Salmon Chase to assail Grant as a "drunken, stupid . . . ass." When Grant died in July 1885, while Conkling was in Europe, Conkling correctly anticipated that publication of the letter would discredit Halstead in the public eye. Once again Chase's private secretary and biographer, Jacob Schuckers, denied that Kate or Conkling had played any role in the letter's publication, this time with the ludicrous explanation that it was stolen from his desk in Philadelphia. In arranging for Conkling to obtain the letter, Kate may have simply been doing a favor for her old lover, but there remains the possibility that some romantic embers still burned.

Kate's political fires certainly had not been extinguished. She provided secret diplomatic advice to Conkling's old friend Levi Morton, now the US minister to France and the same person she once described to President Arthur as too small a man for the Senate. She praised Napoleon as nearly the greatest man the world had known and spoke out in praise of the exiled French monarchy, saying its princes had "suffered the martyrdom of a popular prejudice" (perhaps a subliminal reference to her own experience) and predicting their eventual return to power. She accompanied a French woman to witness a duel, and when the woman began to scream, Kate put her hand over her friend's mouth and told her to keep still, lest their presence be discovered at the illegal encounter. Invitations to Parisian duels were highly sought after and hard to come by, but Kate managed to procure one for Conkling's old antagonist, Blaine, who, while visiting Paris, wanted to watch a French statesman and Russian count fire upon each other. Blaine repaid the favor when he became secretary of state again, securing a diplomatic position for one of Kate's friends.

Popular opinion, now more than ever, she held in low regard. She explained why she did not take part in the women's suffrage movement. "Women do not appreciate their own power in the world," she said. They would "do whatever they want to do; whenever they want to vote they will vote, and no power on earth will stop them."

In August 1886 she again returned briefly to the United States for the removal of her father's remains from Washington, where they had lain in a borrowed vault of the Cooke family, for reburial in Spring Grove Cemetery in Cincinnati. Nettie was there—the first time the estranged sisters had met in many years. In a brief display of reconciliation they clasped hands as they stood around the casket. But the scandal of eight years earlier continued to dog Kate. President Cleveland had received her courteously in Washington, but his wife, supposedly indisposed, would not come down to greet their visitor. In Columbus the ex-First Lady, Lucy Hayes, also shunned Kate, and she further advised the current First Lady of Ohio, Governor Joseph Foraker's wife, Julia, not to meet with "the notorious" Kate. "Why should it be you?" Lucy Hayes asked Mrs. Foraker. "We must not judge her—let the Lord do that—but I think—in your position—to countenance even the appearance is a mistake."

More sympathetic, if bizarre and self-serving, were the comments by Kate's ex-husband. Asked about her return to America, William Sprague called her "a woman of rare attainments" and "ardent affections" to whom the world had been "very inconsiderate in its treatment." He said she deserved to be free from "intrusion of public comment or scandal." Sprague had taken a temperance vow in 1882 after divorcing Kate, but his comments displayed the same old addled thought process. Kate was "always a high-spirited woman accustomed to exercising her own will, and she will always do that," he avowed. The public would probably accept every word she uttered, he said, "but can the children live it down?" Always a critic of her spending habits, he inexplicably said that "judging from her usual conservatism in money matters and her business tact," she probably had enough money to live comfortably with her new, plain style of living near Paris. If Sprague was trying to be complimentary, his second wife was having none of it: she issued a public letter angrily denying that Sprague had made the favorable statements about Kate attributed to him and extending to Kate the "united pity" of the married couple.

Kate's son, Willie, had had little contact with her since his parents' divorce, but just after the birth of the baby Inez he decided to renew relations with his mother. He wrote her, saying he was reluctant to have her see him in his "shabby and generally dilapidated" condition. But Kate welcomed him back unreservedly and helped him get a printing job with the *New York World* and, after that, a divorce from Avice Weed to relieve him from what Kate termed the "inhumanity" that had been practiced upon him. Avice promptly married the millionaire Colonel Wheaton, the man who may have fathered her child.

Back in America after four years abroad, Kate kept up a steady correspondence with Willie, trying to bolster his confidence and helping him financially to the extent she could. She assisted a newspaperman in preparing a story about her boy, then rewrote it herself when it was not to her liking. She and Willie discussed their unsuccessful efforts to pry loose some money from Sprague, who had recently been soundly defeated for reelection to the Narragansett district council, finally ending his political career. Willie drifted from one odd job to the next, from time to time writing Kate to say his days of drinking and hard living were behind him (an echo of his father's letters of years past).

But inwardly he was on a slow, steady decline. He left an electrical mechanic's job in Chicago to head west, writing his father a rambling, incoherent letter referring to the Governor's "diversions" in the "matrimonial line" and accusing him of being "cold and chilling" in his last letter. "With my very sensitive and highly considerate nature," Willie wrote, "I cannot conceive how a man can so ruthlessly knock a man down, gouge his eye and otherwise figuratively abuse him, with so little, or, in fact, no cause." Willie wrote of how he longed for love and affection but said his feelings were "practically of no use, except to myself." This "sentimental 'biz,'" he called it, would "never do." He had a "boozy recollection" of having written his father about some business proposition . . . and there his letter abruptly ends, in the middle of the page.

It was found in his boarding room in Seattle, where he had gone to take a newspaper engraving job. Along with it lay the dead body of Willie, who, in early October 1890, took his own life by slitting his wrists. He apparently had changed his mind when the blood began gushing and tried, without success, to stop its flow with a shirt, then resignedly wrapped a chloroform-soaked sheet around his head to die. The boy with the "slight figure and poetic face," described as an "erratic genius, at times exceptionally brilliant, always impulsive, loving and affectionate," was dead at the age of twenty-five.

Kate lashed out at her ex-husband, writing him to say that "at your door lies this unnatural crime." It was a harsh statement but an understandable reaction from a grief-stricken mother. She telegraphed the morgue in Seattle with instructions to "embalm the body and prepare it in the best possible manner for shipment, and draw on his father for expenses." The funeral at St. Peter's by-the-Sea in Narragansett was a bleak affair, with Kate and her daughters sitting on one side of the church and Sprague and his wife, Inez, along with Willie's ex-wife, Avice, and her new husband, Gerrit Wheaton, together with three-year-old Inez, on the other. Both sides had their lawyers present. Sprague glanced a few times over at Kate's pew, but she did not look back. Her normal composure deserted her as she wept and trembled during the service. Appearing unmoved by her suffering and stung, perhaps, by her letter blaming him for Willie's death, Sprague refused Kate's plaintive request to open the casket for a final view of the boy. Kate and her girls made the trip out to Swan Point Cemetery in Providence for the burial; the boy's father sent only representatives.

The depths of Kate's despair became clear when this normally levelheaded woman consulted a spiritualist medium to whom she sent a short note. "Is my son William Sprague present today and does he know how I mourn him and can he advise me what it is best for me to do for his sisters' benefit?" she wrote. History does not record what, if any, answer she received. Ironically, Mary Lincoln, who had died in 1882, shortly after Kate's divorce was finalized, attempted to contact her son Willie in the afterworld, and now Kate was doing the same with her own Willie.

In Kate's sorrow over her son's death her thoughts turned, as they so often did, to her late father. During Willie's decline she had written to Whitelaw Reid to say that her son had inherited "the blood of a great and good man." She was referring, of course, not to Willie's father but to his grandfather, whose "great heart would ache could he know of this sad and blighted young life."

Death had now claimed her father and her son—and Roscoe Conkling. The ex-senator had lapsed into a fatal coma after stubbornly walking three hours through New York's great Blizzard of 1888 when a cabbie proposed to overcharge him. Learning of his condition, Kate went to New York to see him, but his friends refused her permission to go to his bedside at the hotel where he died, probably on the instruction of his wife, who had come down from Utica to be present.

Kate once again returned to Edgewood. She had enjoyed the peace and quiet of France but felt like "an exile" there. Continually hounded by creditors, she had considered selling Edgewood, but she changed her mind when the extension of an electric street railway in the direction of her property greatly increased its value. More importantly, Edgewood was her home and she was comfortable there. "She dresses modestly, but elegantly, and is as much at ease with herself and those about her as in the old days, when the national capital was at her feet," a New York newspaper reporter wrote. Her life was "simple compared with the luxury which at times has surrounded her, but there is an air of contentment in her face which is worthier than the old smile of conquest which I have seen on her lips in other days."

CHAPTER 29

# "What We Have Is Good"

The day after Willie's suicide Kate's daughter Ethel made her stage debut in a one-act classical comedy, *Lesbia*, at the Madison Square Theatre in New York. A few weeks later she played an Irish maid in Richard Mansfield's *Beau Brummel* at an opera house in Washington, with President Benjamin Harrison as well as Kate and her other two daughters in attendance. An accomplished equestrian in Washington, Ethel took up acting at age eighteen, with Kate's full support, to earn money for the family. After studying under David Belasco, Ethel joined Mansfield's company and spent more than a decade on stage, in New York and on tour. She was a character actress, as her self-described "*jolie laide*" appearance (literally, both "pretty" and "ugly") kept her from landing ingénue and leading-lady roles. But she acquired a lifelong love of the theater and an ability to "recite Shakespeare and Gilbert and Sullivan by the yard," recalled her granddaughter Ann Donaldson.

In July 1896 Ethel secretly married Dr. Frank Donaldson Jr. of Baltimore, a physician-turned-playwright who had recently left his wife and three sons. He and Ethel were married in San Francisco without a license, only days after his divorce was finalized, creating a stir in Donaldson's prominent Baltimore family and his first wife's old-line Virginia family. "Since the newspapers have found us out, we will be married at once in the orthodox way," Donaldson told a reporter in October, and a hasty ceremony was arranged. In marrying Dr. Donaldson, Ethel defied Kate, who, knowing something about the effects of scandal, had strongly opposed the union. Nonetheless Ethel remained loyal to her mother. Ethel went on to be awarded a special medal by President Theodore Roosevelt for hospital service at Montauk, Long Island's Camp Wikoff, during the Spanish Civil War, in which her husband, a friend and former Harvard classmate of Roosevelt, served as an Army surgeon in Cuba with Roosevelt's Rough Riders.

Other than at Willie's funeral, Ethel saw her father only once more, at a brief meeting in New York in 1897. But that same year Portia reconciled with her father. She wrote to Sprague in Rhode Island and, together with Kitty, had a tearful reunion with him in Washington. Soon afterward Portia went to Canonchet to live with him and his wife, Inez. Portia was courted by Inez's rakish brother, Orestes, until he exited the premises under the misapprehension that Sprague was going to shoot him.

Portia was slender and graceful, like her mother, though plainer looking and lacking Kate's charisma. Unlike the attention-seeking Ethel, Portia was withdrawn in manner. She was described as "a fine French scholar, a musician and an artist," a testament to the education Kate provided her. To painter Nicholas Brewer, a visitor at Canonchet, it seemed that Sprague—by then a recluse who saw his family only at meals—was especially reticent around his youngest daughter, as if "the old wound was reopened by the presence of this sweet girl, whose every step and smile and gesture was but a duplicate of those which beguiled him in his younger days and brought him to the feet of the most captivating feminine personality of that time." Brewer, there to paint a portrait of the ex-governor, also thought that although Sprague treated his second wife most courteously, Kate "carried away with her his broken heart." Sprague kept Kate's old bedroom under lock and key, untouched from the day she left. On walks along the beach with Portia, Brewer sensed that "she felt most deeply the sad tragedy in the lives of her parents."

After taking a government clerkship in the Treasury Department, where she toiled quietly for many years, Portia would marry twice. The first time was in Atlantic City at age thirty-six to a recently widowed, seventy-three-year-old coworker and Civil War pensioner who died within eighteen months. Two years later she wed a divorced house carpenter and lived with him in Narragansett. She had no children.

Meanwhile Kitty, the daughter who most closely resembled Kate, continued living with her mother. She never developed a mental capacity beyond that of a child, always retaining an innocent, vacant look. But she was beloved by her family, as evidenced by a photograph of Ethel inscribed to eighteen-year-old Kitty: "To our high kicker and champion humorist, Katharine Chase No. 2, with love from her 'Sister the Actress.'"

Kate avoided the limelight in her later years, going so far as to deny to newspapermen that Ethel was her daughter when Ethel sued Richard Mansfield for unpaid salary in 1897. Kate led a simple retired life, and the few people who knew her well called her "soberer, less spirited, more kindly" than in prior years. She mingled more easily with the sort of ordinary people—tradesmen, small farmers—she had never had much contact with in her heyday. She talked much of her late father and never tired of showing her few visitors at Edgewood the portraits and busts of him she kept there.

Kate's daughter Portia described her as "very sensitive and proud" in her last years, living "in almost complete seclusion from society." She was no longer a fashion plate, and her figure, though not fat, was rounder than it was in her days as a belle. Kate's eating habits are basically unknown, and although her father was portly, we can never know what genetics had in store for her mother in later years. Other than horseback riding in her youth as well as croquet, at which she was once pronounced the best player in Washington, Kate had had little outlet for physical exercise during her life. (Moreover, given the heavy dresses and tight corsets and undergarments nineteenth-century women wore, they were not running or working out the way they would a century and a half later.) And the bicycle craze that swept the country in the mid-1890s, which Susan B. Anthony said did more to emancipate women than anything else, came a bit late for Kate.

Kate's one later foray into politics came when she anonymously caused a bill to be introduced in Congress prohibiting liquor establishments within one mile of the Soldiers' Home in Washington. Kate had never been a cause-oriented woman, and this effort arose less from identification with the growing women's temperance movement than from her desire not to have saloons in her backyard—Edgewood's grounds were within the one-mile protected zone. Not until the quietly enacted bill was passed and signed by President Harrison did the public learn of the involvement of "the brilliant and distinguished woman who had kept in the background and adroitly manipulated the entire matter."

Kate's most pressing concern during the "Gay Nineties" was money. The modest amount she inherited from her father and whatever financial gifts she received over the years from her mother-in-law, Fanny Sprague (who died in 1883, herself besieged by creditors) had long since been eaten up. Edgewood was a cash drain, and fending off debt collectors was a constant struggle. She mortgaged the property again and again for loans totaling $44,000, an amount she was unable to repay. A sale of Edgewood for $115,000 fell through when the buyer was mugged and died. After her creditors foreclosed on the mortgages in 1895 and began auctioning off her personal effects, she sued for an injunction to stop the auctions, alleging the loans were usurious. Although her petition was denied, the court granted her a temporary stay against further sales of her household goods. The trust company holding the mortgages gave her another six months to raise the money to buy back the property but required that, in the meantime, she vacate the premises.

Kate was forced to find care for Kitty while she traveled to Ohio and New York in search of financial aid from her father's old admirers. She appealed to them to save a historic landmark in appreciation of the value of her father's public service. In New York she persuaded Henry Villard, a journalist from the old days, to organize a consortium of investors, including banker J. P. Morgan, to provide her with relief. They came up with a trust fund of $80,000—sufficient to redeem the mortgage out of foreclosure and provide a modest income to Kate for a few years until the property could be profitably sold. The arrangement almost fell through when a couple of the subscribers reneged on their commitments, but Villard made up the difference with additional personal contributions. For the time being Kate could return to Edgewood with her head above water, if only barely.

Villard remembered Kate for her kindness to him as a young reporter, and in early 1896, when she was in New York seeking money, he invited her to his country home in Westchester County. Villard's wife, who thought Kate "the most bewitching of queens" thirty years earlier, could hardly recognize her at fifty-five. "The glorious eyes were dull and inflamed as though scalded by salt tears; she apologized for her looks, saying that she had been on the coast of Maine and the air did not agree with her—a subterfuge, I felt sure. Poor broken woman! She elicited my pity but not my admiration."

While awaiting the outcome of Villard's rescue plan, Kate ventured into Manhattan. She had scarcely known any poor people her entire life, and now she was one of them, gazing upon a city that had become a place of immense wealth, whereas hers had disappeared. Kate could look at but no longer afford the finest hotels and dining establishments or the latest fashions at Stewart's department store. Theater tickets to see Sarah Bernhardt or Eleanora Duse were too expensive, but she could take in the poultry-and-pigeon show at Madison Square Garden. It was also a more practical option, given that she was now trying to help make ends meet by raising hens and selling milk, eggs, and home-grown fruit and vegetables in suburban Washington. Her hand-to-mouth existence is aptly captured in a letter she wrote to Mrs. Jay Bancroft in 1897:

> I was sorry not to be able to send you the asparagus and rhubarb for your dinner today. Kindly give your order at night for the next day and we will be glad to fill it if we have what you wish. . . . What we have is good and I am pleased to send it to one so appreciative as you always are. We have now milk—2 fresh cows and a good deal of milk and cream. Are there any of your neighbors who would care to have our milk and cream? My work this year is largely field work. My men go to work early and are constantly busy until 6 p.m. and we run no wagon so can only serve after working hours.

This letter can be read as either reflecting the tragedy of Kate's decline or her resiliency in the face of misfortune. History has mostly chosen to view Kate as a tragic figure. Certainly Nettie thought so, as she would later write to a relative shortly after Kate's death:

> I feel as if an unhappy chapter of my life has been closed. What grieved me beyond everything, more than any injustice to me, was the way Kate (though she did not realize the harm she was doing) injured our father's memory. The unjust and grossly exaggerated criticisms of his great desire

> for "the presidency" came all through her intrigues with second rate politicians during the latter part of his life. And since his death it was very very hard for me to have her beg money in his name. However all that is all over now. Poor soul, her life was certainly a tragic one.

Nettie herself prospered for a time after her marriage, and for a number of years lived on the grounds of the original Westchester Country Club, where she and her husband were founding members. But Nettie was as hard hit financially as Kate by the Panic of 1873, which destroyed Will Hoyt's business even more completely than it did William Sprague's. With their money running out, Nettie and her husband went to colonize the fledgling community of Southampton, New York, on Long Island, where they became involved in real estate development. Herself an amateur landscape painter, Nettie was instrumental in starting a famous summer outdoor artists' school in Southampton run by impressionist painter William Merritt Chase (no relation). She also helped found the Shinnecock Hills Golf Club, the home course of her daughter Beatrix, who, at age sixteen, became the youngest woman to win the US Women's Amateur Golf Championship. (She went on to capture the same title the following two years, retiring from competitive golf in 1900.)

Nettie was an energetic, resourceful arts patron and civic booster, but a severe national economic depression in 1893 devastated the Southampton real estate market and ushered in another painful period for the Hoyts. Will Hoyt, an alcoholic, could not hold a job and "drank up most of the family fortunes," abandoning his family for "health" reasons by 1900 to go to Puerto Rico, where he died alone in 1905. Nettie and Beatrix were reduced to boarder status in Southampton and spent much of their remaining years in a tiny dirt-floor cottage in Thomasville, Georgia, where they pursued painting and sculpture. As one of her great-grandsons attests, far from living a life of luxury, Nettie was always in extremis financially during the same period Kate was, but through parsimony was able to make her money last and keep up appearances.

Nettie never reconciled with Kate, but that is more due to the legal and financial rift that developed between the families, in which Nettie naturally sided with her own, than to any inherent lack of empathy on Nettie's part. The money battles, following shortly upon the death of their father, may also have exposed long-submerged feelings of jealousy between the two half-sisters, whose relationship had been remarkably free of contention as they were growing up.

Was Nettie right to label Kate a tragic figure? The answer is not a simple one. Under Aristotle's classic definition, a tragic hero or heroine is a mostly good person of royal blood or other high station—with much to lose—who suffers unexpected downfall as a result of some character flaw, such as hubris, or an error of judgment. The punishment is greater than he or she deserves, evoking in the audience a reaction of pity and fear and an emotional release or purging known as catharsis. The hero's suffering leads him or her to a gain in awareness or self-knowledge, though too late to prevent the reversal of fortune.

Several of these elements apply in Kate's case, although it is an imperfect fit. She was not a born royalist, although she virtually became one. She was often described as proud and ambitious, but it is hard to see how those traits caused her misfortune, unless one adheres to the simplistic theory that she married Sprague only to further her father's presidential aspirations. In hindsight her marriage can be viewed as a mistake, but if every poor choice in marriage constitutes a tragedy, the word would lose much of its meaning. Whatever mistakes she made did not justify her dire circumstances, so it was natural to feel pity for her, but there were those who took satisfaction from her decline and saw it as retribution for her supposed sins. The tragic element that appears most applicable is the last one—the acquisition of self-knowledge. Thrust before the spotlight at an early age, a female celebrity when the rules for being one were not well defined, she found satisfaction later in the quieter pleasures of private life. Though Kate surely would have preferred not to lose her status and fortune, doing so taught her that all that once glittered was in many ways illusory and that peace of mind had to be found within herself.

Kate did not talk or act as if she considered hers a tragic life. She bore her misfortune without complaint or apology, and with her few remaining friends she retained her old charm of manner. True, the eyes that once had a liquid look now looked weary, half-closed, and red. But her voice was still full of sentiment, and as she drove her carriage about Washington to sell her garden produce, she sat erect as ever, with the same stately poise of head. A survivor, she lived on her own terms and continued to go after what she wanted with the same determination of old. When she and

Kitty, living alone, were sick one winter night in the late 1890s and the snowdrifts became too deep for Kate to get out, she fired a pistol to seek help from her rural neighbors.

The Southern belle Scarlett O'Hara had once vowed that even if she had to lie, steal, cheat, or kill, she would never be hungry again, and after all was lost she went back to the dilapidated Tara. The former Belle of the North would likewise live out her final years in the ruins of her father's home.

CHAPTER 30

# "None Outshone Her"

*"The old woman held the reins of the rickety, one-horse carriage with her soiled, white kid gloves . . . "*

In her last years, as she gazed out from her carriage at the great glistening Capitol dome in the distance, Kate Chase could have recalled any number of shining moments from her Washington past. There was the first White House state dinner, when she arrived in a horse-drawn carriage far handsomer than the one she now drove, entered the reception room on the arm of her father, and outshone Mary Lincoln to the talk of the town. There were the breakfasts at the house at Sixth and E Streets with men like Charles Sumner as well as the elegant Wednesday afternoon dinner-dances Kate choreographed to entertain the politically powerful. There were the visits to the troops and generals and to a young Rhode Island warrior-governor who, like Kate, seemed to have a limitless future. How ironic it was that his camp, where he showed off for Kate on his white horse, was near the site of the estate where Kate was living out her final years.

Edgewood was now a place of decay and desolation—its roof leaking, its floors rotting, its interior dusty and cobwebbed, its many bare rooms evoking ghosts from the past. Kate had only Kitty to keep her company, along with occasional visits from the now-married Ethel and her one-year-old son, Chase, who delighted in chasing chickens around the property.

Born in California in April 1897, nine months after Ethel's secret marriage to Frank Donaldson, Chase Donaldson was christened Salmon Portland Chase Donaldson by his mother in honor of the chief justice. It was a source of gratification to Kate, who had wanted to name her own son after his grandfather before agreeing to call him Willie, after his father.

In May 1899, with the real estate market having recovered, the Edgewood trustee decided to sell the property, expecting to realize enough to pay off the investor group and provide Kate with an annuity to live comfortably somewhere else. Her farming venture had lost money, and the investors thought they could make a greater profit by subdividing Edgewood into city lots and selling them off. One reason her dairy farm failed was her deteriorating health. She seemed to have aged ten years in the previous twelve months and showed symptoms of Bright's disease, the general name then for kidney ailments. She grew steadily worse over the summer but did not see a doctor. She declined all offers of assistance and, without a servant, continued preparing the meals for herself and Kitty. She was offered a clerkship position in the Treasury Department at $1,200 a year—fittingly, as her father had been the first treasury secretary to employ women clerks. But she had to turn it down because of her illness and the need to care for Kitty. (Portia ended up accepting the job in Kate's place.)

In late July Kate finally sent for a doctor, but by that time she was in the final stages of kidney failure with liver complications. She died at Edgewood at three in the morning on July 31, 1899, two weeks short of her fifty-ninth birthday. She was surrounded by her three daughters, Ethel having rushed from her home in Brooklyn and Portia from Narragansett Pier to be at her bedside. Kate suffered convulsions earlier in the day, but they subsided, and she died peacefully and in little pain.

The simple funeral, conducted at Edgewood by a local Episcopal minister, was attended by her daughters and a few friends. (Nettie was absent.) The casket was placed in the library, near a large marble bust of her father. Several of Kate's former African American servants acted as pallbearers, among them William Joice, Salmon Chase's longtime valet. He had asked his current employer for permission to return to Kate to attend her in her last days. "There are so many little things that she needs now and I can do for her," he explained. He recalled his former household mistress as "a queen then, a saint now, and no man can dispute that with me."

After being placed in a vault at nearby Glenwood Cemetery in Washington, Kate's remains were transferred, at government expense, per instruction of President McKinley, in a special car to Cincinnati. There she was laid to rest beside her father in the family plot at Spring Grove Cemetery, near the Clifton area of her youth, seven miles from where she was born. Her simple gravestone reads "Kate Chase Sprague, 1840–1899." It is not known whether she chose the name under which she was to be buried, but it seems unlikely.

Her death made front-page news across the country. Many of the obituaries and follow-up articles told a cautionary tale of a highly ambitious woman who tried and failed to become First Lady, married for money, and, as a result of scandal, was an outcast in her later years and died in poverty. But nearly all paid tribute to her dazzling beauty, charm, and political acumen. "The homage of the most eminent men in the country was hers," said the *New York Times*. "The most brilliant woman of her day . . . none outshone her," wrote the *Washington Evening Star*. Among her predecessors she was most often compared to Dolley Madison, although the *Washington Post* thought Kate's achievements greater. As the *Post* pointed out, Dolley Madison had the advantage of being the wife of a president, whereas Kate "won her way by her beauty and her talents." She "held court as if she had been a queen, instead of the daughter of a citizen of a republic."

Kate's personal possessions were auctioned off in New York eight months after her death, bringing $44,000 in proceeds over five days. The items sold included the fan given Kate at her wedding by Abraham Lincoln and the lace Kate wore when she was presented to Queen Victoria at the Court of St. James. Kate's daughter Ethel, appointed administratrix of the intestate estate, paid $25 for a portrait of her mother. Some other unique relics avoided going under the hammer and are still in the possession of Kate's descendants: her wedding box; her Conkling "306" pin; albums of photographs and notes signed by various famous people, such as Longfellow, Emerson, and the actress Ellen Terry; and, most striking of all, a lifelike statuette of Kate, about eighteen inches tall and two feet wide, sculpted during one of her first trips to Paris. The white, marble-like piece shows Kate wearing her wedding tiara and the flowing gown she wore when she was presented at the French royal court.

Ethel, who divided her mother's mementoes with Portia, reportedly burned as much of Kate's correspondence as she was able to find. That helps explain why so few of Kate's letters have survived, especially compared with the hundreds written by her father and Sprague. But Ethel did not destroy Kate's diary, which was passed down to one of Kate's great-granddaughters and later donated to Brown University. And auction goers, thumbing through Kate's library, turned up other intriguing papers hidden between the pages of her books. One, an undated note from "C" (presumably Conkling) apologized for not being able to see Kate in Washington the previous day and carried the valediction, "Truly your admirer." A similar letter, dated April 16, 1882, which Kate used to bookmark a French novel, read, "My dear Kate: I wanted to come over and see you today. One moment with you is better than a thousand in town. But I was called home. Hastily, H.T.M." The author was almost certainly Hugh T. McCulloch, a former colleague of Kate's father who became treasury secretary himself and had long known and admired Kate.* Kate, a lifetime lover of poetry, also left behind the following bit of verse entitled "Love's Reality," from Coventry Patmore's *The Angel in the House*. In that work the Englishman Patmore popularized the ideal of the Victorian wife and mother, selflessly devoted to her children and submissive to her husband:

*I walk, I trust, with open eyes;*
*I've travelled half my worldly course,*
*And in the way behind me lies*
*Much vanity and some remorse;*
*I've lived to feel how pride may part*
*Spirits, tho' matched like hand and glove;*
*I've blushed for love's abode, the heart,*
*But have not disbelieved in love—*
*And love is my reward.*

---

*Does this fawning letter, written just before Kate's divorce was finalized, evidence a romantic relationship with McCulloch? It seems unlikely, as he was married and seventy-three at the time (Kate was forty-one), and she was then still attached to Conkling. McCulloch may have simply sent Kate the note to apologize for canceling a planned social visit. Or maybe he was smitten with her in the same way other older men, such as Charles Sumner and Carl Schurz, had been. In his autobiography, written in 1888, he extolled her father as among the greatest of Americans, without mentioning Kate.

The phrase "half my worldly course" suggests Kate may have fancied this poem in midlife, when her affair with Conkling blossomed and she filed for divorce against Sprague. Although she and Sprague had been a spirited match, their pride and tempers had driven them apart. But she had not "disbelieved in love" and so was rewarded with the love of another man, Conkling.

* * *

If these personal papers remain cryptic, Kate's historical legacy is also difficult to assess. She was at or near the center of more major events—war, presidential elections, impeachment, assassinations—than any woman and most men of her time. In her forty-plus years of adulthood there was scarcely a famous American she did not know. True, for all her Zelig-like appearances on the stage of history and for all her considerable talents, she left little in the way of tangible, substantive accomplishments. And despite her political skills, she could not make her father president, could not turn her husband into a respected public official, could not make others appreciate Conkling the way she did. But searching for perceptible achievements is the wrong way to measure her influence. As a woman, she was limited, by definition, to the periphery of the political world. Accordingly, her contribution to history was more as a behind-the-scenes orchestrator who brought the right people together in the same room. Whether at elegant parties or small meetings, she swayed people with her charm, but she was no mere decorative figure: she always had her own political agenda to push and made sure her views received a thorough hearing. Her impact undoubtedly was felt in many ways we can never know.

Kate Chase was a woman ahead of her time. Her inherent abilities were such that in a later century she could have run for office herself, become a trial lawyer or a television news anchor. Or, given her language and diplomatic skills, she could have ably served as a foreign ambassador. As far back as 1886 a journalist recounted that Kate "frequently wished herself that she had been of the other sex, for then she would have enjoyed more freedom and could have had an individual career, from which she was debarred by her gender." That she was thus constrained is less her tragedy than ours.

She was also constrained by the choices she made—or that were forced upon her. She was raised from an early age to "ornament any society," as her father had put it, and that was a role for which she was supremely well qualified. She admired and loved her father and greatly wanted to please him and serve as the companion and confidante he had lost in the deaths of three wives. She knew he loved her as well, but Salmon Chase was, as one man described him, "light without heat." He could not offer Kate the warm maternal love she had lacked or even the unconditional love of a father; his love was always accompanied by the expectation of a certain level of performance. Kate accepted and rose to his challenge and, in so doing, entered into a sort of implied bargain whereby she enthusiastically advanced his political career and he never remarried so Kate could have him to herself. Theirs was a symbiotic relationship.

Still, she sought unconditional love and thought—or at least hoped—she had found it with William Sprague, who courted and flattered her with the most adoring love letters. He had been, she recorded in her diary, the only man to inhabit her heart. But a month into the marriage, when her new husband declined to be with her at Christmas and then New Year's, Kate had to realize that something was wrong, and it only became worse with time.

In marrying the multimillionaire Sprague, Kate embraced the life of an American queen. She enjoyed the trappings of royalty, as evidenced by the clothes, the jewelry, and the grandiose mansion she built in Narragansett. It was important to her that she look and act the part. She also became accustomed to thinking that, as with any monarch, the rules governing ordinary people did not apply to her. Going back to her earlier days in Columbus, Kate believed she was immune to public scrutiny and criticism, that somehow she could survive it unscathed. But only a true queen wields the kind of absolute power capable of stifling her severest critics.

A true queen also has life tenure, and Kate did not. When she realized the man she thought was her prince could never be a king and that her royalty was only transitory, she was left exposed to the world. The confident exterior had masked a vulnerable, even fragile interior. After her broken marriage and financial catastrophe, she turned for a time to a white knight, the senator from New York. But when that relationship exploded in scandal and her dethroning became complete, doors began closing all around her. Fair or not, the rules of society, it turned out, did apply.

There was another constraint operating on her, one that she rarely talked about. A year before the Panic of 1873 that started the decline in her fortunes, Kate bore a child who, though sharing her name and beauty, lacked the same mental gifts Kate and most other people enjoyed. In an era when it would have been easy to hide her child away or place her in an institution, Kate did neither. Kate, who had been left motherless herself, would not abandon Kitty. It was a heavy responsibility being the sole caregiver for a special needs child, and it restricted Kate's movement and options. But she never complained about the sacrifice it required. In a little-noticed interview she gave in 1886, shortly after she moved to Fontainebleau, she explained that she went to France "on account of the health of my dear little Kitty, for whom the physicians prescribed a more equable climate, and the benefit it has wrought for her is truly marvelous." In this new place, where she was the only American, Kate disappeared, leaving behind a life that had become too volatile and complex. And in caring for her innocent child, so dependent upon her, Kate finally found a cause to take up that went beyond herself. To her precious Kitty she gave, and from her received, unconditional love. As much as her other daughters, Kitty was, to Kate, an earthly jewel.

By her final years Kate, who once reigned as America's queen, had been chastened by numerous disappointments. She had not seen her father become president, despite her best efforts. Her marriage had been a painful failure. She had suffered disgrace and social ostracism. The wealth, the gowns, the wedding tiara, and Canonchet, the home of her dreams—all were gone. She had lost her beloved only son by his own hand. In those senses her life was indeed tragic.

But in a larger sense it was not. She may have lost her worldly possessions and discarded her once-burning ambition, but she traded them for a life of greater freedom and independence. She became entirely her own person, a rare feat for women of her day. And through it all she displayed a resilient and indomitable spirit. The jewel was inside her all along. Her legacy was her life story and the example she set. Humbled but still proud, Kate Chase died exhibiting all the strength and valor of a true queen.

# EPILOGUE

## Kate's Family

**Kitty Sprague** was the first of Kate's daughters to succeed her in death. She lived in Washington under Portia's care before dying of tuberculosis on June 22, 1910, at age thirty-eight. She is buried in Washington's Rock Creek Park, in the lot owned by Joseph Whitney, Portia's first husband, where Whitney's first wife had been interred the previous year.

**Portia Sprague** married Joseph Whitney just nine days after Kitty died. Widowed in 1912, she married her second husband, Frank Browning, in 1914 and lived quietly with him in Narragansett until her death there from a stroke on February 23, 1932. She was fifty-eight, the same age as Kate at her death. Portia is buried in Riverside Cemetery in Wakefield, Rhode Island, alongside her second husband, who died two months after she did.

After Kate's death **Ethel Sprague Donaldson** returned occasionally to the stage, cowriting and producing with her husband, Frank Donaldson, a play called *The Last Act*, in which she also appeared. But she ran into hard times. Frank Donaldson, who contracted yellow fever in Cuba during the Rough Rider campaign, never recovered and died at age forty-nine in San Francisco on April 13, 1906. Five days later the San Francisco earthquake burned Ethel out of her home and destroyed most of her possessions. She was reported missing for a time and, shattered by the events, spent a number of years in St. Elizabeth's psychiatric hospital in Washington. Her son, Chase, who had lived with Portia and Kitty for a time in Washington after his mother was first institutionalized, eventually procured Ethel's release. She lived her final years with a friend on New York's Upper East Side and spent several summers in Narragansett, often recalling for her granddaughter her theater days but never talking about her mother or father. Ethel died at her apartment in New York on December 19, 1936, at age sixty-seven, of a cerebral hemorrhage and is buried next to her mother in Spring Grove Cemetery in Cincinnati.

Ethel's only child and Kate's grandson, Chase Donaldson, became an accomplished equestrian like his mother, served in the US cavalry in France during World War I, and ran track at the University of Wisconsin. Handsome and entrepreneurial, he ran businesses in Washington, DC, worked on Wall Street, and made and lost several fortunes over an eighty-three-year lifetime. A widower at age thirty-two, he married twice more and had a total of six children, four of whom were still living in 2014, the time of this book's composition. Ann Donaldson, the oldest of Chase's children, celebrated her ninety-second birthday in August 2014. She followed in her grandmother Ethel's footsteps, graduating from the American Academy of Dramatic Arts in New York. She married and divorced an actor and had one child, a son, William Chase McQuade, who died in 2010 after a successful business career. Ann—who knew both Ethel and Portia—still maintains an active interest in her famous great-grandmother, Kate Chase, whose portrait as a young child hangs on the wall of Ann's apartment overlooking Central Park in New York. It was Ann who donated Kate's diary and correspondence to Brown University in the 1950s, and it is to her that historians are indebted for her wise and generous decision.

Ann's younger half-sister, Aura Donaldson Carr, is also the proud keeper of many articles of Kate Chase memorabilia, including a number of the photographs appearing and artifacts mentioned in this book. Aura, who lives in Connecticut, was for many years a successful corporate events planner, a career at which her great-grandmother Kate Chase would have excelled as well. Her daughter, Kristin Carr, became a well-known cancer survivor and motivational speaker, whose 2007 documentary film, *Crazy Sexy Cancer*, and *New York Times* best-selling books on nutrition and wellness have garnered worldwide attention. Some of Kate Chase's indomitable spirit can be seen in her great-great-granddaughter Kris Carr.

## Nettie and Family

**Janet Ralston Chase Hoyt** lived to be seventy-seven, dying on November 19, 1925, in Thomasville, Georgia, where she was buried. She spent her last years there with her daughter Beatrix in their cottage, "Pinerift," which Nettie built next door to her friend Candace Wheeler, the well-known artist and interior design pioneer. Nettie had met Wheeler in Dresden, Germany, almost sixty years earlier, and in the late 1870s and 1880s worked closely with Wheeler's Society of Decorative Art in New York. Nettie also founded her own decorative and industrial arts school in Pelham, New York.

Nettie had four children: Janet Ralston Hoyt (1872–1932), who ran a real estate business in Manhattan and was later committed to the Bloomingdale Insane Asylum in New York; Edwin Chase Hoyt (1873–1954), a successful New York corporate lawyer who turned to apple farming on Long Island later in life; Franklin Chase Hoyt (1876–1937), a lawyer and judge who founded the Children's Court of the City of New York; and, lastly, Beatrix Hoyt, the golfer (1880–1963).

## Sprague and Family

**William Sprague** told a reporter at Canonchet in 1905 that he had found quiet after years of turbulence and bore no man any grudge. He would not go back to the old days even if he could, he said, as his mind then had been absorbed in his business, whereas now he had developed new parts of his brain that enabled him to memorize thousands of lines of Homer and Virgil. He had also worked out a "philosophy of national life" that held that "increased production, wealth, is but one of the results of accelerated motion or energy," which "unless controlled by a balance, is certain to bring disaster." The philosophical quietude did not last long. A few months later nineteen-year-old Inez Sprague, officially Willie's daughter and Sprague's granddaughter, broke off her engagement to a high-society Philadelphia man in order to elope with lawyer Harry Stiness, the son of one of Sprague's old judicial enemies. An incensed Sprague announced he was disowning the girl, selling Canonchet to prevent her from inheriting it, and moving to Europe with his second wife.

Canonchet stayed within the family but burned to the ground in 1909 as a result of a defective fireplace flue. The now white-bearded Sprague nearly lost his life in the blaze, as he insisted on returning to the mansion to retrieve his rare Civil War papers. His coachman found him on an upper floor, engulfed by smoke and suffocating, and carried him to safety. Devastated, Sprague moved with his wife to Paris.

Not long after relocating to Paris Sprague suffered a stroke that left him partially paralyzed. But he had not lost his flair for the dramatic. When the First World War broke out he and his wife converted their apartment on the Rue de la Pompe to a convalescent hospital for the wounded of all nationalities. When the Germans threatened Paris in August 1914 the Spragues fled for the Normandy seacoast, the ex-governor packing an American flag to wrap his body in should he not survive the journey. A German fighter plane soon appeared above and began to trail their car, whereupon Sprague unfurled the flag and draped it over the back of the vehicle, knowing the Germans would not attack a then-neutral American contingent. After the danger passed they returned to Paris, which Sprague now considered "the only civilized place to live."

He was near the end, though, and on September 11, 1915, one day short of his eighty-fifth birthday, William Sprague died of complications from meningitis. The last of the Civil War governors, he had outlived every member of Lincoln's cabinet and every Senate colleague from the war period. After a simple funeral service in Paris, his body was brought to New York on the French steamer *Rochambeau*, then to Rhode Island, where he received the full hero's treatment: a state funeral, seventeen-gun salute, and flags at half-mast. A family service was held at St. Peter's by-the-Sea in Narragansett, the same church where Willie Sprague's funeral had taken place a quarter-century earlier. Sprague's daughter Portia attended; Ethel did not. Sprague was buried in the family crypt in Swan Point Cemetery in Providence.

History has not treated William Sprague kindly. Clearly he was a troubled person who caused much pain to himself and many around him. Whether that was due entirely to alcohol or also to some mental disturbance can only be guessed at. He did live happily for more than thirty years with his second wife, a fact that has always been inconvenient for those seeking to portray him as an unmitigated monster. Still, he will always be defined more by his first marriage. As one newspaper put it, "One almost wishes that with him at the end could have been Kate Chase, that restless ambitious spirit," as "the two must always be linked in our history, and together they illustrated some of the most dramatic as well as the most sobering possibilities of American life in the 19th century."

## Places

The **Chase-Sprague mansion** at Sixth and E Streets in Washington, home to Kate's Civil War salons, became an Eagles clubhouse and stood until 1936, when it was torn down for a department store parking garage. Today the corner is occupied by the national headquarters of the American Association of Retired Persons (AARP).

Where **Canonchet** once stood is now the site of the South County Museum in Narragansett. The only surviving elements of the original estate are the Robinson Cemetery (past which Kate and her children escaped in 1879), the stone ruins of the Sprague stables, and some tiles and stones that are part of a private residence now standing on the spot the mansion once occupied.

Shortly after Kate's death **Edgewood** was sold and became the site of St. Vincent's Orphan Asylum for girls. Today it is the location of Edgewood Terrace Apartments, a low- and mixed-income housing development at the intersection of Fourth and Edgewood Streets, NE. Due to the heavy concentration of buildings, the original estate is unrecognizable except for the magnificent view of the Capitol dome from which Kate Chase drew inspiration for so long.

# Acknowledgments

My deepest gratitude goes to Aura Carr, who from the very early stages supported this book about her great-grandmother Kate Chase with all her heart and soul. In addition to commenting on drafts, transcribing Kate's diary for me, and giving me access to family photographs and artifacts, Aura was a constant source of inspiration and insight into Kate's personality and relations with her father, husband, and children. Aura was always urging me to "go deeper" in trying to understand Kate, and to the extent I have managed to do so, a large amount of the credit belongs to Aura, my muse.

Aura's half-sister, Ann Donaldson (ninety-two as of this writing), was a font of stories about Kate and her family and a generous source of unique memorabilia. I am grateful to Ann for her cooperation, assistance, and keen observations and wit.

Frank Moore, a great-grandson of Nettie Chase and genealogist extraordinaire, was extremely helpful in illuminating the family history of Nettie and her descendants. Frank also gave me several previously unpublished photographs, read and commented on chapter drafts, and provided general encouragement throughout. I also received much useful information about the Hoyt family from Tom Stokes, another great-grandson of Nettie (who emphasizes that "Nettie" was a *Chase* family nickname and that the Hoyts called her by her real first name, Janet).

Professor Emeritus Richard Vangermeersch, the world's leading expert on William Sprague, generously shared with me his learning on the Spragues and the various Rhode Island environs they inhabited as well as made many helpful comments on the manuscript. Richard, the librettist for the opera *William Sprague and His Women* (music by Geoffrey Gibbs), also graciously hosted me at the opera's world premiere at the University of Rhode Island in 2012, which helped raise money for the beautifully restored portrait of William Sprague that hangs in the Rhode Island State Capitol.

Jim Hall, curator of the Cranston Historical Society at the Governor Sprague Mansion, made available a wealth of new material his institution recently obtained. As volunteers with a limited budget, Jim and his staff deserve credit for turning the society into an important research center on the Chases and Spragues.

I owe special thanks to the Conklingites of Utica, led by Fiona O'Downey and her fellow intrepid grave seekers, Karen Day and Ellen Cucci; other members of the Landmarks Society of Greater Utica: Mike Bosak, Pam Jardieu, Cam Sullivan, Steve Grant, Bob Sullivan, Michelle Klosek, and Boyd Bissell; and Brian Howard and Frank Tomaino from the Oneida County Historical Society.

Several other people were kind enough to review the manuscript and provide editorial comments and corrections. Larry Kamin read with care and interest and offered many valuable suggestions, as did Cathy McCandless, Valerie Townsend, Ruthanne

McCormack, and Susan Manchester. Thanks also to Gary Malone for his very helpful comments. Any errors in the book, of course, remain mine.

I wish also to thank Ken Graff for his terrific photographic work.

I am grateful in particular to the following libraries, archives, and other institutions for their resources and assistance:

*Rhode Island*: Cranston Historical Society (Jim Hall); Cranston Public Library (Lisa Zawadzki); John Hay Library, Brown University, Providence; Rhode Island Historical Society, Providence (Katherine Chansky, Jim DaMico, Kirsten Hammerstrom); Maury Loontjens Memorial Library, Narragansett; Providence Public Library; South County Museum, Narragansett. Thanks also to the Orwig Music Center (Nancy Jakubowski) and University Archives at Brown University (Gayle Lynch).

*Ohio*: Ohio Historical Society Archives/Library, Columbus (Lisa Long); Cincinnati History Library and Archives (Cincinnati Museum Center at Union Terminal), Cincinnati (M'Lissa Kesterman, Linda Bailey, Rick Kesterman); Rutherford B. Hayes Presidential Center, Fremont (Nan Card); Ohio Statehouse, Columbus.

*Pennsylvania*: Historical Society of Pennsylvania, Philadelphia.

*Washington, DC, and vicinity*: Library of Congress Manuscript Division; District of Columbia Public Library (Martin Luther King Jr. Memorial Library) (Andrea Cheney); National Archives at College Park, Maryland (Still Picture Unit).

*New York City*: New-York Historical Society Library; Columbia University Rare Book and Manuscript Library; Bobst Library, New York University; New York Public Library (Stephen A. Schwartzman Building, Mid-Manhattan Library, and Library for the Performing Arts at Lincoln Center); Pierpont Morgan Library (Morgan Library and Museum).

*New York State*: Warner Library, Tarrytown; Oneida County Historical Society, Utica; Saratoga Springs History Museum.

*Michigan*: University of Michigan Special Collections Library, Ann Arbor (Peggy Daub, Kate Hutchens).

*Wyoming*: American Heritage Center, University of Wyoming, Laramie (Ginny Kilander, Sharon Bowen Maier).

*North Carolina*: David M. Rubenstein Rare Book and Manuscript Library, Duke University, Durham (Stephanie Barnwell).

*Paris, France*: Bibliothèque nationale de France.

Other individuals and institutions I wish to thank for helping in various ways, large and small (alphabetically): Biographers International Organization (Jamie Morris and company); Ken Carr; Molly Hoyt Cashin; Phyllis Gershon; Allison B. Goodsell, Rare Books, Kingston, Rhode Island; Dr. Thayer Greene; William B. Hoyt; Bevis and Clara Longstreth; Alison Macor; Chase McQuade; Mark Mitchell; the Ollers of Huron and South Vienna; Howard Palmer; Lydia Rapoza; Kit St. John;

Sue Sutton; Williamstown Art Conservation Center (Matthew Hamilton); Willkie Farr & Gallagher LLP.

This book would scarcely have been possible without the pioneering efforts of the late John Niven and others who edited the voluminous correspondence contained in the five-volume *Salmon P. Chase Papers* and the more recent *"Spur Up Your Pegasus": Family Letters of Salmon, Kate, and Nettie Chase, 1844–1873*, both published by The Kent State University Press. As the notes to this book can attest, I have benefited immensely from the transcriptions of the letters published in these volumes. Thanks to the painstaking work by the editors of these books, Kate and her family will provide grist for future biographers for many years.

Just as my book will not be the last word on Kate Chase, neither is it the first. That honor belongs to Mary Merwin Phelps, whose 1935 biography of Kate rescued her from relative obscurity and has been followed by several other books about Kate as well as prominent treatment of her in some others (including Doris Kearns Goodwin's *Team of Rivals* and, more recently, Jennifer Chiaverini's novel, *Mrs. Lincoln's Rival*). I am indebted to all of Kate's biographers, each of whom has had his or her own take on this fascinating woman, who continues to arouse spirited debate among those who examine her life.

I cannot close without thanking my agent, Jim Donovan, who worked indefatigably on behalf of the book and provided valuable editorial suggestions (in addition to frequent hand-holding). Thanks also to his colleague, Melissa Shultz.

Finally, I wish to thank my editor, Robert Pigeon and the entire Da Capo team for understanding this book from the start and bringing it to fruition.

# Notes

## Abbreviations Used in the Notes

*People*

**KC.** Kate Chase/Kate Chase Sprague

**NC.** Janet Ralston ("Nettie") Chase/Janet Ralston Chase Hoyt

**SPC.** Salmon Portland Chase

**WS.** William Sprague IV (Kate Chase's husband)

*Manuscript Collections*

**Arthur LC.** Chester Alan Arthur Papers, Manuscript Division, Library of Congress

**BUL.** William and Catherine Chase Sprague Papers, Brown University, John Hay Library, Providence, RI

**Chase LC.** Salmon P. Chase Papers, Manuscript Division, Library of Congress

**Chase OHS.** Salmon P. Chase Collection, Ohio Historical Society Archives/Library, Columbus, OH

**Chase HSP.** Salmon P. Chase Papers, Historical Society of Pennsylvania, Philadelphia

**CHS.** Chase/Sprague collection, Cranston Historical Society, Cranston, RI

**Conkling LC.** Roscoe Conkling Papers, Manuscript Division, Library of Congress

**Phelps UM.** Mary Merwin Phelps Papers, University of Michigan Special Collections Library, Ann Arbor, MI

*Books*

***ANB.*** John A. Garraty and Mark C. Carnes, eds., *American National Biography*, 24 vols. (New York: Oxford University Press, 1999)

**Beldens.** Thomas Graham Belden and Marva Robins Belden, *So Fell the Angels* (Boston: Little, Brown, 1956)

**Blue.** Frederick J. Blue, *Salmon P. Chase: A Life in Politics* (Kent, OH: Kent State University Press, 1987)

***CP1–5.*** *The Salmon P. Chase Papers*, ed. John Niven et al., 5 vols. (Kent, OH: Kent State University Press, 1993–1998)

***CP1.*** Vol. 1, *Journals, 1829–1872*

***CP2.*** Vol. 2, *Correspondence, 1823–1857*

***CP3.*** Vol. 3, *Correspondence, 1858–March 1863*

***CP4.*** Vol. 4, *Correspondence, April 1863–1864*

***CP5.*** Vol. 5, *Correspondence, 1865–1873*

**Hart.** Albert Bushnell Hart, *Salmon Portland Chase* (Boston, 1899)

**Lamphier.** Peg A. Lamphier, *Kate Chase and William Sprague: Politics and Gender in a Civil War Marriage* (Lincoln: University of Nebraska Press, 2003)

**Niven.** John Niven, *Salmon P. Chase: A Biography* (New York: Oxford University Press, 1995)

***Pegasus.*** *"Spur Up Your Pegasus": Family Letters of Salmon, Kate, and Nettie Chase, 1844–1873*, ed. James P. McClure, Peg A. Lamphier, and Erika M. Kreger (Kent, OH: Kent State University Press, 2009)

**Phelps.** Mary Merwin Phelps, *Kate Chase, Dominant Daughter: The Life Story of a Brilliant Woman and Her Famous Father* (New York: Thomas Y. Crowell, 1935)

**Ross.** Ishbel Ross, *Proud Kate: Portrait of an Ambitious Woman* (New York: Harper & Brothers, 1953)

**Schuckers.** Jacob W. Schuckers, *The Life and Public Services of Salmon Portland Chase* (New York, 1874)

**Sokoloff.** Alice Hunt Sokoloff, *Kate Chase for the Defense* (New York: Dodd, Mead, 1971)

**Warden.** Robert B. Warden, *An Account of the Private Life and Public Services of Salmon Portland Chase* (Cincinnati, 1874)

## Prologue: A Woman in the Arena

ix **old woman held the reins**: *New York Herald*, Aug. 6, 1899; *Washington Herald*, Mar. 8, 1908; *New York World*, Mar. 16, 1900; Mary L. Bisland, "Confidential Talks," *The Illustrated American* 4, no. 40 (Nov. 22, 1890): 502; *Chicago Tribune*, Aug. 4, 1895, May 24, 1896; Phelps, 275, 278–280; Ross, 274–276, 279; Sokoloff, 11, 289.

x **"No Queen . . . any American woman has"**: *Cincinnati Enquirer*, Aug. 6, 1899.

x **"slightly . . . pug"**: Allan Peskin, *Garfield* (Kent, OH: Kent State University Press, 1978), 154.

x **"something of the strangeness . . . highest order"**: *Boston Herald*, Aug. 16, 1886.

x **"Poor, weak Mrs. Lincoln . . . great secretary"**: Bisland, "Confidential Talks," 502.

x **hush would fall**: Mildred McLean Hazen Dewey, "Memoir" [1896], 132, Mildred McLean Hazen Dewey Collection, GA 52, Folder 1, AC 5142, Rutherford B. Hayes Presidential Center, Fremont, OH (hereafter cited as McLean Hazen Dewey, "Memoir").

x **"when she is talking . . . an afterthought"**: *Washington Times*, Feb. 21, 1896.

xi **"She could talk . . . convention rigger"**: Donald Barr Chidsey, *The Gentleman from New York: A Life of Roscoe Conkling* (New Haven, CT: Yale University Press, 1935), 118.

xi **"mastered the art . . . men's minds"**: H. Donald Winkler, *The Women in Lincoln's Life: How the Sixteenth American President Was Shaped by Fascinating Women Who Loved, Hated, Helped, Charmed, and Deceived Him* (Nashville: Rutledge Hill Press, 2001), 165.

xi **1897**: KC to Mrs. Jay Bancroft, May 7, June 24, 1897, Phelps UM.

xii **"force back the old bitterness of spirit"**: KC Diary, Dec. 27, 1868, BUL.

xii **"proud, passionate . . . never learned to submit"**: KC Diary, Nov. 11, 1868, BUL.

xii **"Day before yesterday . . . work on hand here"**: KC to SPC, July 5, 1868 (*Pegasus*, 370).

xii **"There is a noble work . . . *timid*"**: Ibid.

xii **"immediately sent for"**: *Cincinnati Daily Enquirer*, July 4, 1868.

xiii **"the airiest . . . in the Convention"**: *New-York Tribune*, July 6, 1868.

xiii **"I knew . . . come up"**: *San Francisco Morning Call*, Oct. 15, 1893.

xiii **relative's townhouse**: Kate was staying in the home of Edwin Hoyt at 94 Fifth Avenue, between Fourteenth and Fifteenth Streets. Hoyt had married a cousin of Kate's husband, William Sprague, and was a business partner of the Spragues. (*Pegasus*, 369n1, 457–458).

xiii **at the Fifth Avenue Hotel**: Eugene L. Didier, "Salmon P. Chase," *The Chautauquan: Organ of the Chautauqua Literary and Scientific Circle* 11 (April 1890–September 1890): 183; *Pegasus*, 215n1, 369n1. The hotel's address was 190 Fifth Avenue, at the corner of Broadway and Twenty-Third Street.

xiii **"vertical steam engine"**: Jeff Hirsh, *Manhattan Hotels 1880–1920* (Charleston, SC: Arcadia, 1997), 84–85.

xiii **Kate was visibly in charge**: William C. Hudson, *Random Recollections of an Old Political Reporter* (New York: Cupples & Leon, 1911), 18.

xiii **"Some delegates . . . irresistible beauty"**: Didier, "Salmon P. Chase," 183.

xiii **"What a Magnificent woman . . . overwhelming majority"**: Hamilton Smith to SPC, July 5, 1868 (*CP5*:254–255).

xiv **"There, in supreme control . . . national figure"**: Hudson, *Random Recollections*, 18.
xiv **"cap in hand . . . a nomination"**: Ibid., 19.
xiv **"a debased . . . servitude"**: Democratic National Convention, *Official Proceedings of the National Democratic Convention, Held at New York, July 4–9, 1868*, rep. George Wakeman (Boston, 1868), 1–5 (hereafter cited as *Official Proceedings*).
xiv **"fell under . . . captive"**: Hudson, *Random Recollections*, 19.
xiv **"the most graceful . . . queenly woman"**: Emily Edson Briggs, *The Olivia Letters: Being Some History of Washington City for Forty Years as Told by the Letters of a Newspaper Correspondent* (New York: Neale Publishing, 1906), 400.
xiv **"the absence . . . devoted love"**: KC Diary, Mar. 29, 1868, BUL.
xiv **"if I cannot . . . this man's mistress"**: one-page fragment in Kate Chase's handwriting, n.d., ca. Mar. 1868, BUL.
xv **"The young men . . . in the convention"**: KC to SPC, July 2, 1868 (*Pegasus*, 368).
xv **"Mr. Hunter . . . very fractious"**: Ibid., 369.
xv **"patriotic negro eccentricities"**: *New York Herald*, July 4, 1868.
xvi **"My parlors . . . all the time"**: Frederick Aiken to SPC, July 3, 1868 (*CP5*:251–252n2).
xvi **"All the Southern men . . . his nomination"**: *New-York Tribune*, July 4, 1868.
xvi **"I am so glad . . . Katie"**: KC to SPC, July 5, 1868 (*Pegasus*, 371).
xvi **"acting too much the politician"**: SPC to KC, July 7, 1868 (*CP5*:259).
xvii **"I really . . . just now"**: KC to SPC, July 5, 1868 (*Pegasus*, 370).
xvii **"the *Courage* . . . Statesman"**: KC to SPC, July 7, 1868 (*Pegasus*, 371–372).
xvii **"a little insane"**: Michael Burlingame, *Abraham Lincoln: A Life* (Baltimore: Johns Hopkins University Press, 2008), 1:735.
xvii **"almost to a mania"**: *Cincinnati Daily Gazette*, Mar. 19, 1868.
xvii **"You know how little . . . secure it"**: SPC to KC, July 7, 1868 (*CP5*:258).
xvii **Ohio friends advised**: Roeliff Brinkerhoff, *Recollections of a Lifetime* (Cincinnati: Robert Clarke, 1900), 118–120.
xviii **"entranced by White House dreams"**: Julia Bundy Foraker, *I Would Live It Again* (New York: Harper & Brothers, 1932), 46–47.
xviii **"I am glad . . . do as well?"**: KC to SPC, July 2, 1868 (*Pegasus*, 369).
xviii **devoted to preliminaries**: Charles H. Coleman, *The Election of 1868: The Democratic Effort to Regain Control* (New York: Columbia University Press, 1933), 195–198.
xviii **"ignorant negroes"**: *Official Proceedings*, 47–48. See also ibid., 30, 49–50, 92.
xviii **"Read it! . . . without their consent"**: *Official Proceedings*, 28–30. See also Coleman, *Election of 1868*, 197.
xviii **regarded as a joke**: *New York Times*, June 15, 1924.
xviii **decline to add her name**: Ross, 221.
xix **not allowed on the convention floor**: Hart, 420; *Washington Herald*, Mar. 8, 1908.

xix **like "taking the lieutenant . . . against the captain"**: *New York Herald*, May 18, 1868.

xix **"as dry . . . bygone age"**: *New York Herald*, May 18, 1868.

xix **pepper Tilden with letters**: *Letters and Literary Memorials of Samuel J. Tilden*, ed. John Bigelow (New York: Harper & Brothers, 1908), 1:216–217, 222–224, 229–230.

xx **sincere in his intention**: KC to SPC, July 2, 1868 (*Pegasus*, 368–369).

xx **"It is all a question . . . blunder"**: Hudson, *Random Recollections*, 19–20.

xx **sat at his Senate desk:** *Cong. Globe*, 40th Cong., 2nd Sess. 3733–3738, 3769–3770 (July 6, 7, 1868).

xx **"Adonis of the Senate"**: *Frank Leslie's Illustrated Newspaper*, Oct. 13, 1877.

xx **"The excitement . . . Tammany Hall"**: KC to SPC, July 7, 1868 (*Pegasus*, 371).

xx **"snares and pitfalls . . . the choice"**: Ibid., 372.

xxi **inability to locate Van Buren**: KC to SPC, July 10, 1868 (*Pegasus*, 376).

xxi **Aiken . . . committee**: Ben [Benjamin] Perley Poore, *Perley's Reminiscences of Sixty Years in the National Metropolis* (Philadelphia, 1886), 2:238–239; *Pegasus*, 372n2.

xxi **Chanler House**: Calling card of "Friends of Chief Justice Chase" Executive Committee, Alexander P. Long Papers, Cincinnati History Library and Archives, Cincinnati Museum Center at Union Terminal; *New York Herald*, June 16, July 3, 1868. Hudson erroneously recalled it as the Clarendon Hotel. Hudson, *Random Recollections*, 18.

xxi **"too indiscreet . . . in any way"**: KC to SPC, July 7, 1868 (*Pegasus*, 371).

xxi **"negro supremacy . . . void"**: *Official Proceedings*, 59–60.

xxi **"such a telegram . . . in *open Convention*"**: KC to SPC, July 7, 1868 (*Pegasus*, 372).

xxi **"in the main . . . very good"**: SPC to Van Buren, July 8, 1868, quoted in Schuckers, 590.

xxi **"I can accept . . . can't say that I like it"**: SPC to KC July 7, 1868 (*CP5*:258).

xxii **"do or say . . . housetops"**: Ibid., 259.

xxii **"not yet . . . gaining time"**: SPC to KC, July 7, 1868 (*CP5*:257–258).

xxii **was visiting relatives . . . budding artistic talent**: *St. Paul Daily Press*, July 9, 1868; NC to SPC, July 21, 1868 (*Pegasus*, 377–379).

xxii **"Do you know . . . envelope best of all"**: NC to SPC, July 21, 1868 (*Pegasus*, 377–379).

xxii **"on the back . . . burnt match"**: Ibid., 377–378.

xxiii **seventh . . . through eleventh ballots**: *Official Proceedings*, 108–118; Coleman, *Election of 1868*, 224–226, 237–238, 382, app. B.

xxiii **Kate was waiting for a letter**: KC to SPC, July 10, 1868 (*Pegasus*, 375–376).

xxiii **one-half vote would go to . . . Chase**: *Official Proceedings*, 119.

xxiii **"a scene . . . the convention"**: Schuckers, 565.

xxiii **she joined in the applause**: *New York Times*, June 15, 1924.

# PART ONE: MISS CHASE

## Chapter 1: "Qualified to Ornament Any Society"

3 **Henriette Desportes**: "Henriette Desportes Field," *Find a Grave*, June 1, 2009, www.findagrave.com/cgi-bin/fg.cgi?page=gr&GRid=37793248; passenger list for *Zurich*, arrival New York, Sept. 13, 1849, *Ancestry.com*, record for Henriette Desportes; Mrs. Henry M. [Henriette Deluzy-Desportes] Field, *Home Sketches in France, and Other Papers*, ed. Henry M. Field and Andrew Dickson White (New York, 1875), 22–24.

3 **10 Gramercy Park**: *New-York Tribune*, Aug. 29, 1849; Phelps, 68, 74. Ishbel Ross's 1953 biography of Kate mistakenly placed the school at Forty-Ninth Street and Madison Avenue, an error repeated by several subsequent biographers. Haines opened her original school in lower Manhattan at 68 Warren Street and moved it uptown, to 10 Gramercy Park, by August 1848, where it remained for thirty years. *New-York Tribune*, Aug. 26, 1848, Sept. 6, 1878 (advertisements).

4 **January term in 1850**: John Garniss to SPC, Jan. 2, 7, 15, 1850, Chase HSP; KC to Willie Sprague, Jan. 13 [or 18], 1877, BUL.

4 **daily walks**: Phelps, 74; *Julia Newberry's Diary*, ed. Margaret Ayer Barnes and Janet Ayer Fairbank (New York: W. W. Norton, 1933), 35–36; Catharine Beekman to her brother, Feb. 2, 1854, Beekman Family Papers, New-York Historical Society MSS Collection (hereafter cited as Beekman NYHS).

4 **a brief marriage**: Joseph Tracy et al., *History of American Missions to the Heathen, from Their Commencement to the Present Time* (Worchester, MA, 1840), 271, 298, 331; Sarah Josepha Hale, *Woman's Record: or, Sketches of All Distinguished Women, from the Creation to A.D. 1850 . . .* (New York, 1853), 892.

4 **was only thirty-three**: US Passport Application for Henrietta B. Haines, issued July 21, 1866, *Ancestry.com* (b. June 24, 1816). She died in 1879. *New York Herald*, May 9, 1879.

4 **boasted of its new setting**: The slightly modified townhouse still stands on Gramercy Park South (then known as East Twentieth Street), just east of Park Avenue (formerly Fourth Avenue).

4 **school regimen**: Catharine Beekman's letters to her mother, Mar. 2, 16, 1854; brother, Feb. 2, 1854; and father, Feb. 9, Mar. 9, 1854, Beekman NYHS; Phelps, 74–75; *Julia Newberry's Diary*, 35–37.

4 **"pretty severe . . . hardly breathe"**: *Julia Newberry's Diary*, 36.

5 **"*taught table manners* . . . Manners School"**: Sarah M. Reilay to Morrison V. R. Weyant, June 6, 1928, Miss Haines'[s] School, Gramercy Park, New York, collection at New-York Historical Society (hereafter cited as Haines NYHS).

5 **violent temper**: Sara Upton Edwards to Morrison V. R. Weyant, Apr. 24, 1928, Haines NYHS.

5 **"*supremely* gracious . . . eyes twinkled"**: *Julia Newberry's Diary*, 30.

5 **Kate studied**: Phelps, 75; Ross, 20–21; SPC to KC, Feb. 6, 1853 (*Pegasus*, 126); SPC to KC, Dec. 10, 1853 (*Pegasus*, 135); Catharine Beekman's letters to her father, Feb. 9, Mar. 9, 28, 1854; and her mother, Feb. 2, 16, 1854, Beekman NYHS; *Julia Newberry's Diary*, 32, 36.

5 **"develop a parlor-based . . . entire nation"**: Gail Collins, *America's Women: Four Hundred Years of Dolls, Drudges, Helpmates, and Heroines* (2003; repr., New York: Harper Perennial, 2007), 92.

5 **hear Jenny Lind**: Phelps, 77; Ross, 22.

6 **"at least . . . getting them up"**: Catharine Beekman to her mother, Mar. 2, 1854, Beekman NYHS.

6 **"24 yds . . . C.J. Chase"**: Phelps, 79.

6 **four and a half years Kate spent**: Some biographers have mistakenly written that Kate spent nine years there, from 1847 to 1856. Phelps, 68, 74, 79; Ross, 20; Beldens, 15. In fact, she began there in January 1850 and left in approximately June 1854. SPC to KC, July 5, 1854 (*Pegasus*, 138).

6 **later express pride**: *San Francisco Morning Call*, Oct. 15, 1893.

6 **"a little devil"**: Mary Merwin Phelps, "A Fashionable School of the Last Century, Henrietta B. Haines," 7 (long version), Phelps UM.

6 **had to curtsy . . . "three deadly sins"**: Ibid., 4, 6.

6 **"What little prigs we were!"**: Ibid., 6.

6 **de Janon**: Phelps, 71; Sokoloff, 29; *Pegasus*, 7; Catharine Beekman to her mother, Mar. 16, 1854, Beekman NYHS.

6 **Desportes married . . . salon hostess**: *New York Times*, Mar. 8, 14, 1875; Field, *Home Sketches*, 24–25.

6 **"She would frankly . . . like men"**: *Washington Times Magazine*, Sept. 6, 1908.

6 **Kate was lonely**: SPC to KC, Aug. 10, 1852 (*Pegasus*, 121).

6 **headmistress denied Kate's request**: SPC to KC, Dec. 21, 1852 (*Pegasus*, 123–124).

7 **not to be selfish**: SPC to KC, July 22, 1850 (*Pegasus*, 79).

7 **"You have said . . . ruin forever"**: SPC to KC, Aug. 13, 1850 (*Pegasus*, 82–84).

7 **"You have not . . . very thoughtless"**: SPC to KC, Sept. 5, 1850 (*Pegasus*, 86–87).

7 **spelled "Tuesday" as "tewsday"**: SPC to Sarah Bella Chase, Mar. 16, 1850 (*Pegasus*, 78).

8 **"not nearly as good . . . no older than you are"**: SPC to NC, Sept. 13, 1857 (*CP*2:459).

8 **ragged looking**: SPC to NC, Aug. 19, 1863 (*Pegasus*, 221).

8 **"heedlessness"**: SPC to NC, Nov. 23, 1863 (*Pegasus*, 247).

8 **two letters were among her best**: SPC to KC, Jan. 15, Feb. 1, 1851 (*Pegasus*, 90–92).

8 **too small and pinched**: SPC to KC, Mar. 2, 1851 (*Pegasus*, 93).

8 **wrote "pleasure" as "pleas ure"**: SPC to KC, Mar. 25, 1852 (*Pegasus*, 116).

8 **"follow my precept . . . practice"**: SPC to KC, Mar. 4, 1852 (*Pegasus*, 115).

8 **"You set down . . . without any embellishment whatever"**: SPC to KC, Jan. 22, 1851 (*Pegasus*, 91).

8 **"I hope the other little girls . . . with them"**: SPC to KC, Sept. 10, 1851 (*Pegasus*, 97).

8 **"write exactly . . . wish to know"**: SPC to KC, Apr. 3, 1852 (*Pegasus*, 118).

8 **"mere dry bones . . . your father's wishes"**: SPC to KC, Jan. 23, 1853 (*Pegasus*, 125).

8 **Haines read . . . correspondence**: *Pegasus*, 108; SPC to KC, July 31, 1854 (*Pegasus*, 142).

9 **"rather a poor . . . lady of thirteen"**: SPC to KC, Sept. 6, 1853 (*Pegasus*, 132).

9 **"I am afraid . . . do well"**: SPC to KC, Dec. 10, 1853 (*Pegasus*, 135).

9 **"short and not *very* funny"**: SPC to KC, Oct. 8, 1853 (*Pegasus*, 133).

9 **"the most winsome . . . can imagine"**: SPC to KC, Oct. 19, 1853 (*Pegasus*, 134).

9 **"Artless . . . what it is?"**: SPC to KC, Sept. 15, 1854 (*Pegasus*, 150).

9 **report card . . . unacceptable**: SPC to KC, July 5, 1854 (*Pegasus*, 138).

9 **"first wherever I may be"**: SPC to Charles Cleveland, Feb. 8, 1830 (*CP*2:48).

9 **"The time has come . . . in society"**: SPC to KC, July 5, 1854 (*Pegasus*, 138).

9 **"I desire . . . or elsewhere"**: SPC to KC, Dec. 20, 1853 (*Pegasus*, 136).

10 **"Were you not helped . . . how much was?"**: SPC to KC, July 5, 1854 (*Pegasus*, 139).

10 **"Your last letter . . . not perfect"**: KC to NC, July 25, 1860 (*Pegasus*, 174).

10 **"Grandpapa would complain . . . *meat* on *them*'"**: KC to Willie Sprague, Jan. 13 [or 18], 1877, BUL.

10 **"I repeat . . . every little act"**: Ibid.

10 **"You . . . are like me"**: SPC to KC, Jan. 22, 1851 (*Pegasus*, 91).

10 **"I wish . . . little life in mine"**: Ibid.

10 **death pursuing him**: SPC to C. Sumner, Jan. 28, 1850 (*CP*2:278).

10 **"I wish to see . . . must not lose any of them"**: SPC to KC, Aug. 4, 1853 (*Pegasus*, 129).

## Chapter 2: "I Shall Strive to Be First Wherever I May Be"

12 **disliked farm work**: SPC to John T. Trowbridge, Dec. 27, 1863, Jan. 19, [1864], Chase HSP.

12 **"an almost childlike little lisp"**: *The Reminiscences of Carl Schurz* (New York: McClure Company, 1907), 2:170.

12 **father . . . country boy's schooling**: SPC to J. Trowbridge, Dec. 27, 1863, Jan. 19, [1864], Chase HSP.

12 **it sounded "fishy"**: SPC to Charles Cleveland, Feb. 8, 1830 (*CP*2:48).

12 **others were learned**: Niven, 5; Schuckers, 3; William H. Child, *History of the Town of Cornish, New Hampshire, with Genealogical Record, 1864–1910* (Concord, NH: Rumford Press, 1911), 1:284–285, 2:62.

12 **Ithamar, was a successful farmer . . . died**: Simon G. Griffin, *A History of the Town of Keene: From 1732 . . . to 1874. . . .* (Keene, NH: Sentinel Printing, 1904), 363, 380, 572–573; Child, *History of Cornish*, 1:131, 158, 162, 164–165, 2:62, 64; SPC to J. Trowbridge, Dec. 27, 1863, Jan. 19, [1864], Chase HSP; Niven, 8.

13 **Philander Chase . . . bring the fatherless**: Schuckers, 9–10, 15–16; Niven, 9, 12–14.

13 **pious and cultured woman**: Griffin, *History of Keene*, 406; Child, *History of Cornish*, 1:300; *Pegasus*, 453.

13 **"tyrannical"**: SPC to J. Trowbridge, Jan. 25, 1864 (*CP4*:263).

13 **Bishop Chase beat the boy**: Niven, 13; Warden, 89–90.

13 **hated his time in Ohio**: Warden, 85.

13 **resigned . . . Kenyon college**: Blue, 5; Schuckers, 16–19, 21.

14 **cracked him on the head**: Blue, 5–6.

14 **clever nicknames, . . . lifelong friends**: Arthur M. Schlesinger, *Salmon Portland Chase: Undergraduate and Pedagogue* (Columbus, OH: F. J. Heer, 1919), 123–127; Doris Kearns Goodwin, *Team of Rivals: The Political Genius of Abraham Lincoln* (New York: Simon & Schuster, 2005), 38.

14 **too many novels**: SPC to Thomas Sparhawk, July 8, 1827, in Schlesinger, *Undergraduate*, 138.

14 **"the shortness . . . must perform"**: SPC to T. Sparhawk, Sept. 18, 1927, in ibid., 140.

14 **successful one-man protest**: *CP2*:7n3; Niven, 18–19; Schuckers, 19–20.

14 **"would sooner . . . our enlightened land"**: SPC to T. Sparhawk, Feb. 6, 1826, in Schlesinger, *Undergraduate*, 128.

14 **"old Bison's . . . 99th time"**: SPC to T. Sparhawk, Nov. 29, Dec. 14, 1825, Feb. 6, 1826, in ibid., 123–128.

14 **"give the end . . . this match"**: SPC to T. Sparhawk, May 15, 1828, in ibid., 145.

14 **"I regard . . . his fellowman"**: SPC to T. Sparhawk, Nov. 10, 1828, in ibid., 151.

14 **"I am not sorry . . . one's youth"**: SPC to T. Sparhawk, Sept. 30, 1829, in ibid., 155.

15 **"a shining ornament to the profession"**: Alexander Chase to SPC, Nov. 4, 1825 (*CP2*:5).

15 **"I once obtained . . . in a clerkship"**: SPC to J. Trowbridge, Feb. 10, 1864 (*CP4*:280–281).

15 **sons of Senator Henry Clay**: SPC to T. Sparhawk, Jan. 2, 1828, in Schlesinger, *Undergraduate*, 143.

15 **more obedient than the "brats"**: Ibid.

15 **"as well . . . any school"**: SPC to T. Sparhawk, Jan. 13, 1827, in ibid., 136.

15 **"the petty vexations . . . good resolutions"**: SPC to KC, Apr. 13, 1855 (*Pegasus*, 158).

15 **"miserable set"**: SPC to T. Sparhawk, Jan. 15, 1830 (*CP2*:46).

15 **Hindu caste system**: SPC to Hamilton Smith, May 31, 1827 (*CP2*:17–18).
15 **"stiff . . . Automaton chess-Player"**: SPC to T. Sparhawk, Jan. 2, 1828, in Schlesinger, *Undergraduate*, 142.
15 **"ignoramus . . . chief"**: SPC to T. Sparhawk, Nov. 10, 1828, in ibid., 151.
15 **"contemptible intriguer"**: SPC Diary, Dec. 29, 1829 (*CP1*:34).
15 **views on slavery . . . colonize**: SPC to Hamilton Smith, July 30, 1828 (*CP2*:31).
16 **"see this Union dissolved . . . an event"**: SPC to T. Sparhawk, Nov. 10, 1828, in Schlesinger, *Undergraduate*, 151.
16 **young man's superficial study**: SPC Diary, Dec. 1–2, 1829 (*CP1*:30).
16 **"ruled by . . . mildest means"**: SPC to J. Trowbridge, Jan. 19, [1864], Chase HSP.
16 **daughters, Elizabeth and Catharine**: SPC to Hamilton Smith, Mar. 31, 1828 (*CP2*:27); SPC Diary, Jan. 28, 29, 31, Mar. 20, 1829 (*CP1*:7–8, 12); SPC to J. Trowbridge, Feb. 10, 1864 (*CP4*:282–283).
16 **"bright raven locks . . . thing over the earth"**: SPC Diary, Jan. 10, 1829 (*CP1*:5).
16 **unfair to her**: SPC to T. Sparhawk, Apr. 20, 1829, in Schlesinger, *Undergraduate*, 153.
16 **"The Sisters"**: Schuckers, 25–26n1.
16 **"She was not . . . and yet"**: Ibid.; William Turner Coggeshall, *The Poets and Poetry of the West: With Biographical and Critical Notices* (Columbus, 1860), 170–171; SPC Diary, Jan. 10, 1829 (*CP1*:5).
17 **"slight and frail . . . any earthly possession"**: SPC Diary, Jan. 7, 1830 (*CP1*:37).
17 **"always the seducer . . . upon our own"**: SPC to Hamilton Smith, Mar. 31, 1828 (*CP2*:26).
17 **"Are they deceitful . . . naturally it is not so"**: SPC to Hamilton Smith, July 30, 1828 (*CP2*:29).
17 **"two agreeable . . . Thomas Aquinas"**: SPC Diary, Jan. 7, 1830 (*CP1*:39).
17 **"argumentative ladies"**: Ibid.
17 **"entitled to . . . in the world"**: Ibid.
18 **Elizabeth Hannah Cabell**: *CP1*:7n12; Alexander Brown, *The Cabells and Their Kin: A Memorial Volume of History, Biography, and Genealogy* (Boston, 1895), 258, 574.
18 **"a pretty young lady . . . timid as a fawn"**: SPC Diary, Apr. 7, 1829 (*CP1*:13).
18 **allowed him to escort . . . would not consider marrying**: Didier, "Salmon P. Chase," 184.
18 **"the aroma . . . years afterward"**: Ibid.
18 **"recalled . . . it was interesting"**: Ibid., 184–185.
18 **reason for his move**: SPC to T. Sparhawk, Apr. 20, 1829, in Schlesinger, *Undergraduate*, 153.
18 **"to pass once more . . . I went home"**: SPC Diary, Apr. 20, 1829 (*CP1*:14).

18 **"I would rather be *first* . . . twenty years hence"**: SPC to C. Cleveland, Feb. 8, 1830 (*CP2*:48).

19 **"And as I have . . . Spencer Payne Cheyce"**: Ibid.

19 **"I have always thought . . . men to achieve"**: SPC to Hamilton Smith, Apr. 7, 1829 (*CP2*:38).

## Chapter 3: "How Short Then Is This Life!"

20 **interests ranged far beyond**: Niven, 29–40; Blue, 15–22; Schuckers, 34–37; Hart, 17–20.

20 **"Semi-Colon" literary society**: Joan D. Hedrick, *Harriet Beecher Stowe: A Life* (New York: Oxford University Press, 1995), 82.

20 **planned each day's activities**: SPC Diary, June 26, 1840 (*CP1*:126–128).

20 **"½ past 4 . . . accomplished all" . . . next day's plan**: SPC Diary, June 27, 1840 (*CP1*:128–129).

21 **disgusted observers**: Hedrick, *Harriet Beecher Stowe*, 105–107; Debby Applegate, *The Most Famous Man in America: The Biography of Henry Ward Beecher* (New York: Doubleday, 2006), 128–131.

21 **book that made him cry**: SPC Diary, Jan. 9, 1853 (*CP1*:233).

21 **"I told him . . . at any time"**: Niven, 48.

21 **authorities had acted shamefully**: SPC to C. Cleveland, Oct. 22, 1841 (*CP2*:79).

21 **letter to the editor**: SPC to *Cincinnati Daily Gazette*, Aug. 4, 1836 (*CP2*:62–63).

21 **"denounced . . . a burglar"**: Donn Piatt, *Memories of the Men Who Saved the Union* (New York, 1887), 97.

21 **not technically an abolitionist**: SPC to C. Cleveland, Oct. 22, 1841 (*CP2*:80); SPC to Hamilton Smith, Sept. 15, 1851 (*CP2*:337); SPC to Theodore Parker, July 17, 1856 (*CP2*:445); SPC to Robert Warden, Oct. 23, 1863 (*CP4*:156).

21 **"He was to speak . . . his appointment"**: Piatt, *Memories of the Men*, 100.

22 **"Chase was no . . . political war"**: George Hoadly, "Address at Music Hall . . . October 14, 1886" (Cincinnati, 1887), 6, Chase OHS (hereafter cited as Hoadly, "Address at Music Hall").

22 **"contrary to natural right"**: "Speech of Salmon P. Chase in the Case of the Colored Woman, Matilda . . . March 11, 1837" (Cincinnati, 1837), 8–9, Chase OHS.

22 ***Van Zandt* case**: Schuckers, 53–66; Hart, 75–80; Niven, 76–83.

22 **"zealous . . . color or condition"**: Blue, 39.

22 **"The movement . . . host of Liberty"**: SPC to C. Cleveland, Oct. 22, 1841 (*CP2*:80).

23 **married Catharine Jane "Kitty" Garniss**: *CP1*:72n56; SPC "Family Memoranda," n.d., ca. 1844–1846, Chase LC, reel 32 (hereafter cited as "Family Memoranda," Chase LC).

23 **"pretenders to style"**: SPC Diary, Nov. 1835 (*CP1*:82).
23 **"an affected and shallow girl"**: Ibid.
23 **regal carriage**: Warden, 238.
23 **need of some polishing**: Ibid., 242.
23 **near-deadly bout . . . "live a more godly life"**: SPC Diary, Jan. 18, 1833 (*CP1*:67–68).
23 **"How mistaken . . . underrate her!"**: SPC Diary, Nov. 1835 (*CP1*:82).
23 **she dreamed the night before**: SPC Diary, Feb. 8, 1834 (*CP1*:79).
23 **they named Catharine Jane**: *CP1*:85n26; "Family Memoranda," Chase LC; SPC genealogy note, Chase LC, reel 32 (hereafter cited as genealogy note, Chase LC).
23 **go by Kate**: SPC to C. Cleveland, Feb. 7, 1840 (*CP2*:67); *CP1*:85n26.
23 **baby's mother was dead**: Niven, 42–43; SPC Diary, Nov. 18–Dec. 1, 1835 (*CP1*:86–94).
24 **"implored God . . . but clay"**: SPC Diary, Dec. 1, 1835 (*CP1*:94).
24 **without a struggle or even a sigh**: SPC Diary, Nov. 30–Dec. 1, 1835 (*CP1*:90–93).
24 **"But I procrastinated . . . she is gone"**: SPC Diary, Dec. 27, 1835 (*CP1*:97–98).
24 **Eliza Ann Smith**: *CP1*:120n40; "Family Memoranda," Chase LC; Niven, 71; Phelps, 21.
24 **"very lovely . . . marvelously bright eyes"**: Mrs. Richard [Julia M. Corbitt] Crowley, *Echoes from Niagara: Historical, Political, Personal* (Buffalo, NY, 1890), 99.
24 **died within days**: SPC to C. Cleveland, Feb. 7, 1840 (*CP2*:67–69 and n1); SPC Diary, May 2, 1840 (*CP1*:120 and n39); "Family Memoranda," Chase LC; Niven, 72.
24 **"Her animated playfulness . . . reference to her"**: SPC to C. Cleveland, Feb. 7, 1840 (*CP2*:67–68).
25 **home in downtown**: Chase was living near the southeast corner of Fourth Street and Broadway, two doors north of his in-laws the Garnisses. David Henry Shaffer, *The Cincinnati, Covington, Newport and Fulton Directory, for 1840* (Cincinnati, 1839), 136, 190; Niven, 50.
25 **"suffering . . . pain"**: SPC Diary, Aug. 12, 1840 (*CP1*:142).
25 **"and kneeling down . . . keep his commandments"**: Ibid.
25 **119th Psalm**: Ibid., 143.
25 **Catharine Jane Chase**: *CP1*:142n37; "Family Memoranda," Chase LC; genealogy note, Chase LC.
25 **spelled with a "K"**: See, e.g., KC to Rutherford B. Hayes, May 23, 1877, CHS; KC to NC, Oct. 13, 1874, BUL; KC to William T. Sherman, Jan. 22, 1875, BUL; KC to Frederick Douglass, Jan. 13, 1881, CHS; KC to Chester Alan Arthur, Oct. 21, 1881, Arthur LC.
25 **"a certain interesting . . . this stage"**: SPC to C. Cleveland, Aug. 29, 1840 (*CP2*:69).
25 **"indeed . . . child of God"**: SPC Diary, May 23, 1841 (*CP1*:161).

25 **"looking back . . . earthly existence!"**: SPC to C. Cleveland, Aug. 29, 1840 (*CP2*:70).

26 **Lizzie . . . another Lizzie**: *Pegasus*, 448; *CP1*:164n44; "Family Memoranda," Chase LC; genealogy note, Chase LC.

26 **succumbed to tuberculosis**: Niven, 76; SPC "Family Memoranda," Chase LC.

26 **"The Lord hath . . . we are desolate"**: SPC to C. Cleveland, Oct. 1, 1845 (*CP2*:121).

26 **"Is Christ precious . . . answered 'yes.'"**: Ibid., 121–122.

26 **"listened . . . understand very little"**: SPC Diary, Nov. 24, 1845 (*CP1*:174).

26 **"Remember . . . preparation for another!"**: SPC to KC, Dec. 5, 1851 (*Pegasus*, 100).

## Chapter 4: The Belle of Columbus

28 **"Belle" . . . passed away**: Niven, 144; *Pegasus*, 112n1.

28 **married Belle**: Chase and Belle were married on November 6, 1846. *Pegasus*, 449; genealogy note, Chase LC.

28 **"untrue representation"**: SPC Diary, Apr. 25, 1847 (*CP1*:193).

28 **"your affectionate mother . . . darling little daughter"**: Belle Chase to KC, Aug. 29, 1850, Chase HSP.

28 **brought Kate a baby sister**: Genealogy note, Chase LC. A second daughter of Salmon and Belle—Josephine Ludlow Chase, usually referred to as "Zoe"—died in July 1850, a few weeks after her first birthday. Ibid.; SPC to Belle Chase, July 28, 1850 (*Pegasus*, 80).

28 **"I wish sometimes . . . little Nettie"**: SPC to KC, June 15, 1852, Chase HSP.

29 **coined the party's slogan**: Niven, 110.

29 **defended his conduct**: Hart, 112; SPC to John F. Morse, Jan. 19, 1849 (*CP2*:216–217); SPC to George Bradburn, July 4, 1849 (*CP2*:243).

29 **cause was more important**: SPC to Morse, Jan. 19, 1849 (*CP2*:217).

29 **searching for a cure**: Niven, 132.

30 **hung a picture of him**: SPC to Sumner, May 1, 1857 (*CP2*:449, 451–452, and n13).

30 **another girls' boarding school**: *Pegasus*, 8–9, 145.

30 **"You complain . . . you may deserve it"**: SPC to KC, Apr. 13, 1855 (*Pegasus*, 158).

30 **allowing card playing**: SPC to KC, Sept. 15, 1854 (*Pegasus*, 149).

30 **"freer . . . spirit"**: SPC to KC, July 31, 1854 (*Pegasus*, 142).

30 **favor of sitting next to him**: note, n.d., from "Joe," BUL.

30 **"Whose face . . . rival thine?"**: poem, n.d., "To Katie" from Charlie Buchanon, BUL.

30 **"so queenly . . . named Kate Chase"**: *St. Louis Republic*, Nov. 25, 1900.

30 **"Take care . . . Suppress it then at once"**: SPC to KC, May 27, 1855 (*Pegasus*, 162).

31 **if the people wanted him**: SPC to Oran Follett, May 4, 1855 (*CP2*:408–409).
31 **wrote Kate a long letter**: SPC to KC, Sept. 30, 1855 (*CP2*:421–425).
31 **Republican Party was unlikely to last**: SPC to James Grimes, Apr. 13, 1855 (*CP2*:405–406).
31 **"Independent Democrat"**: Ibid., 406; Niven, 158.
31 **Heyl's Esther Institute**: Phelps, 85; *Pegasus*, 9–10.
31 **private French lessons**: SPC Diary, Jan. 23–May 25, 1857 (*CP1*:257–281); *Pegasus*, 278n4.
31 **official hostess . . . chess and backgammon**: Virginia Tatnall Peacock, *Famous American Belles of the Nineteenth Century* (Philadelphia: J. B. Lippincott, 1901), 210–211; Phelps, 90; Ross, 37; SPC Diary, May 17, 1857 (*CP1*:277–278).
31 **played the piano**: Phelps, 89; *White Cloud (KS) Chief*, Jan. 28, 1869.
31 **Howells's first dinner . . . "My fear and pride . . . my inability"**: William Dean Howells, *Years of My Youth* (New York: Harper & Brothers, 1916), 154–155.
32 **slight crush on her . . . intelligent daughter**: Phelps, 90; SPC to KC, Jan. 8, 1855 (*Pegasus*, 152); Ross, 39.
32 **almost forgave her English father**: [Isabella Strange Trotter], *First Impressions of the New World on Two Travellers from the Old* (London, 1859), 191.
32 **"missiles . . . words were most deadly"**: Phelps, 87.
32 **offend the women members**: Ibid.; Peacock, *Famous American Belles*, 212–213.
32 **hated her female persecutors**: *Cincinnati Enquirer*, Aug. 1, 1899.
32 **"a magnificent girl . . . cherished purpose"**: *Cincinnati Enquirer*, Aug. 13, 1879.
32 **reckless disregard of opinion**: *Brooklyn Eagle*, Jan. 25, 1881.
32 **"opinion or goodwill . . . hurt the head"**: Peacock, *Famous American Belles*, 207.
32 **Richard Nevins**: *Crisis* (Columbus, OH), Mar. 14, 1861; 1860 US Census, Clinton, Franklin, Ohio, *Ancestry.com*, record for Richard Nevins.
32 **Nevins was a handsome**: *Cincinnati Enquirer*, Aug. 13, 1879; *St. Paul Daily Globe*, Aug. 14, 1879; *Indianapolis Daily Sentinel*, Nov. 8, 1879; *Brooklyn Eagle*, Jan. 25, 1881; Phelps, 89.
32 **go nowhere and do nothing**: SPC to KC, July 25, 1856 (*Pegasus*, 164).
33 **waltzing too closely**: SPC Diary, Jan. 15, 1857 (*CP1*:255).
33 **"Trouble at dinner . . . Nevins walking with Kate"**: SPC Diary, Jan. 28, 1857 (*CP1*:260).
33 **asked how she had offended . . . "false conduct" . . . repentant**: SPC Diary, Feb. 5, 6, 1857 (*CP1*:263–264).
33 **"I fear . . . safely trust yours"**: SPC to KC, Dec. 5, 1857 (*Pegasus*, 167).
33 **"Have I mentioned . . . buy in Columbus"**: Ibid.
33 **"Remember this . . . have it done"**: SPC to KC, Dec. 4, 1857 (*Pegasus*, 165).
34 **he granted a pardon**: Phelps, 89–90.

34 **Jessie Frémont**: Melanie Susan Gustafson, *Women and the Republican Party, 1854–1924* (Urbana: University of Illinois Press, 2001), 19–20.

34 **failure to gain the 1856 nomination**: Blue, 112–115; Niven, 185–187.

34 **newly dedicated Ohio statehouse**: Cheryl J. Straker and Chris Matheney, *Ohio Statehouse: A Building for the Ages* (Virginia Beach, VA: Donning Company, 2011), 12–20.

34 **dedication ceremonies**: Niven, 193–194; Straker and Matheney, *Ohio Statehouse*, 18.

35 **"Of course . . . this information"**: SPC to C. Cleveland, Nov. 3, 1857 (*CP2*:462–463).

35 **Schurz . . . told Chase**: Schurz, *Reminiscences*, 2:171–172.

35 **continued to write letters**: Niven, 214.

35 **"Soon she came . . . Governor's library"**: Schurz, *Reminiscences*, 2:169–170.

36 **she convinced him to visit Washington**: Ross, 42; Goodwin, *Team of Rivals*, 220; Niven, 216; *CP3*:26–27 and n4.

36 **Jessie Frémont . . . a better candidate**: Gustafson, *Women and the Republican Party*, 20.

36 **"Freedom forever . . . attempted to do"**: Janet Chase Hoyt, "A Woman's Memories: Salmon P. Chase's Home Life," *New-York Tribune*, Feb. 15, 1891.

36 **condemning his Harper's Ferry expedition**: *CP3*:xvi.

37 **campaigned for Lincoln . . . Douglas would be defeated**: Niven, 210; SPC to KC, Oct. 28, 1858 (*Pegasus*, 169).

37 **Chase turned down a similar invitation**: Niven, 215.

37 **After the first ballot in Chicago**: Blue, 125; Goodwin, *Team of Rivals*, 248–249.

37 **self-pitying reference**: SPC to Lincoln, May 17, 1860 (*CP3*:28).

37 **lingering bitterness . . . Ben Wade**: SPC to Benjamin Wade, Nov. [sic, Dec.] 21, 1860 (*CP3*:42); SPC to James Monroe, Mar. 3, 1862 (*CP3*:142–143); SPC to Wade, July 30, 1862 (*CP3*:233).

38 **Chase was miffed . . . lobbied for the position**: Niven, 223–224; Goodwin, *Team of Rivals*, 290–293, 317–318; SPC to Charles Dana, Nov. 10, 1860 (*CP3*:32); SPC to George Opdyke, Jan. 9, 1861 (*CP3*:44–46); SPC to Lincoln, Jan. 11, 1861 (*CP3*:48).

38 **Kate's would claim**: *San Francisco Morning Call*, Oct. 15, 1893.

## Chapter 5: The Belle of Washington

39 **evening military ball**: "The Lincoln Log: A Daily Chronology of the Life of Abraham Lincoln" (entry for Feb. 13, 1861), *The Papers of Abraham Lincoln*, www.thelincolnlog.org (hereafter cited as "Lincoln Log").

39 **Chases had already left . . . peace conference**: Janet Chase Hoyt, "A Woman's Memories: Washington in War Time," *New-York Tribune*, Mar. 8, 1891; Catherine Clinton, *Mrs. Lincoln: A Life* (New York: Harper, 2009), 121;

Lucius Eugene Chittenden, *A Report of the Debates and Proceedings . . . Held at Washington, D.C., in February, A.D. 1861* (New York, 1864), 9–43.

39 **"Mrs. Lincoln was piqued . . . did not like me at Washington"**: *San Francisco Morning Call*, Oct. 15, 1893.

39 **for a celebration**: Cleveland City Council, *Inauguration of the Perry Statue: At Cleveland, on the Tenth of September, 1860. . . .* (Cleveland, 1861); *Cleveland Plain Dealer*, Aug. 1, 1899.

39 **"I shall be glad . . . me at any time"**: *Cincinnati Enquirer*, Aug. 1, 1899.

40 **Mrs. Charles Walker**: Ibid.; *Pegasus*, 244–245n4; SPC Diary, Sept. 3, 8, 10, 1864 (*CP1*:499, 501); *Daily Constitutional Union* (Washington, DC), June 12, 1863.

40 **"exhibited toward me . . . never loved"**: *Cincinnati Enquirer*, Aug. 1, 1899.

40 **first White House levee**: "Lincoln Log" (entry for Mar. 8, 1861); Clinton, *Mrs. Lincoln*, 127.

40 **last public event**: Clinton, *Mrs. Lincoln*, 128.

40 **left in a mass exodus**: Kathryn Allamong Jacob, *Capital Elites: High Society in Washington, D.C., After the Civil War* (Washington, DC: Smithsonian Institution Press, 1995), 44, 48.

40 **"the titular head . . . sovereign in fact"**: Ibid., 49.

40 **"rattled . . . shook hands"**: Ross, 64.

40 **At that initial levee**: Ross, 63–66; Phelps, 97–98.

40 **"more of a professional beauty . . . to watch her"**: Mrs. Daniel Chester [Mary] French, *Memories of a Sculptor's Wife* (Boston: Houghton Mifflin, 1928), 147–148.

41 **Kate to cross-examine her**: Ross, 66.

41 **Mary Lincoln's expensive shopping**: Ross, 75–76; Clinton, *Mrs. Lincoln*, 134–136; Goodwin, *Team of Rivals*, 359–360.

41 **Mrs. Lincoln held regular**: Goodwin, *Team of Rivals*, 598–599; Clinton, *Mrs. Lincoln*, 164; Daniel Mark Epstein, *The Lincolns: Portrait of a Marriage* (2008; repr., New York: Ballantine Books, 2009), 324.

41 **private Chase gatherings**: Phelps, 111–112; Ross, 78, 93; Beldens, 33; *New York Herald*, Aug. 6, 1899; *San Francisco Morning Call*, Aug. 1, 1899.

42 **alcohol and tobacco were always**: Niven, 340.

42 **"She had a wonderful memory . . . heard or read"**: *Cincinnati Enquirer*, Aug. 1, 1899.

42 **"I never spoke . . . piquancy and flavor"**: *Washington Times Magazine*, Sept. 6, 1908.

42 **Kate's personal influence**: Phelps, 113–114.

42 **"in conversation she never came out second"**: *Cleveland Plain Dealer*, Aug. 6, 1899.

43 **"one of the most intelligent . . . energy and power"**: William Howard Russell, *My Diary North and South* (Boston, 1863), 42.

43 **handful of women**: *Cleveland Morning Leader*, Mar. 30, 1861.

43 **"very attractive . . . and sprightly"**: Russell, *My Diary*, 42.

43 **office seekers were pestering her**: Ibid., 45–46.

43 **Lincoln had been regaling**: Ibid., 43.

43 **discuss a serious matter**: Niven, 245.

43 **had previously waffled . . . now supported**: SPC to Lincoln, Mar. 16, 1861 (*CP3*:53–54); David Herbert Donald, *Lincoln* (New York: Simon & Schuster, 1995), 286–289.

43 **In a letter to Lincoln**: SPC to Lincoln, Mar. 29, 1861 (*CP3*:55).

43 **Kate went to New York with Nettie**: Hoyt, "Washington in War Time," *New-York Tribune*, Mar. 8, 1891.

43 **rally in Union Square**: Ric Burns and James Sanders, with Lisa Ades, *New York: An Illustrated History* (New York: Knopf, 1999), 118–119.

43 **watched the first wave . . . a packed sermon**: Hoyt, "Washington in War Time," *New-York Tribune*, Mar. 8, 1891.

44 **Kate and Nettie undertook a dangerous journey**: Janet Chase Hoyt, "A Woman's Memories: A Privateer—General Scott—Charles Sumner," *New-York Tribune*, Apr. 5, 1891.

44 **military camp**: Hoyt, "A Privateer," *New-York Tribune*, Apr. 5, 1891.

44 **Mary Lincoln, who regularly visited**: Clinton, *Mrs. Lincoln*, 143, 196.

44 **Kate shied away from**: Briggs, *Olivia Letters*, 70.

44 **helped convince the surgeon general**: Joseph R. Smith, "Hammond, the Surgeon-General," *Post-Graduate, A Monthly Journal of Medicine and Surgery* 15, no. 5 (May 1900): 627.

## Chapter 6: The Boy Governor

45 **at five feet five**: *Alexandria (VA) Gazette*, Apr. 7, 1869. Other sources say he was five feet six. Beldens, 42, 236.

45 **inch or two shorter**: Her 1866 passport application records her at five feet seven. US Passport Application for Mrs. Kate C. Sprague, issued Mar. 31, 1866, *Ancestry.com*.

45 **spent more than $100,000**: Charles Hoffmann and Tess Hoffmann, *Brotherly Love: Murder and the Politics of Prejudice in Nineteenth-Century Rhode Island* (Amherst: University of Massachusetts Press, 1993), 171n21; Zechariah Chafee Jr., "Weathering the Panic of '73: An Episode in Rhode Island Business History," *Proceedings of the Massachusetts Historical Society*, Third Series 66 (Oct. 1936–May 1941): 270, 272.

45 **"small, insignificant . . . certainly all right now"**: John Hay Diary, Apr. 26, 1861, in *Inside Lincoln's White House: The Complete Civil War Diary of John Hay*, ed. Michael Burlingame and John R. Turner Ettlinger (Carbondale: Southern Illinois University Press, 1997), 12.

45 **first Union governor to offer troops**: John Russell Bartlett, *Memoirs of Rhode Island Officers Who Were Engaged in the Service of Their Country During the Great Rebellion of the South* (Providence, 1867), 110–111; *Cleveland Plain Dealer*, Apr. 13, 1861.

45 **making his way south . . . arrived in late April**: Bartlett, *Rhode Island Officers*, 112; Charles Carroll, *Rhode Island: Three Centuries of Democracy* (New York: Lewis Historical Publishing, 1932), 1:598, 2:600; John Hay Diary, Apr. 26, 1861, in Burlingame and Ettlinger, *Inside Lincoln's White House*, 12.

45 **paraded past the White House**: John Hay Diary, Apr. 29, 1861, in Burlingame and Ettlinger, *Inside Lincoln's White House*, 14; Bartlett, *Rhode Island Officers*, 111–112; WS to William Seward, Apr. 29, 1861, CHS; Carroll, *Rhode Island*, 2:600; *Providence Evening Press*, May 7, 1861; Schurz, *Reminiscences*, 2:227; *New York Times*, July 3, 1898.

46 ***Little Rhody***: *Cleveland Plain Dealer*, June 5, 1861; Mathias P. Harpin, *The High Road to Zion* (Rhode Island: Harpin's American Heritage Foundation, 1976), 150; "Little Rhody," *Littell's Living Age* 71, no. 909 (Nov. 2, 1861): 239.

46 **became a favorite of the president**: Phelps, 103n1; Ross, 65, 78.

46 **Visiting the Rhode Island troops**: *New York Times*, July 3, 1898; Margaret Leech, *Reveille in Washington, 1860–1865* (1941; repr., New York: New York Review Books, 2011), 84.

46 **first met in Cleveland**: *Narragansett Times*, May 25, 1883; *Cleveland Plain Dealer*, Aug. 1, 1899; Ross, 51.

46 **"It was . . . mutual infatuation"**: *Narragansett Times*, May 25, 1883.

46 **"in that celebrated dress . . . if it was yesterday"**: WS to KC, May 27, 1866, BUL.

47 **"you were then . . . mere friendship"**: WS to KC, June 8, 1863, BUL.

47 **worth around $10 million**: *Baltimore Sun*, May 31, 1861; *Richmond (VA) Daily Dispatch*, June 3, 1861.

47 **Sprague grew up**: Sprague was born on September 12, 1830. Warren Vincent Sprague, *Sprague Families in America* (Rutland, VT: Tuttle Company, 1913), 299, 389.

47 **William Sprague III**: Ibid., 299; Oliver Payson Fuller, *The History of Warwick, Rhode Island* (Providence, 1875), 255; Paul Goodman, *Towards a Christian Republic: Antimasonry and the Great Transition in New England, 1826–1836* (New York: Oxford University Press, 1988), 207, 213.

47 **Old Governor Sprague's Whiggism**: Carroll, *Rhode Island*, 1:573.

47 **reasonably well schooled . . . Providence Conference Seminary**: Bartlett, *Rhode Island Officers*, 107; Daniel Howland Greene, *History of the Town of East Greenwich and Adjacent Territory: From 1677 to 1877* (Providence, 1877), 202–224.

47 **Smithfield Seminary**: Bartlett, *Rhode Island Officers*, 107; Florence Simister, "Research Notes on the Sprague Family," ca. 1950, MSS 736, Rhode Island Historical Society (hereafter cited as Simister, "Research Notes," RIHS).

47 **Smithfield**: Thomas B. Stockwell, ed., *A History of Public Education in Rhode Island, from 1636–1876 . . .* (Providence, 1876), 412–413. It was later renamed the Lapham Institute.

47 **attended the Irving Institute**: Bartlett, *Rhode Island Officers*, 107; Jeff Canning and Wally Buxton, *History of the Tarrytowns, Westchester County, New*

*York: From Ancient Times to the Present* (Harrison, NY: Harbor Hill Books, 1975), 150.

47 **organized a company of forty boys . . . Artillery Company**: Bartlett, *Rhode Island Officers*, 108–109.

48 **bookkeeper . . . A. & W. Sprague**: Ibid., 107; Carroll, *Rhode Island*, 1:521.

48 **Spragues owned . . . Spragueville**: Bartlett, *Rhode Island Officers*, 105–108; Hoffmann and Hoffmann, *Brotherly Love*, 17–20; Robert Eliot Freeman, *Cranston, Rhode Island Statewide Historical Preservation Report P-C-1, September 1980* (Providence: Rhode Island Historical Preservation Commission, 1980), 19–20; *Cincinnati Daily Gazette*, Mar. 25, 1869. A neighborhood rather than an official town, it has sometimes been called "Spraguesville," but almost all nineteenth-century sources refer to it as "Spragueville." See, for example, *Providence Evening Press*, Oct. 30, 1860, June 23, 1866; *Manufacturers' and Farmers' Journal* (Providence), Apr. 13, 1865.

48 **worked side by side . . . ate around same table**: Carroll, *Rhode Island*, 1:521; Goodman, *Towards a Christian Republic*, 208.

48 **William IV started**: Bartlett, *Rhode Island Officers*, 107.

48 **traced it to Amasa's body**: Hoffmann and Hoffmann, *Brotherly Love*, 2–5; Paul F. Caranci, *The Hanging and Redemption of John Gordon: The True Story of Rhode Island's Last Execution* (Charleston, SC: History Press, 2013), 68–77.

48 **"shockingly mangled . . . two places"**: *Easton (MD) Star*, Jan. 9, 1844.

49 **brought back home and laid on the floor**: Hoffmann and Hoffmann, *Brotherly Love*, 4–5; Goodman, *Towards a Christian Republic*, 208.

49 **Gordon was convicted and hanged**: Hoffmann and Hoffmann, *Brotherly Love*, xv–xvii, 6–12.

49 **crime remains unsolved**: According to one rumor, Amasa was murdered while on his way to see his mistress. Hoffmann and Hoffmann, *Brotherly Love*, 5. The Hoffmanns hypothesize that it was Amasa's brother William who plotted the murder from his Senate office in Washington, which he resigned to personally take over the investigation to divert attention from himself. His motive, according to these authors, was that he was a bold visionary who wanted to greatly expand the family business, whereas his brother Amasa, content with the status quo, stood in the way of his grandiose plans. Ibid., 136–146.

49 **William III was a reticent**: Fuller, *History of Warwick*, 126–127, 255; Carroll, *Rhode Island*, 1:521; Hoffmann and Hoffmann, *Brotherly Love*, 138–139.

49 **Amasa Sprague, by contrast**: Hoffmann and Hoffmann, *Brotherly Love*, 138–139; Caranci, *Hanging of John Gordon*, 25.

49 **who eventually sold his shares**: Freeman, *Cranston Preservation Report*, 19; Benjamin Knight Sr., *History of the Sprague Families of Rhode Island, Cotton Manufacturers and Calico Printers, from William I to William IV . . .* (Santa Cruz, CA, 1881), ch. 7.

49 **brother Amasa . . . racehorses**: Knight, *History of Sprague Families*, ch. 8; "The American Trotting Association," *Harper's New Monthly Magazine* 47 (Sept. 1873): 612.

49 **took a business valued**: Bartlett, *Rhode Island Officers*, 106; Fuller, *History of Warwick*, 254; Knight, *History of Sprague Families*, ch. 9; Chafee, "Weathering the Panic," 274.

49 **No Irishmen . . . abolished death penalty**: Hoffmann and Hoffmann, *Brotherly Love*, xvii, 135; Caranci, *Hanging of John Gordon*, 171–172.

50 **"Rhode Island . . . Spragues' property"**: *Brooklyn Eagle*, Aug. 13, 1879.

50 **considered déclassé . . . champions of masses**: Hoffmann and Hoffmann, *Brotherly Love*, 18; Goodman, *Towards a Christian Republic*, 207–208.

50 **did visit Europe . . . for his health**: Bartlett, *Rhode Island Officers*, 109; Sokoloff, 63–64.

50 **impregnated a young neighbor**: Phelps, 300–301; Sokoloff, 70–71; *Indianapolis Daily Sentinel*, Dec. 28, 1880.

50 **named Mary Eliza Viall**: 1870 US Census, Providence Ward 3, Providence, RI, *Ancestry.com*, record for Mary Viall; *Brown's Providence Directory, 1841–'42* (Providence, 1841), 166, 202; *Indianapolis Daily Sentinel*, Dec. 28, 1880; Phelps, 300–301; *Wheeling Register*, Dec. 27, 1880. Mary Viall, the daughter of William Viall, grew up on Power Street in Providence, near the Sprague residence on Young Orchard Avenue. *Brown's Providence Directory, 1847–'48* (Providence, 1847), 202, 217; *Brown's Providence Directory, 1853–'54* (Providence, 1853), 273, 293.

50 **went to Paris . . . free love advocate . . . worshipped Sprague**: Isaac Pitman Noyes, *Reminiscences of Rhode Island and Ye Providence Plantations, 2d Supplement* (Washington, DC, 1905), 22–23; *Wheeling Register*, Dec. 27, 1880; *Indianapolis Daily Sentinel*, Dec. 28, 1880; Lamphier, 34–35, 149; Sokoloff, 70–71.

50 **"Lancelot . . . Hamlet" . . . loved her too much**: [Mary Eliza Viall Anderson], *The Merchant's Wife, or, He Blundered: A Political Romance of Our Own Day and Other Miscellanies, by "A Looker-On Here in Vienna"* (Boston: printed for the author, 1876), on file at Rhode Island Historical Society (hereafter cited as Viall, *The Merchant's Wife*), 18, 21, 23–24.

50 **hero's welcome**: Beldens, 54.

50 **nature always to hide . . . no political knowledge**: *Cong. Globe*, 41st Cong., 1st Sess. 614, 618 (Apr. 8, 1869).

51 **"it was of national importance . . . suppressed"**: Ibid., 618.

51 **political cipher**: *New York Times*, Mar. 30, 1860.

51 **"initiate no . . . grand enterprise"**: *New York Times*, Apr. 6, 1860.

51 **"Of all the States . . . most erratic political leaders"**: *New York Times*, Mar. 29, 1861.

51 **support Lincoln's Emancipation . . . radical Republicans**: Henry Wharton Shoemaker, *The Last of the War Governors: A Biographical Appreciation of Colonel William Sprague* (Altoona, PA: Altoona Tribune, 1916), 15–23; Carroll, *Rhode Island*, 2:642–643, 691.

51 **"lords of the loom . . . lash"**: Patrick T. Conley and Paul Campbell, *Providence: A Pictorial History* (Norfolk, VA: Donning Company, 1982), 85.

51 **hundred-gun salute**: Ibid.

51 **"but one course . . . put down rebellion"**: *Providence Evening Press*, Apr. 15, 1861, quoting *Boston Atlas*.
52 **intercepted a bouquet**: Julia Taft Bayne, *Tad Lincoln's Father* (Boston: Little, Brown, 1931), 81–83; Phelps, 100.
52 **"hesitating kiss . . . such in life"**: WS to KC, May 27, 1866, BUL.
52 **newspapers began reporting . . . Kate the one**: *New York Times*, May 30, 1861; *Baltimore Sun*, May 31, 1861.
52 **battle at Bull Run**: Carroll, *Rhode Island*, 2:601–602, 614–615.
52 **"wanted to feel . . . not twenty paces off"**: *Cong. Globe*, 41st Cong., 1st Sess. 618 (Apr. 8, 1869).
53 **"I am not dead . . . Rhode Island!"**: *Newport (RI) Mercury*, July 27, 1861.
53 **"one after another . . . strength again"**: Janet Chase Hoyt, "A Woman's Memories: The Battle of Bull Run—General McDowell," *New-York Tribune*, June 7, 1891.
53 **returned safely to Willard's**: Beldens, 48; Sokoloff, 67.
53 **turned down commission . . . Butler**: Beldens, 45.
53 **cordial correspondence with Lincoln . . . additional troops**: "Abraham Lincoln and Rhode Island," *Abraham Lincoln's Classroom*, The Lehrman Institute/The Lincoln Institute, www.abrahamlincolnsclassroom.org/Library/newsletter.asp?ID=40&CRLI=120; *New York Times*, June 29, July 4, 1862; Bartlett, *Rhode Island Officers*, 112–113.
53 **corresponded directly with Mary Lincoln . . . earnest suggestions**: Carl Sandburg, *Abraham Lincoln: The War Years* (New York: Harcourt, Brace, 1939), 2:247.
53 **fire a big gun**: Thomas M. Aldrich, *The History of Battery A, First Regiment Rhode Island Light Artillery* (Providence: Snow & Farnham, 1904), 33.
54 **"good man . . . protector you need"**: SPC to KC, n.d., ca. Aug. 1861, Chase HSP.
54 **she hoped Kate would marry**: NC to KC, Sept. 29, 1861, Jan. 28, 1862 (*Pegasus*, 184, 196).
54 **attracted much attention at a grand review**: *Augusta (GA) Chronicle*, Oct. 6, 1861.
54 **"magnificent creature . . . as she rode"**: *Philadelphia Inquirer*, Feb. 25, 1894.
54 **"habits of order"**: WS to Willie Sprague, Nov. 15, 1877, CHS.
55 **schooling for Nettie**: From 1861 to 1862 she attended Maria Eastman's female seminary in Media, Pennsylvania. *Pegasus*, 180; Sokoloff, 69. In September 1862 Nettie entered a boarding school on Madison Avenue in Manhattan run by Mary Macaulay. *Pegasus*, 15, 211; Sokoloff, 74–75.
55 **Nettie contracted scarlet fever . . . Kate went**: SPC Diary, Jan. 9, 1862 (*CP1*:324); Sokoloff, 69; SPC to John A. Stevens Sr., Jan. 17, 1862 (*CP3*:120).
55 **"how futile . . . name you bear"**: SPC to KC, Jan. 10, 1862 (*Pegasus*, 192).
55 **in Philadelphia first**: SPC to Jay Cooke, Oct. 23, 1861, in Ellis Paxson Oberholtzer, *Jay Cooke: Financier of the Civil War* (Philadelphia: George W. Jacobs, 1907), 1:179–180.

55 **ordered carpeting**: Phelps, 106.
55 **Bypassing her father**: SPC to KC, June 25, 1862 (*Pegasus*, 200).
55 **"You will easily remember . . . not doing so"**: SPC to KC, July 6, 1862 (*Pegasus*, 205).
56 **$1.5 million a day**: SPC to Thaddeus Stevens, Feb. 25, 1862 (*CP3*:141–142); Oberholtzer, *Jay Cooke*, 1:149.
56 **"Chase has no money . . . What shall I do?"**: Donald, *Lincoln*, 330.
56 **"You understand . . . I do not"**: SPC Diary, Sept. 11, 1863 (*CP1*:440).
56 **"Gentlemen . . . buy a breakfast"**: Hart, 223.
56 **"Old Greenbacks" . . . face on the one-dollar bill**: Niven, 336, 338.
56 **Kate's picture on notes . . . "positively forbade"**: *San Francisco Morning Call*, Oct. 15, 1893.
56 **"a success as great . . . wonders of history"**: Ibid.
57 **Cooke to sell war bonds . . . intimate friend**: Oberholtzer, *Jay Cooke*, 1:153–156; M. John Lubetkin, *Jay Cooke's Gamble: The Northern Pacific Railroad, the Sioux, and the Panic of 1873* (Norman: University of Oklahoma Press, 2006), 4–8; Niven, 262–263, 353, 397.
57 **dollars from Hiram Barney . . . port collector**: Phelps, 105; Niven, 240, 256; Blue, 232–233.
57 **needed a new carriage**: SPC to KC, Oct. 25, 1861 (*CP3*:102).
57 **"a glorious girl"**: Oberholtzer, *Jay Cooke*, 1:154.
57 **could accept the gift . . . it was too light**: Ibid., 1:179–184; *CP3*:103n1.
57 **bookshelves . . . mild reprimand**: Oberholtzer, *Jay Cooke*, 1:184.
57 **"In order to . . . *be* right"**: SPC to Cooke, June 2, 1863, in Oberholtzer, *Jay Cooke*, 1:274–275.
58 **lamented to Kate**: SPC to KC, Oct. 25, 1861 (*CP3*:102–103).
58 **"Not that . . . to be honest"**: SPC to KC, Aug. 17, 1863 (*Pegasus*, 218).
58 **man of action, not words**: *Harrisburg (PA) Weekly Patriot*, Nov. 21, 1861; *New York Herald*, Nov. 19, 1861.
58 **"sadly disconnected"**: WS to KC, May 18, 1866, CHS.
58 **"very limited mental capacity"**: Henry Villard, *Memoirs of Henry Villard: Journalist and Financier, 1835–1900* (Boston: Houghton, Mifflin, 1904), 1:175.
58 **"handsome cavalier . . . merchant's wife"**: Viall, *The Merchant's Wife*, 24, 39, 48.
58 **"You discover tact . . . does not magnetize"**: Ibid., 48–50.
58 **"sense of ineffable rest . . . found a lodgment there!"**: KC Diary, Nov. 11, 1868, BUL.
59 **"My fate"**: *San Francisco Morning Call*, Oct. 15, 1893.

## Chapter 7: Mrs. Lincoln's Rival

60 **Jim Garfield**: J. M. Bundy, *The Life of James Abram Garfield* (New York, 1880), 21.

60 **future president . . . moved in**: James Garfield to Lucretia Garfield, Sept. 27, 1862, quoted in Theodore Clark Smith, *The Life and Letters of James Abram Garfield* (New Haven, CT: Yale University Press, 1925), 1:242; SPC Diary, Sept. 27, 30, Oct. 11, 1862 (*CP1*:404, 406, 420).

60 **stopped seeing William Sprague**: Lamphier, 45; US Senate, 41st Cong., Third Sess. 1870–1871, *Senate Executive Document vol. 1, no. 10* (Washington, 1871), pt. 3:24.

60 **"vacillation of purpose"**: Adam Goodheart, *1861: The Civil War Awakening* (New York: Knopf, 2011), 96.

60 **Chase adopted**: Peskin, *Garfield*, 151–156; Niven, 307–308; Smith, *Life and Letters of Garfield* (New Haven, CT: Yale University Press, 1925), 1:242, 255–256.

61 **most impressive woman**: Smith, *Life and Letters of Garfield*, 1:242.

61 **Kate and Garfield together**: Ibid., 242–243, 265; Peskin, *Garfield*, 153–154; Steven D. Engle, *Yankee Dutchman: The Life of Franz Sigel* (1993; repr., Baton Rouge: LSU Press, 1999), 147.

61 **Sigel . . . sent . . . ornament**: *Boston Evening Transcript*, Oct. 15, 1862.

61 **he was married . . . Lucretia**: Peskin, *Garfield*, 29, 75.

61 **extramarital affair**: Ibid., 160, 634n21; John T. Noonan Jr., *Bribes* (1984; repr., Berkeley: University of California Press, 1987), 774n49; John Shaw, *Lucretia* (Hauppauge, NY: Nova History Publications, 2004), 45–46.

61 **Calhoun**: *Springfield (MA) Weekly Republican*, June 22, 1867; *Cincinnati Commercial*, Dec. 29, 1869; 1870 US Census, New Providence, NJ, *Ancestry.com*, record for Lucia G. Runkle.

61 **good form . . . "pretty good culture" . . . pug nose**: James Garfield to Lucretia Garfield, Oct. 12, 1862, quoted in Smith, *Life and Letters of Garfield*, 1:242.

61 **"you and Miss Kate . . . *jealous* if she is"**: John M. Taylor, *Garfield of Ohio: The Available Man* (New York: W. W. Norton, 1970), 75.

61 **would long suspect**: Allan Peskin, "Lucretia Rudolph Garfield," in *American First Ladies: Their Lives and Their Legacy*, ed. Lewis L. Gould, 2nd ed. (New York: Routledge, 2001), 157–158.

62 **litany of complaints**: Hart, 291–300; Donnal V. Smith, *Chase and Civil War Politics* (Freeport, NY: Books for Libraries Press, 1972), reprinted from the *Ohio Archaeological and Historical Quarterly* for July and October 1930, 46–51; SPC to Alexander S. Latty, Sept. 17, 1862 (*CP3*:273–274); SPC to Oran Follett, Sept. 25, 1862 (*CP3*:284–285); SPC to Charles P. McIlvaine, Jan. 25, 1863 (*CP3*:372–373).

62 **"trifled with . . . kid gloved rebellion"**: SPC to KC, July [14], 1862 (*CP3*:227).

62 **"as if . . . supplying shoes or cloth"**: SPC to John Sherman, Sept. 20, 1862 (*CP3*:278).

62 **"a cordial support . . . can possibly claim"**: SPC to Zachariah Chandler, Sept. 20, 1862 (*CP3*:275).

62 **Kate also denigrated the president**: *Through Five Administrations: Reminiscences of Colonel William H. Crook, Body-Guard to President Lincoln*, ed. Margarita Spalding Gerry (New York: Harper & Brothers, 1910), 31–32.

62 **"Miss Kate"**: Winkler, *The Women in Lincoln's Life*, 165.

62 **point out through a spyglass**: Charles O. Paullin, "Alexandria County in 1861," in *Records of the Columbia Historical Society, Washington, D.C.* 28 (1926): 107, 121–122.

63 **to meet a delegation of . . . tribes**: *New York Times*, Mar. 28, 1863; Philip B. Kunhardt Jr., Philip B. Kunhardt III, and Peter W. Kunhardt, *Lincoln: An Illustrated Biography* (New York: Knopf, 1992), 207.

63 **"Miss C . . . practice deceit"**: Elizabeth Keckley, *Behind the Scenes, or, Thirty Years a Slave, and Four Years in the White House* (New York, 1868), 124–126.

63 **ignored his wife's edict**: Winkler, *The Women in Lincoln's Life*, 166.

63 **Sumner**: Hoyt, "A Privateer," *New-York Tribune*, Apr. 5, 1891; Clinton, *Mrs. Lincoln*, 199; Jean H. Baker, *Mary Todd Lincoln* (New York: W. W. Norton, 1987), 232–233.

63 **"The Lincoln-Chase contest . . . yet today"**: *Crisis* (Columbus, OH), Nov. 11, 1863.

64 **more "kindred spirits than rivals"**: The theme is developed more fully by Nina Mae Gradia in "Rivals or Kindred Spirits? Mary Todd Lincoln, Katharine (Kate) Jane Chase, and Their Parallel Lives" (master's thesis, University of Maryland, 2010), UMI Dissertation Publishing no. 1477250.

64 **"hostility . . . bitter"**: Keckley, *Behind the Scenes*, 128.

64 **by invitation only**: Goodwin, *Team of Rivals*, 415; Epstein, *The Lincolns*, 354; Baker, *Mary Todd Lincoln*, 205–206.

64 **"jubilant . . . in the cold"**: Clinton, *Mrs. Lincoln*, 164–165.

64 **the event featured**: *Cincinnati Daily Press*, Feb. 10, 1862; Baker, *Mary Todd Lincoln*, 206–207; Clinton, *Mrs. Lincoln*, 165; Epstein, *The Lincolns*, 355, 359–362.

65 **Kate . . . silk gown**: *Cincinnati Daily Press*, Feb. 10, 1862.

65 **"La belle des belles"**: *Frank Leslie's Illustrated Newspaper*, Feb. 22, 1862.

65 **Hutchinson Family**: Scott Gac, *Singing for Freedom: The Hutchinson Family Singers and the Nineteenth-Century Culture of Reform* (New Haven, CT: Yale University Press, 2007), 4–5; Christian McWhirter, *Battle Hymns: The Power and Popularity of Music in the Civil War* (Chapel Hill: University of North Carolina Press, 2012), 8.

65 **they were banned**: *Fremont (OH) Journal*, Feb. 7, 1862; McWhirter, *Battle Hymns*, 8–11; Joseph W. Hutchinson, *The Book of Brothers (Second Series): Being a History of the Adventures of John W. Hutchinson and His Family in the Camps of the Army of the Potomac (1864)* (Boston, 1864), 10–14, 20–21.

65 **"What gives . . . Slavery!"**: Hutchinson, *Book of Brothers*, 12–13.

65 **encored**: *Cincinnati Daily Press*, Feb. 13, 1862.

66 **illness of . . . Willie**: Baker, *Mary Todd Lincoln*, 207–209; Ross, 96.

66 **"Well Nicolay . . . actually gone"**: Stephen B. Oates, *With Malice Toward None: The Life of Abraham Lincoln* (1977; repr., New York: Mentor, 1977), 314.

66 **Mary Lincoln . . . overcome with grief**: Ibid., 315–317.

66 **"made veiled . . . humanity"**: Ross, 90.

67 **is not repeated**: Ishbel Ross, *The President's Wife: Mary Todd Lincoln* (New York: G. P. Putnam's Sons, 1973).
67 **"equality notions . . . Mississippi"**: *Urbana (OH) Union*, Oct. 16, 1867.
67 **"an old negress . . . *odorous*"**: SPC to Stanley Matthews, Jan. 27, 1849 (*CP2*:220–221).
67 **"little darkey" children**: SPC to KC, May 5, 1865 (*Pegasus*, 273).
67 **servants**: Phelps, 106; *Pegasus*, 25, 208n6, 400–401n2; *CP3*:126n8.
67 **serve as pallbearers**: *Boston Herald*, Aug. 3, 1899; Phelps, 282.
67 **"saint"**: Isabel McKenna Duffield, *Washington in the 90's* (San Francisco: Press of Overland Monthly, 1929), 10–11.
67 **kept him sitting**: Ibid.; Didier, "Salmon P. Chase," 184; Ross, 166–167.
68 **Joan Crawford**: *New York Times*, Sept. 23, 1940. According to Ann Donaldson, her father (Kate's grandson Chase Donaldson), threatened to sue MGM for libel if it made the film, but was told by lawyers he had no grounds because Kate was deceased. Most likely the project simply fell by the wayside as so many Hollywood ideas do.
68 **"bitter as gall"**: Elizabeth Blair Lee to Samuel Phillips Lee, May 20, 1862, in *Wartime Washington: The Civil War Letters of Elizabeth Blair Lee*, ed. Virginia Jeans Laas (1991; repr., Urbana: University of Illinois Press, 1999), 151n2.
68 **"Pretty Katie . . . Her father's old game"**: John Hay Diary, Oct. 21, 1863, in Burlingame and Ettlinger, *Inside Lincoln's White House*, 97.
68 **"the country . . . much vanity?"**: SPC to George McClellan, July 7, 1861 (*CP3*:74–75).
68 **"Why don't he *move*?"**: NC to SPC, June 25, 1862 (*Pegasus*, 199).
68 **another "Wendell Phillips"**: Elizabeth Blair Lee to Samuel Phillips Lee, May 20, 1862, in Laas, *Wartime Washington*, 151n2.
68 **"Contact . . . white race"**: Elizabeth Blair Lee to Samuel Phillips Lee, Dec. 31, 1862, in ibid., 223.
68 **"not so nonresistant . . . Pequo[t]s"**: Elizabeth Blair Lee to Samuel Phillips Lee, May 20, 1862, in ibid., 151n2.
69 **"to keep . . . quiet"**: SPC to Benjamin F. Butler, July 31, 1862 (*CP3*:237–238 and n6).
69 **"He never drinks . . . license"**: SPC to W. C. Bryant, Sept. 4, 1862 (*CP3*:259–260).
69 **"Miss Kate's father . . . Commander in Chief"**: Elizabeth Blair Lee to Samuel Phillips Lee, Apr. 14, 1862, in Laas, *Wartime Washington*, 130.
70 **"no white-gloved handling"**: *New York Times*, Aug. 17, 1862.
70 **"Strike him . . . their places"**: Ibid.
70 **Sprague . . . declared war on the state of Georgia**: Evan C. Jones, "Sullivan Ballou: The Macabre Fate of a[n] American Civil War Major," *Weider History Group Historynet.com*, June 12, 2006, www.historynet.com/sullivan-ballou-the-macabre-fate-of-a-american-civil-war-major.htm; Claire Peracchio, "Revisiting Headless Ballou and RI's Civil War

Years," *WPRI.com*, Apr. 18, 2011, http://blogs.wpri.com/2011/04/18/revisiting-headless-ballou-and-ris-civil-war-years/.

70 **regiment of black troops**: Irving H. Bartlett, *From Slave to Citizen: The Story of the Negro in Rhode Island* (Providence: Urban League of Greater Providence, 1954), 47; Carroll, *Rhode Island*, 2:607.

70 **"accepted as . . . men"**: Irving Bartlett, *From Slave to Citizen*, 47.

70 **"wild goose chase" . . . garrison duty**: Ibid., 48. See also Carroll, *Rhode Island*, 2:625–626.

70 **most determined men**: WS to SPC, June 12, 1863, Chase LC, reel 3.

70 **"Please give . . . fair hearing"**: Curt Anders, *Henry Halleck's War: A Fresh Look at Lincoln's Controversial General-in-Chief* (Carmel, IN: Guild Press of Indiana, 2000), 141–144.

71 **"Our hours . . . does not agree with her"**: Phelps, 121.

71 **Saratoga Springs**: Ibid.; Ross, 104.

71 **life . . . "very dull" without her**: SPC to KC, June 2 [4], 1862 (*CP3*:220).

71 **"I try . . . the present"**: KC to Hiram Barney, Sept. 4, 1862, Chase HSP.

71 **wrote to Lincoln . . . Stahel**: KC to A. Lincoln, Feb. 17, 1863, quoted in "Kate Chase Sprague (1840–1899)," *Mr. Lincoln's White House*, The Lehrman Institute/The Lincoln Institute, www.mrlincolnswhitehouse.org/inside.asp?ID=711&subjectID=2; Engle, *Yankee Dutchman*, 147.

71 **Joe Hooker**: SPC Diary, Sept. 23–25, 1862 (*CP1*:396–397, 400).

71 **Chase pooh-poohed the accomplishment**: SPC to Zachariah Chandler, Sept. 20, 1862 (*CP3*:275); SPC to John Sherman, Sept. 20, 1862 (*CP3*:277–278).

72 **"The first . . . like it?"**: SPC to Benjamin Butler, Sept. 23, 1862 (*CP3*:283–284).

72 **Sprague . . . endorsed the edict**: *New York Times*, Sept. 25, 27, 1862, Sept. 12, 1915.

72 **Chase was more guarded**: SPC Diary, July 22, Sept. 22, 1862 (*CP1*:350–352, 393–396); Niven, 304–306, 320–321.

72 **adding the words**: *New York Times*, Sept. 24, 1912.

72 **serenaders . . . "a few old fogies . . . insanity"**: John Hay Diary, Sept. 24, 1862, in Burlingame and Ettlinger, *Inside Lincoln's White House*, 41.

72 **"gleefully . . . horrible name"**: Ibid.

72 **Garfield had accepted . . . invitation**: SPC Diary, Sept. 27, 1862 (*CP1*:404).

72 **more than six weeks**: SPC Diary, Nov. 13, 1862 (*CP1*:423–424).

72 **moved into bachelor quarters**: Smith, *Life and Letters of Garfield*, 1:255.

73 **"the blank"**: WS to KC, May 27, 1866, BUL.

73 **"turn a *restless* eye upon us all"**: Elizabeth Blair Lee to Samuel Phillips Lee, May 24, 1863, in Laas, *Wartime Washington*, 269.

73 **Hooker . . . "wholly undependable"**: WS to SPC, May 25, 1863, CHS.

73 **"the Governor . . . my battles"**: WS to Hiram Barney, May 18, 1863, Chase HSP.

73 **word hit the newspapers**: *Jamesville (WI) Daily Gazette*, June 8, 1863, citing *Newport (RI) News*.

73 **"remember me kindly to Miss Kate"**: Garfield to SPC, May 5, 1863 (*CP4*:23).

73 **broke the news**: SPC to Garfield, May 31, 1863 (*CP4*:47–48).
73 **"Why can't you be here?"**: SPC to Garfield, Aug. 17, 1863 (*CP4*:104).
73 **Garfield was in . . . Baltimore**: Peskin, *Garfield*, 218, 640n41.

## Chapter 8: Wedding of the Decade

74 **"She is to be . . . with life"**: John Hay to Charles G. Halpine, Oct. 24, 1863, in *At Lincoln's Side: John Hay's Civil War Correspondence and Selected Writings*, ed. Michael Burlingame (Carbondale: Southern Illinois University Press, 2006), 67.
74 **"only a little lovelier . . . great future"**: Ibid.
74 **"I have been . . . for both"**: Gideon Welles Diary, May 19, 1863, in *Diary of Gideon Welles*, (Boston: Houghton Mifflin, 1911), 1:306.
75 **"In America . . . a cloister"**: Alexis de Tocqueville, *Democracy in America*, trans. Henry Reeve, rev. ed. (New York, 1899), 2:211.
75 **"the women . . . minds of men"**: Ibid., 222.
75 **"in the full flush . . . happiness and love"**: KC Diary, Nov. 11, 1868, BUL.
75 **average age**: Clinton, *Mrs. Lincoln*, 32.
75 **"childish" and "unmanly"**: WS to KC, Oct. 22, 1863, BUL; WS to KC, Oct. 28, 1863, CHS.
75 **"infirmities . . . eccentric"**: WS to SPC, Nov. 4, 1863 (*CP4*:176).
75 **attributed . . . improprieties to alcohol**: WS to SPC, June 12, 1863, Chase LC, reel 3.
75 **cross and ugly . . . "disgusting habit"**: WS to KC, Oct. 28, 1863, CHS.
75 **"Don't influence me . . . no war"**: WS to KC, Nov. 4, 1863, BUL.
76 **"indulge in . . . to be mine" . . . Kate's objection**: WS to KC, Oct. 19, 1863, CHS.
76 **do nothing that would diminish**: SPC to KC, Aug. 12, 1863 (*Pegasus*, 216).
76 **she gave in . . . "weakness . . . sin"**: KC Diary, Nov. 4, 1868, BUL. See also Lamphier, 110; Sokoloff, 155.
76 **strange behavior**: WS to KC, Sept. 20, 1863, BUL.
76 **"I trust . . . control us"**: WS to KC, Sept. 19, 1863, CHS.
76 **"You know . . . tenacious of everything"**: WS to SPC, Dec. 2, 1863 (*Pegasus*, 249).
76 **no longer her own person**: WS to KC, June 3, 1863, CHS.
76 **"I shall expect . . . the lecture"**: WS to KC, Oct. 23, 1863, BUL.
76 **his preference for . . . September**: SPC to WS, June 6, 1863 (*CP4*:55–56); WS to SPC, June 8, 1863 (*CP4*:59); SPC to KC, Oct. 3, 1863 (*Pegasus*, 232).
76 **"Must I wait . . . Angels guard you"**: WS to KC, Oct. 23, 1863, BUL.
77 **"*To get . . . what I shall do*"**: WS to KC, Nov. 2, 1863, BUL.
77 **"sickening twaddle"**: *White Cloud (KS) Chief*, Nov. 12, 1863.
77 **Cabinet Crisis**: Niven, 310–313; Goodwin, *Team of Rivals*, 486–495.
77 **"I can ride . . . my bag"**: Donald, *Lincoln*, 405.
77 **not losing a daughter**: SPC to Garfield, May 31, 1863 (*CP4*:47).

77 **"I expect . . . only son?"**: SPC to KC, Oct. 3, 1863 (*Pegasus*, 232).
78 **"delightful"**: SPC to Hiram Barney, Nov. 7, 1863 (*CP4*:178). See also SPC to WS, June 6, 1863 (*CP4*:55).
78 **"I love him . . . patriotism"**: SPC to KC, Sept. 30, 1863 (*Pegasus*, 231).
78 **"if they both live . . . change their minds"**: Oberholtzer, *Jay Cooke*, 1:276.
78 **"To get the esteem . . . satisfaction to me"**: WS to KC, June 7, 1863, CHS.
78 **"We must be guided . . . affectionate interest"**: WS to KC, June 7, 1863 (second letter), CHS.
78 **"Writing is not . . . in kind"**: WS to SPC, July 19, 1863, Chase LC, reel 3.
78 **invigorating ocean air**: WS to KC, July 19, 1863, CHS; WS to SPC, July 22, 1863, Chase LC, reel 3.
78 **visit the McDowell country home:** WS to SPC, June 24, 1863, Chase LC, reel 3; Sokoloff, 81.
78 **"old womanly view"**: WS to Hiram Barney, July 7, 1863, Chase HSP. See also Ross, 130–131.
78 **"I have written . . . *three* letters"**: WS to KC, July 16, 1863 (second letter), BUL.
78 **"I am afraid . . . grateful"**: WS to KC, July 19, 1863, CHS.
79 **visit to . . . Providence**: Lamphier, 54; Sokoloff, 82–83; SPC to KC, Aug. 27, 1863 (*Pegasus*, 223–224); *CP4*:107n1.
79 **"lady . . . genuine dignity"**: SPC to KC, Aug. 17, 1863 (*Pegasus*, 218).
79 **"known almost . . . mother's care"**: SPC to WS, Oct. 31, 1863 (*CP4*:164).
79 **he blew up . . . Sprague, knew nothing**: SPC to NC, Sept. 19, 1863 (*CP4*:141); WS to SPC, Sept. 15, 1863, Chase LC, reel 3.
79 **"You and Sister . . . a good deal"**: SPC to NC, Sept. 19, 1863 (*CP4*:141).
79 **accept the blame**: WS to KC, Sept. 23, 1863, BUL.
79 **"as free . . . until marriage"**: Lois Banner, *American Beauty: A Social History . . . Through Two Centuries of the American Idea, Ideal, and Image of the Beautiful Woman* (New York: Knopf, 1983), 80.
79 **Chase suggested . . . move out**: SPC to WS, June 6, 1863 (*CP4*:55–56).
79 **"the delicate link . . . daughter"**: WS to SPC, Nov. 4, 1863 (*CP4*:176).
79 **a compromise**: WS to SPC, May 31, 1863 (*CP4*:49–50); SPC to WS, July 14, 1863 (*CP4*:79–80); WS to SPC, July 18, 1863, Chase LC, reel 3; WS to KC, July 22, 1863, BUL.
80 **"What *they* are doing . . . *to* enquire"**: SPC to NC, Aug. 19, 1863 (*Pegasus*, 221).
80 **concern . . . renovation costs**: SPC to KC, Aug. 27, Sept. 9, 17, 1863 (*Pegasus*, 223–225, 228).
80 **buying the townhouse**: SPC to WS, Nov. 26, 1863 (*CP4*:204–205 and n3).
80 **a second carriage**: Niven, 342; WS to SPC, July 18, 1863, Chase LC, reel 3.
80 **Chase was exasperated with the bills**: SPC to KC, Sept. 17, 1863 (*Pegasus*, 228).
80 **overdrew his checking account**: Phelps, 145.
80 **"some inequalities of temper"**: SPC to WS, Nov. 26, 1863 (*CP4*:204).

80 **"with trembling . . . dark days"**: SPC to KC, Nov. 18, 1863 (*Pegasus*, 243).
80 **too materialistic**: SPC to WS, Nov. 26, 1863 (*CP4*:204).
80 **become good Christians**: SPC to KC, Nov. 18, 1863 (*Pegasus*, 244).
80 **"all the fine 'things' . . . from the reality"**: WS to KC, Oct. 20, 1863, CHS.
80 **did not expect all would run smoothly**: WS to SPC, June 8, 1863 (*CP4*:59).
81 **"receives no detriment . . . given to me"**: WS to SPC, May 31, 1863 (*CP4*:49–50).
81 **"all the liberty . . . heart desires"**: WS to KC, Nov. 2, 1863, CHS.
81 **"This is indeed . . . being lovers"**: Ibid.
81 **systematic effort to sever**: WS to KC, Sept. 23, 1863, BUL.
81 **"Your Ohio friends are getting desperate"**: WS to KC, Oct. 22, 1863, BUL.
81 **read . . . toss them out**: WS to KC, June 7, 1863 (second letter), CHS; WS to KC, Sept. 23, 1863, BUL.
81 **Sprague's gift**: WS to KC, Sept. 19, 1863, CHS; Sokoloff, 84.
81 **"I wish not . . . right to do this"**: WS to KC, Sept. 23, 1863, BUL.
81 **ceded . . . the invitations**: WS to KC, Nov. 1, 1863, CHS.
81 **serenaded**: John Hay Diary, Nov. 11, 1863, in Burlingame and Ettlinger, *Inside Lincoln's White House*, 111.
81 **wedding box**: possessions of Aura Carr, viewed by the author.
82 **wedding ceremony**: *New York Times*, Nov. 15, 1863; Niven, 342–343; *Harper's Weekly*, Nov. 28, 1863, 440; Lamphier, 58, 60, 63–64.
82 **Mary, who pleaded**: *Wooster (OH) Republican*, Apr. 15, 1869.
82 **He kissed the bride**: *Salt Lake Herald*, Oct. 19, 1890; Ross, 140.
82 **a small fan**: Sandburg, *Lincoln: The War Years*, 2:456; Ross, 140.
82 **bridesmaids . . . groomsmen**: *New York Times*, Nov. 15, 1863.
82 **Betty Blair . . . "a great display . . . very lame"**: Elizabeth Blair Lee to Samuel Phillips Lee, Nov. 12, 1863, in Laas, *Wartime Washington*, 319.
82 **"Aladdin . . . princess"**: *New York World*, Nov. 16, 1863.
83 **child labor**: Hoffmann and Hoffmann, *Brotherly Love*, 20–21; Caranci, *Hanging of John Gordon*, 45; John Ker Towles, "Factory Legislation of Rhode Island," *American Economic Association Quarterly* 9, no. 3 (Oct. 1908): 9–11; *Cincinnati Daily Gazette*, Mar. 25, 1869.
83 **"Lords of the Loom"**: SPC to C. Sumner, Nov. 27, 1848 (*CP2*:196).
83 **"tired out . . . *arrived*"**: John Hay Diary, Nov. 12, 1863, in Burlingame and Ettlinger, *Inside Lincoln's White House*, 111.
83 **Maggie Mitchell in *Pearl of Savoy***: *Daily National Republican* (Washington, DC), Oct. 27, 1863.
83 **"the statuesque . . . a baby"**: John Hay Diary, Oct. 22, 1863, in Burlingame and Ettlinger, *Inside Lincoln's White House*, 98.
83 **melodramatic story**: *The Pearl of Savoy: A Domestic Drama, in Five Acts, French's Standard Drama, the Acting Edition* (New York, [1864]).
83 **follower of newspaper gossip**: *New York Times*, Aug. 19, 1879.
83 **upbraided Sprague . . . old flames**: Elizabeth Blair Lee to Samuel Phillips Lee, Nov. 12, 1863, in Laas, *Wartime Washington*, 319.

## PART TWO: MRS. SPRAGUE

### Chapter 9: "Imagine My Disappointment"

87 **"horse fair" decorations**: Phelps, 141; Sokoloff, 92.
87 **old line families declined to show**: Phelps, 142–143.
87 **Niagara Falls**: *Cleveland Morning Leader*, Nov. 30, 1863.
87 **heading to Ohio**: Ibid.; Ross, 145–146.
87 **"The sunshine . . . hard to bear"**: KC to WS, Dec. 11, 1863, CHS.
87 **"the one . . . my life"**: KC to WS, Dec. 12, 1863, BUL.
87 **father was driving her crazy**: KC to WS, Dec. 11, 1863, CHS.
88 **"To you . . . all joy"**: Ibid.
88 **"Forgotten so soon!"**: KC to WS, Dec. 12, 1863, BUL.
88 **bitterly disappointed**: KC to WS, Dec. 29, 1863, CHS.
88 **needed her sympathy**: WS to KC, Dec. 31, 1863, BUL.
88 **"Imagine my disappointment"**: KC to WS, Dec. 29, 1863, CHS.
88 **"the absent one"**: KC to WS, Dec. 24, 1863, BUL.
88 **dismissive . . . his father's murder**: WS to KC, Dec. 30, 31, 1863, BUL.
88 **enthusiastic reception**: Niven, 338; SPC to Edward D. Mansfield, Oct. 18, 1863 (*CP4*:154).
88 **"The Next Presidency . . . Secretary Chase"**: *White Cloud (KS) Chief*, Nov. 12, 1863.
88 **asked his last surviving sister**: SPC to Helen Walbridge, Jan. 2, 1864, in Warden, 560–561.
88 **"controlled merely . . . that man"**: SPC to WS, Nov. 26, 1863 (*CP4*:204).
89 **"necessary to have . . . well laid plan"**: WS to KC, Dec. 12, 1863, BUL.
89 **"maybe a little too . . . must not be so"**: SPC to WS, Nov. 26, 1863 (*CP4*:204).
89 **her receptions . . . politician from the hinterlands**: Burton Jesse Hendrick, *Lincoln's War Cabinet* (Boston: Little, Brown, 1946), 382.
89 **cross . . . off the list**: John G. Nicolay to John Hay, Jan. 18, 1864, in *With Lincoln in the White House: Letters, Memoranda, and Other Writings of John G. Nicolay, 1860–1865*, ed. Michael Burlingame (Carbondale: Southern Illinois University Press, 2000), 124.
89 **"Rhode Island . . . arose such a rampage . . . for a year"**: Ibid.
89 **"at work . . . laying pipe"**: John Hay Diary, Nov. 28, 1863, in Burlingame and Ettlinger, *Inside Lincoln's White House*, 120.
89 **"like the bluebottle fly . . . can find"**: John Hay Diary, Oct. 29, 1863, in ibid., 103.
89 **Chase-for-President committee**: Goodwin, *Team of Rivals*, 605; Niven, 357; Oberholtzer, *Jay Cooke*, 1:363–364.
90 **Pomeroy Circular . . . withdrawal . . . presidential contest**: Blue, 223–226; Niven, 360–362; SPC to Lincoln, Feb. 22, 1864 (*CP4*:303–304); Lincoln to SPC, Feb. 29, 1864 (*CP4*:305n3); SPC to William Orton, Mar. 4, 1864 (*CP4*:316n5); SPC to NC, Mar. 15, 1864 (*Pegasus*, 255).

90 **private criticism**: SPC to George S. Denison, Mar. 16, 1864 (*CP4*:330–332); SPC to Cyrus W. Field, Apr. 6, 1864 (*CP4*:364–365).

90 **continued to supply material:** SPC to John T. Trowbridge, Mar. 20, 21, 22, 1864 (*CP4*:332–250, 356–258).

90 **"modestly . . . quick of wit"**: Sandburg, *Lincoln: The War Years*, 2:646.

90 **"Kate seems . . . as she does"**: SPC to Helen Walbridge, Jan. 2, 1864, in Warden, 560.

90 **"the distinguished honor . . . Mrs. Sprague"**: Josiah Marshall Favill, *The Diary of a Young Officer Serving with the Armies of the United States During the War of the Rebellion* (Chicago: R. R. Donnelley, 1909), 280.

90 **"Don't neglect . . . very long"**: KC to WS, Mar. 4, 1864, CHS.

91 **"was all devotion . . . to be so petted" . . . almost worthwhile**: SPC to NC, May 5, 1864 (*Pegasus*, 256).

91 **"go out among . . . and why"**: SPC to KC, Aug. 26, 1864 (*Pegasus*, 262).

91 **patronage appointment . . . resignation**: Goodwin, *Team of Rivals*, 518, 631–633; Hart, 314–317; SPC to Lincoln, June 29, 1864 (*CP4*:409–410); Lincoln to SPC, June 30, 1864 (*CP4*:411); SPC Diary, June 29–30, 1864 (*CP1*:468–472).

91 **Lincoln confided**: John Hay Diary, June 30, 1864, in Burlingame and Ettlinger, *Inside Lincoln's White House*, 212.

91 **"a good deal . . . could not imagine"**: SPC Diary, June 30, 1864 (*CP4*:470).

91 **"too earnest . . . radical"**: SPC Diary, July 4, 1864 (*CP4*:476).

91 **"The truth . . . this war"**: Hart, 318.

91 **people never sympathize**: SPC to KC, July 11, 1864 (*Pegasus*, 260).

91 **feel sorry for himself and complain**: SPC to William Curtis Noyes, July 11, 1864 (*CP4*:418–419); SPC Diary, July 13, 1864 (*CP1*:479); SPC to Samuel Hooper, Sept. 16, 1864 (*CP4*:428–430); SPC to Sumner, Nov. 12, 1864 (*CP4*:438–440).

91 **Chase went east**: Niven, 370–371; SPC Diary, July 13–Sept. 13, 1864 (*CP1*:479–502).

91 **Kate and her husband arguing**: SPC Diary, Sept. 9–10, 1864 (*CP1*:501).

91 **"I hope . . . cannot be healed"**: WS to KC, n.d., BUL.

92 **Adele Cutts Douglas**: Niven, 204; Clinton, *Mrs. Lincoln*, 108; Epstein, *The Lincolns*, 212.

92 **Susan Walker**: Niven, 203–204; *Journal of Miss Susan Walker, March 3d to June 6th, 1862*, ed. Henry Noble Sherwood, in *Quarterly Publication of the Historical and Philosophical Society of Ohio* 7, no. 1 (Jan.–Mar. 1912): 3–4; Willie Lee Rose, *Rehearsal for Reconstruction: The Port Royal Experiment* (1964; repr., Athens: University of Georgia Press, 1999), 53; *Pegasus*, 194n4.

92 **Charlotte Eastman**: Niven, 204; Goodwin, *Team of Rivals*, 544–545; *Pegasus*, 171n1.

92 **opposed to her father remarrying . . . intercept their letters**: Blue, 211; Hart, 419; Eugene L. Didier, "Personal Recollections of Chief-Justice Chase," *The Green Bag* 7, no. 7 (July 1895): 315–316; Beldens, 88–89.

92 **disliked Mrs. Eastman . . . rumored to be engaged**: Ross, 147, 187, 193–194; Niven, 441–442; SPC to Jacob W. Schuckers, Sept. 24, 1866 (*CP5*:124–125).
92 **"wipe out . . . both sides"**: SPC to KC, n.d., ca. 1861 (*Pegasus*, 183).
92 **"so sorry . . . don't exactly *jee*"**: SPC to Charlotte Eastman, Aug. 22, 1863 (*CP4*:112).
92 **visits to Mrs. Eastman**: SPC Diary, July 24, 29, 1864; Aug. 19, 22, 25, 26, 1864 (*CP1*:483–484, 491–492, 494–495); Ross, 161.
92 **Greeley and . . . Reid**: Whitelaw Reid to SPC, Aug. 22, 1864 (*CP4*:423–424).
92 **Chase . . . open to the nomination**: SPC to George Opdyke, Aug. 19, 1864 (*CP4*:423).
92 **denigrating Grant's efforts . . . meet his "Moscow"**: SPC to Alfred P. Stone, May 23, 1864 (*CP4*:386–387).
93 **"He talked feelingly . . . Mr. Chase's daughter"**: Crook, *Through Five Administrations*, 31.
93 **"I feel that I do not know him"**: SPC to KC, Sept. 17, 1864 (*CP4*:432). See also SPC Diary, Sept. 15–16, 1864 (*CP1*:503–504).
93 **"enough like . . . on himself"**: Joseph B. Foraker, "Address of Hon. J. B. Foraker, on the Life, Character and Public Services of Salmon P. Chase . . . at Springfield, Illinois, October 7, 1905," 24, Chase OHS (hereafter cited as Foraker, "Address on Chase").
93 **"enough unlike . . . duty so required"**: Ibid.
93 **would despise himself**: Goodwin, *Team of Rivals*, 679–680.
93 **Crook**: *New York Times*, Mar. 14, 1915.
93 **"I ought not . . . said about me"**: Crook, *Through Five Administrations*, 32.
94 **Chase . . . was greeted . . . thanked the president**: Schuckers, 488; SPC to Lincoln, Dec. 6, 1864 (*CP4*:445).
94 **sworn in . . . "gorgeously dressed"**: Noah Brooks, *Washington in Lincoln's Time* (New York, 1895), 194.
94 **"And you, too . . . defeat you all!"**: Warden, 630.
94 **"experiment" . . . resign in two or three years**: Hiram Calkins to James Gordon Bennett, Dec. 25, 1864, Chase OHS.
94 **"how Mrs. Sprague . . . on the bench'"**: Piatt, *Memories of the Men*, 120–123.
94 **forgot their first anniversary**: KC Diary, Nov. 11, 1868, BUL.
94 **Christmas and New Year's apart**: WS to KC, Jan. 1, 1865, CHS; WS to KC, Jan. 3, 1865, BUL.
94 **appreciated . . . her loving notes . . . to do his part**: WS to KC, Jan. 3, 1865, BUL.
95 **"very uneasy"**: SPC Diary, Jan. 17, 1865 (*CP1*:518).
95 **suddenly indisposed . . . damper on the evening**: SPC Diary, Jan. 13, 1865 (*CP1*:517).
95 **"she either . . . very ungracious"**: SPC Diary, Jan. 9, 1865 (*CP1*:515–516).
95 **"'trip the light . . . *or ball*"**: Mary Lincoln to Madame Alfred Berghmans, [Feb. 1865], autographed letter, Lot 131, Sale 9262, *Christie's*, Dec. 10, 1999, www.christies.com/lotfinder/LotDetailsPrintable.aspx?intObjectID=1632878.

95 **robe . . . Frederick Douglass**: Frederick Douglass, *The Life and Times of Frederick Douglass: From 1817–1882*, ed. John Lobb (London, 1882), 316.

95 **matinee reception**: *Cleveland Morning Leader*, Mar. 4, 1865.

95 **She attended . . . ball**: Clinton, *Mrs. Lincoln*, 236.

95 **Sprague returned to Providence**: SPC Diary, Mar. 17, 1865 (*CP1*:522).

95 **Booth . . . on Kate's wedding day**: *Daily National Republican* (Washington, DC), Nov. 12, 1863.

## Chapter 10: "Our Accomplished Countrywoman"

96 **funeral service**: *New York Times*, Apr. 20, 1865; Clinton, *Mrs. Lincoln*, 248–249; Dorothy M. Kunhardt and Philip B. Kunhardt Jr., *Twenty Days* (1965; repr., Secaucus, NJ: Castle Books, 1993), 123–127; Philip B. Kunhardt Jr., Philip B. Kunhardt III, and Peter W. Kunhardt, *Lincoln: An Illustrated Biography* (New York: Knopf, 1992), 370–371; SPC Diary, Apr. 15, 17, 1865 (*CP1*:529–531).

96 **"Now only . . . beauty's presence"**: *Cleveland Morning Leader*, Apr. 22, 1865.

96 **tour of . . . South . . . letters to President Johnson**: Niven, 384–393; SPC Diary, May 3, 1865 (*CP1*:537); Janet Chase Hoyt, "Sherman and Chase: An Interview at Beaufort," *New-York Tribune*, Feb. 22, 1891; SPC to Andrew Johnson, May 17, 1865 (*CP5*:47–52).

97 **Adolphus Mot**: SPC to KC, May 20, 1865 (*Pegasus*, 277).

97 **baby boy . . . "bright . . . handsome"**: SPC Diary, June 23, 1865 (*CP1*:579). Willie Sprague was born on or about June 20, 1865 at Narragansett Pier (South Kingstown), Rhode Island. SPC to KC, June 24, 1865 (*Pegasus*, 284–286 and n8).

97 **"the name . . . 'adjudged'"**: SPC to KC, June 24, 1865 (*Pegasus*, 284).

97 **"even the clever speeches . . . far and wide"**: *New York Herald*, Aug. 6, 1899.

97 **advertised . . . Kate to be in better health**: SPC Diary, July 6, 1865 (*CP1*:586–587).

97 **visited the Sprague offices . . . comfortable conditions**: SPC Diary, July 12, 1865 (*CP1*:590).

98 **would spend less time on business**: SPC to KC, June 19, 1865 (*Pegasus*, 283).

98 **books . . . about Rhode Island**: SPC to KC, Sept. 8, 1865 (*Pegasus*, 292).

98 **Sprague . . . bought up cotton plantations**: Lawrence N. Powell, *New Masters: Northern Planters During the Civil War and Reconstruction* (New Haven, CT: Yale University Press, 1980), 14–15, 44, 73–74, 125; *Daily Phoenix* (Columbia, SC), June 8, 1866.

98 **"actually employing . . . not to be trusted"**: *Daily Phoenix* (Columbia, SC), June 8, 1866.

98 **Sprague preferred leasing**: Powell, *New Masters*, 6, 42–44, 48; WS to SPC, Feb. 8, 1862 (*CP3*:130–131).

98 **"Let them . . . with them"**: Powell, *New Masters*, 48.

98 **immigrant workers**: Ibid., 73–74.

98 **whites harder to provide for**: John Floyd King to Georgia [King] Smith, Feb. 19, 1866, quoted in Matthew Pratt Guterl, *American Mediterranean: Southern Slaveholders in the Age of Emancipation* (Cambridge, MA: Harvard University Press, 2008), 172.

99 **"at least one third . . . work"**: John Floyd King to Mallery Page King, Jan. 18, 1866, quoted in Powell, *New Masters*, 73–74.

99 **turned back to . . . African American freedman**: Powell, *New Masters*, 74–75; Guterl, *American Mediterranean*, 172.

99 **to support black suffrage**: *Cong. Globe*, 39th Cong., 1st Sess. 1934 (Apr. 13, 1866); O. P. G. Clarke to WS, Apr. 16, 1866, William Sprague Papers, Columbia University Rare Book and Manuscript Library.

99 **"independent, and manly . . . these days"**: SPC to KC, June 19, 1865 (*Pegasus*, 283).

99 **Resuming her receptions**: *Saturday Evening Post*, Jan. 27, 1866.

99 **"the picture . . . in her arms"**: Phelps, 177.

99 **postwar social season**: Mrs. E. F. [Elizabeth Fries] Ellet, *The Court Circles of the Republic, or the Beauties and Celebrities of the Nation* (Hartford, CT, 1870), 550–553.

99 **French Ambassador's ball**: Ibid., 552; *National Tribune* (Washington, DC), Dec. 23, 1897; Sue A. Kohler and Jeffrey R. Carson, *Sixteenth Street Architecture* (Washington, DC: US Commission of Fine Arts, 1978), 1:14–15.

99 **"our accomplished countrywoman, Mrs. Senator Sprague"**: Briggs, *Olivia Letters*, 17.

99 **drew out the taciturn**: Claude G. Bowers, *The Tragic Era: The Revolution After Lincoln* (Cambridge, MA: Riverside Press, 1929), 255.

100 **George Armstrong Custer**: SPC Diary, Mar. 22, 1866 (*CP1*:608); Shirley A. Leckie, *Elizabeth Bacon Custer and the Making of a Myth* (Norman: University of Oklahoma Press, 1993), 82.

100 **regular news coverage**: *The Independent* (Oskaloosa, KS), Sept. 9, 1865; *The Caledonian* (St. Johnsbury, VT), Sept. 1, 1865; *Democrat and Sentinel* (Ebensburg, PA), June 28, 1866. See also *Saturday Evening Post*, Jan. 27, 1866; *Boston Daily Journal*, Nov. 12, 1867.

100 **female society reporters**: Jacob, *Capital Elites*, 65, 94; "Maria Austine ('Miss Grundy') Snead," *Find a Grave*, Oct. 25, 2009, www.findagrave.com/cgi-bin/fg.cgi?page=gr&GRid=43517532.

100 **Sprague . . . back to Providence . . . rarely accompanied**: SPC Diary, Jan. 7, 1866 (*CP1*:602); Phelps, 178; Ross, 176, 183.

100 **"a pair of bright eyes . . . ashamed of you"**: *Cleveland Plain Dealer*, Feb. 25, 1870.

100 **absence might help**: KC Diary, Nov. 4, 1868, BUL.

## Chapter 11: "More Unfitness Day by Day"

101 **Sprague had tears**: WS to KC, Apr. 14, 1866, CHS.

101 **"taken to whiskey . . . deserted me?"**: Ibid.
102 **odd couple . . . horseback rides**: WS to KC, May 8, 14, 1866, CHS.
102 **father-in-law bashful . . . Sprague accused Kate of forgetting**: WS to KC, May 8, 1866, CHS.
102 **"a slave . . . to hate"**: WS to KC, July 6, 1866, CHS.
102 **"more unfitness day by day"**: WS to KC, Apr. 30, 1866, CHS.
102 **getting control of drinking**: WS to KC, May 9–12, 1866, BUL.
102 **"physical infirmities . . . cannot remember"**: WS to KC, May 18, 1866, CHS.
102 **commenting on his drinking**: *Urbana (OH) Union*, Mar. 28, July 25, 1866.
102 **"shirt collar . . . funnel"**: Ibid., July 25, 1866.
102 **stories were on target**: WS to KC, May 18, 1866, CHS.
102 **"He does not understand . . . discourage anyone"**: Ibid.
103 **"doleful letter . . . the separation"**: WS to KC, May 22, 1866, BUL.
103 **Kate stayed in Europe**: Phelps, 183–184; Ross, 184–185; *Pegasus*, 297–299.
103 **letter-writing contest**: SPC to NC, May 14, June 18, 22, July 2, 1866 (*Pegasus*, 303–304, 311–315); SPC to KC, June 15, 1866 (*Pegasus*, 308–309).
103 **"a real treat "**: SPC to NC, June 18, 1866 (*Pegasus*, 311).
103 **"Katie seems to think . . . any degree of perfection"**: SPC to NC, Aug. 9, 1866 (*Pegasus*, 317).
103 **his opinion on women's rights**: SPC to KC, June 15, 1866 (*Pegasus*, 308–309).
104 **"encouragement . . . liberal with you"**: WS to KC, June 8, 1866, BUL.
104 **"Dearie . . . similar liberty?"**: WS to KC, June 11, 1866, BUL.
104 **"with the rustle . . . women's dresses"**: Ibid.
104 **buxom woman . . . obtain a full view**: WS to KC, June 29, 1866, BUL.
104 **"Mama and Papa . . . between them"**: WS to Willie Sprague, July 8, 1866, BUL.
104 **"poor show . . . very sluggish"**: Lamphier, 82–83, quoting WS to KC, July 12, 1866, BUL.
104 **talked of quitting . . . "cowardly act"**: WS to KC, July 19, 1866, CHS.
104 **"neatness in dress . . . great things"**: Ibid.
105 **gave thought to studying law**: SPC to WS, July 25, 1866 (*CP5*:121).
105 **traveled east . . . Charlotte Eastman**: SPC Diary, July 14–Sept. 2, 1866 (*CP1*:612–631); SPC to J. Schuckers, Sept. 24, 1866 (*CP5*:124–125).
105 **knocking . . . no answer**: SPC Diary, Aug. 13, 1866 (*CP1*:624).
105 **left him the key . . . was barred**: SPC Diary, Aug. 14, 1866 (*CP1*:624–625).
105 **"would have yielded"**: SPC Diary, Aug. 15, 1866 (*CP1*:625).
105 **bar . . . would have given way . . . grieving at his scheduled departure**: Ibid.
105 **"the most astonishing . . . news" . . . Sumner was to be married**: SPC to KC, Sept. 10, 1866 (*Pegasus*, 323–324 and n8).
105 **authorizing him to deny**: SPC to J. Schuckers, Sept. 24, 1866 (*CP5*:125).
105 **"But I am . . . grandmothers?!"**: Ibid., 125.
106 **"but for . . . I lead"**: Ross, 194.
106 **Sumner's suffering**: *San Francisco Morning Call*, Oct. 15, 1893.

106 **"a little wanting . . . the conquest"**: WS to KC, Sept. 17, 1866, BUL.

106 **rumors of . . . divorce**: *New York World*, Sept. 14, 1866; *Albany Journal*, Sept. 28, 1866; *Vinton Record* (M'arthur, Vinton County, OH), Nov. 1, 1866.

106 **"in consequence . . . his part"**: *Burlington (VT) Free Press*, Oct. 26, 1866.

106 **print a denial without mentioning Kate's name**: SPC to J. Schuckers, Oct. 16, 1866, Chase LC, reel 25.

106 **"the shameful libel . . . domestic relations"**: *Providence Journal*, Oct. 19, 1866.

106 **"infamous calumnies . . . votes always right"**: *New-York Tribune*, Oct. 31, 1866.

107 **Sprague . . . met up in Germany**: SPC to KC, Oct. 12, 1866 (*Pegasus*, 324); SPC to NC, Oct. 15, 18, 1866 (*Pegasus*, 326–331).

107 **Kate's father . . . joyful**: SPC to NC, Dec. 12, 1866 (*Pegasus*, 342).

107 **Kate's new curled hair**: SPC to KC, Oct. 12, 1866 (*Pegasus*, 324).

107 **chagrined that Nettie**: SPC to KC, Sept. 10, 1866 (*Pegasus*, 322); SPC to NC, Oct. 18, Nov. 27, 1866 (*Pegasus*, 329, 335–336).

107 **Maggie English**: *New York Times*, Dec. 20, 1880; *Wheeling Register*, Dec. 27, 1880; WS to KC, May 28, 1866, BUL; WS to Willie Sprague, July 8, 1866, BUL; SPC to NC, Oct. 15, 1866 (*Pegasus*, 326–327).

107 **Mary Viall**: *New York Times*, Dec. 20, 1880.

## Chapter 12: "I Am Told That She Actually Controls the Entire Affair"

108 **Canonchet**: *New York Sun*, Aug. 21, 1882; *New York Times*, Aug. 22, 1881; Sallie W. Latimer, *Narragansett in Vintage Postcards* (Portsmouth, NH: Arcadia, 1999), 108; Warren Vincent Sprague, *Sprague Families*, 389; Carroll, *Rhode Island*, 2:1173; *New York Sun*, Sept. 3, 1879; Monroe C. Beardsley, *Aesthetics: Problems in the Philosophy of Criticism* (Indianapolis: Hackett, 1981), 484; William H. Jordy, *Buildings of Rhode Island* (Oxford: Oxford University Press, 2004), 368; WS to KC, Apr. 14, 1866, CHS; SPC Diary, July 31, 1872 (*CP1*:695 and n96); *St. Paul Daily Globe*, Mar. 28, 1883.

109 **apart again at Christmas**: SPC to NC, Dec. 24, 1866 (*Pegasus*, 344–345).

109 **"I am glad . . . husband and child"**: SPC to KC, Jan. 4, 1867 (*Pegasus*, 346–347).

109 **"a little speech"**: SPC to NC, Dec. 12, 1866 (*Pegasus*, 343–344 and n3).

109 **"a great deal from dyspepsia" . . . couldn't even come downstairs**: SPC to NC, Jan. 24, 1867 (*Pegasus*, 350–351).

109 **"no woman . . . *facile princeps*"**: Ibid.

109 **Saturday afternoon receptions**: *Cincinnati Daily Gazette*, Jan. 16, 1868.

110 **she stayed out . . . impairing her health**: SPC to NC, Jan. 31, 1867 (*Pegasus*, 352).

110 **Kate . . . visited him the prior summer**: SPC to KC, Sept. 10, 1866 (*Pegasus*, 322–323 and n3).

110 **"never seen . . . a roomful"**: John Hay Diary, Feb. 11, 1867, in William Roscoe Thayer, *The Life and Letters of John Hay* (Boston: Houghton Mifflin, 1915), 1:268.

110 **"like an idiot . . . table"**: Thayer, *Life and Letters of John Hay*, 1:257.

110 **"plain people . . . national calamity"**: Mrs. John A. [Mary] Logan, *Thirty Years in Washington; or, Life and Scenes in Our National Capital* (Hartford, CT: A. D. Worthington, 1901), 659.

110 **"slept on it and said no"**: Thayer, *Life and Letters of John Hay*, 1:258–259. See also Beldens, 169; John Taliaferro, *All the Great Prizes: The Life of John Hay, from Lincoln to Roosevelt* (New York: Simon & Schuster, 2013), 114.

110 **housewarming . . . Ogontz**: SPC to NC, Feb. 15, 1867 (*Pegasus*, 355); *Pegasus*, 295 n1. Ogontz was located in what is now the suburb of Elkins Park.

110 **"costly dressing . . . what nots"**: *National Republican* (Washington, DC), Feb. 25, 1867.

111 **"Oh how . . . simplicity of tastes!"**: SPC to NC, Feb. 15, 1867 (*Pegasus*, 355).

111 **"There could not . . . possibly imagine"**: Mary Logan, *Reminiscences of a Soldier's Wife* (New York: Charles Scribner's, 1913), 300.

111 **"has the look . . . Holland maiden"**: *Cincinnati Daily Gazette*, Mar. 20, 1868.

111 **"large and blonde . . . Flemish Venus"**: John Hay to John Nicolay, Dec. 8, 1868, in *Lincoln and the Civil War, in the Diaries and Letters of John Hay*, ed. Tyler Dennett (1939; repr., New York: Da Capo Press, 1988), 297.

111 **April . . . Kate went back**: *New York Times*, Apr. 7, 1867; Phelps, 192.

111 **brought her sister back . . . forgot Kate's birthday**: SPC to NC, Sept. 12, 1867 (*Pegasus*, 359).

111 **"not quite certain . . . 13th of September"**: SPC to KC, Oct. 12, 1866 (*Pegasus*, 324).

111 **try his hand**: SPC to J. Schuckers, Sept. 24, 1866 (*CP5*:128).

111 **"it does look . . . fall upon me"**: SPC to NC, July 11, 1867 (*CP5*:169).

112 **"irksome"**: Blue, 247, 283.

112 **Sprague "came to the rescue"**: Susie Lee Owens, "The Union League of America: Political Activities in Tennessee, the Carolinas, and Virginia 1865–1870" (PhD diss., New York University, Apr. 1943), 480, on file at Bobst Library, New York University, quoting excerpt from Annual Report of the National Executive Committee of the Urban League of America, December 1867.

112 **Sprague secured a commitment**: James Edmunds to WS, July 26, Aug. 7, 1867, William Sprague Letters, Columbia University Rare Book and Manuscript Library; Michael W. Fitzgerald, *The Union League in the Deep South: Politics and Agricultural Change During Reconstruction* (Baton Rouge: LSU Press, 2000), 12–13.

112 **Chase acknowledged Sprague's efforts . . . public mood was favorable**: SPC to WS, Aug. 7, 1867, CHS.

112 **paid $100 a week**: William Perrine, "The Dashing Kate Chase," *Ladies Home Journal*, June 1901, 12.

112 **"the most splendid woman . . . of Washington"**: *New York Herald*, Jan. 20, 1868.
113 **"unreservedly . . . with Congress"**: *Lincoln County Herald* (Troy, MO), Apr. 2, 1868.
113 **"the time . . . the Constitution"**: *Lincoln County Herald* (Troy, MO), Apr. 2, 1868.
113 **privately told Kate**: SPC to KC, May 10, 1868 (*Pegasus*, 367).
113 **mostly favored Johnson's defense**: Michael Gerhardt, "Impeachment," in *The Concise Princeton Encyclopedia of American Political History* (Princeton, NJ: Princeton University Press, 2011), 303; Blue, 279.
113 **"To me . . . seems wrong"**: SPC to Gerrit Smith, Apr. 19, 1868 (*CP5*:208).
113 **Wade, ascend to the presidency**: Coleman, *Election of 1868*, 79; Blue, 281.
113 **never forgiven Wade**: SPC to Benjamin Rush Cowen, Nov. 8, 1866 (*CP5*:137).
114 **"coquetting with the Democrats"**: Coleman, *Election of 1868*, 81.
114 **Swisshelm . . . accused Kate**: *Cincinnati Daily Gazette*, Mar. 19, 1868.
114 **Swisshelm . . . challenged anyone**: *New York Herald*, Jan. 28, 1869.
114 **"Can it be . . . controls the entire affair"**: *Augusta (GA) Daily Constitutionalist*, June 5, 1868.
114 **"no reward . . . underhanded schemings"**: *Massachusetts Spy* (Worcester, MA), June 12, 1868.
114 **Kate . . . attended every session**: Briggs, *Olivia Letters*, 50–51, 69–70; *New-York Tribune*, Mar. 14, 1868; Niven, 423–424.
115 **"a Parisian suit . . . its appointments"**: Briggs, *Olivia Letters*, 400.
115 **"Paris has . . . immortality"**: Ibid., 70.
115 **"dangerous . . . removed"**: *Cleveland Plain Dealer*, Apr. 11, 1868.
115 **thought to be drunk**: *Fayetteville (TN) Observer*, Apr. 9, 1868; *White Cloud (KS) Chief*, Apr. 23, 1868.
115 **"just as Papa Chase tells him"**: *Brooklyn Eagle*, Nov. 14, 1863.
115 **Kate reportedly gave**: *Charleston (SC) Daily News*, Mar. 12, 1868.
115 **more afraid of . . . wife**: *Nashville Union and Dispatch*, Apr. 23, 1868.
115 **"hen pecked"**: *Cleveland Plain Dealer*, April 24, 1868.
115 **rumored Kate would leave him**: Sokoloff, 137; *Flake's Bulletin* (Galveston, TX), May 13, 1868.
115 **"Sprague was not . . . influence him"**: SPC to Greeley, May 19, 1868 (*CP5*:216–217).
115 **demonstrate his independence**: *Augusta (GA) Daily Constitutionalist*, June 5, 1868.
116 **Stanton . . . secret report**: Beldens, 148–149, 159–160, 188–189; Lamphier, 94–95.
116 **Rhode Island was also heavily Republican**: Edward McPherson, *A Political Manual for 1868 . . . From April 1, 1867, to July 15, 1868* (Washington, DC, 1868), 112; Carroll, *Rhode Island*, 2:643.
116 **left Washington**: SPC to KC, May 10, 1868 (*Pegasus*, 366–368).
116 **"I never saw . . . moved to tears"**: Ibid., 367.

116 **"I see now . . . nearly perfect"**: Ibid.
117 **"pulling the wires with great effect"**: *Macon (GA) Weekly Telegraph*, June 5, 1868.
117 **case she was making**: Ibid.
117 **"an even one"**: *San Francisco Morning Call*, Oct. 15, 1893.
117 **Grant . . . "slave of . . . revenge"**: *New York Herald*, May 7, 1868.
117 **Chase as an opportunist**: Coleman, *Election of 1868*, 68; Foraker, "Address on Chase," 5–6.
117 **"It is probably . . . has produced"**: Foraker, "Address on Chase," 6.
117 **"I can perceive . . . availability"**: Thomas F. Bayard to James A. Bayard, May 31, 1868, quoted in Joel H. Silbey, *A Respectable Minority: The Democratic Party in the Civil War Era, 1860–1868* (New York: W. W. Norton, 1977), 203.
117 **Democrat at heart**: SPC to August Belmont, May 30, 1868 (*CP5*:221–224).
118 **"compromise subterfuge"**: Coleman, *Election of 1868*, 138.
118 **"most discreet friends"**: SPC to KC, July 7, 1868 (*Pegasus*, 373).
118 **his motives were also suspect**: Blue, 286; Thomas S. Mach, "George Hunt Pendleton, The Ohio Idea and Political Continuity in Reconstruction America," *Ohio History, The Scholarly Journal of the Ohio Historical Society* 108 (Summer–Autumn 1999): 125, 137.

## Chapter 13: "You Have Been Most Cruelly Deceived"

120 **ovation for Chase**: Schuckers, 565.
120 **"no power . . . bad conduct"**: *Official Proceedings*, 119.
120 **balloting . . . through the eighteenth . . . adjournment**: Ibid., 125–139; Beldens, 211; *New-York Tribune*, July 10, 1868.
120 **"Seymour in favor . . . in the Ascendant"**: *New York Herald*, July 9, 1868.
120 **at Delmonico's restaurant**: *New York Sun*, Sept. 5, 1868.
120 **Seymour . . . buttonholing**: Coleman, *Election of 1868*, 227.
121 **Seymour and Van Buren convinced**: *New York Sun*, Sept. 5, 1868; Blue, 294.
121 **Seymour read . . . Seymour fully expected**: *New York Sun*, Sept. 5, 1868.
121 **Pendleton withdrew . . . a few hisses**: *Official Proceedings*, 140–151.
121 **"Many thought . . . Chase"**: *New-York Tribune*, July 10, 1868.
121 **McCook . . . enemy of Chase**: Charles Whalen and Barbara Whalen, *The Fighting McCooks: America's Famous Fighting Family* (Bethesda, MD: Westmoreland Press, 2006), 28, 33, 45–46; Thomas Edward Powell, ed., *The Democratic Party of the State of Ohio: A Comprehensive History of Democracy in Ohio from 1803 to 1912* (n.p.: Ohio Publishing Company, 1913); 1:198–199.
121 **"Mr. Chairman . . . New York"**: *Official Proceedings*, 152.
121 **"*meant* it . . . I cannot be"**: Ibid., 153.
122 **Vallandigham favored Chase, who welcomed**: F. Aiken to SPC, July 3, 1868 (*CP5*:251–52n1); SPC to F. Aiken, July 4, 1868 (*CP5*:251).
122 **"every personal . . . his name"**: *Official Proceedings*, 154.

122 **Kernan seconded . . . Seymour . . . chosen by acclamation**: Ibid., 154–161; *New-York Tribune*, July 10, 1868; *New York Sun*, July 10, 1868.

122 **playing croquet**: Schuckers, 566.

122 **"Does Mrs. Sprague . . . bear it?"**: Warden, 705–706.

122 **"My dearest Father . . . without a recognition"**: KC to SPC, July 10, 1868 (*CP5*:263).

123 **"answer no questions . . . outraged and deceived"**: Ibid.

123 **"I am perfectly well . . . the depression here"**: Ibid., 263–264.

124 **Van Buren . . . fifteen-point statement**: Coleman, *Election of 1868*, 115–117, 125, 136–140; Van Buren to SPC, June 25, 1868 (*CP5*:244–245 and n1); Blue, 290; Niven, 430.

124 **"throw back the nomination . . . my guest"**: Van Buren to A. Long, July 24, 1868, Alexander Long Papers, Cincinnati History Library and Archives at Cincinnati Museum Center (hereafter cited as Long Papers, Cincinnati History Library).

124 **some notes and a letter**: *CP5*:251n1; note in unidentified handwriting received from SPC, n.d., "3:30 p.m.," Long Papers, Cincinnati History Library; SPC to Long, July 4, 1868 (*CP5*:252).

124 **retracted . . . made Van Buren promise . . . err on the side of caution**: SPC to Van Buren, July 1 [sic, 4], 1868 (*CP5*:253); Van Buren to SPC, July 6, 1868 (*CP5*:256–257).

124 **"I know you would not deceive"**: SPC to Van Buren, July 10, 1868, Chase LC, reel 28.

125 **Tilden . . . cooled to the idea**: Alexander Clarence Flick, *Samuel Jones Tilden: A Study in Political Sagacity* (New York: Dodd, Mead, 1939), 167, 173, 175, 177; Blue, 286, 289; Coleman, *Election of 1868*, 227; Warden, 707–710; Van Buren to A. Long, July 24, 1868, Long Papers, Cincinnati History Library.

125 **"Chase is out of the question . . . must not think of nominating him"**: Sanford E. Church to Tilden, June 10, 1868, in Bigelow, *Tilden Letters*, 1:228–229.

125 **Chase came to believe**: SPC to Gerrit Smith, July 26, 1868 (*CP5*:269–270). See also SPC to Jay Cooke, July 11, 1868 (*CP5*:265); SPC to William B. Thomas, July 17, 1868 (*CP5*:268).

125 **Tilden . . . surprised as anyone**: Tilden to F. Kernan, n.d., ca. late July 1868, in Bigelow, *Tilden Letters*, 1:239–240.

125 **Van Buren had warned Chase**: Van Buren to SPC, June 25, 1868 (*CP5*:244).

125 **"setting back against you"**: Van Buren to SPC, July 2, 1868, quoted in Coleman, *Election of 1868*, 223–224.

126 **"was on every man's tongue . . . no man's heart"**: Coleman, *Election of 1868*, 231, quoting *The Independent* (New York), July 16, 1868.

126 **movement to replace Seymour**: Blue, 299–300; Coleman, *Election of 1868*, 344–359; Flick, *Samuel Jones Tilden*, 186–188.

126 **not really sought . . . could honorably give up politics**: SPC to Elizur Wright, July 9, 1868 (*CP5*:260–261); SPC to Murat Halstead, July 14, 1868 (*CP5*:266–267); SPC to Daniel Butterfield, July 2, 1869 (*CP5*:311–312).

126 **Douglass . . . welcomed to Chase's dinner table**: Douglass, *Life and Times of Frederick Douglass*, 317.
126 **"any of his predecessors in treachery"**: *National Anti-Slavery Standard*, July 18, 1868, quoted in *CP5*:271n4.
126 **"ambition was consuming . . . his nature"**: *New York Times*, July 11, 1868.
126 **"disgusting . . . overweening desire"**: Oberholtzer, *Jay Cooke*, 2:68.
126 **shorn of . . . respect**: Foraker, "Address on Chase," 34.
127 **interview in 1893**: *San Francisco Morning Call*, Oct. 15, 1893.
127 **"acting too much the politician"**: SPC to KC, July 7, 1868 (*CP5*:259).
127 **"Mrs. Sprague's disappointment . . . wife of William Sprague"**: Didier, "Salmon P. Chase," 184.

## Chapter 14: "I Almost Hate This Man"

128 **"Well my old friend . . . more than I can bear"**: KC Diary, Nov. 4, 1868, BUL.
129 **"there can be but one head to a family"**: SPC to KC, Aug. 9, 1868 (*Pegasus*, 380).
129 **Kate found a satisfying occupation**: KC to SPC, Oct. 5, 1868 (*Pegasus*, 382–383).
129 **horse riding accident**: *New York Times*, Oct. 9, 1868.
129 **"a simple act . . . I respect"**: KC Diary, Nov. 4, 1868, BUL.
129 **"Sometimes I have almost . . . it is heavy"**: Ibid.
129 **"remembering it is . . . inflicted it"**: Ibid.
130 **Fanny Kemble**: Catherine Clinton, *Fanny Kemble's Civil Wars* (2000; repr., Oxford: Oxford University Press, 2000), 9–11, 135–138, 140, 142, 146–156.
130 **"What a lifetime . . . I feel for Mrs. K"**: Ross, 115–116.
130 **"which if true . . . life for us?"**: KC Diary, Nov. 4, 1868, BUL.
130 **"some little token . . . dirty boor"**: KC Diary, Nov. 11, 1868, BUL.
130 **"a matter of wonder . . . title to the name"**: Ibid.
130 **"William thinks . . . disappointment"**: KC Diary, Nov. 4, 1869, BUL.
131 **"far superior . . . every way"**: Villard, *Memoirs*, 1:175.
131 **"beautiful and intellectual . . . my full appreciation"**: WS to KC, June 8, 1866, BUL.
131 **compare Kate to Fanny Sprague**: WS to Willie Sprague, Nov. 15, 1877, CHS.
131 **"interfere . . . think fit"**: Lucia Gilbert Calhoun, ed., *Modern Women and What Is Said About Them* (New York, 1868), 146–147.
132 **"vapid, flippant . . . dispense with"**: Ibid., 102–103.
132 **December . . . southern business trip**: *Cleveland Plain Dealer*, Dec. 17, 1868; *New York Times*, Dec. 23, 26, 1868, Jan. 10, 11, 15, 1869; *Alexandria (VA) Gazette*, Dec. 31, 1868; Henry W. Hilliard to SPC, Dec. 5, 1868, Henry Washington Hilliard Papers, Duke University, David M. Rubenstein Rare Book and Manuscript Library, Durham, NC; *Commercial Advertiser* (New York), Jan.

5, 1869; *Anderson Intelligencer* (Anderson Court House, SC), Jan. 28, 1869; *Macon (GA) Weekly Telegraph*, Feb. 12, 1869.

132 **"long and pleasant sojourn"**: KC Diary, Dec. 27, 1868, BUL.

132 **Tiffany jewel . . . "was a bitter disappointment"**: Ibid.

132 **"he would think me . . . my humiliations"**: Ibid.

133 **few blocks away**: Sprague's office was at 3 Exchange Place in Providence, now Kennedy Plaza. *Providence City Directory*, 1868 (Providence, 1868), 191.

## Chapter 15: "She's Capable of Hitting Him"

134 **told almost no one**: SPC to KC, Sept. 15, 1869 (*Pegasus*, 394–395); Niven, 443.

134 **Grant . . . and Fish**: Jacob, *Capital Elites*, 87–88, 98–99.

134 **"Her reign is undisputed"**: Ellet, *Court Circles*, 581.

135 **"Nothing . . . you *can't* do"**: Viall, *The Merchant's Wife*, 40.

135 **in his usual . . . manner**: *New York Herald*, Mar. 20, 1869.

135 **went on to attack**: Sprague gave a series of five lengthy Senate speeches, on March 15, 19, 24, and 30, and April 8, 1869. *Cong. Globe*, 41st Cong., 1st Sess. 64–66, 156–161, 242–246, 358–363, 613–624 (1869) (hereafter cited as *Cong. Globe*).

135 **indictment of the radical**: *Harrisburg (PA) Patriot*, Mar. 26, 1869; *Charleston (SC) Daily News*, Apr. 2, 1869; *Cleveland Plain Dealer*, Apr. 6, 1869.

135 **"aggressive and spirited . . . invisible woes"**: *Alexandria (VA) Gazette*, Apr. 7, 1869.

135 **"highly eccentric verbal pyrotechnics"**: *Montana Post* (Helena), May 7, 1869.

135 **petition for women's suffrage**: *Cong. Globe* 204 (Mar. 23, 1869).

135 **"any other . . . world"**: Ibid.

135 **produced laughter**: *Cong. Globe* 159 (Mar. 19, 1869).

136 **visitors . . . frivolous**: Ibid., 243 (Mar. 24, 1869).

136 **"wine . . . our exact situation"**: Ibid., 475 (Apr. 3, 1869).

136 **"would rather . . . bayonets"**: Ibid., 157 (Mar. 19, 1869).

136 **"aroused . . . to their affairs"**: Ibid., 614 (Apr. 8, 1869).

136 **"Americans who travel . . . their own society"**: *Cong. Globe* 361 (Mar. 30, 1869).

136 **"Where is there . . . with satisfaction?"**: Ibid., 245 (Mar. 24, 1869).

136 **"any more virtue . . . less luxuriant quality"**: Ibid., 243 (Mar. 24, 1869).

136 **looking up at Kate**: *Cleveland Plain Dealer*, Apr. 9, 1869.

136 **"the pallor of her icily-beautiful face"**: *Frank Leslie's Illustrated Newspaper*, Apr. 24, 1869, 82.

136 **"It was like . . . her parasol"**: Viall, *The Merchant's Wife*, 41–42.

137 **Kate . . . in Aiken**: *Pegasus*, 393n2; *New York Herald*, Apr. 6, 1869; *Charleston (SC) Daily News*, Apr. 17, 1869.

137 **"sorely tried . . . unkind acts"**: SPC to KC, Apr. 15, 1869 (*CP5*:298).

137 **"that out . . . peace for you"**: SPC to KC, Apr. 17, 1869 (*Pegasus*, 385).
137 **"You have both erred . . . on your side"**: Ibid., 386.
137 **"Overcome . . . transparently truthful"**: SPC to KC, May 4, 1869 (*CP5*: 303–304).
137 **"much of your trial . . . yourself"**: SPC to KC, Apr. 15, 1869 (*CP5*:298).
137 **"I don't want . . . human Species"**: SPC to KC, Apr. 17, 1869 (*Pegasus*, 386).
137 **Leary . . . "avoid all . . . evil tongues"**: SPC to KC, Apr. 26, 1869 (*Pegasus*, 388–389 and n5).
137 **warning had not been "in distrust"**: SPC to KC, May 4, 1869 (*CP5*:303).
138 **package of letters . . . to search his pockets**: Ibid., 304.
138 **bore her second child**: SPC to KC, Nov. 7, 1869 (*Pegasus*, 397–398); genealogy note, Chase LC; burial record for Ethel Chase Sprague Donaldson, no. 119183, Spring Grove Cemetery, Cincinnati, www.springgrove.org/stats/119183.tif.pdf (birth date Oct. 23, 1869).
138 **"Esbelle"**: Genealogy note, Chase LC.
138 **remained friends with Crosby**: An unidentified man who closely resembles Crosby was photographed with Kate during a visit to Mount Vernon, Washington's home, in the late 1880s or early 1890s. Photographs, possession of Aura Carr and Ann Donaldson, viewed by the author.
138 **Crosby**: 4 *Dictionary of American Biography*, 568–569; "John Schuyler Crosby," *Find a Grave*, Sept. 2, 2005, www.findagrave.com/cgi-bin/fg.cgi?page=gr&GRid=11663805; *New York Times*, Aug. 9, 1914.
138 **fighting Indians**: *Philadelphia Evening Telegraph*, Nov. 5, 1868; *Holt County Sentinel* (Oregon, MO), Dec. 11, 1868; *New York Herald*, Jan. 5, 1869; *Warren (OH) Western Reserve Chronicle*, Jan. 13, 1869; *Public Ledger* (Memphis, TN), Mar. 11, 1869; *Emporia (KS) News*, Mar. 12, 1869; *National Republican* (Washington, DC), Mar. 13, 1869.
138 **Maine woods**: *Cincinnati Daily Gazette*, Jan. 18, 1869; *Daily Eastern Argus* (Portland, ME), Jan. 19, 1869; *New York Times*, Jan. 31, 1869; *Commercial Advertiser* (New York), Feb. 26, 1869.
139 **"fond of the ladies"**: WS to KC, Apr. 14, 1866, CHS.
139 **"a very fine . . . no other women here?"**: SPC to WS, May 2, 1869, Chase LC, reel 28.
139 **"Harriet Brown . . . at Washington"**: *New York Times*, Dec. 20, 1880.
139 **no longer . . . "loving me and trusting me"**: SPC to KC, Oct. 1, 1869 (*Pegasus*, 397).
139 **he and Nettie were moving**: Ibid., 396–397.
139 **"Edgewood"**: Niven, 443; Phelps, 230–231; SPC to KC, Nov. 7, 1869 (*CP5*:319–320 and nn2–3); *Washington Star*, Oct. 7, 1882; *Washington Times*, Sept. 12, 1894; *New York Herald*, Aug. 6, 1899; Michael J. Henderson and Karin Bleeg, webmasters, "History," *Edgewood Neighborhood, Washington, D.C.*, www.edgewooddc.org/id12.html.
140 **hundreds of admiring letters**: *Cong. Globe* 745–776 (Apr. 22, 1869).
140 **"I don't exactly comprehend his views"**: SPC to NC, Apr. 12, 1869 (*CP5*:297).

140 **"for, if I am not mistaken . . . ambitious for him"**: SPC to KC, Apr. 15, 1869 (*CP5*:299).

140 **"can be summed up . . . more greenbacks.'"**: Briggs, *Olivia Letters*, 113.

140 **"the inspired Cassandra . . . disaster"**: *Pittsfield (MA) Sun*, Apr. 15, 1869.

140 **"somewhat long . . . malady called craziness"**: *New York Herald*, Apr. 16, 1869.

140 **serenaded**: *Manufacturers' and Farmers' Journal* (Providence, RI), Apr. 15, 1869; Chafee, "Weathering the Panic," 276.

141 **Sprague-for-President**: *New York Herald*, Apr. 16, 1869.

141 **"both as parties are rotten"**: Ibid.

141 **"a Sprague Party . . . Chase Sprague Party"**: Henry T. Johns to WS, Aug. 14, 1869, CHS; Marion D. Shutter and John S. McLain, eds., *Progressive Men of Minnesota* (Minneapolis, 1897), s.v. "Henry T. Johns."

141 **"pukes . . . mutton head"**: *New York Herald*, Apr. 16, 1869.

141 **"mongrel puppy . . . mastiff"**: *Cong. Globe* 745, 776 (Apr. 22, 1869); *National Republican* (Washington, DC), Apr. 23, 1869; *New-York Tribune*, Apr. 23, 1869.

141 **mediators averted**: *Memphis Daily Appeal*, Apr. 27, 1869; SPC to KC, Apr. 26, 1869 (*CP5*:300); Chafee, "Weathering the Panic," 276.

141 **"Little Spraguey . . . put to bed"**: *New York Herald*, Apr. 23, 1869.

141 **sharp rebuke . . . "dog and pup" story**: SPC to KC, Apr. 29, 1869 (*Pegasus*, 389–390).

## Chapter 16: Some Dared Call It Treason

142 **"I do not see . . . or South?"**: Mary Lincoln to Mrs. J. H. Orne, Feb. 18, 1870, quoted in Carl Sandburg, *Mary Lincoln: Wife and Widow* (1932; repr., New York: Harcourt, Brace, 1960), 294–295.

142 **"truly kind-hearted"**: Ibid., 295.

142 **"the Governor . . . every night"**: SPC to NC, Oct. 15, 1870 (*Pegasus*, 400).

143 **"most laborious and trying"**: KC to Clinton Rice, Oct. 14, 1870, Pierpont Morgan Library Dept. of Literary and Historical Manuscripts, New York.

143 **"a solitary existence . . . tears"**: Didier, "Personal Recollections of Chief-Justice Chase," 313–314.

143 **Nettie . . . lacking discipline . . . erratic**: Maria Eastman to SPC, June 23, 1862 (*Pegasus*, 198); Mary Macaulay to SPC, Sept. 9, 1863 (*Pegasus*, 227).

143 **tried to set up**: KC to Hay, Feb. 21, 1871, CHS; NC to Hay, Dec. 17, 1872, CHS.

143 **"more art . . . than the *ainée*"**: Dennett, *Lincoln and the Civil War*, 297.

143 **"more universally . . . haughty sister"**: *New York World*, Feb. 20, 1870.

143 **Nettie's recently released book**: Ibid.; *New York World*, Mar. 24, 1871; *Pegasus*, 16, 57n68; *The Publishers' Weekly* 10 (July–Dec. 1876): 840; [Janet Ralston Chase Hoyt], *Janet et ses Amis* (New York: D. Appleton, 1876).

143 **"old maidism and forty cats"**: NC to KC, Feb. 15, 1864 (*Pegasus*, 251).

143 **"a very nice girl . . . no end of cash"**: John Hay to John Bigelow, Mar. 12, 1871, in John Bigelow, *Retrospections of an Active Life* (Garden City, NY: Doubleday, Page, 1913), 4:480. See also *New York World*, Mar. 24, 1871.

144 **"In the darkest days . . . munitions of war"**: *Providence Journal*, Oct. 31, 1870.

145 **Grant and Sherman**: David G. Surdam, "Traders or Traitors: Northern Cotton Trading during the Civil War," *Business and Economic History* 28, no. 2 (Winter 1999): 301, 308–309; William T. Sherman to SPC, Aug. 11, 1862, in *Memoirs of Gen. William T. Sherman* (New York, 1889), 1:294–296.

145 **Lincoln . . . more liberal**: Surdam, "Traders or Traitors," 302–303; Ludwell H. Johnson, *Red River Campaign: Politics and Cotton in the Civil War* (1958; repr., Kent, OH: Kent State University Press, 1993), 3–5.

145 **as moderate as possible**: Niven, 258; Blue, 167, 169; SPC to Ulysses S. Grant, July 4, 1863 (*CP4*:75); SPC to William P. Mellon, July 4, 1863 (*CP4*:76).

145 **"given to *anyone* . . . general rush?"**: WS to SPC, June 23, 1863, Chase LC, reel 3. See also Jonathan D. Sarna, *When General Grant Expelled the Jews* (New York: Schocken Books, 2012), 31–32.

145 **treasury agents . . . Chase did little to probe**: Surdam, "Traders or Traitors," 301, 305, 309; Johnson, *Red River Campaign*, 53–54, 59–64, 70; Niven, 353–354.

145 **Blair . . . attack on Chase**: Niven, 346–351; Albert Gallatin Riddle, *Recollections of War Times: Reminiscences of Men and Events in Washington, 1860–1865* (New York, 1895), 266–269; SPC to Jay Cooke, May 5, 1864 (*CP4*:379–380).

145 **Chase edited . . . special privileges**: *Cong. Globe*, 38th Cong., 1st Sess. 3543 (July 4, 1864); SPC Diary, June 27, July 4, 1864 (*CP1*:465, 475).

145 **"a union man . . . a few goods"**: WS to SPC, Oct. 14, 1862 (*CP3*:297). The development and carrying out of the plan are described in detail in US Senate, 41st Cong., 3rd Sess. 1870–1871, *Senate Executive Document vol. 1, no. 10* (Washington, DC, 1871) (hereafter cited as *SED*).

146 **had broken off relations**: *SED* pt. 3:24.

146 **Hoyt . . . others were arrested**: US Naval War Records Office, "Report of Commander Guest . . . of the Capture of the British Schooner *Sybil*," Nov. 21, 1864, in *Official Records of the Union and Confederate Navies in the War of the Rebellion, Series I–Vol. 11: North Atlantic Blockading Squadron, Oct. 28, 1864–Feb. 1, 1865* (Washington, DC: GPO, 1900), 80; *SED* pt. 2:1–6, pt. 3:46–47, 58–60.

146 **confidential statement . . . disappeared**: *SED* pt. 1:1–2, pt. 2:1–2, 4, pt. 3:1; S. Rep. No. 377, 41st Congress, 3d Sess. 9, 14, 16 (Mar. 3, 1871) (hereafter cited as S. Rep. 377).

146 **"mistaken information . . . unjust suspicion"**: S. Rep. 377:5–6.

146 **"nothing . . . implicating Senator Sprague"**: S. Rep. 377:18.

146 **fictionalized scene**: Gore Vidal, *Lincoln* (New York: Random House, 1984), 600; *Lincoln*, dir. by Lamont Johnson (1988; Chris/Rose Productions and The Finnegan/Pinchuck Co.; A Vision Entertainment, 1993 video).

## Chapter 17: End of an Era

148 ***carte de visite***: NC to KC, Nov. 27, 1861 (*Pegasus*, 189).
148 **looked like her "noble" father**: NC to KC, [Nov.] 1861 (*Pegasus*, 187).
148 **Nettie turned to Kate for advice**: Ibid.; NC to KC, Nov. 27, 1861 (*Pegasus*, 189).
148 **spelling . . . "perfect"**: KC to NC, July 25, 1860 (*Pegasus*, 174).
148 **"quietly and affectionately"**: SPC Diary, Mar. 15, 1865 (*CP1*:522).
148 **"be *very* kind . . . her thoughtlessness"**: SPC to KC, Mar. 28, 1865 (*Pegasus*, 264).
148 **"Katie thinks . . . for clothing"**: SPC to Mary Macaulay, Oct. 21, 1863 (*Pegasus*, 233).
149 **rector to object**: *Albany Argus*, Mar. 25, 1871; Richard F. Grimmett, *St. John's Church, Lafayette Square: The History and Heritage of the Church of the Presidents, Washington, D.C.* (Minneapolis: Mill City Press, 2009), 65–66.
149 **"objectionable features . . . most inexcusable way"**: Grimmett, *St. John's Church*, 66–67.
150 **Nettie . . . filmy white gown**: *New York World*, Mar. 24, 1871; *New York Herald*, Mar. 24, 1871; *Albany Argus*, Mar. 25, 1871.
150 **"if possible . . . more graceful than ever"**: *New York World*, Mar. 24, 1871.
150 **"Why would he not . . . this emergency?"**: Parsons to SPC, Feb. 16, 1871 (*CP5*:342).
150 **Tower Hill House**: Oliver H. Stedman, *A Stroll Though Memory Lane with Oliver H. Stedman: Stories of South County's Past* (West Kingston, RI: Kingston Press, 1978), 2:78.
150 **"I fear . . . things yet"**: KC to SPC, Aug. 29, 1871 (*Pegasus*, 418).
150 **"I want Grandpa . . . hurrah for Chase"**: Ibid., 418–420 and nn10–11.
150 **"advocating a Mutual friend . . . serve his Country"**: Ibid., 418.
151 **Kate's third child**: SPC to NC, Feb. 4, 1872 (*Pegasus*, 422–423 and nn1–2); Sokoloff, 194.
151 **inherited her mother's beauty . . . mental disability**: Phelps, 241; Ross, 230; Sokoloff, 202, 282; *Washington Herald*, July 7, 1910; *Washington Tribune*, July 21, 1910; Willie Sprague to KC, Sept. 7, 1880, BUL.
151 **April 1872 . . . reception**: Niven, 447–448; *New York Herald Tribune*, Apr. 26, 1872; *San Francisco Bulletin*, May 17, 1872; SPC Diary, Apr. 25, 1872 (*CP1*:677); *Springfield (MA) Republican*, Nov. 26, 1877.
151 **"futile efforts . . . pathetically evident"**: Schurz, *Reminiscences*, 2:187.
151 **same old line**: SPC to M. C. C. Church, Mar. 26, 1872; SPC to Flamen Ball, Apr. 8, 1872, in Warden, 728–729.
151 **Sprague . . . poured money**: *Cincinnati Daily Gazette*, June 2, 1877.
152 **Chase entertained some hope**: SPC Diary, May 29, 1872 (*CP1*:685).
152 **"continued to nurse . . . bestowed upon him"**: Schurz, *Reminiscences*, 2:187.
152 **"arose more . . . his own"**: Brinkerhoff, *Recollections*, 118.
152 **"her . . . wild ambition"**: *Cincinnati Daily Gazette*, June 2, 1877.

152 **Greeley had become . . . eccentric**: Jean Edward Smith, *Grant* (New York: Simon & Schuster, 2001), 548.

152 **"an easy, worthless race . . . the morrow"**: Ibid., 549.

153 **Greeley opposed giving women the vote**: Robert C. Williams, *Horace Greeley: Champion of American Freedom* (New York: NYU Press, 2006), 274–278; Gustafson, *Women and the Republican Party*, 45–51.

153 **to Kate, Greeley's policies**: *Frank Leslie's Illustrated Newspaper*, Apr. 24, 1872; Ross, 226.

153 **Chase . . . massive stroke . . . funeral**: Schuckers, 622–625; *New York Times*, May 8, 13, 1873; *New-York Tribune*, May 13, 1873; *Cincinnati Daily Gazette*, May 8, 1873; *Oregon State Journal* (Eugene, OR), May 24, 1873.

154 **"great financiers in our history"**: "Eulogy on Chief-Justice Chase, Delivered by William M. Evarts, before the Alumni of Dartmouth College, at Hanover, June 24, 1874" (New York, 1874), 17.

154 **"join . . . Liberty"**: SPC to C. Cleveland, Oct. 22, 1841 (*CP*2:80).

154 **started a biography**: *Salt Lake Herald*, June 16, 1889; *Pittsburgh Dispatch*, July 27, 1890; *San Francisco Morning Call*, Jan. 31, 1891.

154 **cooperate only with . . . Schuckers**: Frederick Blue, "Kate's Paper Chase: The Race to Publish the First Biography of Salmon P. Chase," *The Old Northwest* 8, no. 4 (Winter 1982–1983): 353–363.

154 **"distress of returning . . . my dear father"**: KC to John Nicolay, Nov. 3, 1876, quoted in Beldens, 276.

155 **"she seemed to die in his death"**: Piatt, *Memories of the Men*, 131. See also *Saline (KS) County Journal*, July 24, 1873.

## Chapter 18: End of an Empire

156 **$18,000 French silk dress**: *Macon (GA) Weekly Telegraph*, Aug. 1, 1871; *Memphis Daily Appeal*, Aug. 8, 1871.

156 **floral ornament**: *Chicago Sunday Times*, Mar. 9, 1873; *Annapolis (MD) Gazette*, Mar. 18, 1873.

156 **issued a blank check**: Ernest M. Hoyt, "Historical Sketch of St. Peter's by-the-Sea of Narragansett, Rhode Island, 1852–1956" (Narragansett, 1956), 9.

156 **$250,000 . . . Kate's children**: *Rapides Gazette* (Alexandria, LA), July 27, 1872; Phelps, 241.

157 **Cooke's bank had gone bust . . . Panic of 1873**: Oberholtzer, *Jay Cooke*, 2:419–439; Smith, *Grant*, 575.

157 **Sprague's company . . . collapse**: *New-York Tribune*, Oct. 31, 1873; *New York Times*, Nov. 1, 2, 1873; Chafee, "Weathering the Panic," 276–278; Carroll, *Rhode Island*, 2:762–764, 863–864; Capers Jones, *The History and Future of Narragansett Bay* (Boca Raton, FL: Universal Publishers, 2006), 216.

157 **fiscal policies caused**: Oberholtzer, *Jay Cooke*, 2:431.

158 **trusteeship . . . Sprague . . . an employee**: Carroll, *Rhode Island*, 2:764–765; Chafee, "Weathering the Panic," 277–284, 288; *New York Times*, Nov. 2, 1873.

158 **an allowance for her**: KC to George Riggs, Nov. 1875, BUL; *Providence Journal*, Aug. 14, 1879; *New York Times*, Dec. 20, 1880.

158 **Kate . . . named Kitty last**: Certification of Vital Record for Portia Sprague Browning, State of Rhode Island (b. Nov. 3, 1873); Certificate of Death for Katherine Chase Sprague, Government of the District of Columbia, Dept. of Health, No. 193.106 (age 38 at June 22, 1910); 1880 US Census, Washington, DC, *Ancestry.com*, records for Kitty Sprague and Portia Sprague (Kitty age 8, Portia age 6 at June 12, 1880).

158 **Portia was named . . . grandfather**: Kate once explained that she wanted Portia "to bear a name that would recall my father's, for he was dead then, and I loved and admired him more than anything else on earth." *Sacramento Daily Record-Union*, Aug. 28, 1886.

159 **rift . . . Kate and Nettie . . . Edgewood**: Clarkson N. Potter to KC, Sept. 14, 1874, BUL; NC to KC, Sept. 20, Oct. 13, 1874, BUL; KC to NC, Oct. 13, 1874, BUL; WS to Clarkson N. Potter, Oct. 28, Nov. 4, 1874, BUL; KC to J. Ralston Skinner, Jan. 1875, May 5, 1875, CHS; Clarkson N. Potter to KC, May 3, 1875, BUL; WS to Clarkson N. Potter, Nov. 15, Dec. 13, 1875, BUL; KC to NC, Nov. 22, 1875, BUL; KC to Clarkson N. Potter, Nov. 22, 1875, BUL; Sokoloff, 200–206.

159 **put up for auction**: Phelps, 242–243; Ross, 236–237.

159 **"little people . . . Locusts"**: KC to George Riggs, Nov. 1875, BUL.

159 **"of unbalanced intellect . . . any business"**: Chafee, "Weathering the Panic," 288.

159 **"with the strength of intellect"**: *Daily Graphic* (New York), Jan. 29, 1874.

160 **"created on purpose to diminish their husbands"**: *Daily Graphic* (New York), Nov. 20, 1873.

160 **defying . . . Grant . . . sole Republican**: Smith, *Grant*, 581–582; James Ford Rhodes, *History of the United States from the Compromise of 1850 to the Final Restoration of Home Rule at the South in 1877* (New York: Macmillan, 1906), 7:71n2.

160 **withdrew from the Republican caucus**: *New York Times*, Mar. 4, 1875.

160 **"a brave . . . at present staggering"**: KC to William T. Sherman, Jan. 22, 1875, BUL.

160 **"a rare fund . . . time for his work"**: KC to Amasa Sprague, May 26, 1875, BUL.

160 **"peculiar and difficult . . . hope lies in him"**: KC to Will Hoyt, Dec. 2, 1875, BUL.

161 **modest little apartment**: KC to George Riggs, Nov. 1875, BUL.

161 **"Why is this not . . . Faithfully always your wife"**: KC to WS, Dec. 2, 1875, BUL.

162 **"with the same . . . the lawyers"**: Viall, *The Merchant's Wife*, 42–43.

162 **"No more . . . listen to him"**: Ibid., 39.

162 **"great fires . . . statesman's daughter"**: Ibid., 6, 8, 39.

162 **"The expression . . . somewhat calculating"**: Ibid., 4.

162 **"malachite clock . . . traces of himself"**: Ibid., 3, 6.
162 **"willing never . . . reunited one day"**: Ibid., 21–22, 29.

## Chapter 19: "Intended by Their Creator for Each Other"

163 **turned down . . . chief justice**: Conkling explained that he would be "forever gnawing at [his] chains" if he accepted the judicial position. *The Autobiography of Thomas Collier Platt*, ed. Louis J. Lang (New York: B. W. Dodge, 1910), 68.

163 **Conkling . . . most powerful man**: David M. Jordan, *Roscoe Conkling: Voice in the Senate* (Ithaca, NY: Cornell University Press, 1971), 3–5, 11, 35–36, 110, 143, 145; Platt, *Autobiography*, 55; Chauncey M. Depew, *My Memories of Eighty Years* (New York: Charles Scribner's, 1922), 79.

164 **"veritable bird of paradise"**: Robert C. Byrd, *The Senate: 1789–1989*, ed. Mary Sharon Hall (Washington: GPO, 1988), 1:319; Chidsey, *Gentleman from New York*, 119.

164 **"turkey gobbler strut"**: Jordan, *Roscoe Conkling*, 80.

164 **Conkling was an orator**: Ibid., 12, 144, 181–182, 258; Chidsey, *Gentleman from New York*, 39, 151; *Cleveland Plain Dealer*, May 1, 1879; James Dabney McCabe, *Behind the Scenes in Washington* (New York, 1873), 158–159.

165 **widespread rumors . . . estranged early on**: Chidsey, *Gentleman from New York*, 116; Jordan, *Roscoe Conkling*, 13–14, 51–52, 145, 164–165; *Utica Press*, Oct. 19, 1893.

165 **young daughter, Bessie**: 1870 US Census, Utica, Ward 4, Oneida, New York, *Ancestry.com*, record for Roscoe Conkling; Jordan, *Roscoe Conkling*, 20, 51.

165 **"Even to be invited . . . one man"**: Chidsey, *Gentleman from New York*, 118.

165 **"these two people . . . for each other"**: Hamilton Gay Howard, *Civil-War Echoes: Character Sketches and State Secrets* (Washington, DC: Howard Pub. Co., 1907), 130.

165 **attended Grant's inaugural balls**: *New York World*, Mar. 24, 1871; *Roanoke (VA) Times*, Aug. 12, 1891; *Chicago Times*, Mar. 9, 1873; *Oregon State Journal* (Eugene, OR), May 24, 1873; Ross, 235–236; Jordan, *Roscoe Conkling*, 213; Jacob, *Capital Elites*, 113.

165 **sources contend**: Jordan, *Roscoe Conkling*, 205; Phelps, 243–244; Ross, 231–232. More recently, author Peg Lamphier makes the case that Kate's affair with Conkling did not start until her return from Europe in the fall of 1876. Lamphier, 136–137, 145, 149. Sokoloff, alone among Kate's biographers, dismisses the claim of an affair as based on nothing more than rumor and gossip. Sokoloff, 249–250, 305n32.

165 **hanging around . . . infatuated**: *Oregon State Journal* (Eugene, OR), Oct. 4, 1879.

165 **1875 or early 1876**: *Cincinnati Daily Gazette*, Aug. 12, 1879.

166 **dinner party . . . early 1878**: *New York Evening Press*, Sept. 1, 1879.

166 **February 1878**: *Cleveland Plain Dealer*, Feb. 18, 1878; Phelps, 247.

166 **election . . . 1876 . . . tasked his man Conkling**: Smith, *Grant*, 598–602; John Bigelow, *The Life of Samuel J. Tilden* (New York, 1895), 2:60–61, 83–84, and n1.

166 **Conkling had thrown his support to Hayes**: Kenneth D. Ackerman, *Dark Horse: The Surprise Election and Political Murder of President James A. Garfield* (New York: Carroll & Graf, 2003), 74.

166 **"snivel service" reform**: Peskin, *Garfield*, 453.

167 **Conkling barely lifted a finger**: Ari Hoogenboom, *Rutherford B. Hayes: Warrior and President* (Lawrence: University Press of Kansas, 1995), 271–272, 280–281; Roy J. Morris, *Fraud of the Century: Rutherford B. Hayes, Samuel J. Tilden, and the Stolen Election of 1876* (New York: Simon & Schuster, 2003), 99–106, 209–210.

167 **electoral commission . . . no one knew**: Jordan, *Roscoe Conkling*, 256; Smith, *Grant*, 601–602; Peskin, *Garfield*, 415–416; Flick, *Samuel Jones Tilden*, 381–382.

167 **"Senator Conkling . . . a speech"**: Hudson, *Random Recollections*, 23.

167 **"From one . . . habits of you boys"**: Ibid., 22.

167 **she revealed to him Conkling's plans**: Ibid., 22–23.

168 **"egotistical coxcomb"**: Welles, *Diary*, 3:558.

168 **"vain . . . czar in arrogance"**: Chidsey, *Gentleman from New York*, 40.

168 **ace poker playing**: Howard, *Civil-War Echoes*, 43–47.

168 **"pursued . . . slaughtered"**: Chidsey, *Gentleman from New York*, 147.

168 **"powers of sarcasm . . . vital spot"**: Crowley, *Echoes from Niagara*, 191.

168 **"with a spirit . . . ordinary men"**: Perrine, "The Dashing Kate Chase," 12.

168 **"once again . . . in order"**: Jordan, *Roscoe Conkling*, 258–259.

169 **Garfield rejoiced**: Peskin, *Garfield*, 416.

169 **party-line votes . . . to support the Democrats**: Jordan, *Roscoe Conkling*, 259–262; Hoogenboom, *Hayes*, 288, 290; Alexander K. McClure, *Our Presidents and How We Make Them* (New York: Harper & Brothers, 1900), 268–269; *Louisiana Democrat* (Alexandria, LA), Mar. 7, 1877.

169 **Conkling was nowhere**: Hoogenboom, *Hayes*, 290; McClure, *Our Presidents*, 269; *Louisiana Democrat* (Alexandria, LA), Mar. 7, 1877.

169 **friends felt deceived**: Bigelow, *Retrospections*, 5:301.

169 **supposedly to visit friends**: Jordan, *Roscoe Conkling*, 261–262.

169 **to summon Conkling**: Hudson, *Random Recollections*, 23.

170 **"open secret . . . Mrs. Sprague"**: McClure, *Our Presidents*, 269.

170 **"I got even . . . for defeating my father"**: Simon Wolf, *The Presidents I Have Known from 1860–1918* (Washington, DC: Press of Byron S. Adams, 1918), 101.

170 **"utter fantasy" . . . Hayes promised**: Jordan, *Roscoe Conkling*, 262 and n26.

170 **meeting at Wormley's**: Peskin, *Garfield*, 418; Hoogenboom, *Hayes*, 292.

170 **Kate's biographers**: Sokoloff, 229; Lamphier, 151.

170 **"I know . . . quicker than mine"**: Peacock, *Famous American Belles*, 213–214.

170 **"perfectly true" . . . 2 a.m. meeting**: Bigelow, *Tilden Letters*, 2:511–513.

171 **Hoadly disputed . . . admitted he was unaware**: Ibid.

171 **she was in Washington**: Sokoloff, 230; *Vicksburg (MS) Daily Commercial*, Mar. 24, 1877.
171 **the sole basis . . . Hoadly's great fondness**: Bigelow, *Tilden Letters*, 2:513.

## Chapter 20: "Mrs. Conkling Is Not Here This Winter"

172 **Kate and . . . Conkling both went to Europe**: Jordan, *Roscoe Conkling*, 274–275; *National Republican* (Washington, DC), July 7, Dec. 21, 1877; *Saline (KS) County Journal*, Aug. 30, Oct. 18, 1877; *Inter Ocean* (Chicago), Aug. 11, 1877; *New-York Tribune*, Aug. 11, 1877; Roscoe Conkling to Bessie Conkling, July 11, 1877, Conkling LC; *Cleveland Plain Dealer*, Sept. 3, 1877.
172 **February 1877**: *New York Times*, Dec. 20, 1880.
172 **"Your Mama thinks . . . times a day"**: KC to Willie Sprague, Feb. 10, 1877, BUL.
172 **"beau boy . . . bear's cubs"**: KC to Willie Sprague, Jan. 13 [or 18], 1877, BUL.
173 **criticized her handwriting . . . needed to pursue his Latin and German**: KC to Willie Sprague, Apr. 20, 1879, BUL.
173 **after making his corrections**: SPC to NC, Nov. 23, 1863 (*CP4*:197).
173 **"I shall send . . . *on my list*"**: KC to Willie Sprague, Apr. 30, 1879, BUL.
173 **"throw away . . . useless things"**: Ibid.
173 **"'The apparel . . . shows for himself"**: KC to Willie Sprague, Jan. 13 [or 18], 1877, BUL.
173 **"Indeed, at your age . . . by a good deal"**: WS to Willie Sprague, Nov. 15, 1877, CHS.
173 **"rigid" mother . . . "constantly reminding . . . when you come home"**: Ibid.
174 **exhausted and haggard**: *New-York Tribune*, Aug. 11, 1877; Jordan, *Roscoe Conkling*, 274.
174 **investigation . . . Custom House**: Jordan, *Roscoe Conkling*, 270–274, 287, 292, 297–301; Thomas C. Reeves, *Gentleman Boss: The Life and Times of Chester Alan Arthur* (Newtown, CT: American Political Biography Press, 1975), 62–63, 73, 87–88, 112–123, 145–148.
174 **she sublet Edgewood to . . . Schurz**: *National Republican* (Washington, DC), July 7, 1877; *Saline (KS) County Journal*, Aug. 30, Oct. 18, 1877; *Inter Ocean* (Chicago), Aug. 11, 1877.
174 **"He had not read . . . never be enforced"**: *New York Herald*, Aug. 6, 1899.
174 **wrote President Hayes a warm letter**: KC to Hayes, May 23, 1877, CHS.
174 **"very nervous . . . touched by others"**: Alfred R. Conkling, *The Life and Letters of Roscoe Conkling: Orator, Statesman, Advocate* (New York, 1889), 44.
175 **hero's welcome . . . torchlight parade**: *New-York Tribune*, Aug. 11, 1877; *Utica Daily Observer*, Aug. 15, 1877; *Daily Critic* (Washington, DC), Aug. 15, 1877; *Cincinnati Commercial*, Aug. 17, 1877.
175 **"a starry canopy . . . no city like Utica"**: *Utica Daily Observer*, Aug. 15, 1877.
175 **Worth costume**: Note from Phelps UM.

175 **bracelet with an inscription**: possession of Aura Carr, viewed by the author.
175 **"land of the Rhine"**: *New-York Tribune*, Aug. 11, 1877.
175 **giving weekly receptions**: *New-York Tribune*, Jan. 23, 1878.
176 **"gave a new light . . . his face"**: *Independent* (New York), Feb. 28, 1878.
176 **"Mr. Conkling would write . . . the answer"**: *Cincinnati Daily Gazette*, Aug. 12, 1879.
176 **Her reply . . . "a deep flush of pleasure"**: Ibid.
176 **she was his mistress**: Jacob, *Capital Elites*, 111.
176 **"Senator Conkling and the fair lady . . . say of us'"**: *Springfield (MA) Republican*, May 13, 1878.
176 **"the scandal-mongers . . . very free way"**: *Idaho Avalanche* (Owyhee, ID), June 1, 1878.
176 **ejectment suit**: *Brooklyn Eagle*, June 9, 1878; Chafee, "Weathering the Panic," 289.
177 **"a selfish politician . . . her will"**: *Cleveland Plain Dealer*, May 28, 1879.
177 **she could evict**: *New-York Tribune*, June 6, 1878.
177 **Miss Grundy saw**: *Springfield (MA) Republican*, May 13, 1878.
177 **"Mrs. Sprague is a born diplomat . . . haughtily aside"**: *Cincinnati Daily Gazette*, May 25, 1878.
177 **"heard distinctly . . . where I was"**: KC to Willie Sprague, Mar. 26, 1878, BUL.
177 **Conkling had dined with her**: Ibid.
177 **Fanny Sprague . . . visit**: Sokoloff, 220–221; Lamphier, 156.
177 **Willie's return**: KC to Willie Sprague, July 18, 1878, BUL.
177 **"disgraceful orgy"**: *Providence Journal*, Aug. 14, 1879.
178 **drunk and disorderly**: *Indianapolis Daily Sentinel*, Dec. 28, 1880; *Warren (MN) Sheaf*, Mar. 16, 1881.
178 **agricultural academy . . . regressed**: KC to Willie Sprague, Feb. 28, Apr. 20, 1879, BUL; *New York Sun*, Sept. 3, 1879; Sokoloff, 222–223.
178 **"liberally furnished . . . filled it himself"**: KC to Willie Sprague, Mar. 30, 1879, BUL.
178 **"inspired more . . . his loves"**: Peskin, *Garfield*, 452–453.
178 **escorted . . . Bruce**: Blanche Kelso Bruce to Roscoe Conkling, Sept. 21, 1879, Conkling LC; Nicholas Patler, "A Black Vice President in the Gilded Age? Senator Blanche Kelso Bruce and the National Republican Convention of 1880," *The Journal of Mississippi History* (Summer 2009): 106–116; Stanley Turkel, *Heroes of the American Reconstruction: Profiles of Sixteen Educators, Politicians and Activists* (Jefferson, NC: McFarland, 2005), 34–35.
178 **"Excuse me . . . my name is Conkling"**: Patler, "A Black Vice President," 112–113.
178 **named him**: *New York Times*, May 20, 1879; Turkel, *Heroes*, 35.
178 **"He never said . . . we all run!"**: Briggs, *Olivia Letters*, 420.
178 **"Mrs. Conkling . . . Mrs. Kate Sprague"**: *Ohio Democrat* (New Philadelphia, OH), Feb. 20, 1879.

179 **"all the Washington peasantry"**: *Weekly Kansas Chief* (Troy, KS), Apr. 3, 1879.
179 **"the most open . . . social transaction"**: *Indianapolis Daily Sentinel*, Nov. 8, 1879.
179 **Bessie was getting married**: *New York Times*, May 1, 1879.
179 **"a worthy gentleman," possessed little wealth**: Ibid.
179 **Conkling disapproved of Oakman**: Jordan, *Roscoe Conkling*, 313.
179 **Oakman**: *New York Times*, May 1, 1879, Mar. 19, 1922; *National Cyclopedia of American Biography*, 3:58.
179 **refused to invite Kate**: *Sedalia (MO) Weekly Bazoo*, Mar. 15, 1881.
179 **daughter sided with mother**: *Cleveland Plain Dealer*, Feb. 18, 1880.
179 **owed $3,700**: *Indianapolis Daily Sentinel*, May 9, 1879.
179 **"unjust bill"**: *Cleveland Plain Dealer*, May 28, 1879.
179 **"the Mrs. Sprague bill"**: *Boston Evening Journal*, June 20, 1878.
179 **Conkling who got the bill passed . . . limited the exemption**: *Indianapolis Daily Sentinel*, May 9, 1879; Chafee, "Weathering the Panic," 289; Beldens, 300.
180 **"all the thugs . . . incite them"**: Jordan, *Roscoe Conkling*, 303–304.
180 **Kate watching from the gallery . . . stormy scene**: *Inter Ocean* (Chicago), June 21, 26, 1879; *New York Times*, June 20, 1879; Jordan, *Roscoe Conkling*, 307.
180 **"a falsehood . . . man would wear"**: Jordan, *Roscoe Conkling*, 305–306.
180 **Kate . . . nearly fainted**: Jordan, *Roscoe Conkling*, 307; Sokoloff, 226.
181 **Kate was still there**: *Inter Ocean* (Chicago), June 26, 1879.
181 **Hayes . . . signed it**: *New York Times*, June 21, 24, 1879; Hoogenboom, *Hayes*, 400–402.
181 **no duel**: Jordan, *Roscoe Conkling*, 307; *New York Times*, June 20, 21, 1879; *Anderson Intelligencer* (Anderson Court House, SC), July 3, 1879.
181 **"exceedingly rich! . . . quite so red"**: Jordan, *Roscoe Conkling*, 307.
181 **Kate would later deny . . . "warm personal friend"**: *New York Sun*, Aug. 17, 1879.
181 **rumor was insistently denied**: *New York Sun*, Aug. 11, 1879; *Cincinnati Daily Gazette*, Aug. 12, 1879; Jordan, *Roscoe Conkling*, 296.
181 **made his animosity clear**: *New York World*, Aug. 13, 1879; *New York Sun*, Aug. 13, 1879.

## Chapter 21: "The Now Notorious Outbreak"

182 **senator landed . . . husband was not expected**: *New York Times*, Aug. 12, 19, 1879; *Cincinnati Enquirer*, Aug. 13, 1879; *New York World*, Aug. 10, 11, 12, 1879; *Cincinnati Commercial Tribune*, Aug. 14, 1879; *New York Sun*, Aug. 16, 1879.
182 **sleepy little village**: *A Guide to Narragansett Bay: Newport, Narragansett Pier . . . and All the Famous Resorts Along the Shore* (Providence, 1878), 5–6,

48–52 (hereafter cited as *Guide to Narragansett Bay*); Carroll, *Rhode Island*, 2:1173.

182 **railroad was extended**: James N. J. Henwood, *A Short Haul to the Bay: A History of the Narragansett Pier Railroad* (Brattleboro, VT: Stephen Greene Press, 1969), 5–12; WS to Willie Sprague, Nov. 17, 1876, CHS.

182 **her husband adjust his affairs**: *Providence Journal*, Aug. 11, 14, 1879; *Cincinnati Enquirer*, Aug. 11, 1879.

183 **were sketched**: Charles Stanley Reinhart, "On the Beach," cover of *Harper's New Monthly Magazine* 59, no. 350 (July 1879).

183 **Conkling stayed . . . through Thursday**: *New York World*, Aug. 11, 1879; *New York Sun*, Aug. 13, 17, 1879; *Narragansett Times*, Aug. 15, 1879; *Cincinnati Enquirer*, Aug. 13, 1879. Seventy-year-old Enos Thompson Throop Martin and his wife, Cornelia, were friends of Roscoe Conkling. *Narragansett Herald*, Aug. 16, 1879; *New York Sun*, Aug. 17, 1879.

183 **promenading around Narragansett**: *Cincinnati Enquirer*, Aug. 12, 1879.

183 **hired a German professor . . . off to Canonchet**: *Providence Journal*, Aug. 11, 1879; *New York Sun*, Aug. 12, 1879.

183 **Sprague objected to . . . tutor**: *New York Times*, Aug. 16, Sept. 2, 1879; *New York Sun*, Aug. 13, 16, 17, Sept. 3, 1879.

183 **ordered Linck off his property**: *Providence Journal*, Aug. 11, 1879.

184 **bearded professor . . . "prime of life"**: *Narragansett Herald*, Aug. 23, 1879; *New York Sun*, Aug. 16, Nov. 27, 1879.

184 **now bearded himself**: *Narragansett Herald*, Aug. 23, 1879.

184 **"mixed up and muddled"**: *Providence Journal*, Aug. 11, 1879.

184 **"If I find you . . . take my word for it"**: Ibid.

184 **Linck . . . at a boardinghouse**: Ibid.; *New York Times*, Aug. 12, 16, 1879.

184 **"on important business" . . . drove off with the coachman**: *New York Sun*, Aug. 16, 1879.

184 **"The Governor . . . the information"**: *Providence Journal*, Aug. 11, 1879.

185 **"was not prepared . . . out of harm's way"**: *Providence Journal*, Aug. 11, 1879.

185 **"scarcely anything . . . family matter"**: *New York Sun*, Aug. 11, 1879.

185 **"on some legal business"**: *New York Times*, Aug. 10, 1879.

185 **he was in the library . . . "like a wild man"**: *New York Sun*, Aug. 11, 1879.

185 **Conkling took the train . . . Fifth Avenue Hotel**: Ibid.; *Cincinnati Enquirer*, Aug. 11, 1879.

185 **"The report . . . no foundation whatever"**: *New York Sun*, Aug. 11, 1879.

186 **"too thin"**: *Washington Post*, Aug. 11, 1879.

186 **failed to mention Conkling**: *New York Times*, Aug. 13, 1879; *Cincinnati Enquirer*, Aug. 13, 1879.

186 **political enemy of Sprague**: Carroll, *Rhode Island*, 2:695; Lamphier, 113, 122, 168–169.

186 **also Conkling's good friend**: *New York Times*, Aug. 13, 1879.

186 **business partner of Conkling**: *Cincinnati Daily Gazette*, Aug. 15, 1879; Charles Dana, *Recollections of the Civil War, with the Leaders at Washington*

*and in the Field in the Sixties* (New York: D. Appleton, 1902), 17; James Harrison Wilson, *The Life of Charles Dana* (New York: Harper & Brothers, 1907), 195, 380.

186 **Conkling had helped write**: *New York Times*, Aug. 13, 1879; *Brooklyn Eagle*, Aug. 13, 1879.

186 **Linck went to the *Journal*'s office**: *New York Times*, Aug. 12, 13, Sept. 2, 1879; *New York Sun*, Aug. 13, 1879.

186 **Kate called on him**: *New York World*, Aug. 13, 15, 1879; *Narragansett Herald*, Aug. 16, 1879.

186 **made numerous substantive changes**: *New York Times*, Aug. 16, Sept. 1, 1879; *Cincinnati Enquirer*, Aug. 19, 1879.

186 **"No German Teacher Concerned"**: *New York World*, Aug. 11, 1879.

186 **"Sprague's Shotgun . . . My Lord Roscoe"**: *Cincinnati Enquirer*, Aug. 13, 1879.

186 **"Professor Conkling . . . missing Link"**: *St. Paul Daily Globe*, Aug. 14, 1879.

187 **in Newport visiting a friend**: *New York World*, Aug. 12, 13, 1879; 15 *ANB* 953; *Guide to Narragansett Bay*, 73.

187 **"for I will not . . . tall row"**: *New York World*, Aug. 13, 1879; *Cincinnati Commercial Tribune*, Aug. 14, 1879.

187 **custom of dueling**: *New York World*, Aug. 10, 12, 1879.

187 **just missed Conkling**: *New York World*, Aug. 12, 1879.

187 **Carrying a trunk and large valise**: *New York World*, Aug. 11, 1879; *New York Times*, Aug. 12, 1879.

187 **Conkling arrived at Narragansett**: *New York Times*, Aug. 12, 1879; *Cincinnati Enquirer*, Aug. 13, 1879; *New York World*, Aug. 10, 1879. Kate and Linck said he arrived on Wednesday. *New York Sun*, Aug. 16, 17, 1879.

187 **Sprague returned unexpectedly**: *New York World*, Aug. 11, 1879; *New York Sun*, Aug. 13, 16, 1879; *Cincinnati Enquirer*, Aug. 13, 1879; *Cincinnati Daily Gazette*, Aug. 15, 1879.

187 **tipped him off**: Nicholas R. Brewer, *Trails of a Paintbrush* (Boston: Christopher Publishing House, 1938), 159.

187 **he got up early . . . went to a restaurant**: *Cincinnati Enquirer*, Aug. 13, 1879; *New York Sun*, Aug. 13, 15, 16, 1879.

187 **Sprague was inebriated**: *New York Times*, Aug. 13, 1879; *New York Sun*, Aug. 15, 16, 1879.

187 **"sober but dreadfully in earnest"**: *New York Times*, Aug. 13, 1879.

187 **got himself worked up**: *New York Sun*, Aug. 15, 17, 1879.

187 **confrontation . . . with Linck . . . and Conkling**: *Providence Journal*, Aug. 11, 1879; *New York Sun*, Aug. 13, 16, 17, 1879; *Cincinnati Enquirer*, Aug. 13, 15, 1879; *New York Times*, Aug. 14, Sept. 2, 1879; *Narragansett Times*, Aug. 15, 1879.

188 **ordered Conkling to leave**: *New York Times*, Aug. 12, Sept. 2, 1879; *Cincinnati Enquirer*, Aug. 13, 1879.

188 **five minutes**: *New York World*, Aug. 11, 1879; *Cincinnati Enquirer*, Aug. 12, 1879.

188 **thirty seconds**: *New York Sun*, Aug. 17, 1879.
188 **was debunked**: *New York World*, Aug. 11, 1879.
188 **Conkling left . . . waited at Billington's**: *New York Sun*, Aug. 13, 1879; *Cincinnati Enquirer*, Aug. 13, 1879.
188 **drove his carriage into town**: *New York Sun*, Aug. 13, 17, 1879; *Cincinnati Daily Gazette*, Aug. 12, 1879.
188 **something exciting**: *New York Times*, Aug. 13, 1879; *Cincinnati Enquirer*, Aug. 13, 1879.
188 **"Have you not gone . . . I shall kill you"**: *New York Sun*, Aug. 13, 1879; see also *New York Times*, Sept. 2, 1879.
188 **inside Billington's . . . strolled the beach**: *New York Sun*, Aug. 13, 1879; *New York Times*, Aug. 13, 1879; *Cincinnati Enquirer*, Aug. 13, 1879.
189 **she and the girls would spend the night**: *Cincinnati Daily Gazette*, Aug. 12, 1879; *Narragansett Times*, Aug. 15, 1879; *Narragansett Herald*, Aug. 16, 1879.
189 **short walk to the depot . . . worked with Danielson**: *Cincinnati Enquirer*, Aug. 11, 13, 1879; *New York Sun*, Aug. 13, 1879; *Providence Journal*, Aug. 9, 1879; *New York Times*, Aug. 13, 1879.
189 **"less irritable than usual"**: *New York Times*, Aug. 13, 1879.
189 **"For what reason . . . seeks to do it here"**: *New York Times*, Aug. 12, 1879.
189 **When pressed . . . would know why**: Ibid.
189 **The only wonder**: *Brooklyn Eagle*, Aug. 12, 1879.
189 **Conkling . . . scandals**: *St. Paul Daily Globe*, Aug. 14, 1879; *Cincinnati Daily Gazette*, Aug. 12, 1879.
189 **Dick Nevins**: *St. Paul Daily Globe*, Aug. 14, 1879; *Cincinnati Enquirer*, Aug. 13, 1879.
189 **"decided in their opinion . . . greatly provoked"**: *New York Times*, Aug. 16, 1879.
189 **not "so flagrant . . . the affair"**: *Brooklyn Eagle*, Aug. 13, 1879.
189 **"has the sympathy . . . the people"**: *Cincinnati Enquirer*, Aug. 12, 1879.
189 **"the weight of expression . . . attempted to do"**: Ibid., quoted in Sokoloff, 237.
190 **private letter to a friend**: *Providence Journal*, Aug. 14, 1879.
190 **"As you must have surmised . . . murder to be done"**: Ibid.
190 **"absurd . . . in the newspapers"**: Ibid.
191 **"The design . . . turned against her"**: *New York Times*, Aug. 16, 1879.
191 **Some have assumed**: Sokoloff, 241–242; Lamphier, 171.
191 **"we presume . . . unavoidable"**: *Cincinnati Commercial Tribune*, Aug. 15, 1879.
191 **"no longer his property"**: *New York Times*, Aug. 16, 1879.
191 **"talked to him . . . stronger way"**: *Cincinnati Enquirer*, Aug. 19, 1879.
191 **he could no longer recognize it**: *New York Times*, Sept. 1, 1879.
192 **"not . . . cat's paw of"**: *New York Sun*, Aug. 16, 1879.
192 **"found ridiculous by Mrs. Sprague"**: Ibid.

192 **husband should be the one**: Ibid.
192 **"his wife's persistency . . . her point"**: Ibid.
192 **"proud spirit" not gotten in the way**: *New York Sun*, Aug. 17, 1879.
192 **"for his senseless . . . that only"**: Ibid.
192 **living in seclusion**: *New York Sun*, Aug. 13, 15, 1879; *New York Times*, Aug. 14, 1879.
192 **"never sleep . . . again"**: *New York Sun*, Aug. 15, 1879.
192 **ill-advised summit meeting**: *New York Sun*, Aug. 15, 1879; *New York World*, Aug. 15, 1879.
192 **to the nearby cottage**: *New York Sun*, Aug. 15, 1879; *New York World*, Aug. 15, 1879; *New York Times*, Aug. 16, 1879.
192 **cousin, Ralston Skinner**: *New York Sun*, Aug. 15, 16, 1879; *New York World*, Aug. 15, 1879; Sokoloff, 242–243; Lamphier, 174–175; *Pegasus*, 455.
192 **"This is your work . . . and painful"**: *New York World*, Aug. 15, 1879.
192 **"tissue of falsehoods"**: *New York Sun*, Aug. 15, 1879.
192 **accused her of poisoning the minds**: Ibid.; *New York World*, Aug. 15, 1879.
192 **"general brutality . . . alcohol"**: *New York Sun*, Aug. 15, 1879.
192 **"Where is that $5,000 . . . squandered all that"**: *New York Sun*, Aug. 17, 1879. See also *New York World*, Aug. 15, 1879; *New York Times*, Aug. 16, 1879.
193 **"Your man . . . didn't he?"**: *New York Sun*, Aug. 17, 1879.
193 **bore these remarks**: Ibid.; *New York World*, Aug. 15, 17, 1879.
193 **"I fear . . . you are safe"**: *New York Sun*, Aug. 15, 1879. See also *New York World*, Aug. 15, 1879.
193 **loaded pistol**: *New York Sun*, Aug. 16, 17, 1879.
193 **he merely acknowledged**: *New York World*, Aug. 15, 1879.
193 **demands for surrender of the children**: *New York Sun*, Aug. 15, 16, Sept. 1, 1879; *New York Times*, Aug. 16, 1879.
193 **"deeply wrapped up"**: *New York Times*, Aug. 16, 1879.
193 **"soothing and comforting"**: *New York Times*, Sept. 2, 1879.
193 **to follow them to Canonchet**: *New York Sun*, Aug. 15, 1879.
193 **in the mansion overnight . . . refused to allow**: *New York Sun*, Aug. 15, 16, Sept. 1, 1879; *New York World*, Aug. 15, 1879.
193 **"Is His Wife . . . lock and key"**: *New York Sun*, Aug. 16, 1879.
193 **opening every telegram**: Ibid.
194 **sympathetic maid**: *New York Sun*, Aug. 17, 1879.
194 **denied that Kate was a prisoner**: *New York Sun*, Aug. 17, Sept. 1, 2, 1879; *New York World*, Sept. 2, 1879; *New York Times*, Sept. 2, 1879.
194 **"prevent her communication . . . hostile to him"**: *New York Sun*, Aug. 17, 1879.
194 **story was overblown**: *Cincinnati Enquirer*, Aug. 19, 1879.
194 **keeping his wife composed . . . better understanding**: *New York Sun*, Aug. 17, 1879.
194 **Sprague greeted him cordially**: Ibid.

194 **Watson, a younger relative**: *New York Sun*, Aug. 17, Sept. 3, 1879. A local businessman, twenty-nine-year-old Watson, was married to the daughter of William Sprague's cousin Byron.
194 **elegantly furnished suite**: *New York Sun*, Aug. 17, 1879.
194 **"extremely pale . . . trace of agitation"**: Ibid.
194 **"with a degree . . . most obdurate"**: Ibid.
194 **"I have sent . . . no reason to fear the truth"**: Ibid.
195 **"For thirteen . . . none for years"**: Ibid.
195 **"whole miserable affair . . . a child"**: *New York Sun*, Aug. 17, 1879.
195 **"who has not . . . should have been"**: Perrine, "The Dashing Kate Chase," 12, 30.
195 **"There is not a word of truth . . . his monomania"**: *New York Sun*, Aug. 17, 1879.
195 **"How did . . . under the circumstances?"**: Ibid.
196 **"He came . . . for that purpose"**: Ibid.
196 **Sprague disputed . . . *Times* dismissed it**: *New York Times*, Aug. 19, 1879.
196 **room on the third floor**: *New York Sun*, Aug. 17, 1879.
196 **"I paid no attention . . . disquieting manner"**: Ibid.
196 **"He walked slowly . . . whatever the consequences"**: Ibid.
196 **"spoke in a very calm voice . . . lead to violence"**: Ibid.
196 **"'Don't go . . . desperate way"**: Ibid.
196 **"Mr. Sprague took his gun . . . kill them sure'"**: Ibid.
196 **best not to give them**: Ibid.
196 **"reason to be grateful that no one was murdered"**: Ibid.
197 **Sprague himself admitted**: *Cincinnati Enquirer*, Aug. 13, 1879; *New York World*, Aug. 15, 1879; *New York Sun*, Aug. 17, 1879.
197 **"the story . . . with it"**: *Cleveland Plain Dealer*, Dec. 24, 1880.
197 **"the yarn . . . whole cloth"**: *New York Herald*, Dec. 23, 1880.
197 **"sensibly silent"**: *New York World*, Aug. 18, 1879.
197 **leaving it to representatives**: *Cincinnati Enquirer*, Aug. 13, 1879; *New York Sun*, Aug. 17, 1879.
197 **"another falsehood . . . disapproved of it"**: *New York Sun*, Aug. 17, 1879.
197 **approved by Conkling**: *New York Times*, Aug. 13, Sept. 1, 1879.
197 **"apocryphal"**: *New York Times*, Sept. 2, 1879.
197 **"not consistent"**: *New York World*, Sept. 2, 1879.
198 **"outrageous slanders . . . the persecution"**: *New York Sun*, Aug. 17, 1879.
198 **"she looks . . . man's standpoint"**: *Indianapolis Daily Sentinel*, Nov. 8, 1879.
198 **Beecher's adultery**: Applegate, *Most Famous Man*, 382–383, 395–397, 402–408, 442–464.
198 **"lucky dog"**: Beldens, 297.
198 **"peculiarly tempted . . . excuse it"**: SPC to KC, Aug. 13, 1850 (*Pegasus*, 83).
199 **"more sinned against than sinning"**: *Cincinnati Enquirer*, Aug. 13, 1879.
199 **"vain Senator . . . nor the manliness"**: *New York Times*, Aug. 21, 1879.
199 **accompanied by a loyal servant**: *New York Sun*, Sept. 1, 1879.
199 **surveillance system . . . in constant fear**: Ibid.

199 **started sending jewelry**: *New York Times*, Sept. 2, 1879; *New York World*, Sept. 2, 1879.
199 **Sprague knew**: *New York Times*, Sept. 2, 1879; *Narragansett Herald*, Sept. 6, 1879.
199 **wanted to eject Sprague . . . Chafee objected**: *New York Sun*, Aug. 16, 1879; *New York Times*, Aug. 19, 1879.
199 **tried to throw her out window**: *New York Sun*, Sept. 1, 1879.
199 **"Leave and take . . . your daughters"**: *Daily Arkansas Gazette* (Little Rock), Oct. 7, 1879.
199 **closeted at Canonchet**: *Cincinnati Daily Gazette*, Nov. 15, 1880.
199 **Kate arranged for**: *New York Sun*, Sept. 5, 1879.
200 **next morning, Saturday**: Ibid.; see also *New York World*, Sept. 2, 1879.
200 **sensing a conspiracy . . . Jerome Greene**: *Cincinnati Daily Gazette*, Nov. 15, 1880; *Providence Journal*, July 28, 1906.
200 **matters looked smooth enough**: *New York World*, Sept. 2, 1879; *Cincinnati Daily Gazette*, Nov. 15, 1880.
200 **Sprague walked to the beach**: *New York Sun*, Sept. 5, 1879.
200 **to the rear of the house**: Ibid.

## Chapter 22: "The Bird Has Flown"

201 **Morris the overseer**: *New York Times*, Aug. 12, 13, 1879.
201 **Ernest the black cook**: *New York Times*, Sept. 2, 1879; *New York Sun*, Sept. 3, 1879.
201 **Watson**: *New York Sun*, Aug. 17, Sept. 3, 1879.
201 **took their flight**: *New York World*, Sept. 2, 1879; *New York Times*, Sept. 2, 1879; *New York Sun*, Sept. 1, 3, 5, 1879; *Narragansett Herald*, Sept. 6, 13, 1879; *Cincinnati Daily Gazette*, Nov. 15, 1880; *Providence Journal*, n.d., ca. 1935, "Gaius Smith Saw It All That Night at Canonchet," CHS.
202 **Sitting alone in her carriage**: *New York Sun*, Sept. 3, 5, 1879; *Narragansett Herald*, Sept. 6, 1879.
202 **Sprague had been catnapping**: *New York Sun*, Sept. 3, 1879.
202 **"The bird has flown"**: *New York World*, Sept. 2, 1879.
203 **went over to Tower Hill House**: *New York Sun*, Sept. 1, 3, 1879; *New York Times*, Sept. 2, 1879.
203 **in a speedy yacht**: *New York Sun*, Sept. 1, 1879; *Narragansett Herald*, Sept. 6, 1879.
203 **steamer to Europe**: *New York Times*, Sept. 2, 1879.
203 **bound for Boston**: *New York Times*, Sept. 2, 1879; *New York World*, Sept. 2, 1879; *New York Sun*, Sept. 3, 5, 1879.
203 **as much in his possession**: *New York Times*, Sept. 2, 1879.
203 **race all over the country**: *New York Sun*, Sept. 3, 1879.
203 **"surreptitiously"**: *New York World*, Sept. 2, 1879.
203 **sent Willie to carry a note**: *Cincinnati Daily Gazette*, Sept. 2, 1879.

203 **went on to deny . . . well provided with money**: *New York World*, Sept. 2, 1879; *New York Times*, Sept. 2, 1879; *New York Sun*, Sept. 3, 1879.
203 **transferred $5,000**: *New York Times*, Aug. 19, 1879.
204 **unfrequented road to Wickford**: *New York Sun*, Sept. 5, 1879; *Cincinnati Daily Gazette*, Nov. 15, 1880; *Narragansett Herald*, Sept. 13, 1879.
204 **land at Bristol . . . home of Austin Corbin**: *New York Sun*, Sept. 5, 1879; *Cincinnati Daily Gazette*, Nov. 15, 1880; *New York World*, Sept. 2, 1879; *New York Herald*, Dec. 23, 1880.
204 **Corbin harbored Kate**: 5 *ANB* 498–499; *New York Times*, June 5, 1896; *New York Herald*, Dec. 23, 1880.
204 **"would have made . . . molest them"**: *New York Herald*, Dec. 23, 1880.
204 **way back to Edgewood**: *Washington Post*, Sept. 20, 1879.
204 **petition to appoint a trustee . . . Thompson**: *New York Sun*, Sept. 6, 27, 1879; *New York Times*, Oct. 20, 1880.
205 **"the salacious . . . this transaction"**: *Columbus (NE) Journal*, Aug. 20, 1879.
205 **Hillsboro**: *Pegasus*, 452; *CP*2:425n1.
205 **"such as no . . . any other man"**: *Highland Weekly News* (Hillsboro, OH), Aug. 28, 1879.
205 **"maligned . . . totally innocent"**: *Washington Post*, Sept. 20, 1879.
205 **"because I was a woman . . . not unmerited"**: Ibid.
205 **ostracism she faced postshotgun**: McLean Hazen Dewey, "Memoir," 134–135; *New York World*, Mar. 16, 1900; *Big Stone Post* (Big Stone Gap, VA), May 15, 1891.
206 **"that his career . . . then and there"**: *Cincinnati Commercial Tribune*, Aug. 12, 1879.
206 **"exposure of Conkling's . . . only bad"**: Hoogenboom, *Hayes*, 408.
206 **"treasure" . . . no detriment**: WS to SPC, May 31, 1863 (*CP*4:50).
206 **"as if he . . . dreadful innuendoes"**: *New York Times*, Aug. 16, 1879.
207 **most widely advertised tutor**: *New York World*, Aug. 12, 1879.
207 **he ended up suing Kate**: *Cleveland Plain Dealer*, Nov. 26, 1879; *Washington Post*, Nov. 27, 1879; *New Ulm (MN) Weekly Review*, Dec. 3, 1879.
207 **avoided paying for some professional photographs**: *Alton (IL) Telegraph*, May 29, 1879; Chafee, "Weathering the Panic," 289.
207 **"She travels . . . her children"**: *New York Sun*, Nov. 27, 1879.
207 **reserved decision**: Ibid.

## PART THREE: KATE CHASE AGAIN

### Chapter 23: "A Dinner with the Queen"

211 **dinner party . . . press saw through the event**: *Lancaster (PA) Daily Intelligencer*, Jan. 26, 27, 29, 1880; *St. Paul Daily Globe*, Jan. 29, Feb. 17, 1880; *Cleveland Plain Dealer*, Feb. 18, 1880.
211 **"the suppliant air . . . Mrs. Conkling"**: *St. Paul Daily Globe*, Jan. 29, 1880.

211 **"Mrs. Conkling does not pretend . . . his request"**: *St. Paul Daily Globe*, Feb. 17, 1880.

211 **write Kate a letter**: Ibid.; *Cleveland Plain Dealer*, Feb. 18, 1880.

212 **"brutality of Conkling . . . Mrs. Sprague appeared"**: William Henry Smith, notes of Aug. 9, 1890, meeting with Rutherford B. Hayes, William Henry Smith Papers, Rutherford B. Hayes Presidential Center, Fremont, OH.

212 **"I made up . . . and suffering"**: John Hay to Clara Stone Hay, Jan. 19, 1880, in *Books at Brown, 1988–1989, Vols. 35–36, John Hay Sesquicentennial*, ed. Jennifer B. Lee (Providence: Friends of the Library of Brown University, 1990), 113.

212 **"A Dinner with the Queen . . . English language"**: Briggs, *Olivia Letters*, 403–408.

212 **"bring the old . . . governor of Rhode Island"**: Ibid., 404.

213 **went incognito, with the sister-in-law**: KC to Chester Alan Arthur, June [4], 1880, Arthur LC. Kate identified "Miss Corbett," her traveling companion, as Richard Crowley's "sister," but she was probably Crowley's sister-in-law. See Blake v. Crowley and Corbitt, 12 N.Y.S. 650 (1887); 1850 US Census, Lockport, Niagara, New York, *Ancestry.com*, records for Julia Corbit[t] and Isabella Corbit[t].

213 **good friends of Kate . . . entertained her**: Crowley, *Echoes from Niagara*, 90–102, 188–189, 192–193; *St. Paul Daily Globe*, May 13, 1883.

213 **"When asked what state . . . apple tree"**: Jordan, *Roscoe Conkling*, 334–336.

214 **"the Trickster of Mentor"**: Ackerman, *Dark Horse*, 128.

214 **"funereal" voice**: *New York World*, June 9, 1880.

214 **"immortal 306 . . . Old Guard"**: Peskin, *Garfield*, 476–177; Ackerman, *Dark Horse*, 115–116.

214 **small breastpins**: *Morning Star* (Glens Falls, NY), May 5, 1893.

214 **wearing her "306" pin**: *Macon (GA) Telegraph*, Aug. 5, 1886.

214 **"Mrs. Sprague . . . Comment unnecessary"**: *New Haven (CT) Register*, Nov. 10, 1880.

214 **"Mrs. Sprague suddenly appeared"**: *Kansas City Star*, Oct. 28, 1880.

214 **together at Pierce's Palace**: *Lancaster (PA) Daily Intelligencer*, Nov. 5, 1880; *St. Paul Daily Globe*, Nov. 23, 1880.

214 **"positive proof . . . many years"**: *St. Paul Daily Globe*, Nov. 23, 1880.

214 **reported, falsely**: *Salt Lake Herald*, Aug. 27, 1880; *Los Angeles Herald*, Aug. 27, 1880.

214 **"Were not your lungs . . . cure them?"**: Willie Sprague to KC, Sept. 7, 1880, BUL.

## Chapter 24: "As Much Alone as Cleopatra"

216 **found the house barricaded**: *New York Sun*, Nov. 5, 1880.

216 **"shot down like a cur"**: *Kansas City Star*, Oct. 28, 1880.

216 **Britton left**: *Cincinnati Commercial Tribune*, Nov. 1, 1880; *New York Sun*, Nov. 5, 1880.

216 **Willie allegedly fired a pistol**: *New York Times*, Nov. 7, 9, 14, 1880; *New York Sun*, Nov. 14, 1880; *Providence Journal*, Nov. 15, 1880.

216 **"for fun"**: *New York Sun*, Nov. 14, 1880.

216 **"long-haired bushwhackers . . . enjoyed his discomfiture"**: Ibid.

217 **"frequently attempted . . . maiden name, Katherine Chase"**: *New York Times*, Dec. 20, 1880; Lamphier, 253–256, app. A.

218 **"improper intimacy . . . and at hotels"**: *National Republican* (Washington, DC), Jan. 28, 1881; Lamphier, 257–258, app. B.

218 **"little better . . . strumpet"**: *The Globe* (Atchison, KS), Jan. 28, 1881.

218 **"infamous lie . . . received from him"**: *Wheeling (WV) Register*, Dec. 27, 1880.

218 **offering to apologize**: *Macon (GA) Telegraph and Messenger*, Jan. 25, 1881. In June 1880 the Irish-born Mrs. McCue was still living as a housekeeper at Canonchet, married to "farm overseer" Morriss McCue, almost certainly the property overseer mentioned in newspaper articles at the time of the shotgun incident. 1880 US Census, South Kingstown, Washington, RI, *Ancestry.com*, record for Elizabeth McCue. The McCues had a nine-month-old child at the time, which may have aroused Kate's suspicions.

218 **Jerome Greene**: *Providence Journal*, July 28, 1906.

218 **"thought to be dead . . . charges in person"**: *Wheeling Register*, Dec. 27, 1880. Mary Viall would live to age sixty-seven, dying in 1908. Rhode Island Deaths, 1630–1930, *Ancestry.com*, record for Mary E. Anderson.

219 **"a breaker . . . law of God"**: *Los Angeles Herald*, Dec. 8, 1880.

219 **"God may have . . . never did"**: *Warren (PA) Ledger*, Jan. 14, 1881.

219 **"You have no idea . . . social queens"**: Ibid.

220 **"likely to effectually squelch . . . strut"**: *Indianapolis Daily Sentinel*, Mar. 18, 1881.

220 **"the chief force . . . Sprague case"**: *Springfield (MA) Daily Republican*, Mar. 12, 1881.

220 **"follow him and expose him"**: *Omaha Daily Bee*, Jan. 18, 1881.

220 **"an interesting story . . . Senator Conkling"**: *Indianapolis Daily Sentinel*, Dec. 28, 1880.

220 **writing for the *New-York Tribune* . . . savaged Conkling**: Taliaferro, *All the Great Prizes*, 133, 141, 158–159, 199–200, 202–203.

220 **"until you fight them *dead* . . . kept peaceable"**: Reeves, *Gentleman Boss*, 211.

220 **"peacock . . . his own wife"**: Shaw, *Lucretia*, 96.

220 **children had become good friends**: KC to Willie Sprague, Feb. 28, Apr. 20, 30, 1879, BUL; Ruth Stanley-Brown Feis, *Mollie Garfield in the White House* (Chicago: Rand McNally, 1963), 62.

220 **still the vacillator of years past**: Jordan, *Roscoe Conkling*, 360–361, 368–372; Ackerman, *Dark Horse*, 229–240; Crowley, *Echoes from Niagara*, 194–195.

220 **"How willing Garfield was . . . save the day!"**: Jordan, *Roscoe Conkling*, 354.

221 **three-way contest**: Reeves, *Gentleman Boss*, 209–210; Jordan, *Roscoe Conkling*, 363–366; Crowley, *Echoes from Niagara*, 195–198; Ackerman, *Dark Horse*, 242–244.

221 **"Chet" Arthur**: Reeves, *Gentleman Boss*, 33, 40–41, 68, 85, 190, 273.

221 **"well-fed Briton"**: Ibid., 85.

221 **"last man . . . any company"**: Ibid., 72.

221 **"master in all the arts . . . 'best society.'"**: Depew, *My Memories*, 116.

221 **"The Ohio men . . . majority of the delegation"**: Hudson, *Random Recollections*, 96–99.

222 **"*Strictly Confidential*"**: KC to Chester Arthur, Jan. 10, 1881, Arthur LC.

222 **"mutual friend . . . man to man"**: Ibid.

222 **"But my dear . . . long run?"**: Ibid. Lamphier reads the word before "Mr. Crowley" as "independent" and a possible reference to Crowley's Catholicism. Lamphier, 207–208. I believe the word is "improvident," which also squares with the *New York Times*' reference to Crowley's "absolute indifference to the value of money. He has spent several fortunes and is today poor, although he has always had a lucrative law practice." *New York Times*, Aug. 21, 1895.

222 **"too small . . . decorate the Senate"**: KC to Arthur, Jan. 10, 1881, Arthur LC.

222 **"Could anything . . . autocratic Senator?"**: *Sacramento Daily Record-Union*, Jan. 3, 1881.

222 **"would be to think Cleopatra . . . poisoned by one"**: Crowley, *Echoes from Niagara*, 206.

222 **continued to socialize**: *Fort Worth Daily Gazette*, Mar. 18, 1883; *Saline (KS) County Journal*, May 3, 1883; *St. Paul Daily Globe*, May 13, 1883.

223 **"never much for ideology . . . ignored more substantive problems"**: Jordan, *Roscoe Conkling*, 434, 437.

223 **"crush him . . . which it is to be"**: KC to Arthur, Jan. 10, 1881, Arthur LC.

223 **strike a deal . . . promptly elected**: Reeves, *Gentleman Boss*, 210–211; Ackerman, *Dark Horse*, 243–244; Crowley, *Echoes from Niagara*, 198–199; Depew, *My Memories*, 111–112; *New York Times*, Jan. 14, 1881, Aug. 21, 1895.

223 **never had to apologize**: *New York Times*, Jan. 14, 1881; Platt, *Autobiography*, 142.

223 **dinner party . . . Stalwarts**: *Los Angeles Herald*, Apr. 9, 1881; *Salt Lake Herald*, Apr. 5, 1881.

223 **in the Senate gallery**: Poore, *Perley's Reminiscences*, 2:404; *Brooklyn Eagle*, Apr. 10, 1881; Briggs, *Olivia Letters*, 401.

224 **infuriated some cabinet wives**: *Kalamazoo (MI) Gazette*, Apr. 17, 1881.

224 **"care-worn . . . more subdued style than usual"**: *Carbon Advocate* (Lehighton, PA), Apr. 9, 1881.

224 **"she smiles . . . half a dozen others"**: *Brooklyn Eagle*, Apr. 10, 1881.

224 **"cold, stately . . . dusky Nile"**: Briggs, *Olivia Letters*, 399–400.

224 **"history is full . . . the Empress Eugénie"**: Ibid., 401.

224 **Pryor**: *New York Sun*, Feb. 24, 1881; Applegate, *Most Famous Man*, 442–443.

224 **Britton**: *Brooklyn Eagle*, May 23, 1872; *New York Times*, Dec. 2, 1873, Oct. 27, 1874, Nov. 5, 1876; *New-York Tribune*, Feb. 28, Oct. 28, 29, 1874; *Daily Graphic* (New York), Feb. 16, 1886.

225 **"indefensible"**: *New York Times*, Nov. 4, 1877.

225 **zealous and skilled litigator**: Edward Earl Britton and Florence Evelyn [Pratt] Youngs, *Genealogy Britton* (Brooklyn: J. W. Gunnison, 1901), 12.

225 **Moore and his wife**: *Salt Lake Herald*, Apr. 5, 1881.

225 **Olive Logan**: *Boston Herald*, Apr. 29, 1909; 11 *Dictionary of American Biography*, 365.

225 **popular book**: Olive Logan (Mrs. Wirt Sikes), *Get Thee Behind Me, Satan!* (New York, 1872).

225 **"removing a cancer with a knife"**: Ibid., 183.

225 **"When I look . . . so few do"**: Ibid., 184.

225 **"noble dignity . . . her honor"**: *Belmont Chronicle* (St. Clairsville, OH), Mar. 31, 1881.

225 **called upon Mrs. Moore**: *Salt Lake Herald*, Apr. 5, 1881; *National Republican* (Washington, DC), Apr. 12, 1881.

225 **"one of the handsomest . . . money could buy"**: *Salt Lake Herald*, Apr. 5, 1881.

225 **Conkling was anxious to take the stand**: *Indianapolis Daily Sentinel*, Apr. 18, 1881.

225 **"Do you not think . . . contradicting each other"**: Roscoe Conkling to Julia Conkling, June 29, 1881, Conkling LC.

226 **"family difficulties," expressing dismay**: Julia Conkling to Roscoe Conkling, July 1881, Conkling LC.

226 **"the turning point . . . never withdraw him"**: Ackerman, *Dark Horse*, 309.

226 **"Roscoe is finished"**: Jordan, *Roscoe Conkling*, 396.

226 **with his pants down**: Chidsey, *Gentleman from New York*, 350; Ackerman, *Dark Horse*, 368–369.

227 **pep talk Kate gave**: *People and New Hampshire Patriot* (Concord, NH), June 30, 1881.

227 **"I am a Stalwart and Arthur will be president"**: Ackerman, *Dark Horse*, 365–366, 377–379.

## Chapter 25: Gilded Age Woman

228 **"His death . . . Stalwart of the Stalwarts"**: Peskin, *Garfield*, 592.

228 **incompetent doctoring**: See generally Candice Millard, *Destiny of the Republic: A Tale of Madness, Medicine and the Murder of a President* (New York: Doubleday, 2011).

228 **died in the summer home**: *New York Times*, Sept. 5, 6, 19, 22, 1881, Apr. 7, 1932.

228 **"Arthur for President! . . . the throne!"**: Hoogenboom, *Hayes*, 470.

229 **fishing buddies . . . soul mates**: Gregory J. Dehler, *Chester Alan Arthur: The Life of a Gilded Age Politician and President* (New York: Nova Science Publishers, 2007), 23.
229 **Arthur's "cowardice"**: Crowley, *Echoes from Niagara*, 232.
229 **wasn't good old "Chet Arthur . . . the President"**: Reeves, *Gentleman Boss*, 260.
229 **"For the Vice Presidency . . . the Almighty"**: *Autobiography of Andrew Dickson White* (New York: Century, 1905), 1:194.
229 **"among those . . . stands pre-eminent"**: KC to S. Pomeroy, Oct. 15, 1881, Arthur LC.
229 ***one* man . . . "dreaded by . . . threatens its destruction"**: Ibid.
230 **"this act . . . done quickly'"**: Ibid. The quotation is from *Macbeth*, act 1, scene 7.
230 **"So much gratuitous . . . the Treasury"**: KC to Chester Arthur, Oct. 21, 1881, Arthur LC.
230 **"*notwithstanding* the whirlwind . . . what then?"**: Ibid.
231 **"*the victim of Grantism* . . . Garfield's legatees"**: Ibid.
231 **"speak and speak effectively . . . or should accept"**: Ibid.
232 **"his trusted friend . . . loyalty and friendship"**: Ibid.
232 **power blinded him**: Jordan, *Roscoe Conkling*, 434, 436–439.
233 **"He presented no solutions . . . what he dealt with"**: Ibid., 438.
233 **"he left practically no . . . achievement"**: "Roscoe Conkling," *Oneida County Historical Society*, www.oneidacountyhistory.org/PublicFigures/Conklin/RoscoeConkling.asp.
233 **"Roscoe Conkling was created . . . local issues"**: Depew, *My Memories*, 79.
233 **Conkling brusquely rejected it . . . "His Accidency"**: Jordan, *Roscoe Conkling*, 416.

## Chapter 26: Stalwart Woman

235 **Union lines at Chickamauga**: James M. McPherson, *Battle Cry of Freedom: The Civil War Era* (New York: Oxford University Press, 1988), 671–674; Peskin, *Garfield*, 202–210.
235 **"confused . . . hit on the head"**: John Hay Diary, Oct. 24, 1863, in Burlingame and Ettlinger, *Inside Lincoln's White House*, 98–99.
235 **Chase acquitted himself well**: Niven, 333–335.
235 **Kate had spoken bitterly**: John Hay Diary, Oct. 21, 1863, in Burlingame and Ettlinger, *Inside Lincoln's White House*, 97.
235 **Rosecrans did his best to forget**: William M. Lamers, *The Edge of Glory: A Biography of General William S. Rosecrans, U.S.A.* (New York: Harcourt, Brace, 1961), 440–444.
236 **Dana . . . a private letter**: Ibid., 443; Peskin, *Garfield*, 214.
236 **"in the light . . . your chief"**: Peskin, *Garfield*, 214.

236 **"any charge . . . no particle of truth in it"**: Ibid.; Lamers, *Edge of Glory*, 443–444.
236 **Dana printed . . . "almost fatal delay"**: *New York Sun*, Mar. 8, 1882.
236 **it played a crucial role . . . father had concurred**: Society of the Army of the Cumberland, *Burial of General Rosecrans, Arlington National Cemetery, May 17, 1902* (Cincinnati: Robert Clarke Company, 1903), 97; *New York Sun*, June 12, 1882; Lamers, *Edge of Glory*, 445; SPC to Edward D. Mansfield, Oct. 27, 1863 (*CP4*:159).
236 **"the blackest treachery . . . court martial at once"**: *New York Herald*, Mar. 9, 1882.
236 **"there is much . . . Garfield's duplicity"**: *Columbian and Democrat* (Bloomsburg, PA), Mar. 17, 1882.
236 **Chase's private secretary**: Ibid.; *Sacramento Daily Record-Union*, Mar. 16, 1882; *New York Sun*, June 12, 1882.
236 **Kate had furnished the letter**: *Weekly Graphic* (Kirksville, MO), Mar. 17, 1882.
236 **"equivalent to an admission . . . 'by direction of Mrs. Kate Chase Sprague'"**: *Washington Herald*, Mar. 19, 1882.
237 **Schuckers denied that Kate**: *Cincinnati Daily Gazette*, Mar. 22, 1882.
237 **his belated explanation**: *New York Sun*, June 12, 1882.
237 **supplied a glowing tribute**: Schuckers, 626–627.

## Chapter 27: An Unmarried Woman

239 **two sides reached a settlement**: *Providence Journal*, Feb. 21, 22, 1882; *Providence Press*, Feb. 22, 23, 1882; *New York Herald*, Feb. 21, 1882.
239 **credited Kate's lawyer . . . "threatened to outrival the Beecher-Tilton affair"**: *Providence Press*, Feb. 22, 1882.
239 **"Divorce Made Easy"**: *Daily Astorian* (Astoria, OR), Mar. 16, 1882.
239 **"While it is . . . not immaculate"**: *Warren (MN) Sheaf*, Mar. 9, 1882.
240 **"both sides . . . their own lives"**: *Los Angeles Herald*, Mar. 22, 1882.
240 **Sprague turned the facts**: *New York Times*, Apr. 18, 1883; *Brooklyn Eagle*, Apr. 18, 1883; *New York Sun*, Apr. 19, 1883.
240 **"partisan act . . . in her life"**: Lamphier, 205–206, 251; see ibid., 202–204.
240 **retained much of her former beauty**: *Washington Star*, Oct. 7, 1882.
240 **"an expression . . . but momentary"**: Ibid.
241 **Conkling in Manhattan . . . his wife Julia**: Jordan, *Roscoe Conkling*, 412.
241 **spent the winter of 1882–1883 in New York . . . be near Conkling**: *Lancaster (PA) Daily Intelligencer*, Jan. 3, 1883; *St. Paul Daily Globe*, Jan. 9, Mar. 19, 1883; *Burlington (VT) Free Press*, Feb. 16, 1883; *Stark County Democrat* (Canton, OH), Mar. 3, 1883; *Fort Worth Daily Gazette*, Mar. 18, 1883; *Sedalia (MO) Weekly Bazoo*, Oct. 30, 1883.
241 **trip to Yellowstone**: Jordan, *Roscoe Conkling*, 412.
241 **Conkling sent her a package**: Jordan, *Roscoe Conkling*, 313n5; Phelps, 261n3.

241 **"To be thus . . . safely thus"**: note in possession of Aura Carr, reviewed by the author.

241 **"scorpion tongues"**: Gail Collins, *Scorpion Tongues: Gossip, Celebrity, and American Politics*, rev. ed. (New York: Harper Perennial, 2007), 61–62.

## Chapter 28: An Independent Woman

243 **sailed to Europe**: *People and New Hampshire Patriot* (Concord, NH), July 12, 1883; *Lancaster (PA) Daily Intelligencer*, Aug. 4, 1883.

243 **wintered in Germany**: *Sacramento Daily Record-Union*, Nov. 3, 1883.

243 **Avenue du Bois de Boulogne . . . receptions**: *Cleveland Plain Dealer*, Apr. 4, May 15, 1884. Today the street is known as Avenue Foch.

243 **tired of that scene**: *Cincinnati Commercial Gazette*, Jan. 5, 1885; *Boston Herald*, Aug. 16, 1886.

243 **Avon . . . Dussaut's boarding school**: *Boston Herald*, Dec. 29, 1884; *Cincinnati Commercial Gazette*, Jan. 5, 1885; *San Francisco Bulletin*, Jan. 17, 1885; *Macon (GA) Weekly Telegraph*, Jan. 26, 1886; *Columbus (GA) Daily Enquirer-Sun*, July 31, 1886; Margaret Isabel White, *Daisy in Exile: The Diary of an Australian Schoolgirl in France, 1887–1889*, introd. and anno. Marc Serge Rivière (Canberra: National Library of Australia, 2003), 28–36, 110, 182–184.

243 **"offering high French culture to foreign young women"**: White, *Daisy in Exile*, 34. The school still stands today on the renamed Avenue Franklin Roosevelt in Avon. Ibid., 184.

243 **French census . . . "rentière"**: Dénombrement de 1886, List Nominative des Habitants de la Commune d'Avon, Department de Seine-et-Marne, Arrondissement de Fontainebleau, www.archinoe.fr/cg77/index.php/rechercheTheme/requeteConstructor/17/1/A/1191/FONTAINEBLEAU. The entry for Kate is at page 39 of the digital image "10M311 1886."

243 **"France is superlatively . . . could not enjoy"**: *Columbus (GA) Daily Enquirer-Sun*, July 31, 1886.

244 **"an expression of pensiveness . . . extraordinary following"**: *Boston Herald*, Aug. 16, 1886.

244 **"very punctilious . . . name of Sprague"**: *Baltimore Sun*, Nov. 6, 1883.

244 **married Dora Inez Weed Calvert**: *New York Times*, Mar. 10, 1883; *Cleveland Plain Dealer*, Mar. 20, 1883; *Summit County Beacon* (Akron, OH), Mar. 21, 1883; *Wheeling Register*, Aug. 1, 1884.

244 **twenty-something divorcée**: 1880 US Census, Guyandotte, Cabell, WV, *Ancestry.com*, record for Dora I. Calvert (b. about 1858); 1870 US Census, Guyandotte, Cabell, WV, *Ancestry.com*, record for Dora Weed (b. about 1857).

244 **"wild yet beautiful"**: *Cleveland Plain Dealer*, July 30, 1885.

244 **sold the mansion . . . denied admission**: *Providence Journal*, Aug. 16, 1882; *New York Times*, Aug. 26, 1882; Applegate, *Most Famous Man*, 402–410, 418–420, 440–448.

244 **futile attempt . . . continue living at Canonchet**: Carroll, *Rhode Island*, 2:654, 765, 772.

244 **Inez converted . . . sold the property back**: *Macon (GA) Telegraph*, Jan. 27, 1885; *New York Times*, Mar. 17, 18, 19, 1887, Oct. 12, 1909; *Boston Daily Advertiser*, Aug. 21, 1899; *Ogden (UT) Standard*, Sept. 11, 1915; Phelps, 272; Ross, 268, 270; Sokoloff, 271.

245 **barefoot and poorly clad**: *Baltimore Sun*, July 27, 1885.

245 **"a chip off the old block"**: Ibid.

245 **seventeen-year-old sister**: Avice was born in Connecticut on November 3, 1867. US Passport Application for Mrs. Avice Wheaton, issued Oct. 24, 1900, *Ancestry.com*.

245 **daughter, Inez**: Inez was born at Narragansett Pier on November 3, 1886. US Passport Applications for Inez Sprague Stiness, issued June 3, 1915, Jan. 3, 1919, *Ancestry.com*.

245 **Gerrit Smith Wheaton**: Sokoloff, 273–277; Lamphier, 223; *Washington Post*, Feb. 13, 1899; *Providence Journal*, Oct. 9, 1890.

245 **Chase family lore**: The rumor also appears in Mary Merwin Phelps's book, *Dominant Daughter*, which was written with Ethel's cooperation. Phelps, 269; Mary Merwin Phelps, "How I Happened to Write Kate Chase," Phelps UM.

245 **"detestable parasites"**: Willie Sprague to KC, Jan. 15, 1890, BUL.

245 **inauguration of George Hoadly**: *St. Paul Daily Globe*, Dec. 6, 1883.

245 **"Blaine . . . will not be elected"**: *Wichita Daily Eagle*, Nov. 24, 1893.

245 **took up painting**: *Wheeling Register*, July 21, 1884; *Grit* (Washington, DC), July 26, 1884.

245 **not wishing to mingle**: *Cincinnati Commercial Gazette*, Jan. 5, 1885.

245 **"to be retired and secluded"**: *Rochester (NY) Democrat and Chronicle*, Aug. 1, 1886.

246 **"gayety in fashionable life . . . leave nothing"**: Ibid.

246 **"buoyancy . . . her face"**: *Columbus (GA) Daily Enquirer-Sun*, July 31, 1886.

246 **"that queenly air . . . through it all"**: *Daily Graphic* (New York), July 9, 1886.

246 **"I was so young . . . fun for myself in my life"**: *Columbus (GA) Daily Enquirer-Sun*, July 31, 1886.

246 **rendezvous with Roscoe Conkling . . . obtaining an old letter**: *Trenton (NJ) Times*, June 25, 1885; *Patriot* (Harrisburg, PA), Oct. 15, 1885; *Kansas City Times*, Oct. 18, 1885.

247 **"drunken, stupid . . . ass"**: *New York Herald*, Sept. 28, 1885; *Kalamazoo (MI) Gazette*, Sept. 30, 1885.

247 **Schuckers, denied . . . stolen from his desk**: *Cincinnati Commercial Tribune*, Oct. 3, 1885.

247 **secret diplomatic advice**: *Cincinnati Enquirer*, Aug. 1, 1899.

247 **praised Napoleon**: *Boston Herald*, Aug. 16, 1886.

247 **princes had "suffered . . . prejudice"**: Lamphier, 225, quoting unidentified newspaper clipping, BUL.

247 **to witness a duel**: *Cincinnati Enquirer*, Aug. 1, 1899.

247 **managed to procure one**: *New York Times*, July 21, 1895.
247 **"Women do not . . . power in the world"**: *Columbus (GA) Daily Enquirer-Sun*, July 31, 1886.
247 **"do whatever . . . stop them"**: Ibid.
247 **reburial in Spring Grove**: *Critic* (Washington, DC), July 26, 1886; *Rochester (NY) Democrat and Chronicle*, Aug. 1, 1886; *Springfield (OH) Globe-Republic*, Aug. 14, Oct. 14, 1886; *Daily Evening Bulletin* (Maysville, KY), Oct. 15, 1886.
247 **they clasped hands**: *Daily Inter Ocean* (Chicago), Oct. 15, 1886.
248 **"the notorious . . . a mistake"**: Julia Bundy Foraker, *I Would Live It Again*, 76.
248 **"a woman of rare attainments . . . or scandal"**: Sokoloff, 269; Lamphier, 227.
248 **temperance vow**: *Truth* (New York), Dec. 25, 1882; *Baltimore Sun*, Dec. 26, 1882; *New-York Tribune*, Dec. 25, 1882.
248 **"always a high-spirited woman . . . business tact"**: Sokoloff, 269.
248 **issued a public letter . . . "united pity"**: *Kansas City Star*, Oct. 25, 1886; *Fort Worth Daily Gazette*, Oct. 26, 1886.
248 **"shabby and generally dilapidated"**: Willie Sprague to KC, Nov. 4, 1886, BUL.
248 **Kate welcomed him . . . "inhumanity"**: Sokoloff, 276.
248 **Avice promptly married**: *Providence Journal*, Oct. 9, 1890; *Washington Post*, Feb. 13, 1899, Oct. 25, 1907; *Rice Belt Journal* (Welsh, Calcasieu Parish, LA), Nov. 8, 1907.
248 **steady correspondence with Willie**: Willie Sprague to KC, Feb. 16, 1887, Mar. 24, July 19, 1890, BUL; Sokoloff, 280–282; Lamphier, 231–232.
249 **rewrote it herself**: KC to William E. Curtis, May 21, 1887, BUL.
249 **soundly defeated**: *Narragansett Times*, June 6, 1890.
249 **"diversions . . . boozy recollection"**: *Providence Journal*, Oct. 15, 1890.
249 **took his own life**: *New York Times*, Oct. 9, 1890; *Providence Journal*, Oct. 9, 1890.
249 **"slight figure and poetic face"**: *Boston Herald*, Oct. 17, 1909.
249 **"erratic genius . . . affectionate"**: *Rice Belt Journal* (Welsh, Calcasieu Parish, LA), Nov. 8, 1907.
249 **"at your door lies this unnatural crime"**: KC to WS, Oct. 8, 1890, BUL.
249 **"embalm the body . . . father for expenses"**: *New York Times*, Oct. 10, 1890.
249 **funeral at St. Peter's**: *San Francisco Evening Bulletin*, Oct. 22, 1890; *Boston Herald*, Oct. 22, 1890; *Chicago Tribune*, Oct. 22, 1890; *Salt Lake Herald*, Oct. 23, 1890; *Narragansett Times*, Oct. 24, 1890; *Sunday Inter Ocean* (Chicago), Oct. 26, 1890; Sokoloff, 285–286; Ross, 269.
250 **"Is my son . . . sisters' benefit?"**: note, n.d., in Kate Chase's handwriting, BUL.
250 **"the blood . . . blighted young life"**: Sokoloff, 276, quoting KC to Whitelaw Reid, Nov. 29, 1886.
250 **Kate went to New York**: note, n.d., ca. 1935, Phelps UM.
250 **"an exile"**: *Rochester (NY) Democrat and Chronicle*, Aug. 1, 1886.

250 **hounded by creditors**: *Boston Herald*, Mar. 16, 1884; *Siftings* (Austin, TX), Apr. 10, 1886.

250 **considered selling Edgewood . . . increased its value**: *New York Herald*, June 15, 1886; *St. Paul Daily Globe*, June 16, 1886; *Sacramento Daily Record-Union*, Nov. 9, 1888; *Fort Worth Daily Gazette*, July 3, 1889.

250 **"She dresses modestly . . . other days"**: *Kansas City Star*, Mar. 10, 1890.

## Chapter 29: "What We Have Is Good"

252 **Ethel made her stage debut**: T. Allston Brown, *A History of the New York Stage, from the First Performance in 1732 to 1901* (New York: Dodd, Mead, 1903), 2:432.

252 **played an Irish maid . . . President Benjamin Harrison**: *New York Times*, Nov. 11, 1890; Clyde Fitch, *Beau Brummel: A Play in Four Acts* (New York: Samuel French, 1908), cast list.

252 **equestrian**: *Wichita Daily Eagle*, Sept. 29, 1889; *Pittsburgh Dispatch*, May 11, July 27, 1890.

252 **with Kate's full support, to earn money for the family**: *Omaha Daily Bee*, Mar. 6, 1887; *Springfield (OH) Daily Republic*, Nov. 5, 1887; Ann Donaldson, interview with the author, Nov. 19, 2011.

252 **studying under David Belasco . . . decade on stage**: Ann Donaldson, interviews with the author, Oct. 3, Nov. 19, 2011; *New York Herald Tribune*, Jan. 30, 1937; David Belasco to Ethel Sprague, Feb. 22, 1889 (letter in possession of Aura Carr); *San Francisco Evening Bulletin*, Oct. 25, 1890; *Boston Daily Journal*, Apr. 11, 1891; *Kalamazoo (MI) Gazette*, Dec. 12, 1894; Brown, *History of the New York Stage*, 3:385; *New York Herald*, Oct. 8, 1897; *Colorado Springs Gazette*, Aug. 3, 1902; *Fort Wayne News*, July 20, 1905.

252 **"*jolie laide*"**: Ann Donaldson, interview with the author, Oct. 3, 2011. See also *New York World*, May 25, 1890; *Boston Daily Journal*, Apr. 11, 1891.

252 **"recite . . . by the yard"**: Ann Donaldson, interview with the author, Oct. 3, 2011.

252 **secretly married Dr. Frank Donaldson**: *Baltimore Sun*, July 23, 1896; *Boston Herald*, Oct. 30, 1896; *Washington Evening Star*, Oct. 30, 1896; *Washington Times*, Oct. 29, 1896; *Washington Post*, Oct. 31, 1896; *Houston Daily Post*, Oct. 31, 1896; *Harvard College, Class of 1879, Secretary's Report, No. 4* (Buffalo, NY, 1890), 33–35, 124; Ann Donaldson, interview with the author, Nov. 19, 2011; Landon C. Bell, *Cumberland Parish, Lunenburg County, Virginia, 1746–1816: Vestry Book, 1746–1816* (Richmond, VA: Clearfield Company, 1930), 265.

252 **"Since the newspapers . . . orthodox way"**: *Washington Evening Star*, Oct. 30, 1896.

253 **medal by President . . . Rough Riders**: *Fort Wayne News*, July 20, 1905; *New York Herald Tribune*, Jan. 10, 1937; *Duluth News-Tribune*, July 30, 1905;

Patrick McSherry, with data contributed by Peter Amabile, "Lt. Frank Donaldson, Assistant Surgeon of the Rough Riders," *The Spanish American War Centennial Website*, www.spanamwar.com/rrdonaldson.html; *Boston Herald*, Nov. 19, 1898; *New-York Tribune*, Aug. 24, 1899; Frank Donaldson to Ethel Donaldson, July 9, 1898 (letter in possession of Aura Carr).

253 **Ethel saw father only once**: *Washington Post*, Oct. 3, 1897.

253 **Portia reconciled . . . tearful reunion**: *Washington Times*, Sept. 25, 1897; *New York World*, Sept. 27, 1897; Brewer, *Trails of a Paintbrush*, 153–154; *Washington Herald*, July 7, 1910.

253 **Portia was courted . . . misapprehension**: Brewer, *Trails of a Paintbrush*, 155–158.

253 **withdrawn in manner**: *Washington Times Magazine*, Sept. 6, 1908; Ann Donaldson, interview with the author, Oct. 3, 2011.

253 **"a fine French scholar . . . artist"**: *Washington Tribune*, July 21, 1910.

253 **then a recluse . . . reticent around his youngest daughter**: Brewer, *Trails of a Paintbrush*, 150, 155.

253 **"the old wound . . . of that time"**: Ibid., 155.

253 **"carried away with her his broken heart"**: Ibid., 153.

253 **kept Kate's old bedroom**: *New York Sun*, Aug. 21, 1882.

253 **"she felt . . . her parents"**: Brewer, *Trails of a Paintbrush*, 164.

253 **government clerkship . . . the first time**: *Rockford (IL) Morning Star*, Aug. 22, 1905; *Washington Times Magazine*, Sept. 6, 1908; *Washington Herald*, July 7, 1910; *New York Sun*, July 10, 1910; *Washington Tribune*, July 21, 1910; Rock Creek Cemetery, Section I ("eye"), Lot 69 (Whitney); "Archive: Civil War Pension File, Joseph Newell Whitney," *Whitney Research Group*, http://wiki.whitneygen.org/wrg/index.php/Archive:Civil_War_Pension_File,_Joseph_Newell_Whitney.

254 **later she wed**: Marriage Certificate, Portia Sprague Whitney and Frank Browning, Aug. 10, 1914, Narragansett, RI, Town Records; *New York Times*, Feb. 24, 1932; 1920 US Census, Narragansett, RI, *Ancestry.com*, record for Frank and Portia [Sprague] Browning.

254 **when Ethel sued**: *Lexington (KY) Morning Herald*, Jan. 24, 1897; *Charlotte (NC) Observer*, Jan. 31, 1897.

254 **"soberer, less spirited, more kindly"**: *Washington Times*, Sept. 12, 1894.

254 **talked much of her father**: *Wichita Daily Eagle*, Nov. 18, 1890; *New York Herald*, Aug. 6, 1899.

254 **"very sensitive . . . seclusion from society"**: *Washington Times Magazine*, Sept. 6, 1908.

254 **no longer a fashion plate**: *Princeton (MN) Union*, Aug. 4, 1892.

254 **not fat, was rounder**: *San Francisco Morning Call*, Oct. 15, 1893.

254 **croquet**: Didier, "Salmon P. Chase," 183.

254 **heavy dresses and tight corsets**: Collins, *America's Women*, 122–124.

254 **bicycle craze**: Ibid., 279–280.

254 **prohibiting liquor**: *New-York Tribune*, Mar. 14, 1891.

254 **"the brilliant and distinguished . . . entire matter"**: *Oswego (NY) Daily Times*, Apr. 10, 1891.

255 **Fanny Sprague . . . besieged by creditors**: *Fort Worth Daily Gazette*, July 23, 1883; *New Haven (CT) Register*, Aug. 8, 1883; *Boston Morning Journal*, Oct. 15, 1883.

255 **creditors foreclosed . . . temporary stay . . . trust fund**: *Washington Times*, Aug. 19, 1894; *New York Times*, Jan. 7, July 12, 15, 23, Aug. 2, 1895, Sept. 22, Oct. 6, 1897; *Richmond Dispatch*, Jan. 19, 1895; *Los Angeles Herald*, July 16, 1895, Oct. 3, 1897; *St. Paul Daily Globe*, Aug. 2, 1895; *Washington Evening Star*, July 22, 1895; *Omaha Bee*, Aug. 5, 1895; *Washington Times*, Feb. 21, 1896; *New York Sun*, Sept. 17, 1897; *Marietta (OH) Daily Leader*, Sept. 21, 1897; *Brownsville (TX) Daily Herald*, Feb. 11, 1898; *New York Herald*, Aug. 6, 1899; Phelps, 277–278.

255 **"the most bewitching . . . not my admiration"**: Phelps, 279.

256 **poultry-and-pigeon show**: Ross, 283; *New York Sun*, Feb. 2, 1896 (advertisement).

256 **selling milk, eggs**: *Chicago Tribune*, Aug. 4, 1895; *Washington Times*, Feb. 21, 1896; *San Francisco Morning Call*, Aug. 1, 1899; *New York Herald*, Aug. 6, 1899.

256 **"I was sorry . . . after working hours"**: KC to Mrs. Jay Bancroft, May 7, 1897, Phelps UM. Other evidence of Kate's farming business can be found, in the same papers, in her letter to Mrs. Bancroft of June 24, 1897, and in various receipts from February to October 1898 for payment for vegetables, fruit, and milk (at ten cents a quart).

256 **"I feel as if . . . a tragic one"**: NC to "Aunt Ammie" [Ruhamah Ludlow Hunt], Aug. 17, 1899, typescript, box 1, Ludlow-Dunlop-Chambers Collection, American Heritage Center, University of Wyoming, Laramie, WY. See also *Pegasus*, 444n19.

257 **Westchester Country Club**: *New York Times*, Oct. 16, 1898, Apr. 29, 1905.

257 **went to colonize . . . artists' school . . . Shinnecock Hills**: David Goddard, *Colonizing Southampton: The Transformation of a Long Island Community, 1870–1900* (Albany: State University of New York Press, 2011), 55–56, 240–243, 246–247, 349n59; Cynthia V. A. Schaffner and Lori Zabar, "The Founding and Design of William Merritt Chase's Shinnecock Hills Summer School of Art and the Art Village," *Winterthur Portfolio* 44, no. 4 (Winter 2010): 303–350.

257 **daughter Beatrix**: *Kansas City Star*, Oct. 14, 1896; *New York Times*, Oct. 16, 1898, Aug. 15, 1963; Richard J. Moss, *Golf and the American Country Club* (Urbana: University of Illinois Press, 2001), 26, 69–71.

257 **depression in 1893 devastated Southampton**: Schaffner and Zabar, "Founding and Design," 344, 349–350.

257 **"drank up . . . family fortunes"**: Amelia Peck and Carol Irish, *Candace Wheeler: The Art and Enterprise of American Design, 1875–1900* (New York: Metropolitan Museum of Art/New Haven, CT: Yale University Press, 2001), 76, 86n327. See also Goddard, *Colonizing Southampton*, 55.

257 **"health" reasons**: *New York Times*, Apr. 29, 1905.
257 **by 1900 to go to Puerto Rico**: Goddard, *Colonizing Southampton*, 55; *New York Times*, Apr. 29, 1905.
257 **boarder status**: 1900 US Census, Southampton, Suffolk, NY, *Ancestry.com*, record for Janet [R.] Hoyt and Beatrix Hoyt.
257 **Thomasville**: *New York Times*, Aug. 15, 1963; Peck and Irish, *Candace Wheeler*, 76; 1920 US Census, Thomasville, GA, *Ancestry.com*, record for Janet C. Hoyt; "Mrs. W.S. Hoyt Dead," unidentified newspaper obituary, 1925, CHS; Franklin Hoyt Moore, e-mails to the author, Sept. 12, 21, 2011.
257 **always in extremis**: Thomas Hoyt Stokes, interview with the author, Dec. 2, 2011; Franklin Hoyt Moore, e-mails to the author, Sept. 12, 21, Nov. 15, 2011.
258 **those who took satisfaction . . . retribution**: *Daily Graphic* (New York), July 9, 1886; *Big Stone Post* (Big Stone Gap, VA), Oct. 31, 1890, May 15, 1891; *Anaconda (MT) Standard*, Aug. 6, 1899.
258 **misfortune without complaint . . . old charm of manner**: McLean Hazen Dewey, "Memoir," 135–136; *Niagara Falls Gazette*, May 11, 1887; *Wichita Daily Eagle*, Nov. 18, 1890; *San Francisco Morning Call*, Oct. 15, 1893; *Springfield (MA) Daily Republican*, Aug. 1, 1899; *New York Herald*, Aug. 6, 1899; *Washington Herald*, Mar. 8, 1908; Ross, 279–280; Sokoloff, 292.
258 **eyes that once . . . now looked weary**: *Omaha World-Herald*, Mar. 1, 1891; Ross, 279, 281; Phelps, 279.
258 **voice was still full of sentiment**: McLean Hazen Dewey, "Memoir," 136; *Omaha World-Herald*, Mar. 1, 1891; Ross, 279.
258 **erect . . . same stately poise of head**: *New York World*, Mar. 16, 1900; *Columbus (GA) Enquirer-Sun*, Mar. 8, 1891; Ross, 274; Sokoloff, 289.
258 **fired a pistol**: *New York Herald*, Aug. 6, 1899.

## Chapter 30: "None Outshone Her"

260 **now a place of decay**: *Chicago Tribune*, Aug. 4, 1895, May 24, 1896; *New York Herald*, Aug. 6, 1899; Phelps, 280; Sokoloff, 11, 291.
260 **Ethel and her one-year-old son**: Phelps, 280; Sokoloff, 291; Ann Donaldson, interview with the author, Nov. 19, 2011.
261 **Chase Donaldson**: Register of Births, Santa Clara County, CA, Apr. 10, 1897.
261 **trustee decided to sell**: *Washington Times*, May 13, 1899; *Baltimore Sun*, May 13, 1899; *New York Sun*, May 23, 1899.
261 **venture had lost money**: *New-York Tribune*, May 12, 1899; *Washington Times*, May 13, 1899; Phelps, 275.
261 **Bright's disease . . . declined all offers of assistance**: *New York Herald*, Aug. 6, 1899; *Washington Post*, Aug. 1, 1899; *Washington Evening Star*, July 31, 1899; *Washington Evening Times*, July 31, 1899.
261 **she was offered a clerkship**: *New-York Tribune*, May 12, 1899.
261 **to employ women clerks**: *Chicago Broad Axe*, Oct. 3, 1903; *Pegasus*, 28.

261 **turned it down . . . Portia ended up accepting**: *Washington Post*, Aug. 2, 1899; *New York Times*, Aug. 17, 1899.

261 **She died**: *Washington Evening Star*, July 31, 1899; *Washington Post*, Aug. 1, 1899; *Washington Evening Times*, July 31, 1899; *Washington Times Magazine*, Sept. 6, 1908.

261 **the simple funeral**: *Washington Evening Star*, Aug. 2, 1899; *Boston Herald*, Aug. 3, 1899.

261 **"There are so many little things . . . with me"**: Duffield, *Washington in the 90's*, 10–11.

262 **placed in a vault . . . transferred**: *Washington Times*, Mar. 9, 1900; Phelps, 282; *Cincinnati Enquirer*, Mar. 11, 1900.

262 **gravestone**: Burial record for Katharine Chase Sprague, no. 64465, Spring Grove Cemetery, Cincinnati, lots 10 and 11; "Katherine Jane 'Kate' Sprague," *Find a Grave*, Mar. 3, 1999, www.findagrave.com/cgi-bin/fg.cgi?page=gr&GRid=4642.

262 **obituaries**: *New York Times*, Aug. 1, 27, 1899; *New York World*, Aug. 6, 1899, Mar. 16, 1900; *Cincinnati Enquirer*, Aug. 1, 1899; *Washington Evening Star*, July 31, 1899; *Pawtucket (RI) Times*, Aug. 1, 1899; *The State* (Columbia, SC), Aug. 4, 1899; *Springfield (MA) Daily Republican*, Aug. 1, 1899; *Anaconda (MT) Standard*, Aug. 6, 1899; *San Francisco Call*, Aug. 1, 1899.

262 **"The homage . . . was hers"**: *New York Times*, Aug. 1, 1899.

262 **"The most brilliant . . . none outshone her"**: *Washington Evening Star*, July 31, 1899.

262 **compared to Dolley Madison**: *Washington Post*, Aug. 1, 1899; *New York World*, Aug. 6, 1899; *Cleveland Plain Dealer*, Aug. 6, 1899.

262 **"won her way . . . a republic"**: *Washington Post*, Aug. 1, 1899.

262 **possessions were auctioned**: *New York Sun*, Mar. 18, 1900 (advertisement); *Washington Evening Star*, Mar. 31, 1900; "Legal Notes," *Albany Law Journal: A Weekly Record of the Law and the Lawyers* 61, no. 13 (Mar. 31, 1900): 205; *Washington Times*, Mar. 28, Apr. 1, 1900.

262 **statuette**: possession of Aura Carr, viewed by the author.

262 **at the French royal court**: *New York World*, Mar. 24, 1871.

262 **divided her mother's mementoes**: Portia Sprague to Ethel Donaldson, Mar. 15, 1900, BUL.

262 **burned as much of Kate's correspondence**: *New York World*, Mar. 16, 1900.

263 **Kate's diary**: Ann Donaldson, interviews with the author, Oct. 3, Nov. 19, 2011; donor records, BUL.

263 **note from "C . . . your admirer"**: *New York World*, Mar. 16, 1900.

263 **"My dear Kate . . . H.T.M."**: Ibid.

263 **McCulloch**: *National Republican* (Washington, DC), Feb. 25, 1867; *Washington Times*, Feb. 21, 1896; Hugh McCulloch, *Men and Measures of Half a Century, Sketches and Comments* (New York: J. J. Little, 1900), 181–194.

263 **"I walk . . . my reward"**: *New York World*, Mar. 16, 1900; Coventry Patmore, *The Angel in the House*, 6th ed. (London, 1885), 8.

264 **"frequently wished . . . her gender"**: *Boston Herald*, Aug. 16, 1886.
265 **"light without heat"**: Ross, 26.
266 **"on account of the health . . . truly marvelous"**: *Columbus (GA) Daily Enquirer*, July 31, 1886.

## Epilogue

267 **under Portia's care**: *Rockford (IL) Morning Star*, Aug. 22, 1905; *Washington Times Magazine*, Sept. 6, 1908; *Washington Tribune*, July 21, 1910; 1900 US Census, Washington, DC, *Ancestry.com*, records for Portia C. Sprague and Kitty C. Sprague.
267 **dying of tuberculosis**: Certificate of Death for Katherine Chase Sprague, Government of the District of Columbia, Department of Health, no. 193.106, June 22, 1910; *Washington Herald*, June 23, 1910 (death notice).
267 **She is buried**: Rock Creek Cemetery, Section I ("eye"), lot 69. Her simple gravestone reads, "Kitty Sprague, 1872–1910."
267 **death there from a stroke**: *New York Times*, Feb. 24, 1932; Certification of Vital Record for Portia Sprague Browning, State of Rhode Island, Feb. 23, 1932; Riverside Cemetery, Wakefield, RI, Plot B 0020.
267 **returned occasionally to stage**: She appeared for one performance in *The Storm* at New York's Carnegie Lyceum Theatre on February 2, 1900, and in *The Last Act*, *A Scrap of Paper*, and *Out on Bail* in 1902 at Colorado Springs. In 1905 she announced plans for further productions of *The Last Act*. "The Storm," *Internet Broadway Database*, http://ibdb.com/person.php?id=60715; *Colorado Springs Gazette*, May 5, Aug. 3, 1902; *Duluth News Tribune*, July 30, 1905; *Fort Wayne (IN) News*, July 20, 1905.
267 **Frank Donaldson . . . yellow fever**: *New-York Tribune*, Aug. 24, 1899; Frank Donaldson to Mrs. Frank Donaldson, c/o Catharine Chase, Edgewood, n.d., ca. 1899 (telegram in possession of Aura Carr).
267 **died at age forty-nine**: *San Francisco Call*, Apr. 14, 1906.
267 **San Francisco earthquake**: Ann Donaldson, interviews with the author, Oct. 3, Nov. 19, 2011; *San Francisco Call*, June 29, July 14, 1906.
267 **St. Elizabeth's**: Beldens, 351, 393n2; 1910 US Census, Washington, DC, *Ancestry.com*, record for Ethel S. Donaldson; Ann Donaldson, interview with the author, Oct. 3, 2011.
267 **Chase, who had lived with Portia and Kitty . . . procured Ethel's release**: *Washington Times Magazine*, Sept. 6, 1908; Ann Donaldson, interview with the author, Oct. 3, 2011.
267 **final years . . . Ethel died**: Ann Donaldson, interviews with the author, Oct. 3, Nov. 19, 2011; *New York Times*, Dec. 20, 1936; *New York Herald Tribune*, Jan. 10, 1937; Certificate of Death for Ethel Sprague Donaldson, Dept. of Health of the City of New York, Bureau of Records, no. 27324, Dec. 19, 1936.
267 **Chase Donaldson . . . six children**: Ann Donaldson, interviews with the author, Oct. 3, Nov. 19, 2011; *New York Times*, Sept. 25, 1921, Jan. 2, 1935, Sept.

17, 1936, Jan. 26, 1937, Mar. 31, 1940, Mar. 27, Apr. 28, 1945; *Washington Post and Times-Herald*, Aug. 1, 1959. His first son, Edward Chase Donaldson, was killed in action in Germany in the last month of World War II in Europe. Jimmy Donaldson, his second son, died at age thirty-one in 1959 in Pakistan, where he contracted a polio-like virus while advising the Pakistani government on building low-cost housing for refugees. Two other sons from later marriages survive: Henry Thompson ("Tom") Donaldson, retired in Maine, and Chase Fernando Donaldson, a Louisville, Kentucky, businessman.

268 **Janet Ralston Chase Hoyt . . . Candace Wheeler**: Death certificate for Janet Ralston Chase Hoyt, Georgia State Board of Health Bureau of Vital Statistics, file no. 35441, Nov. 19, 1925; "Janet Ralston 'Nettie' Chase Hoyt," *Find a Grave*, Feb. 26, 2002, www.findagrave.com/cgi-bin/fg.cgi?page=gr&GRid=6216516; Peck and Irish, *Candace Wheeler*, 76; Candace Wheeler, *Yesterdays in a Busy Life* (New York: Harper & Brothers, 1918), 7–14, 197–199; Schaffner and Zabar, "Founding and Design," 310–311; *New York Times*, May 23, 1885.

268 **Nettie had four children**: Franklin Hoyt Moore, e-mails to the author, Sept. 12, 21, 2011; Thomas Hoyt Stokes, interview with the author, Dec. 2, 2011; *Lockport (NY) Daily Journal*, Mar. 24, 1898; *New York Times*, July 1, 1933, Nov. 14, 1937, Oct. 22, 1954, Aug. 15, 1963.

268 **Beatrix Hoyt**: Based on an erroneous entry on Beatrix Hoyt in *American National Biography*, the *Pegasus* authors state that Nettie had a fifth child, "Placidia, the wife of an Episcopal minister." *Pegasus*, 442–443. Nettie's great-grandsons confirm that Placidia White, the woman referred to in the *ANB* entry, was not a child of Nettie's. She was born in North Carolina, in 1881, to John and Laura Bridgers. Isabel Hall Chambers and Overton Chambers, *Remembering Highlands: From Pioneer Village to Mountain Retreat* (Charleston, SC: History Press, 2009), Part II; Monika S. Fleming, *Echoes of Edgecombe County: 1860–1940* (Charleston, SC: Arcadia, 1996), 113; 1930 US Census, Thomasville, GA, *Ancestry.com*, records for Robb White Jr. and Placidia White.

268 **he had found quiet**: *Baltimore American*, Dec. 10, 1905.

268 **"philosophy of national life . . . disaster"**: Ibid.

269 **in order to elope . . . he was disowning**: *Richmond Times Dispatch*, Mar. 14, 1906, Oct. 22, 1907; *Philadelphia Inquirer*, May 17, 1906; *Cleveland Plain Dealer*, June 23, 1907; *Rice Belt Journal* (Welsh, Calcasieu Parish, LA), Nov. 8, 1907.

269 **burned to the ground . . . Sprague nearly lost his life**: *New York Times*, Oct. 12, 1909; *New York Sun*, Oct. 12, 1909.

269 **Sprague suffered a stroke**: Shoemaker, *Appreciation of Sprague*, 1, 26; *New York Times*, Jan. 25, 1911.

269 **converted their apartment**: *New York Times*, Sept. 12, 1915.

269 **Spragues fled . . . returned to Paris**: Shoemaker, *Appreciation of Sprague*, 62–63.

269 **"the only civilized place to live"**: Lamphier, 245.

269 **Sprague died of complications**: *New York Times*, Sept. 12, 1915; *New York Herald*, Sept. 12, 1915.

269 **he had outlived**: *Ogden (UT) Standard*, Sept. 11, 1915.

269 **hero's treatment**: Shoemaker, *Appreciation of Sprague*, 71–87.

269 **"One almost wishes . . . 19th century"**: *Springfield (MA) Republican*, Sept. 12, 1915. Sprague was later joined in burial at Swan Point by his wife, Inez, who died in Narragansett in 1938. Her sister, Avice (Willie Sprague's first wife), inherited $7 million on the death of her second husband, Colonel Wheaton, in 1899, before marrying and later divorcing Wenceslao Borda Jr., a Puerto Rican sugar planter and mysterious former diplomat. Avice died in 1923 in Narragansett at age fifty-five. Avice's daughter, Inez, after divorcing Harry Stiness, married a French military man named du Chazaud, moved to the Riviera, and died in France in 1981 in her nineties. Inez and Harry Stiness's daughter (also named Avice), was briefly married and divorced in Budapest. She died childless in France in 1980. *New York Times*, July 14, 1909, Nov. 27, 1910, Aug. 26, 1911, Jan. 23, 1938; *Narragansett Times*, Mar. 9, 1923, Jan. 28, 1938; *El Paso Herald*, Nov. 3, 1911; *Pawtucket (RI) Evening Times*, Jan. 5, 1920; *Boston Herald*, Sept. 22, 1921; *Charlotte (NC) Observer*, Sept. 21, 1911; *Washington Post*, Feb. 13, 1899, Apr. 23, 1901, Oct. 25, 1907, Apr. 17, 1910; *Washington Times*, Sept. 22, 1917; *Aberdeen (SD) Daily News*, Apr. 6, 1901; *Colorado Springs Gazette*, Aug. 16, 1914; "Inez Sprague," *The Sprague Project*, Feb. 5, 2012, www.sprague-database.org/genealogy/getperson.php?personID=I57992&tree=SpragueProject; *Providence Sunday Journal*, Oct. 10, 1937.

270 **Chase-Sprague mansion**: *Washington Times*, Sept. 20, Oct. 17, 1908; *Pegasus*, 217n3; Alexander D. Mitchell IV, *Washington, D.C., Then and Now* (San Diego: Thunder Day Press, 2000), 98–99.

270 **Canonchet**: "Our Museum: History of the South County Museum," *South County Museum*, www.southcountymuseum.org/About_SCM.html; author visit to site, Apr. 29, 2012.

270 **Edgewood**: *Washington Times*, May 25, 1900; *Baltimore Sun*, Dec. 21, 1900; Henderson and Bleeg, "History," *Edgewood Neighborhood, Washington, D.C.*, www.edgewooddc.org/id12.html; "Catholic Charities of the Archdiocese of Washington, D.C.," *The Catholic University of America*, http://archives.lib.cua.edu/findingaid/ccdc.cfm.

# Selected Bibliography

The works in this list are those cited in shortened form periodically in the notes as well as those consulted more generally in the preparation of this book.

## Books


Ackerman, Kenneth D. *Dark Horse: The Surprise Election and Political Murder of President James A. Garfield.* New York: Carroll & Graf, 2003.

[Anderson, Mary Eliza Viall]. *The Merchant's Wife, or, He Blundered: A Political Romance of Our Own Day and Other Miscellanies, by "A Looker-On Here in Vienna."* Boston: printed for the author, 1876.

Applegate, Debby. *The Most Famous Man in America: The Biography of Henry Ward Beecher.* New York: Doubleday, 2006.

Baker, Jean H. *Mary Todd Lincoln.* New York: W. W. Norton, 1987.

Bartlett, John Russell. *Memoirs of Rhode Island Officers Who Were Engaged in the Service of Their Country During the Great Rebellion of the South.* Providence, 1867.

Belden, Thomas Graham, and Marva Robins Belden. *So Fell the Angels.* Boston: Little, Brown, 1956.

Bigelow, John. *The Life of Samuel J. Tilden.* 2 vols. New York, 1895.

———. *Retrospections of an Active Life.* Vol. 4, *1867–1871*, and Vol. 5, *1872–1879.* Garden City, NY: Doubleday, Page, 1913.

Blue, Frederick J. *Salmon P. Chase: A Life in Politics.* Kent, OH: Kent State University Press, 1987.

Bordman, Gerald, ed. *The Oxford Companion to American Theatre.* 2nd ed. New York: Oxford University Press, 1992.

Bowers, Claude G. *The Tragic Era: The Revolution After Lincoln.* Cambridge, MA: Riverside Press, 1929.

Brewer, Nicholas R. *Trails of a Paintbrush.* Boston: Christopher Publishing House, 1938.

Briggs, Emily Edson. *The Olivia Letters: Being Some History of Washington City for Forty Years as Told by the Letters of a Newspaper Correspondent.* New York: Neale Publishing, 1906.

Brinkerhoff, Roeliff. *Recollections of a Lifetime.* Cincinnati, OH: Robert Clarke, 1900.

Brown, T. Allston. *A History of the New York Stage, from the First Performance in 1732 to 1901.* 3 vols. New York: Dodd, Mead, 1903.

Burlingame, Michael. *Abraham Lincoln: A Life.* Vol. 1. Baltimore: Johns Hopkins University Press, 2008.

Burns, Ric, and James Sanders, with Lisa Ades. *New York: An Illustrated History.* New York: Knopf, 1999.

Calhoun, Lucia Gilbert, ed. *Modern Women and What Is Said About Them*. New York, 1868.

Caranci, Paul F. *The Hanging and Redemption of John Gordon: The True Story of Rhode Island's Last Execution*. Charleston, SC: History Press, 2013.

Carroll, Charles. *Rhode Island: Three Centuries of Democracy*. 4 vols. New York: Lewis Historical Publishing, 1932.

Chase, Salmon P. *The Salmon P. Chase Papers*. Edited by John Niven, James P. McClure, Leigh Johnsen, William M. Ferraro, Steve Leikin, Kathleen Norman, and Holly Byers Ochoa. 5 vols. Kent, OH: Kent State University Press, 1993–1998.

Chase, Salmon P., Kate Chase, and Nettie Chase. *"Spur Up Your Pegasus": Family Letters of Salmon, Kate, and Nettie Chase, 1844–1873*. Edited by James P. McClure, Peg A. Lamphier, and Erika M. Kreger. Kent, OH: Kent State University Press, 2009.

Chidsey, Donald Barr. *The Gentleman from New York: A Life of Roscoe Conkling*. New Haven, CT: Yale University Press, 1935.

Child, William H. *History of the Town of Cornish, New Hampshire, with Genealogical Record, 1864–1910*. 2 vols. Concord, NH: Rumford Press, 1911.

Clinton, Catherine. *Fanny Kemble's Civil Wars*. 2000. Reprint, Oxford: Oxford University Press, 2000.

———. *Mrs. Lincoln: A Life*. New York: Harper, 2009.

Clymer, Kenton J. *John Hay: The Gentleman as Diplomat*. Ann Arbor: University of Michigan Press, 1975.

Coleman, Charles H. *The Election of 1868: The Democratic Effort to Regain Control*. New York: Columbia University Press, 1933.

Collins, Gail. *America's Women: Four Hundred Years of Dolls, Drudges, Helpmates, and Heroines*. 2003. Reprint, New York: Harper Perennial, 2007.

———. *Scorpion Tongues: Gossip, Celebrity, and American Politics*. Rev. ed. New York: Harper Perennial, 2007.

Conkling, Alfred R. *The Life and Letters of Roscoe Conkling: Orator, Statesman, Advocate*. New York, 1889.

Crook, William Henry. *Through Five Administrations: Reminiscences of Colonel William H. Crook, Body-Guard to President Lincoln*. Edited by Margarita Spalding Gerry. New York: Harper & Brothers, 1910.

Crowley, Mrs. Richard [Julia M. Corbitt]. *Echoes from Niagara: Historical, Political, Personal*. Buffalo, NY, 1890.

Dana, Charles. *Recollections of the Civil War, with the Leaders at Washington and in the Field in the Sixties*. New York: D. Appleton, 1902.

Depew, Chauncey M. *My Memories of Eighty Years*. New York: Charles Scribner's, 1922.

Donald, David Herbert. *Lincoln*. New York: Simon & Schuster, 1995.

Douglass, Frederick. *The Life and Times of Frederick Douglass: From 1817–1882*. Edited by John Lobb. London, 1882.

Duffield, Isabel McKenna. *Washington in the 90's*. San Francisco: Press of Overland Monthly, 1929.

Ellet, Mrs. E. F. [Elizabeth Fries]. *The Court Circles of the Republic, or the Beauties and Celebrities of the Nation*. Hartford, CT, 1870.

Engle, Steven D. *Yankee Dutchman: The Life of Franz Sigel*. 1993. Reprint, Baton Rouge: Louisiana State University Press, 1999.

Epstein, Daniel Mark. *The Lincolns: Portrait of a Marriage*. 2008. Reprint, New York: Ballantine Books, 2009.

Field, Mrs. Henry M. [Henriette Deluzy-Desportes]. *Home Sketches in France, and Other Papers*. Edited by Henry M. Field and Andrew Dickson White. New York, 1875.

Field, Rachel. *All This, and Heaven Too*. 1938. Reprint, Chicago: Chicago Review Press, 2003.

Fields, Armond. *Tony Pastor: Father of Vaudeville*. Jefferson, NC: McFarland, 2007.

Flick, Alexander Clarence. *Samuel Jones Tilden: A Study in Political Sagacity*. New York: Dodd, Mead, 1939.

Foner, Eric. *A Short History of Reconstruction, 1863–1877*. New York: Harper Perennial, 1990.

———. *The Story of American Freedom*. New York: W. W. Norton, 1998.

Foraker, Julia Bundy. *I Would Live It Again*. New York: Harper & Brothers, 1932.

Freeman, Robert Eliot. *Cranston, Rhode Island Statewide Historical Preservation Report P-C-1, September 1980*. Providence: Rhode Island Historical Preservation Commission, 1980.

Fuller, Oliver Payson. *The History of Warwick, Rhode Island*. Providence, 1875.

Garmey, Stephen. *Gramercy Park: An Illustrated History of a New York Neighborhood*. New York: Balsam Press, 1984.

Goddard, David. *Colonizing Southampton: The Transformation of a Long Island Community, 1870–1900*. Albany: State University of New York Press, 2011.

Goodman, Dena. *The Republic of Letters: A Cultural History of the French Enlightenment*. 1994. Reprint, Ithaca, NY: Cornell University Press, 1996.

Goodman, Paul. *Towards a Christian Republic: Antimasonry and the Great Transition in New England, 1826–1836*. New York: Oxford University Press, 1988.

Goodwin, Doris Kearns. *Team of Rivals: The Political Genius of Abraham Lincoln*. New York: Simon & Schuster, 2005.

Griffin, Simon G. *A History of the Town of Keene: From 1732, when the Township was Granted by Massachusetts, to 1874, when It Became a City*. Keene, NH: Sentinel Printing, 1904.

*A Guide to Narragansett Bay: Newport, Narragansett Pier, Block Island, Watch Hill, Rocky Point, Silver Spring, and All the Famous Resorts Along the Shore*. Providence, 1878.

Gustafson, Melanie Susan. *Women and the Republican Party, 1854–1924*. Urbana: University of Illinois Press, 2001.

Hacker, Paul LeRoy. *A Story of Kate Chase's Family*. Bloomington, IN: AuthorHouse, 2006.

Hart, Albert Bushnell. *Salmon Portland Chase*. Boston, 1899.

Hay, John. *At Lincoln's Side: John Hay's Civil War Correspondence and Selected Writings.* Edited by Michael Burlingame. Carbondale: Southern Illinois University Press, 2006.

———. *Inside Lincoln's White House: The Complete Civil War Diary of John Hay.* Edited by Michael Burlingame and John R. Turner Ettlinger. Carbondale: Southern Illinois University Press, 1997.

———. *Lincoln and the Civil War, in the Diaries and Letters of John Hay.* Edited by Tyler Dennett. 1939. Reprint, New York: Da Capo Press, 1988.

Hedrick, Joan D. *Harriet Beecher Stowe: A Life.* New York: Oxford University Press, 1995.

Henwood, James N. J. *A Short Haul to the Bay: A History of the Narragansett Pier Railroad.* Brattleboro, VT: Stephen Greene Press, 1969.

Hoffmann, Charles, and Tess Hoffmann. *Brotherly Love: Murder and the Politics of Prejudice in Nineteenth-Century Rhode Island.* Amherst: University of Massachusetts Press, 1993.

Holcombe, John Walker, and Hubert Marshall Skinner. *Life and Public Services of Thomas A. Hendricks.* Indianapolis, 1886.

Hoogenboom, Ari. *Rutherford B. Hayes: Warrior and President.* Lawrence: University Press of Kansas, 1995.

Howard, Hamilton Gay. *Civil-War Echoes: Character Sketches and State Secrets.* Washington, DC: Howard Publishing Company, 1907.

Howells, William Dean. *Years of My Youth.* New York: Harper & Brothers, 1916.

Hudson, William C. *Random Recollections of an Old Political Reporter.* New York: Cupples & Leon, 1911.

Hutchinson, Joseph W. *The Book of Brothers (Second Series): Being a History of the Adventures of John W. Hutchinson and His Family in the Camps of the Army of the Potomac (1864).* Boston, 1864.

Jacob, Kathryn Allamong. *Capital Elites: High Society in Washington, D.C., After the Civil War.* Washington, DC: Smithsonian Institution Press, 1995.

Johnson, Ludwell H. *Red River Campaign: Politics and Cotton in the Civil War.* 1958. Reprint, Kent, OH: Kent State University Press, 1993.

Joki, Robert. *Saratoga Lost.* 3rd ed. Hensonville, NY: Black Dome Press, 2000.

Jordan, David M. *Roscoe Conkling: Voice in the Senate.* Ithaca, NY: Cornell University Press, 1971.

———. *Winfield Scott Hancock: A Soldier's Life.* 1988. Reprint, Bloomfield: Indiana University Press, 1996.

Kale, Stephen. *French Salons: High Society and Political Sociability from the Old Regime to the Revolution of 1848.* Baltimore: Johns Hopkins University Press, 2004.

Katz, Irving. *August Belmont: A Political Biography.* New York: Columbia University Press, 1968.

Keckley, Elizabeth. *Behind the Scenes, or, Thirty Years a Slave, and Four Years in the White House.* New York, 1868.

Knight, Benjamin, Sr. *History of the Sprague Families of Rhode Island, Cotton Manufacturers and Calico Printers, from William I to William IV . . . .* Santa Cruz, CA, 1881.

Kunhardt, Philip B., Jr., Philip B. Kunhardt III, and Peter W. Kunhardt. *Lincoln: An Illustrated Biography*. New York: Knopf, 1992.

Lamphier, Peg A. *Kate Chase and William Sprague: Politics and Gender in a Civil War Marriage*. Lincoln: University of Nebraska Press, 2003.

Lee, Elizabeth Blair. *Wartime Washington: The Civil War Letters of Elizabeth Blair Lee*. Edited by Virginia Jeans Laas. 1991. Reprint, Urbana: University of Illinois Press, 1999.

Logan, Mary. *Reminiscences of a Soldier's Wife*. New York: Charles Scribner's, 1913.

Logan, Mrs. John A. [Mary]. *Thirty Years in Washington; or, Life and Scenes in Our National Capital*. Hartford, CT: A. D. Worthington, 1901.

McClure, Alexander K. *Our Presidents and How We Make Them*. New York: Harper & Brothers, 1900.

McPherson, James M. *Battle Cry of Freedom: The Civil War Era*. New York: Oxford University Press, 1988.

Morris, Roy J. *Fraud of the Century: Rutherford B. Hayes, Samuel J. Tilden, and the Stolen Election of 1876*. New York: Simon & Schuster, 2003.

Newberry, Julia. *Julia Newberry's Diary*. Edited by Margaret Ayer Barnes and Janet Ayer Fairbank. New York: W. W. Norton, 1933.

Nicolay, John G., and John Hay. *Abraham Lincoln: A History*. Vol. 9. New York, 1890.

Niven, John. *Salmon P. Chase: A Biography*. New York: Oxford University Press, 1995.

Oates, Stephen B. *With Malice Toward None: The Life of Abraham Lincoln*. 1977. Reprint, New York: Mentor, 1977.

Oberholtzer, Ellis Paxson. *Jay Cooke: Financier of the Civil War*. 2 vols. Philadelphia: George W. Jacobs, 1907.

Peacock, Virginia Tatnall. *Famous American Belles of the Nineteenth Century*. Philadelphia: J. B. Lippincott, 1901.

Peck, Amelia, and Carol Irish. *Candace Wheeler: The Art and Enterprise of American Design, 1875–1900*. New York: Metropolitan Museum of Art/New Haven, CT: Yale University Press, 2001.

Peskin, Allan. *Garfield*. Kent, OH: Kent State University Press, 1978.

Phelps, Mary Merwin. *Kate Chase, Dominant Daughter: The Life Story of a Brilliant Woman and Her Famous Father*. New York: Thomas Y. Crowell, 1935.

Piatt, Donn. *Memories of the Men Who Saved the Union*. New York, 1887.

Platt, Thomas C. *The Autobiography of Thomas Collier Platt*. Edited by Louis J. Lang. New York: B. W. Dodge, 1910.

Poore, Ben [Benjamin] Perley. *Perley's Reminiscences of Sixty Years in the National Metropolis*. Vol. 2. Philadelphia, 1886.

Powell, Lawrence N. *New Masters: Northern Planters During the Civil War and Reconstruction*. New Haven, CT: Yale University Press, 1980.

Powell, Thomas Edward, ed. *The Democratic Party of the State of Ohio: A Comprehensive History of Democracy in Ohio from 1803 to 1912*. Vol. 1. n.p., Ohio Publishing Company, 1913.

Pryor, Sara Agnes Rice. *Reminiscences of Peace and War*. New York: Macmillan, 1905.

Rapoza, Lydia L., and Bette Miller. *Images of America: Cranston*. Charleston, SC: Arcadia, 1999.

Reid, Whitelaw. *After the War: A Tour of the Southern States, 1865–1866*. 1866. Reprint, New York: Harper Torchbooks, 1965.

Reeves, Thomas C. *Gentleman Boss: The Life and Times of Chester Alan Arthur*. Newtown, CT: American Political Biography Press, 1975.

Rose, Willie Lee. *Rehearsal for Reconstruction: The Port Royal Experiment*. 1964. Reprint, Athens: University of Georgia Press, 1999.

Ross, Ishbel. *Proud Kate: Portrait of an Ambitious Woman*. New York: Harper & Brothers, 1953.

Russell, William Howard. *My Diary North and South*. Boston, 1863.

Safire, William. *Freedom: A Novel of Abraham Lincoln and the Civil War*. New York: Doubleday, 1987.

Sandburg, Carl. *Abraham Lincoln: The War Years*. 4 vols. New York: Harcourt, Brace, 1939.

Schlesinger, Arthur M. *Salmon Portland Chase: Undergraduate and Pedagogue*. Columbus, OH: F. J. Heer, 1919.

Schuckers, Jacob W. *The Life and Public Services of Salmon Portland Chase*. New York, 1874.

Schurz, Carl. *The Reminiscences of Carl Schurz*. Vol. 2, *1852–1863*. New York: McClure Company, 1907.

Shapiro, Henry D., and Zane L. Miller. *Clifton: Neighborhood and Community in an Urban Setting, a Brief History*. Cincinnati, OH: Laboratory in American Civilization, 1976.

Shaw, John. *Lucretia*. Hauppauge, NY: Nova Publishers, 2004.

Sherman, William Tecumseh. *Memoirs of Gen. William T. Sherman*. Vol. 1. New York, 1889.

Shoemaker, Henry Wharton. *The Last of the War Governors: A Biographical Appreciation of Colonel William Sprague*. Altoona, PA: Altoona Tribune, 1916.

Shumaker, Eleanor Harper. *The Belle of Washington: A Civil War Novel About the Life and Times of Kate Chase Sprague and the Eternal Triangle: Political Ambition, Money and Sex*. Tarentum, PA: Word Association Publishers, 2004.

Silbey, Joel H. *A Respectable Minority: The Democratic Party in the Civil War Era, 1860–1868*. New York: W. W. Norton, 1977.

Smith, Donnal V. *Chase and Civil War Politics*. Freeport, NY: Books for Libraries Press, 1972. Reprinted from *Ohio Archaeological and Historical Quarterly* for July and October 1930.

Smith, Jean Edward. *Grant*. New York: Simon & Schuster, 2001.

Smith, Theodore Clark. *The Life and Letters of James Abram Garfield*. Vol. 1, *1831–1877*. New Haven, CT: Yale University Press, 1925.

Sokoloff, Alice Hunt. *Kate Chase for the Defense*. New York: Dodd, Mead, 1971.

Sprague, Warren Vincent. *Sprague Families in America*. Rutland, VT: Tuttle Company, 1913.

Stahr, Walter. *Seward: Lincoln's Indispensable Man*. New York: Simon & Schuster, 2012.

Stebbins, Homer A. *A Political History of the State of New York, 1865–1869*. New York: Columbia University Press, 1913.

Stedman, Oliver H. *A Stroll Through Memory Lane with Oliver H. Stedman: Stories of South County's Past*. Vols. 1 and 2. West Kingston, RI: Kingston Press, 1978.

Stewart, David O. *Impeached: The Trial of President Andrew Johnson and the Fight for Lincoln's Legacy*. 2009. Reprint, New York: Simon & Schuster, 2010.

Straker, Cheryl J., and Chris Matheney. *Ohio Statehouse: A Building for the Ages*. Virginia Beach, VA: Donning Company, 2011.

Taliaferro, John. *All the Great Prizes: The Life of John Hay, from Lincoln to Roosevelt*. New York: Simon & Schuster, 2013.

Taylor, John M. *Garfield of Ohio: The Available Man*. New York: W. W. Norton, 1970.

Thayer, William Roscoe. *The Life and Letters of John Hay*. Vol. 1. Boston: Houghton Mifflin, 1915.

Tilden, Samuel J. *Letters and Literary Memorials of Samuel J. Tilden*. Edited by John Bigelow. 2 vols. New York: Harper & Brothers, 1908.

[Trotter, Isabella Strange]. *First Impressions of the New World on Two Travellers from the Old*. London, 1859.

Unger, Irwin. *The Greenback Era: A Social and Political History of American Finance, 1865–1879*. Princeton, NJ: Princeton University Press, 1964.

Vidal, Gore. *Lincoln*. New York: Random House, 1984.

Villard, Henry. *Memoirs of Henry Villard: Journalist and Financier, 1835–1900*. Vol. 1, *1835–1862*. Boston: Houghton Mifflin, 1904.

Ward, Geoffrey C., with Ric Burns and Ken Burns. *The Civil War: An Illustrated History*. New York: Knopf, 1990.

Warden, Robert B. *An Account of the Private Life and Public Services of Salmon Portland Chase*. Cincinnati, 1874.

Welles, Gideon. *Diary of Gideon Welles*. 3 vols. Boston: Houghton Mifflin, 1911.

Wilson, James Harrison. *The Life of Charles Dana*. New York: Harper & Brothers, 1907.

Winkler, H. Donald. *The Women in Lincoln's Life: How the Sixteenth American President Was Shaped by Fascinating Women Who Loved, Hated, Helped, Charmed, and Deceived Him*. Nashville: Rutledge Hill Press, 2001.

## Articles, Speeches, and Web Pages

Bisland, Mary L. "Confidential Talks." *Illustrated American* 4, no. 40 (November 22, 1890): 497–503.

Blue, Frederick. "Kate's Paper Chase: The Race to Publish the First Biography of Salmon P. Chase." *Old Northwest* 8, no. 4 (Winter 1982–1983): 353–363.

Bodek, Evelyn Gordon. "Salonnières and Bluestockings: Educated Obsolescence and Germinating Feminism." *Feminist Studies* 3 (Spring–Summer 1976): 185–199.

Chafee, Zechariah, Jr. "Weathering the Panic of '73: An Episode in Rhode Island Business History." *Proceedings of the Massachusetts Historical Society*, Third Series 66 (October 1936–May 1941): 270–293.

Chase, Salmon P. "'Going Home to Vote,' Authentic Speeches of S. P. Chase, Secretary of the Treasury, During His Visit to Ohio, with His Speeches at Indianapolis, and at the Mass Meeting in Baltimore, October, 1863." Washington, DC, 1863, 1–36.

Didier, Eugene L. "Personal Recollections of Chief-Justice Chase." *Green Bag* 7, no. 7 (July 1895): 313–317.

———. "Salmon P. Chase." *Chautauquan: Organ of the Chautauqua Literary and Scientific Circle* 11 (April 1890–September 1890): 182–186.

Evarts, William M. "Eulogy on Chief-Justice Chase, Delivered by William M. Evarts, Before the Alumni of Dartmouth College, at Hanover, June 24, 1874." New York, 1874, 1–30.

Foraker, Joseph B. "Address of Hon. J. B. Foraker, on the Life, Character and Public Services of Salmon P. Chase, Late Chief Justice of the United States: Delivered Before the Circuit Court of the United States, at Springfield, Illinois, October 7, 1905," 1–35.

Henderson, Michael J., and Karin Bleeg, webmasters. "History." *Edgewood Neighborhood, Washington, D.C.* www.edgewooddc.org/id12.html.

Hoadly, George. "Address at Music Hall, Cincinnati, Ohio, on the Occasion of the Removal of the Remains of Salmon P. Chase, to Spring Grove Cemetery: Thursday, October 14, 1886." Cincinnati, 1887, 1–24.

Hoyt, Janet Chase. "Sherman and Chase: An Interview at Beaufort." *New-York Tribune*, February 22, 1891.

———. "A Woman's Memories: The Battle of Bull Run—General McDowell." *New-York Tribune*, June 7, 1891.

———. "A Woman's Memories: A Privateer—General Scott—Charles Sumner." *New-York Tribune*, April 5, 1891.

———. "A Woman's Memories: Salmon P. Chase's Home Life." *New-York Tribune*, February 15, 1891.

———. "A Woman's Memories: Washington in War Time." *New-York Tribune*, March 8, 1891.

Lloyd, David Demarest. "The Home-Life of Salmon Portland Chase." *The Atlantic Monthly*, November 1873, 526–538.

McSherry, Patrick, with data contributed by Peter Amabile. "Lt. Frank Donaldson, Assistant Surgeon of the Rough Riders." *Spanish American War Centennial Website*. www.spanamwar.com/rrdonaldson.html.

"Our Museum: History of the South County Museum." *South County Museum*. www.southcountymuseum.org/About_SCM.html.

Perrine, William. "The Dashing Kate Chase." *Ladies Home Journal*, June 1901, 11–12, 30.

"Roscoe Conkling." *Oneida County Historical Society*. www.oneidacountyhistory.org/PublicFigures/Conklin/RoscoeConkling.asp.

"Samuel Clarke Pomeroy Papers." *Kansas Historical Society*. 2013. www.kshs.org/archives/40476.

Schaffner, Cynthia V. A., and Lori Zabar. "The Founding and Design of William Merritt Chase's Shinnecock Hills Summer School of Art and the Art Village." *Winterthur Portfolio* 44 no. 4 (Winter 2010): 303–350.

Surdam, David G. "Traders or Traitors: Northern Cotton Trading During the Civil War." *Business and Economic History* 28, no. 2 (Winter 1999): 301–312.

Vidal, Gore. "Those Whom the Gods Would Disappoint They First Make Charming." In *Books at Brown, 1988–1989, Vols. 35–36, John Hay Sesquicentennial*, edited by Jennifer B. Lee, 1–5. Providence: Friends of the Library of Brown University, 1990.

## Dissertations and Other Unpublished or Informally Published Papers

Dewey, Mildred McLean Hazen. "Memoir" [1896], 131–136. On file at Mildred McLean Hazen Dewey Collection, Rutherford B. Hayes Presidential Center, Fremont, OH.

Gradia, Nina Mae. "Rivals or Kindred Spirits? Mary Todd Lincoln, Katharine (Kate) Jane Chase, and Their Parallel Lives." Master's thesis, University of Maryland, 2010. UMI Dissertation Publishing no. 1477250.

Owens, Susie Lee. "The Union League of America: Political Activities in Tennessee, the Carolinas, and Virginia 1865–1870." PhD diss., New York University, April 1943. On file at Bobst Library, New York University.

Vangermeersch, Richard. "A Sketch of the Life of William Sprague (1830–1915)." Narragansett, June 2012. Presented at the University of Rhode Island Department of Music, September 30, 2012, in connection with the opera, *William Sprague and his Women*, music by Geoffrey Gibbs, libretto by Richard Vangermeersch.

———. "William Sprague: 50 Vignettes." Narragansett, 2013.

# INDEX